A LOOK OVER
MY SHOULDER

A LOOK OVER
MY SHOULDER

——

A Life in the
Central Intelligence
Agency

RICHARD HELMS

with William Hood

RANDOM HOUSE / NEW YORK

To my beloved Cynthia

Library of Congress Cataloging-in-Publication Data
Helms, Richard.
A look over my shoulder : a life in the Central Intelligence Agency / Richard Helms
with William Hood.
p.   cm.
Includes index.
ISBN 0-375-50012-X
1. Helms, Richard.   2. United States. Central Intelligence Agency—Biography.
3. Intelligence officers—United States—Biography.   I. Hood, William.   II. Title.
UB271.U52 H454   2002   327.1273'0092—dc21
[B]   2002035262

Printed in the United States of America on acid-free paper
Random House website address: www.atrandom.com
24689753
First Edition

Book design by J. K. Lambert

PREFACE

This is a memoir that I never expected to write.

On February 2, 1973, I was driven home for the last time in the official car of the director of Central Intelligence (DCI). This followed what for me had been an emotional farewell to hundreds of colleagues in the atrium of the Agency headquarters. They had gathered there on short notice after the unexpected swearing-in of new Nixon appointees earlier that day. James Schlesinger, my successor at CIA, was among those sworn in. So, in a matter of minutes it was over. I was no longer in charge. The velvet curtain had slipped into place. I was on the outside. My life in intelligence was behind me.

When I left government after serving four years as ambassador to Iran, I had no thought of writing about my thirty years in intelligence. I believed in the ban against revelation of intelligence secrets, and while in CIA had enforced it. I had every intention of keeping my mouth shut and my pen in the desk drawer. Although I had been circumspect when interviewed by Thomas Powers, and had limited my answers to correcting personal data he had assembled, when his book was published I realized that some of my former colleagues had been more forthcoming. In the event, the book's title, *The Man Who Kept the Secrets** seemed to bear out my intentions in speaking to Powers.

In 1975 a volcano in the form of the Church and Pike Committees' hearings in Congress erupted. Between the committees' demands for files and Director William Colby's eagerness to volunteer additional data, the hearings turned into a wanton breach of the secrecy under-

*(New York: Knopf, 1979).

standings which had existed between the Congress and the Agency until that time. The published findings of the Senate and House committees weighed some twenty pounds. My impression was that these hundreds of thousands of words were more useful to the KGB and some of our other adversaries than to the American taxpayers who footed the bill.

After leaving Iran and returning to Washington, I decided to catch my breath for a bit while offering myself as a consultant. Although a friend had poked fun at me by saying that "a consultant is a man who borrows your watch to tell you what time it is," I soon found myself once again engaged in an absorbing line of work.

In 1983 when President Ronald Reagan awarded me the National Security medal, probably at the instigation of Vice President George H. W. Bush, the thought of writing my memoirs might well have come to mind. It did not.

A few days later, I opened a congratulatory letter from President Richard Nixon. His note read in part: "The attempt to castrate the CIA in the mid-seventies was a national tragedy." President Nixon and I had not always agreed on everything, but I did concur with this belated judgment. I was amused to find that the former president had taken the occasion of this well-after-the-fact presentation of the highest security service award to write to me. It had been ten years since President Nixon had ended my intelligence career with a handshake at Camp David.

The end of the Cold War, the collapse of the Berlin wall, and the several post-Gorbachev governments in Moscow are at the root of my decision to put some of my impressions of the secret world on paper. It is not my intention to write a history of CIA. Taken as a whole, the existing histories are adequate. But as dated as my experience may be now, I think this memoir might yet serve as background to intelligence as it exists today, and give a glimpse of what happened during my service.

I am not so naive as to expect that anything I say will cause those who would not allow a government any secrecy in the area of foreign policy to change their views. This may be a bit of professional deformation, but to me it has always seemed absurd to question the government's right to secrecy in some aspects of foreign and defense policy while in our national games we accept without a frown the catcher's right to signal the pitcher from behind the batter's back, or the secret council of the quarterback and his team to plan their next offensive move at a safe remove from the opposing defense. Journalists' sources are protected by custom if not by law, yet a secret agent whose reports are of national importance and whose life and the well-being of his family may be at stake is considered fair game for the media. Perhaps this is but another expression of the Agency's alleged "secret culture." Whether it is or not, the events which took place on September 11, 2001, changed all that in the United States.

Past references to CIA's "culture" and one former DCI's expressed determination to destroy it caught me quite by surprise. The notion of a culture had not occurred to me, but, of course, there is a CIA culture. Any circumscribed group of people engaged in a demanding, isolated, and occasionally dangerous activity is likely in time to develop a culture. This is also true of a family whose members have only one another to lean upon, and in consequence must create its own support system. Those on the outside may not know them, may not like them, or even give a damn. In government, those above the group will seek their loyalty but at times may step aside when something goes wrong.

I see no reason to believe that those who followed my contemporaries will have an easier time of it. As in the past, the intelligence consumers will demand results that in many instances may be a long time coming. When goals are achieved and policy is a success, there will be others in a position to claim the victory. For security reasons, praise—should there be any—is likely to be kept in-house. Few statesmen have ever thought to admit that a sound decision was made on anything less than their own good judgment, and no political administration is likely to share its reputation for prescience and wisdom with a few faceless men and women and an obscure culture tucked away a few miles out of town.

Secret intelligence has never been for the fainthearted. This is one aspect of the culture that will never change. Exposures and real or alleged scandals will always be with us. This makes it all the more important that the American people understand why secret intelligence is an essential element in our national defense. These days, terrorists are a more tangible threat and a much more difficult intelligence target than a hostile state armed with nuclear weapons.

I am quite aware that numbers of Americans will never believe that secrecy is essential. To them there is nothing to be said. To others, I hope this book will enlighten and perhaps put to rest some of the bugaboos which spy novels and lurid journalism have created.

There remains a problem. I had first thought to include the names of colleagues at all levels who were involved with me in those years. I soon realized that to mention a score meant that fifty had been left out, and that behind these were another hundred who should be named. Unless the memoir was to read like a telephone directory, there was no alternative but to restrict personal references to an absolute minimum. I can only console myself by saying that you know who you are, and you know I know you all, and that I treasure our work together.

FOREWORD

Henry A. Kissinger

America's relationship to its intelligence activities has always been ambivalent. Because America was secure behind two vast oceans for most of its history, its margin of survival was so great that it felt liberated from the need for precise information required by less fortunate nations. Thus America's attitude toward intelligence was aloof, if not reluctant, leaving it in embryonic form to the military services. "Gentlemen do not read each other's mail" was Secretary of State Henry Stimson's verdict in 1929 when he disapproved funding for the department's code-breaking unit.

World War II and the Cold War changed these attitudes. Long-range nuclear weapons shrank the American margin of safety and created the danger of surprise attack; communist ideology merged foreign and domestic threats. Terrorism added a new dimension of privatized danger. Groups heretofore considered private or at least nongovernmental—such as political parties and, more recently, terrorist cells—were in a position to pose threats to national security and to the global balance of power. Precise information became a condition of survival. And covert operations were needed to deal with threats in the gray area between diplomacy and military strategy—a type of intelligence in which the American government had no expertise and the American public no experience.

Richard Helms was a key figure in the building of America's intelligence capability for this new world. He gives a gripping account of the thirty-five years during which he rose through the ranks at the Central Intelligence Agency, mostly in the Directorate for Plans, which recruits and trains foreign agents and conducts covert operations. Appointed director of Central Intelligence by President Lyndon Johnson in 1965, Helms continued in office under President Richard Nixon until relieved of his position in February 1973 in a move of surpassing pettiness six weeks before he would have reached the automatic retirement age of sixty.

After his death in October 2002, some obituaries snidely described Richard Helms as the holder of secrets, as if this inevitable aspect of intelligence work reflected his character or his predisposition. Those of us who observed Dick over the decades and who admired his patriotism, his dedication, and his character regretted that his sense of duty prevented the nation from sharing his accomplishments. This Helms has now remedied in this thoughtful book.

As national security advisor and later secretary of state under President Nixon, I consulted with Dick on a daily basis as DCI and regularly, under President Ford, in his subsequent post as ambassador to Iran. There was no public servant I trusted more or who contributed more to the understanding of the challenges facing our nation.

No department head has a more difficult assignment than the director of Central Intelligence. He wears two partly incompatible hats: he heads the Agency, which is responsible for the collection of intelligence on foreign countries and the conduct of covert operations; at the same time, he is director of Central Intelligence for the entire United States government. In the latter capacity, he has to coordinate the actions of his own department with the separate—and occasionally competitive—intelligence activities of the State and Defense Departments and other agencies charged with intelligence gathering by technical means.

All department heads are technically under the authority of the President. But the director of Central Intelligence, unlike his colleagues, is not to have a stake in the political fortunes of the administration in office; he represents "objective" truth on matters where objectivity is itself often at issue. The DCI must be prepared to challenge the favorite theses of powerful political personalities.

Dick Helms navigated these shoals with remarkable skill and extraordinary integrity. Each administration presents a unique challenge to the intelligence community, reflecting differences in personality and political outlook. Helms's account is fascinating, acute, and subtle about the various administrations in which he served: the increasing reliance on covert operations in the Eisenhower and Kennedy administrations; Richard Nixon's ambiguous attitude toward the Central Intelligence Agency and its director.

President Nixon's view of Helms reflected his characteristic ambivalence. On the one hand, he considered the position of DCI nonpolitical, and when he assumed the presidency, he emphasized continuity by reappointing Helms. At the same time, he regarded Helms as a member of the "Georgetown social set," which Nixon believed—not incorrectly—to be more sympathetic to Democratic administrations than to his own. He therefore coupled Helms's reappointment with an attempt to insulate him from the policy process: the DCI was to attend National Security Council meetings only to give a briefing; once discussion turned to policy, he was to leave the Cabinet Room. Helms accepted this directive, which it fell to me to convey, with characteristic discipline, albeit with slightly raised eyebrows. In the event, Nixon was so impressed by Helms's briefings that he wanted to hear his views on policy—or at least the CIA's assessment of the consequences of various policy options, which is what policy discussions, in the end, are all about. Nixon solved the problem after an early NSC meeting by inviting Helms after a briefing to join the group for lunch.

From that point on, Dick Helms was an integral member of the NSC team. The Agency under his leadership was indispensable in supplying analyses and—even when I thought they stuck too closely to conventional wisdom—beyond criticism as to its motives. As time went on, Helms was given many opportunities for private meetings at the White House, most frequently with me, to make sure that all the implications of his department's recommendations were available to the President. It was also Helms's responsibility to report which, if any, American agents abroad might cause foreign policy difficulties if exposed. (For reasons of security and deniability, we preferred not to know their names unless they fell into this category.) Helms's conduct with respect to this sensitive issue was impeccable.

The CIA's role in covert operations became controversial at the end of Helms's tenure. Traditional diplomacy seeks to affect the conduct of states; military force exists to sustain the balance of power. But during the Cold War—and now again in today's war against terrorism—the threat often comes from nonstate actors, such as political parties or terrorist groups, financed from abroad.

The CIA did not deserve the opprobrium various investigations heaped on it. Most of its operations were designed to prevent radical forces from taking over countries considered important to American security and interests and where our adversaries had instruments of action not available to us. Not all were well designed, but all were approved—and, in the most controversial cases, ordered—by presidents of every Cold War administration, even when the paperwork was conducted to provide deniability.

After Helms left office, he and some of his colleagues came under attack for having been assigned to defend these new and intangible frontiers—which their superiors had defined for them—on behalf of a society accustomed to more conventional enemies. The men and women who undertook these thankless tasks, veiled in a secrecy imposed on them by their superiors, were deprived of credit and, as it turned out, the protection to which they were entitled. Their actions were often challenged well after the event when the necessities that had given rise to them could be recalled only with difficulty by a new generation.

Dick Helms became one of the most prominent victims. He was charged with having committed perjury while testifying before the Senate Foreign Relations Committee during confirmation proceedings for his appointment as ambassador to Iran. Following established procedures, Helms had denied covert operations before a committee not authorized to receive such information. But in classified hearings, he had already briefed the members of the House and Senate designated by the congressional leadership for that purpose—including the SFRC member who had posed the incriminating questions. It was a grievous injustice, rectified to some extent when President Ronald Reagan awarded Helms the National Security Medal in 1983 and later came to dinner at his house.

Helms discusses this episode that was to blight his life for many years without self-pity. He was proud of all aspects of his service, as he had every right to be. His lodestar was a sense of duty, his motivating force public service. There was no public servant I respected more. It was an honor to be Richard Helms's colleague; it enhanced my life to be his friend.

ACKNOWLEDGMENTS

Many thanks to these and the others who have plundered their memories in helping with this memoir:

Thomas Ahern, Cicely Angleton, Michael Beschloss, James Critchfield, Mia Cunningham, Agnes Gavin, Sam Halpern, Cynthia Helms, Richard Holm, Walter Jessel, Richard Kerr, Vinton Lawrence, Charles McCarry, Scott Miler, Sam Papich, Hayden Peake, James Potts, David Robarge, R. Jack Smith, Hugh Tovar, Bronson Tweedy, John Waller, and Albert "Bud" Wheelon.

And for Robert D. Loomis, whose guiding hand and advice were with us throughout, a special thank you.

CONTENTS

A LOOK OVER
MY SHOULDER

Chapter 1

———

A SMOKING GUN

The telephone call that set in motion the events that would eventually end my intelligence career came as I was preparing for bed, Saturday, June 17, 1972.

"Dick, are you still up?"

"Yes, Howard." It was a familiar voice. At this time of night, Howard Osborn, the CIA chief of security, did not need to identify himself.

"I've just learned that the District police have picked up five men in a break-in at the Democratic Party National Headquarters at the Watergate."

"Yes." Osborn was not given to idle chatter. He obviously had a brick to drop.

"Four Cubans and Jim McCord."

"McCord? Retired out of your shop?"

Osborn drew a deep breath. "Two years ago."

I remembered James McCord as a serious, straitlaced staff security and counter-audio specialist. He had retired with a good record. I was baffled. "What about the Cubans—Miami or Havana?"

"Miami," Osborn said quickly. "Florida . . . exiles, they've been in this country for some time now."

"Do we know them?"

"As of now, I can't say."

"Get hold of the operations people, first thing. Have them get on to Miami. Check every record here and in Miami."

"Okay, first thing tomorrow."

"Is that all of it?"

"No, not half," Osborn said heavily. "Howard Hunt also seems to be involved in some way."

It was my turn for a deep breath. I knew that Hunt, a former CIA officer, was also retired. Marine Lieutenant General Robert E. Cushman, my deputy, had mentioned a year or so previously that he'd been told Hunt was employed at the White House as a security consultant, and involved with the Special Investigations group responsible for looking into security leaks. This was the outfit that became known as the "Plumbers." While with CIA, Hunt had worked in Latin America, Mexico, and Europe. Before his retirement, he served with the task force responsible for the Bay of Pigs operation.

"What in hell were they doing in the Democratic Party offices?"

Osborn paused, almost as if he couldn't quite believe what he was about to say. "I'm not sure what they were doing, but as of now it looks as if they might have been trying to tap the phones and bug the place."

It was a moment before I could say, "Is there any indication that we could be involved in this?"

"None whatsoever," Osborn replied.

"Stay on top of it," I said, "and see me before the staff meeting Monday morning." Despite occasional taunts from congressional members and the press, CIA was a highly disciplined organization. Before Admiral Rufus Taylor gave up his assignment as CIA deputy director to return to the Navy, he remarked that the Agency was "the most disciplined organization" in which he had ever served, "including the U.S. Navy." The notion that the Agency or anyone in it would undertake a caper as bizarre as the break-in and attempted bugging of a national political party was quite simply preposterous.

Still sitting on the edge of the bed, I decided to telephone Patrick Gray, who was acting FBI director while waiting for Senate approval. He'd not had time to gain much knowledge of the internal White House workings, and I wanted to be sure he was in the picture. It took a few more minutes than usual for the ever-efficient White House switchboard to locate Gray in a Los Angeles hotel room.

Gray said that he had been informed of the break-in, but had no details. I filled him in as much as I could and assured him that, despite the background of the apparent perpetrators, CIA had nothing to do with the break-in. I added that I couldn't imagine what anyone could hope to gain by breaking into those offices. Gray listened politely but had little to say.

"You might want to look into the relationship of John Ehrlichman, the President's domestic policy advisor, with McCord and Hunt," I said. "He'll be familiar with the circumstances in which Howard Hunt was hired for work at the White House and with McCord's job on the Committee to Re-elect the President as well." Gray remained unresponsive. After repeating my assurance that CIA was not involved with any of the break-in group, I put the phone down.

When I first heard that Hunt was working as a security consultant at the White House, it struck me as peculiar that no one there had called to verify with me or the Agency his career and reputation. As a matter of common practice, someone would have checked with us—officially or quietly—before hiring any former employee for a sensitive White House job.

The first time the Agency heard from Hunt in his new job was in July 1971 when Ehrlichman telephoned my deputy, General Cushman, to tell him that Hunt would be coming to see him for assistance. Hunt arrived a few days later and asked the general to supply some operational gear— a disguise wig, a voice-altering device, and false personal-identification documents. Cushman did so, and requested that the gear be returned after use.

The decision to supply the equipment might be interpreted as falling within the deputy director of Central Intelligence's area of responsibility, but it was a very close call. As Bob later remarked, he wished he had at the outset left the baby at my doorstep. By the time the break-in scandal was in full flower, it was too late for any Monday-morning quarterbacking on my part.

The gear was not returned, and Hunt's requests for operational material continued to escalate until he asked that his former secretary be detached from her job in Paris to work in his White House office. At this point General Cushman informed me of Hunt's various demands. The petition for a secretary was, of course, refused, as were subsequent requests for telephone answering services, cover for notional offices, and such. Now, after almost a year of silence, we thought we had heard the last of Hunt.

By the time of my Monday-morning staff meeting, the Washington media were aboil with the news of the break-in. It was confirmed that McCord had been arrested at the scene, but neither the *Washington Post* nor the *New York Times* mentioned Hunt. It was all too clear that although the problem apparently rested with the White House, the arrest of a retired Agency officer, the possible involvement of another, and the ties the Cuban-Americans had to the Agency would have an explosive impact on the press.

After a general discussion, I went around the conference table asking each of the senior officers if he knew of any possible CIA involvement in the Watergate break-in. None did, and it seemed obvious to us all that the most CIA could do was quickly to establish rock-solid proof that despite its previous relations with the burglars, the Agency had nothing to do with the break-in, and then to distance itself from the incident.

My instructions in effect were, "Keep cool, do not get lured into any speculation, don't volunteer any information, and just stay the hell away from the whole damned mess." It was not long before the notion of "distancing" became a lame joke. Our exhaustive records search confirmed that the Cuban-Americans arrested at the Watergate had formerly been listed as Agency contacts in the Miami area, and that one was still on a $100-a-month retainer. Press reports that Hunt was deeply involved spread quickly across the front pages and TV screens. A check signed by Hunt was found in the hotel room used as a makeshift observation point, and notebooks with his name and telephone number were taken from the burglars' pockets. Hunt's bizarre involvement was a major embarrassment.

In most circumstances it is difficult enough to prove a negative; it is all but out of the question to do so in secret operations. We were soon to learn that it is impossible to prove anything to an inflamed national press corps already in full cry.

Although we repeatedly denied the accusations, what seemed to be daily leaks to the press kept pointing at CIA. This was not the first time the Agency had been pilloried by self-serving Washington sources. But these incidents had been short-lived, and our denials were accepted by other agencies and in time by well-informed reporters. In this instance, we got no support from the administration or Congress, and the leaks continued relentlessly.

CIA cooperation with the FBI was correct, but seemed unavailing. One question arose repeatedly: were the leaks coming from the FBI? In J. Edgar Hoover's day this would not have been the case. But what about the new Bureau administration? Was discipline as strong as it had been? We did not know.

Today, after the hours of sworn testimony—the FBI file is said to contain 16,000 pages—publication of thousands of pages of memoirs, and the raw evidence exposed in the White House tapes, it seems incredible that at the time the probability that the leaks were coming directly from the White House did not occur to me or to anyone on my staff. Later, when evidence began to emerge showing clearly that the most senior members of the White House staff were involved in this featherbrained crime, none of us realized that from the moment the news of the arrests reached the White House, President Nixon was personally manipulating the administration's effort to contain the scandal.

The day after the first newsbreak, I went to the Capitol for routine testimony before the Senate Foreign Relations Committee. As I entered the hearing room, the committee chairman, Senator William Fulbright, took me to one side and in a low voice asked, "Have you read about the break-in at the Democratic National Committee?"

"Oh, yes," I said. "Yes, indeed."

"What on earth could they have been trying to find?"

"I've no idea," I answered, shaking my head. "It's as nutty an episode as I can recall." I waited a moment before saying, "There's one thing I can tell you, Mr. Chairman."

Senator Fulbright moved a bit closer.

"Despite all the allegations, we didn't have a damned thing to do with it."

"It doesn't read like one of your operations," he said. "But you understand I felt I had to ask." He smiled and took my arm as we moved to take our places. This was the only time the break-in was mentioned at the hearing.

Press reports soon indicated that Hunt and McCord and their confederates were attempting to photograph files, bug the telephones, and arrange electronic monitoring of the Democratic Committee. I could not understand why anyone would think there was anything to be gained from such a half-baked and technically difficult operation that would possibly warrant the risks involved.

On June 23, General Vernon "Dick" Walters (who had replaced General Cushman), with seven weeks on the job, and I were summoned to the White House for a meeting with John Ehrlichman. This was the only time I can recall having been directed to bring my deputy with me to a White House meeting. Because the tone was that of a command rather than an invitation, I suggested that General Walters and I have lunch in a downtown hotel and arrive at the meeting together. It did not take a great gift of imagination to guess what the meeting would be about, and it seemed unfair to risk letting any of the White House heavy hitters catch Dick Walters alone. He agreed with alacrity.

To my knowledge, General Walters's military history is unique. Not only did he rise from private to retire as a lieutenant general, but his entire career as an officer was spent in intelligence-related assignments. Dick Walters was heavyset, with a genial manner, a hearty laugh, and the ability to speak rapidly and eloquently in actual sentences—something of a rarity in the bureaucracy. He was a gifted raconteur, and apparently never forgot a good story. When he repeated an anecdote, it was always in exactly the same manner and in the identical words. I often wondered if this trick of memory contributed to his extraordinary linguistic ability. Walters was fluent in a number of languages, and I suspect could make his way in a great many more. As an interpreter, he had the admirable knack of conveying not only the words he was translating, but also the sense of the message. When Walters came into the Agency, Averell Harriman, former ambassador to the USSR and governor of New York, told me that although their political views were quite different, he had found Walters thoroughly reliable in carrying out instructions.

At the time of Ehrlichman's summons, the Agency's line into the White House was through Henry Kissinger, who was then Nixon's national security advisor. In Kissinger's absence, we worked with his deputy, Alexander Haig, and had had very little contact with any other White House staffers.

A graduate student might write a dissertation on the geography and decor of the rabbit warren of White House offices, and how the frequent reallocation of space and redecoration mark the changing fortunes of the staff. Proximity to the President's offices is the ultimate goal of every ambitious—that is to say *every*—White House aide. Close on the heels of proximity as a mark of favor come the size and aspect of the office space. The bigger the better; a view of anything not a wall or parking lot is next best. But if a visitor has not been around for a couple of months, and if a crisis has intervened, everything is likely to have changed. Office space will have been reallocated, and temporary partitions shifted.

We parked in the visitors' lot beside the West Wing and made our way through a basement entrance to an elevator the size of a telephone booth. On the second floor, we were escorted to what looked like an anteroom, but turned out to be John Ehrlichman's conference chamber.

I am tall; even in those days, Dick Walters had a certain bulk; and Ehrlichman's mere presence took up some space. We had scarcely wedged ourselves onto the straight-backed chairs around the conference table when H. R. "Bob" Haldeman, the White House chief of staff, marched into the room and took over the meeting.

After a few general observations about the serious nature of the allegations involving important people in the President's election campaign, he turned to me and asked very formally what connection CIA might have with the Watergate break-in.

"The CIA had no connection whatever with Watergate," I said.

Haldeman ignored this, and went on to say that the FBI investigation of certain Mexican leads might jeopardize Agency activity there. His tone stiffened as he added, "It has been decided to have General Walters go to see Pat Gray and tell him that further investigation in Mexico could lead to the exposure of certain Agency assets and channels for handling money."

"Just yesterday," I said, "I told Pat Gray *again* that the Agency was not involved and that none of the suspects had worked for us in the past two years." It seemed unlikely that Haldeman could possibly know more about CIA equities and funding channels than I did, but I decided to wait and hear what else he had in mind.

Haldeman pushed on, repeating his insistence that Walters carry the message to Gray. Toward the end of this increasingly baffling session, Haldeman took an even more serious, rather threatening tone, and said that if the FBI didn't cease its investigation of money transfers in Mexico, it would lead to an unraveling of the Bay of Pigs activity.

At this point, enough was quite enough, and I responded vigorously—though not quite as explosively as Haldeman later claimed. "The Bay of Pigs hasn't got a damned thing to do with this," I said. "And, what's more, there's nothing about the Bay of Pigs that's not already in the public domain." Haldeman notwithstanding, I did not shout in the White House, and cannot even remember ever having shouted in my own office.

As we stepped out of Ehrlichman's den, I was still pondering Haldeman's peculiar references to the Bay of Pigs. It baffled me then, and it does today. As my grandmother might have put it, the President had a bee in his bonnet. My guess at the time was that Haldeman was doing what he had been told to do, and might not have known the background of his message, or precisely what was at stake. He was speaking as he always did, and exactly as the President had instructed him. He was not an independent operative in any way. With his crew cut and straightforward manner, Haldeman complemented his chief by issuing the commands and orders which the President, for whatever reason, declined to express himself.

Only later did the White House tapes reveal that Nixon's order to Haldeman for this meeting was the "smoking gun." It was a clear case of the President attempting to obstruct justice, and led directly to Nixon's resignation.

When we got back to the parking lot, I admitted to Walters that I was completely mystified by Haldeman's reference to the Bay of Pigs. "The only thing I can think of is that the President may know something that we don't know. But I'll be damned if I can think what it could be." Because Walters was so new on the job, I mentioned the Agency's agreement with the FBI on work abroad. The Bureau would restrict its activity to criminal matters and leave secret intelligence work abroad to CIA. If either agency found that lines had crossed, the other party was to be informed immediately. I knew of no problem in Mexico. If the FBI sensed any conflict it would be up to them to inform us.

I was, of course, quite aware that the Nixon White House domestic policy staff aides were less than enthusiastic supporters of the Agency and that General Walters's relationship with President Nixon dated from the time he accompanied the then vice president on an extended trip to Latin America in 1958, and their ill-starred and dangerous visit to Caracas. General Walters had served as a high-level interpreter for President Nixon, as well as three of his predecessors in the White House, before being selected as deputy director of Central Intelligence. Whether or not Nixon thought of General Walters as his man in CIA and the only person who could be trusted to carry out his orders, on form if the President wanted a message taken to Pat Gray at the FBI, he should have asked me rather than my deputy to carry it.

More important than the attitudes of the lesser White House aides toward the Agency and to me was President Nixon's opinion. It had long been clear to me that Nixon had disliked CIA from the time that he lost the 1960 election. He was apparently convinced that CIA Director Allen Dulles had given Senator Stuart Symington information which allowed the Democrats to blame the Eisenhower administration for the famous "missile gap"—that is, permitting the Soviets to outdo the United States in the production of long-range missiles. The missile gap did play a role in the Democratic campaign rhetoric, and Nixon's vengeful reaction to what he imagined to have been Dulles's action devolved upon me and the Agency. In my view, it would have been quite unlike Allen Dulles to engage in any such political maneuvering with any senator, Democrat or Republican.

The fact was that in 1960, despite our strenuous efforts, the Agency did not know if there was a missile gap, or if the United States was behind the USSR in the race to develop effective intercontinental ballistic missiles. Our initial overhead reconnaissance flights probing Soviet missile activity were brought to term when the U-2 aircraft piloted by Gary Powers was shot down over the USSR on May 1, 1960. It was not until April 1961, and after President Kennedy's election, that Colonel Oleg Penkovsky's reports to CIA could be tested against the earlier U-2 data and collated. Only then did these evaluated reports show that the American ICBM program was significantly ahead of the Soviet effort. Colonel Penkovsky, a senior officer in Soviet military intelligence (GRU), had excellent access to high-level sources within the Soviet ICBM programs. He was a volunteer spy—as were many of the great agents in history—and was handled jointly by CIA and the British Secret Intelligence Service (SIS).

I was never sure why President Nixon distrusted me, aside from associating me with Allen Dulles and the other East Coast, Ivy League, establishment figures whom he loathed and thought of as dominating the upper brackets of OSS and subsequently CIA. In contrast, I always had an excellent relationship with Lyndon Johnson, who had at least as much claim as Nixon to have been born in a log cabin, and whose views of Ivy Leaguers were, at the best, reserved.

Walters delivered his message and for a while we thought the matter had been put to rest. Not at all. In Washington, allegations and speculation about the Agency's possible role in the break-in continued to pop like kernels of corn on a hot stove.

At a subsequent staff meeting, one of our older hands suggested a way of convincing the press that CIA had nothing to do with the break-in. "Just have someone show it up as the tradecraft mess it actually was. The entry team had no cover for being in the building and no cover story for resisting interrogation. Their clothing hadn't been sanitized—Hunt's check, his White House telephone number, and Lord knows what else were in various pockets. They all knew one another's true name, and everyone knew where everybody else worked. What's more, McCord actually went along with the entry team—it's unbelievable."

There was no one at the table—including those who had no operational experience or responsibility—who did not know that in the real world a team undertaking an operation like this would have been recruited by a cutout—"Mr. Lopez"—who would say he was fronting for some well-heeled émigrés who wanted proof that the Democrats were taking money from Castro. It would have been a cash-and-carry event—all cash and no checks. None of the team would have anything to reveal but a sterile telephone number and a physical description of Señor Lopez, who would have vanished the moment the gong rang.

And from the end of the table someone muttered, "No intelligence service worth the name would run an operation like that." This was too obvious to be helpful.

Three days later, John Dean, the White House counsel, summoned Dick Walters. I told him to listen to Dean but to make no commitments. Dean had one request. The White House wanted money from CIA to make bail for the burglars. I reminded Walters that although the Agency had unvouchered funds, the money could be released only by the director. If the circumstances were unusual or if large amounts were involved, it would be my responsibility to inform the chairmen of the Senate and

House Appropriations Committees in detail. I added that I had no intention of supplying any such money, or of asking Congress for permission to dip into funds earmarked for secret intelligence purposes to provide bail for a band of political bunglers.

The next day, Walters was called back to the White House, and Dean leaned even more heavily on his request for help to the burglars. On his return, Walters, deeply troubled by the situation, reminded me that he had had a long and full career. As he put it, "I've had my ticket punched, and I've got a great place to live in Florida." He then offered, rather boldly in the circumstance, to take the heat by attempting to work out something to pacify Dean's repeated request. This brought me forward in my chair. Speaking as plainly as I could, I told Dick there was no way he could take the fall without destroying his own reputation. Given the nature of our work, I said, CIA's reputation depends on straightforward, honest relations with both the executive branch and the Congress. There was no way that the deputy DCI could furnish secret funds to the Watergate crowd without permanently damaging and perhaps even destroying the Agency.

It has long since become clear to me that President Nixon himself called the shots in the Watergate cover-up, and that Attorney General John Mitchell and H. R. Haldeman were his closest associates. The failed break-in was a considerable jolt to the reelection campaign, but the arrest of former CIA employees and agents at the scene handed Nixon a weapon that he thought would serve his cover-up. He might more plausibly have blamed the burglary on his reelection staff, admitted it was a stupid mistake, and promised that nothing like it would happen again. Had Nixon done so, the headlines would shortly have disappeared, and despite any knowing snickers from within the Beltway, he would have gone on to win the election. But no, Nixon chose to deny all responsibility, and incidentally to protect his good friend Mitchell and the other confederates at the reelection headquarters and the White House. He would blame CIA, an agency he disliked and which he knew would have difficulty defending itself. The cover-up failed, and the effort boomeranged to destroy the Nixon presidency.

Five months later, and a few days after his reelection, President Nixon called me to Camp David. It was the last time we spoke while he was in office.

Chapter 2

—

LUNCH WITH ADOLF

The circumstances of my family life and education might well have been devised for what turned out to be my career. I was born in St. Davids, on the Philadelphia Main Line. After his service as an officer in the First World War, my father moved the family to New York City, then to South Orange, New Jersey, near his office as district manager for the Aluminum Company of America. I had finished my junior year at Carteret Academy when my parents, Herman and Marion, who were convinced that knowledge of foreign languages and culture were essential to a good education, took the family—my older sister, Elizabeth, or Betty, younger brothers Pearsall and Gates, a preschooler whom we called Wuz—to Europe. This was twice lucky. Along with broadening our education, Dad decided to close his margin stock market accounts before leaving, and thus escaped the crash that erased the holdings of so many others.

After a summer in Aix-les-Bains, I was enrolled at the last possible moment in Le Rosey, a preparatory school in Switzerland, with all courses, including geometry and German, given in French. My sister, Elizabeth, and brother Pearsall entered school in Lausanne. Like many Americans whose parents have insisted they study French as children, but who have never heard the language spoken outside the classroom, I experienced a jolt of language shock when I found myself in the beginners' French class after ten weeks in Aix. However humbling, I got the message. My Swiss roommate, Jacques Mallet, was as determined to learn English as I was to conquer French. I'm not sure who won, but Jacques went on to become a diplomat and I received the academic prize for my age-group—a copy of Flaubert's *Salammbô,* a long, complex novel which the faculty may have thought contained enough romance to keep an adolescent turning the pages.

The curriculum at Le Rosey was a creative mix of study and sports. Soccer was dominant in the fall. The game was new to the American contingent, but there were enough Europeans to make it a good team. I qualified as a goalie. In November the school moved to winter quarters at nearby Gstaad, a fine ski area, if even then a fashionable resort. Academic courses continued at full blast, but were arranged to provide ample time for sport. Skiing excellence was not graded, but the competition was such that we all learned quickly. By springtime I was sweating through many exhausting miles as bow oar on a four-man rowing shell on Lake Geneva.

Crown Prince Mohammed Reza Pahlavi, later the Shah of Iran, attended Le Rosey sometime after I had left but, despite what others have written, I never knew or met him there. Our first meeting came years later and in quite a different context.

In the spring, we returned to the United States. It didn't take long for Dad to realize that the depressed economy offered few promising business opportunities and he soon decided to take the family back to Europe. My paternal grandfather had emigrated from Germany and this probably influenced Dad's decision to settle in Freiburg im Breisgau, a pleasant city in southern Germany. This is not far from Basel, Switzerland, where my maternal grandfather, Gates W. McGarrah, had just been appointed the first president of the newly established Bank for International Settlements.

As profitable and pleasant as the year at Le Rosey had been, school in Freiburg was an abrupt change, not only because all classes were in German. As a guest student, I entered the Realgymnasium as an *Unter Primaner,* a junior in a local high school. Education in the Weimar Republic was a dead serious activity. Classes ran five and a half days a week, from early morning until late afternoon with no study periods. Study, and there was a lot of it, was to be done at home. There were few organized sports, and the occasional exercise classes were a poor substitute.

My German gradually became conversational, and I began to read quite easily, but much of the academic classwork was beyond me. Because Williams College—for which I was headed—required four years of Latin, my father found a classics professor to be my tutor. He was a spry, rather affable German academician who taught at the Humanistisches Gymnasium, where classics were emphasized. Although we worked alone in a sparsely furnished room in his house, the professor always wore a tailcoat, perhaps as a badge of office. He had just enough English to read and criticize my translations. But we got on well, and solved any remaining language problems by speaking French with each other.

An examination in European history remained as a final hurdle for admission to Williams. Fortunately this problem and my continuing difficulty at the Gymnasium solved themselves. On a family tour in Italy during Easter recess, I was felled by a nasty case of chicken pox. To protect the immediate family, I was moved to my grandparents' house in Basel and given a bedroom with a ladder leading to the garden. There, with a college syllabus in hand, and capitalizing on a very relaxed sort of quarantine—chicken pox was a serious disease in those days—I plowed through the recommended books. These quiet weeks, the excellent foundation provided by Le Rosey, and freedom from the pressure cooker of the Gymnasium made the final College Board examination in Geneva a relative success.

In four years I'd moved through three languages, and from an American prep school to Le Rosey, and to the Gymnasium. In 1931, Williams College was a fourth terra incognita. I had never visited the campus, been interviewed by any admissions official, or been introduced to anyone at the college. Once I settled down, Williams was even more than I had hoped for, and offered a near-perfect mix of study and a range of nonacademic activity.

In our junior year, Henry Swan, a classmate, and I decided to take advantage of the Honors Work tutorial system by trying an experiment of combining English literature and history as a single major. Although this is now a standard in many liberal arts colleges, in 1933 it took some doing to get the two separate academic departments to collaborate in the experiment. Swan became class valedictorian and later one of the most distinguished pioneers in open-heart surgery. He was by any standard an extraordinary man, with a passion for sixteenth-century music and a strong taste for adventure: after having casually bought a sextant in a junk shop, he became interested in sailing, and piloted a trimaran from Spain along Columbus's route to the New World.

Four years at Williams taught me a lot, not the least of which was the reminder that the boys who note that certain emperors are wearing no clothes are more likely to get a knock on the head than an encouraging pat on the back. This came when as editor of *The Williams Record,* I wrote an editorial urging the elimination of the four-year Latin requirement and compulsory chapel attendance. For good measure, I added that these were probably the reasons the college was sliding downhill, and student admissions were dropping. As a final touch I titled my views "Downhill."

Fortunately, the sulfurous reaction of the college president, the faculty, and the board of trustees to my helpful suggestions and judgment did not result—as some recommended—in my expulsion, or even affect the granting of a magna cum laude degree. Both the chapel and Latin requirements were soon dropped, but my experience was an early lesson in the problems of "speaking truth to power."

Another useful bit of experience came in an American history course given by Professor T. C. Smith, who had written a biography of President James Garfield, the only Williams alumnus to reach that office. He required students to prepare "problem papers" in which we developed sources on both sides of a given subject and then had to decide which represented the best policy or course of action. This is, of course, much the same approach used by CIA in preparing assessments and position papers.

By graduation I had narrowed my immediate plans to Harvard Law School or journalism. In those days one could get into Harvard Law on the strength of a Williams diploma; journalism had a tougher standard. An interview was wangled with Hugh Baillie, president of the United Press. If I could get myself to Europe, there would be a job in the London UP offices. This was exciting enough to suggest rowing across, but the family financed the trip as a graduation present.

As low man in the UP bureau in the *News of the World* building in

London, my job ranged from writing and updating obituaries of British politicians to searching the press for "brighteners"—the odd bits used as fillers in the dailies—and occasionally monitoring telephone calls from other European bureaus. The high point came one morning when an Italian-accented clerk in the Rome office blurted, "Flash! Webb Miller reports the Italian Army invaded Abyssinia today." This, at last, was journalism.

The depression was a dominant factor in England in 1935 and the Home Office was not about to take bread from the tables of English journalists by giving work permits to foreigners, particularly cub reporters. I was no exception, and left London in time for Thanksgiving in Berlin, where Frederick Oechsner, already a well-known foreign correspondent, was in charge of the UP office. Edward W. Beattie, an open-faced and heavyset Yale graduate, and Paul Kecskemeti, a Hungarian, bent-backed and small, were the stars. Beattie became a well-known war correspondent. Kecskemeti, who wrote treatises on mathematical logic in his spare time, emigrated to the States and subsequently joined the Rand Corporation.

It was in Berlin that I began my real training as a newsman. Because my German was reasonably fluent, Oechsner was well disposed, and some work came my way that might otherwise have gone to the more experienced staff. Along with a variety of what we called street assignments, I translated Hitler's speeches for the UP's important Latin American clients, principally *La Prensa* in Buenos Aires, rewrote significant articles from the German press, and chased down queries from various UP clients scattered around the world.

I found an apartment, actually a bed-sitter, in the Wittenberg Platz with rent that could be squeezed within the approximately $25 a week I was earning. This left enough cash to cover occasional evening meals and beer at the foreign press *Stammtisch* in a pleasant restaurant, Die Taverne. Although I was very much a junior member, I got to know some of the best newsmen in Germany at the time. Among those occasionally at the press table were H. R. "Red" Knickerbocker of the Hearst chain, William "Bill" Shirer, Louis Lochner, Ralph Barnes, and H. V. Kaltenborn. There was also a stream of visitors—among them, Bennett Cerf and Frederick Birchall, former managing editor of the *New York Times*.

At the time, my life was pretty much fettered by my wages. When not at Die Taverne, I saved a bit by ordering a plate of borscht at a *Kneipe* (café) on the corner near my apartment. Unlike the borscht usually found in Poland and Russia, the Berlin barroom version was a thick stew of vegetables and meat. Aside from an occasional movie or night at the theater, my social life was a bit thin. The Nazi German population was already becoming leery of open social relations with Americans and other foreigners. As a result, the American community—as too often happens in these days—was to a degree turned in upon itself and even the newsmen spent too much time with the American business and embassy community. One of my friends from the time in Berlin was Wallace Deuel, a correspondent for the *Chicago Daily News.*

Another American I got to know was Martha Dodd, the daughter of William E. Dodd, who was ambassador to Germany from 1933 to 1938. Her story is a curious footnote to the history of that time.

Martha was a lively, intelligent, and aggressive woman who became well known in the international and press community in Berlin. After being initially impressed by some of the Nazi leadership, she became passionately anti-Hitler. Our casual acquaintance—in a moment of transient affluence I once invited her to dinner—must have occurred after she was first courted by Boris Vinogradov, the press secretary at the Soviet embassy in Berlin. She fell deeply in love with Vinogradov, who was well known in Berlin as an attractive and outgoing Russian. Even in those days, he was a notable exception to the usual run of Soviet officials abroad. At the time, I doubt that there was any security official who might have suspected that Vinogradov was an intelligence officer and that whatever his personal feelings, his relationship with Dodd was known and approved of by his NKVD superiors.

Vinogradov was transferred from Berlin in 1934 to Bucharest and subsequently to Warsaw, but continued his relationship with Martha Dodd until he disappeared in Moscow in 1938. He was one of the scores of intelligence officers put to death by Stalin in the purges. Martha often described Vinogradov as the love of her life, and although she married an American businessman, Alfred K. Stern, she continued for years to press Soviet officials and newspaper friends for information about the Russian's disappearance.

In 1957, Boris Morros, a well-known Hollywood producer, testified—very convincingly—that the Sterns were part of a Soviet spy ring. They were both indicted for conspiring to act as agents to transmit military, commercial, and political information to the Soviet Union. Rather than face trial, they fled to Czechoslovakia via Mexico and Cuba. When the case was reviewed in 1979, the Department of Justice asked a federal district court to dismiss the indictment. After twenty-two years, the deaths of various witnesses, and two persons whose testimony was essential, there was not enough evidence to make a prima facie case against the couple. Neither of the Sterns ever returned to this country. Alfred died in 1986. Martha was seventy when she died in Prague in 1990.

The 1995 disclosure of deciphered Soviet intelligence cable traffic (code name VENONA) confirms the allegations that Martha was a recruited Soviet agent who passed classified documents taken from Ambassador Dodd's files in Berlin to her Russian case officer, Boris Vinogradov. She continued to serve as a spy throughout her life. Despite her enthusiastic efforts, her work in Berlin was probably the peak of her spy career. Alfred Stern also remained on the KGB roster throughout his life.

So much happened between 1936 and the defeat of Hitler in 1945 that it is difficult now to capture the atmosphere in Germany in the early days of the Nazi regime, and too easy to forget that despite the street fighting and warring factions, Hitler came to power legally in an open election in 1933. In his first three years in office, the Fuehrer took credit for curbing the disastrous inflation, ending the widespread unemployment, suppressing the flagrant vice in the cities, smashing German communism, and bringing the highly successful Olympics to Berlin. He was rapidly reestablishing the German military, playing heavily on what he dubbed the "*Diktat*" of the Versailles Treaty, and at every opportunity trumpeting the glory of Germany.

On March 7, 1936, Hitler addressed the Reichstag, assembled for the occasion in the Kroll Opera House. For what seemed to be hours, he harangued his audience, inveighing against the Versailles Treaty. Suddenly, from my seat with the press, I noticed that Hitler had become pale, and that he was passing a handkerchief back and forth between his hands beneath the lectern. A few seconds later, he slowed his speech. Leaning forward over the lectern to command special attention, he said slowly,

"At this moment German troops are crossing the Rhine bridges and occupying the Rhineland."

The Reichstag audience erupted: "Sieg Heil, Sieg Heil, Sieg Heil." The Nazi chant rocked the rafters of the old opera house. This was the first of what became known as Hitler's "Saturday surprises." The lightly armed troops which had crossed the Rhine with orders to withdraw immediately if there was any resistance were soon safely in place. The French and British reacted with words. Hitler's first big bluff had worked.

Even in those early days, the entire atmosphere in Germany was dominated by the incessant and effective propaganda produced by Joseph Goebbels. The Nazis had already smothered most dissenting political opinion. Every element of the media was controlled, from the smallest local newspaper to the national dailies, and no countervailing news was easily available to the public. Radio, the theater, and films were equally dominated. Loudspeakers seemed to function twenty-four hours a day; billboards and posters were plastered everywhere. The otherwise immaculate streets were often littered with Nazi Party handouts and flyers. Most of the foreign press corps and the embassy staffs attempted to portray German fascism accurately, but there was no such reporting easily available within the Third Reich.

The German population at large was, of course, well aware of the insistent Nazi anti-Semitism. This had reached such a raucous level in the summer of 1935 that Reichsbank President Hjalmar Schacht warned a group of senior Nazi officials that the continuing mistreatment of Jews had become serious enough to be bad for business. Important export orders were being canceled, and unless things changed, Schacht said, he could not complete the economic rearmament of Germany. Such moderates as there were within the Nazi Party then prevailed and won a brief partial cutback in the most obvious anti-Semitic activity. This relative quiet was to be permanently broken in November 1938 by the riots known as Kristallnacht. Hours after a German diplomat was assassinated by a young German Jew in Paris, the German police and security services stood by as some two hundred synagogues were burned and thousands of shops sacked throughout Germany. Although some of the initial outbursts by radical Nazis may have been spontaneous, it is clear that the rioting that followed was triggered by Goebbels and then hastily encouraged by Heinrich Himmler.

In 1935 the middle and upper levels of Jewish society were so well integrated into the German communities that many, along with a number of otherwise well-informed Germans, still continued to dismiss the increasingly virulent and pervasive anti-Semitism as a vote-catching device rather than fundamental evidence of Hitler's final intention. Even the well-established Jewish leaders, aware of their cultural and economic prominence and hence vulnerability, also tended to take this view. It took the violence and Nazi-encouraged riots of Kristallnacht to expose the Nazi anti-Semitism to an international audience.

In 1936 the Parteitag,* the annual week-long Nazi Party Congress in Nuremberg, was considered a routine event, and Ed Beattie was scheduled to cover it. A last-minute family complication made this impossible and I was sent alone as his replacement. As I walked into my hotel one afternoon, the young SS officer who had recently replaced the amiable Putzi Hanfstaengl as Hitler's press representative handed me an invitation for a "light luncheon" with the Fuehrer. This caught the Berlin office by surprise, but because I was the sole UP man on the scene the assignment fell to me.

It was a real break. Hitler had received few foreign visitors since his rise to power, and the demands of his office and native prudence restricted interviews to well-established dignitaries and a few American publishers with wide audiences. The working press had no choice but to view the Fuehrer from a distance. The U.S. military attaché, the shrewd and intelligent Major Truman Smith, who, on a 1922 assignment as an assistant military attaché, had presciently recognized Hitler as a coming figure, contrived to have Charles Lindbergh visit Hermann Goering and look over the new Luftwaffe. Smith told me that he had arranged the trip because he was convinced that the famous Lone Eagle, then still at the height of his popularity, would learn more about the new air force than anyone else. He was right. The rate and quality of German warplane production alarmed Lindbergh and Smith. For their part, the Nazis were pleased that Lindbergh had taken notice.

The open Mercedes that called for me carried Alfred Rosenberg, who is now best remembered for drafting the Nazi racial laws, and a Polish

---

*Literally "Party Day" but usually translated by American newsmen as "Party Congress."

reporter in the back seat. I sat beside the black-uniformed SS driver as we were whisked through the old town to the Luitpold Wiese, an open field with a massive podium at one end. Tens of thousands of Nazis, gathered in military formation, waited for their leader.

"The wonder of this age is that you have found *me*—an unknown man among millions" was the highlight of the Fuehrer's speech. "Sieg Heils" thundered and echoed across the transformed meadow while Hitler, god-like and alone, flicked a final Nazi salute and walked deliberately down the steps from the podium. He paused dramatically before saluting the black pylons honoring the Nazis who fell in the Munich Beer Hall Putsch in 1923. It was a perfectly executed and stage-managed political pageant.

We followed Hitler out of the stadium to the waiting military and party vehicles. Hitler stood in the familiar, massive, open Horch motor-car directly ahead of us as the cavalcade moved slowly through the city to the Burg, the medieval Nuremberg Castle. Every building was draped with swastika-spattered bunting and flags, the open windows and curbs lined with cheering crowds. Children, their arms rigid in the Nazi salute, edged closer to the moving vehicles. Hitler turned slowly, seeming to study the crowds on each side of the street before offering a slight, almost imperceptible smile, and flipping his customary stylized salute.

There was, I must admit, something mesmerizing about this ride. Only a seasoned movie star might have resisted the weird, vicarious sense that somehow some of the blind adulation of the crowds, who could have had no idea who was riding in the limousine directly behind Hitler, was meant for oneself. It was not difficult to imagine the feelings of the provincial Nazi Party functionaries in the cars that followed.

However much one loathed Nazis, and I certainly did, this was heady stuff. There could be no question about the German people's intoxication with their leader. It is easy today to forget that in his prime—the word sticks on one's tongue—Hitler was a masterful politician. He had studied German grievances from the First World War, and there was little that was irrational or ascetic in his stark identification of causes. Almost instinctively Hitler offered every group what it most wanted. Logic notwithstanding, Jews were simultaneously capitalists, communists, pacifists, and, in a hazy way, those responsible for usurping the influence of the Germanic Balts in Russia. Hitler threaded his obsessive hatred of Jews and communists into the fabric of his ranting against the enemies of whatever group he might be addressing.

The spacious battlement of the medieval castle looked out beyond the red gabled roofs of the town to the spreading farmland of the Franconian plain. In contrast to the emotion roiled by the Fuehrer's passage through the city, the warm autumn sun bathed the bright landscape in a lazy peace. Introductions were made to Rudolf Hess, in uniform, and Joachim von Ribbentrop. We chatted calmly until a throaty voice cut in.

"Das ist ein schoener Blick"—it was a pronouncement, "That *is* a beautiful view," not an observation, "What a beautiful sight."

Adolf Hitler had stepped out onto the balcony and was waiting to be introduced. His greeting—a firm handshake, the stylized Nazi salute, hand flipped almost casually back over the shoulder—came with a slight smile, more practiced than warm. The Germans returned the salute, foreigners did not. It was not expected.

At arm's length, Hitler appeared shorter and less impressive than at a distance. Fine, dark brown hair, rusty in front, slightly graying along the crown; bright blue eyes, coarse skin, with a pinkish tinge. His neatly trimmed mustache was shot slightly with gray. When Hitler spoke face-to-face, active salivary glands seemed to make his voice indistinct, possibly the reason some words were blurred and difficult to understand in his speeches. The lower row of teeth, bordered with gold, were perhaps false. He wore the usual brown shirt, uniform trousers, Sam Browne belt, and brightly polished boots. An Iron Cross was pinned to the shirt, and a brightly embroidered Nazi emblem blazoned on the left sleeve.

Hitler's manner was pleasant, if not exactly at ease. As he stood talking with the handful of correspondents, his knees moved back and forth nervously. His arms and shoulders as well as his hands were involved in every gesture.

When asked why he produced the massive and stunningly staged annual ceremonies of the Parteitag, Hitler smiled. "The party units all over Germany work hard for me and for the cause all year long. What should I do? Money prizes would break the Treasury. So I bring the most effective leaders here for a couple of days, give them this show and a chance to meet us all. They pay their own expenses. If they can't afford it, the local party units help them out. They go home stimulated, ready to work for me again. Then, their places are filled by others." He paused a moment before saying, "Besides, this is exactly the kind of exercise the *Reichsbahn* [German railways] would be required to perform in the event of war." The last word—*Krieg*—hung in the air.

Hitler did not venture opinions or introduce comments with "I believe" or "I think." In response to questions, he simply offered his views as facts.

The Parteitag inflicted more than one learning experience on me. Most of the important speeches at the Nuremberg gathering were signaled to the press well in advance and could be covered from Berlin. Paul Kecskemeti, the gnomelike deskman, would stand at the radio table in the UP Berlin offices, and scribble the highlights in English as the speech went along. After a few sentences, Paul would hand the "takes" to a colleague who would read them over the telephone to the London bureau, where they would be relayed by radio to New York.

The morning after our lunch, I drifted out to the Luitpold Wiese meeting area a few minutes late but in ample time to cover the scheduled events. It was a moment before I learned that Hitler had opted for a surprise speech and that it was not being broadcast. Using an upturned oil barrel which the genie protecting young reporters had stationed beside a fire exit, I managed to hear and make a note of the most dramatic bit of Hitler's hyperbole. In effect, he mused that if Germany had the riches of the Ukraine, the country would be "swimming in plenty."

A few hours later, my hotel phone rang. Half expecting congratulations for my report, I learned that in the lead bulletin covering the speech, the Associated Press had reported that just as Hitler mentioned the Ukraine, a flight of Luftwaffe bombers streaked over Nuremberg, and that the Fuehrer had then pointed east, toward the Ukraine.

"What about it?" my editor demanded.

"Well," I admitted, "some bombers did fly low, right across the crowd, but it was just a peaceful rehearsal for a flyover scheduled for later this week."

"Do you expect me to tell that to the New York office after every newspaper in the United States has featured the AP version of the story?" I must have mumbled some sort of excuse before he said, "In future, you'd better take the time to give this office the quotes that the AP thinks worth featuring."

When I got back to the Berlin office, Paul Kecskemeti grinned, tapped his nose, and said, "So lernt man, Dick." Indeed, and so I did learn to report everything and let the editors do the cutting.

The 1936 Summer Olympic Games were another occasion Hitler and Goebbels used to impress the world press with the reborn Germany, its prosperity and effective reorganization. I was lucky enough to be in the press box atop the stadium the day Jesse Owens won the 200-meter race. He burst into the lead at the turn and never looked back. In August, sixty years later, I was eerily reminded of that incident when I watched the television image of Michael Johnson running almost exactly the same race. In an interview, Johnson said, "Jesse was always my hero, I'll never forget him. His widow wrote me a letter of encouragement before these games."

In setting the world record, Johnson ran faster than Owens, but in 1936 there were no starting blocks or scientific timers—runners troweled holes in the track at the starting line, and stopwatches measured the records. Crossing on the *Queen Mary* after the Games, Owens explained to me one of the means that he and his Ohio State coach had worked out to improve his speed. "At the gun, runners tend to clench their fists. This causes a tension to run through the body, and this slightly slows the first steps. What I do at the start is to place my thumbs on my first finger— it's just enough to keep me from clenching." Owens was a quiet, modest man. He did not feel he had been insulted, as conventional reporting had it, when Hitler failed to award him the gold medal. Hitler followed the track events closely, and on several occasions congratulated the German gold medal winners, but he did not present any of the gold medals.

Berlin was a rewarding experience, and the disciplines involved in the daily struggle to get the news first, get it straight, and get it succinctly across to the reader was to prove useful.

But by mid-1937 it was time to go home.

Chapter 3

—

SIGNING ON

After a few years on the beat some reporters dream of having their own newspaper. My ambition took shape a little earlier. Even before graduation from Williams I had begun to hope that one day I might run or perhaps even own an American newspaper. As it happened, George Hawkins, a fraternity brother whose father, William, was head of Scripps-Howard newspapers, shared the same ambition. It never worked out, but George and I considered joining forces after graduation.

The possibility of running one's own paper stayed with me, and I left the UP in 1937 because the need for hands-on business experience, and a lot of it, had been driven home to me as an essential underpinning to newspaper management. Editorial work was important but I learned that, in the flinty eyes of the owners, reporters were easy to find and a dime a dozen. Good advertising salesmen and topflight circulation managers were comparatively rare. As exciting as my UP job was, I knew I had better get to the business side as soon as possible. Still, it was more of a wrench than I expected at the time to leave the excitement of Berlin to gamble on a future which even then looked remote.

Once home, I went to William Hawkins. He suggested I get out of New York, where newspaper departments were large and relatively compartmented, and go to a paper where the entire operation was under one roof. He recommended the *Indianapolis Times,* a Scripps-Howard property, and the smallest of the three local dailies, as the sort of paper I should seek out. He must have put in a good word, for a job soon opened in the paper's retail advertising staff.

There was much more than the few thousand miles of travel involved in the change from the foreboding atmosphere of Nazi Germany, and the opportunity to observe and mingle with the people who were soon to unleash the most catastrophic war in history, to six weeks as a messenger, trundling advertising material between the more important accounts and the advertising department in downtown Indianapolis. The full significance of the move was underlined when I learned that my wages had plummeted from twenty-five bucks a week in Berlin to a cool twenty-two fifty in Indianapolis. Life has its ways of puncturing one's balloon.

The sweat and shoe leather spent in the first few months on my new job were enough to convince me that news reporting was relatively easy compared to the advertising side of publishing. My first step up what was beginning to seem like a very long ladder was the assignment to manage a rubble of small accounts ranging from chicken merchants to funeral homes. I was also charged with the responsibility for luring other such accounts away from the competing papers. In the blistering summer heat, my funeral home accounts were a blessing. Air conditioning was by no means universal at the time, but even the most modest undertaking parlors were frigid. Although my calls on these potential clients were heavily influenced by the weather, the owners appeared to find me a welcome change from the usual run of bereaved patrons. Unfortunately, the more amiable undertakers were proud of their techniques, and I learned to cut our interviews just short of the inevitable invitation, "Come on downstairs and have a look at a really up-to-date shop." At the critical point I would check my watch, claim intense pressure, and bolt, preserving forever my innocence of embalming techniques.

By the time of my promotion to national advertising manager, I'd learned exactly how hard it was to earn a dollar. Having my knuckles rapped for failure to hustle enough new business was a new experience for me, and incidentally a lesson from which the taxpayers would eventually profit. The notion that secret intelligence budgets are bound only by the occasional need to break open another crate of money is pure Hollywood. Because some intelligence funds are unvouchered, there is stricter budgetary control in CIA than in any government agency I know, and throughout my tenure I remained tightfisted with the taxpayers' money.

In September 1939, in Indianapolis, I married Julia B. Shields, a divorcée with two children, James and Judith. I was introduced to Julia soon after I arrived in Indianapolis, by her lawyer, Bates Johnson, the friend of a friend. Julia had been raised and educated in Indianapolis and was recently divorced from Frank Shields, an entrepreneur who had built the Barbasol Company from a local venture to a nationwide business. Julia's brother, Noble Bretzman, was Indiana's leading portrait photographer.

After a brief honeymoon, actually a long weekend, on a lake in southern Michigan, I settled in with what I suddenly realized was a whole family. The children took the change in stride. I was the one who needed to be housebroken. Julia's connections in the city created a new social life, a welcome change from my bachelor existence. In fact, we saw nothing but a promising future.

Some two years later, on a Sunday, warm for that time of year, we were invited for lunch with Hubert Hickam, a well-known Indianapolis lawyer, and his family. We had left the table and were settling down to listen to the New York Philharmonic concert on the radio when the announcement came. Pearl Harbor had been attacked. Although I had followed the war in Europe closely, I had not considered the possibility of a Japanese attack.

Later, as we moved toward the door, Hubert said softly, "This reminds me of my brother Horace. He was a lieutenant colonel, and killed practicing night landings in Texas seven years ago. I've been told he was one of the coming guys in the Army Air Force. They named that airdrome in Hawaii for him . . . Hickam Field."

We drove home in silence.

—

The Japanese attack on Pearl Harbor brought five hard years' work to an end. I resigned from the *Indianapolis Times,* and in January 1942, volunteered for the U.S. Naval Reserve. In anticipation of my being called up, we moved to South Orange, New Jersey, so that Julia and the children could be near my parents when I left the country. During the early months of that year, I worked for the Navy Relief Society in New York, raising money for the survivors of naval personnel killed at Pearl Harbor. My application for a commission dragged on until, in despair, I asked a friend to see if he could trace it at naval headquarters. The papers had been so wildly misfiled that without this intervention I might have missed World War II entirely.

On July 1, twenty-four hours after a first glimpse of my son Dennis, I reported to the Harvard Naval Training School in Cambridge, Massachusetts. One of our instructors was a lively young ensign who must have come to the school a few hours after the graduation ceremonies at Annapolis. We were all older and outranked Ensign Holloway, but he was very much on the ball. The next time our paths crossed, Admiral James Holloway was chief of naval operations at the Pentagon.

With two months' intensive indoctrination under my belt, I was assigned to the Eastern Sea Frontier headquarters in New York City.

When I volunteered for the Navy, my language qualifications, two years of digging for news in the Third Reich and living in Berlin surrounded by Germans of every stripe might have suggested an intelligence assignment. Apparently they did not. I didn't pursue this because I had the impression that to qualify for assignment to naval intelligence, one had to be a third-generation American. My paternal grandfather had emigrated from Germany, and I assumed this ruled me out. But sixty days' orientation at Harvard had at least officially qualified me as a naval officer with the assignment of helping to plot the positions of Allied ships as they attempted to avoid German submarine wolf packs ravaging the convoys to England.

I had been on the job for only a few weeks when Frederick Oechsner, my boss in the UP bureau in Berlin, asked me to meet him for a drink at the Overseas Press Club. It didn't take long for him to get to the point. After a stiff lecture on the secrecy of what he was about to say, Fred said he had been asked by General William J. Donovan, the head of the recently established Office of Strategic Services, to build a new section, Morale Operations, or MO. I had never heard of General Donovan or his organization, but promised to keep the secret.

"MO," Oechsner whispered, "will be responsible for black propaganda." It was a new term, and my blank expression prompted Fred to explain a bit more loudly, "Black propaganda—misinformation! Stuff that will deceive and confuse the enemy."

After a prudent nod, and more to gain time than any additional Top Secret information, I asked what else General Donovan might be up to.

"Sabotage," Fred said softly. "Espionage, building paramilitary guerrilla armies, resistance operations." Then, with a glance along the bar, he leaned closer. "Counterespionage," he whispered. "But I want you to join us in black propaganda, MO—you're a natural."

At the time it was vitally important to keep the shipping lanes open to England and I was still learning my job. It would be a long war, and if the promise of hoped-for sea duty did not materialize, there would be time enough to consider something as nebulous as MO seemed to be. As it turned out, Fred's generous assessment of my "natural" talent for black propaganda had nothing to do with my eventual transfer.

My career in what Kim Philby always—and in his case with good reason—referred to as "the racket" began on a Sunday morning in 1943 when my commanding officer in New York flipped a cable across his desk and growled, "What the hell is this? I'm the one who decides if you like it here, not you." The secret order transferred me to the Office of Strategic Services in Washington. A Madison Avenue advertising mogul on duty with OSS in Washington required an assistant who spoke French and German, had lived in Europe and worked as a journalist. Of the three officers who qualified, I was the only one on duty in the United States.

A few hours after reporting for duty, I was whisked out of Washington for two weeks' training at OSS Area E—a farmhouse, garage, a few tents, and adjoining fields in nearby Maryland. My classmates varied in age, but were otherwise quite anonymous. We were told to conceal our last names and background, remove labels from clothing, and cache our driving licenses, checkbooks, and other identifying data with the camp commander. One enthusiastic and well-heeled potential operative went so far as to snip the monograms from the bosom of his custom-made shirts. We were also each privately instructed to ferret out the name and background of our fellow acolytes in preparation for a show-and-tell session at our graduation dinner.

Some of the indoctrination intended to prepare newcomers for life in the secret world would have been of more use in a barroom dustup than in Nazi-occupied Europe. Major W. E. Fairbairn, who had organized the Shanghai police riot squad, an outnumbered constabulary that fought the local assassins and gangsters on their own terms, was one of the first instructors of the British commandos, and taught a much-touted OSS course in hand-to-hand combat. The fine points of knife fighting—never hold a knife pointed down, if you miss, you may gut yourself—and the uses of broken bottles were stressed. Targets for below-the-belt kicks were identified.

"Grab my privates," Fairbairn told me. I did so, but prudently. "Not good enough," he commanded. "*Go* for me." I did, and landed flat on my back. The major was short and spare but made up for it with technique.

The rest of the training was more pertinent and gave a firsthand impression of the problems of keeping cover and gaining access to targets. My first test was to apply for a job under an assumed name and with no identification whatsoever in a war-related industry in Baltimore. This done, I was supposed to learn exactly what was going on.

Getting into the personnel office of the target—a Baltimore shipping company—was not difficult. American industry had few if any functioning security precautions, and there was a growing need for warm bodies in the draft-depleted workforce. Despite a dry mouth and tight sphincter, I lied my way through the interview, asked a few questions, scooped up a handful of company stock reports and advertising brochures, and escaped with the promise of a job when I returned with the completed application forms. I was luckier than a member of an earlier class who attracted so much suspicion that he was thoroughly beaten with wet towels before he could convince the Baltimore police to call the emergency number we were given in lieu of the lethal "L" tablet, an optional item sometimes issued to real-life agents. As tame as this exercise was, it served to give us a slight, very slight, taste of the anxiety and stress that are endemic to espionage.

The two weeks' training was less than comprehensive, but in 1943 it was the best OSS had to offer in the Washington area, and some of it was sound enough eventually to be incorporated into the early CIA syllabus.

Back in Washington, I was assigned to the planning staff. My office mate was John W. Gardner, a Marine officer who was handsome, gracious, and very intelligent. He went on to serve in President Johnson's cabinet, to found Common Cause, and to write a number of books.

Working with Gardner was a delight, although neither of us thought much of the dust-dry "plans" we were assigned to write. He managed to shake himself loose by helping Dr. Harry Murray, a Harvard professor, devise a series of tests intended to show a candidate's aptitude for over-seas service. Put into effect, the tests helped to identify individuals un-likely to stand the strain of living a double life abroad. After the war, an expanded version of these tests became common in industry and the government.

By the time I was convinced that none of the plans I was composing were likely ever even to be read, Ferdinand Mayer, a former foreign service officer, came to my rescue by slipping me into his tiny section responsible for coordinating intelligence collection on Germany. Although I didn't recognize it at the time, this assignment brought me face-to-face with two of the root problems of secret intelligence collection—establishing an agent's bona fides, and the veracity and value of his reports.

In Switzerland, Allen Dulles had made contact with Fritz Kolbe, a disaffected member of the Nazi foreign office in Berlin. With incredible pluck, Kolbe had arranged a trip to Bern, where he offered his services to British intelligence. The British head of station scented a provocation, and refused Kolbe's offer. Despite the carbon copies of secret German foreign office cables and dispatches Kolbe had smuggled from Berlin to Bern, London headquarters concurred: Kolbe had probably been sent by German intelligence in a bold move to deceive the British. The gutsy German was shown the door.

Here, as in so many other instances, Dulles's network of contacts and collaborators functioned perfectly. In despair, the bewildered Kolbe turned to a Swiss acquaintance who within hours alerted one of the OSS staff. Allen Dulles immediately recognized the treasure Kolbe had smuggled into Switzerland, and flashed reports to Washington and London.

But London stood firm. No German official would be foolhardy enough even to attempt to sneak such material out of the foreign ministry, let alone smuggle it through the security controls along the railway and at the German border. Kolbe was obviously an instrument of German intelligence, and his documents were probably the opening gambit in a deception scheme.

Dulles was equally adamant. Kolbe was straight. His reports were valid, indeed priceless, copies of highly classified German documents.

This confrontation came at a time when the British intelligence organizations were very much senior in experience and reputation to the fledgling OSS staff. The American cousins were politely tolerated by many of their British colleagues, but in some quarters there was a marked resentment of the open-faced, unsophisticated, and brash American operatives. The elegant British chief in Bern had an extensive wardrobe, and a title and attitude to match. The fact that he resented Dulles as an intruder may have affected local judgment, but London should have seen things more clearly. Unfortunately, Colonel Claude Dansey, the London headquarters officer directing espionage operations in Europe, had been badly stung by a German operation.

Two British intelligence officers who thought they were dealing with German resistance representatives were kidnapped in Holland and hustled across the border to Germany. He was not about to be caught twice by the bloody Boche. Moreover, Dansey, whom another senior British intelligence officer described as "the kind of a shit that gives other shits a bad name," had even less tolerance for upstart Americans than his man in Bern.

On form, there was reason to doubt Kolbe. If German intelligence were to manufacture a gift horse calculated to appeal to Allied intelligence, Kolbe was if anything too perfect a figure. After ten years' diplomatic service in Spain and South Africa, Kolbe returned to Berlin in 1939 to serve as an assistant to Ambassador Karl Ritter, who was the official liaison between the foreign office and the supreme military command. Kolbe's job gave him access to *all* the Nazi diplomatic cable and dispatch traffic, and intimate insights into military planning. He was a profound anti-Nazi, but capable of concealing his views and adroit enough to avoid the almost mandatory membership in the party. Kolbe was a workaholic, able to make himself an indispensable assistant to his Nazi chief while devoting almost as many hours to his own intelligence activity. Along with these blessings, Kolbe came with a communications system which, with the help of some professional tinkering, remained secure for the duration of the war.

However sound the early reports appeared to be, Kolbe had the aspect of a volunteer too good to be true. In Washington and London, counterintelligence staffs were consulted.

In the years that followed I became convinced that no intelligence service can be more effective than its counterintelligence component for very long. I also learned that although the best CI officers possess sound political judgment and insight, these qualities are by no means dominant at all levels in the counterintelligence world. The bona fides of a spy can best be determined by a combined effort, with experienced field operatives and counterintelligence staff evaluating the operation itself, and the substantive analysts concentrating on the intelligence content. Neither element can function effectively without the support of the other.

Kolbe's early reports ranged from the location of rendezvous points for Japanese and German submarines, data on a German cipher system, and proof that confirmed our fear that certain American ciphers had been broken. Subsequent reports detailed air raid damage to the vital Schweinfurt ball-bearing plant and the Ploeşti oil fields, disclosed a German agent (code name CICERO) who had access to the British ambassador's Top Secret cable traffic in the Ankara embassy, the development of a supersonic jet aircraft, and the research on yet other mysterious secret weapons—the self-propelled V-1 "buzz bomb" and the V-2 rocket.

Despite the demonstrable quality of the Kolbe reports, the British remained convinced that the data were but a buildup for future deception. Norman Pearson, chief of the OSS X-2 (counterintelligence) component in London, was less convinced. He urged caution, but pointed out that the reports were of great value and contained no hint of deception. In Washington, OSS gave the Kolbe material a highly restricted circulation. Senior military intelligence officers in the Pentagon rejected Kolbe's reports and refused to allow broader dissemination.

Mayer and I were confounded. We did not see how German intelligence could hope to profit from eventually inserting deceptive data into such a flood of high-level intelligence.

Dulles continued to report Kolbe's material. It was not until April 1944 that the British analysts came around and admitted that they had found that only 4 percent of the reports were inaccurate—an extraordinary record for any agent reporting from within an enemy country. At this point the American military agreed to full dissemination of the Kolbe material. Not only did the cables and dispatches—the final count was some 1600 documents—give vital insights into German policy and plans, but the copies of cables also enabled Allied cryptanalysts to complete the deciphering of the heretofore only partially broken Nazi diplomatic ciphers. And if this were not enough, Kolbe's information included an instance in which, presumably unbeknownst to Hitler, Peter Kleist, a ranking foreign office official, was dispatched to Sweden to approach Soviet diplomats with an offer from Ribbentrop to negotiate an end to the fighting on the eastern front. The Soviet embassy refused to meet Kleist.

Kolbe continued to make his daring trips to Switzerland well into 1944, when in the aftermath of the July 20 attempt to assassinate Hitler, the intensified Nazi security measures made the journey impossible.*

Fritz Kolbe is an authentic hero of the German resistance to Hitler. He survived the war, but was never able to regain his footing with his "denazified" former colleagues who were busily establishing the new German foreign office. After some time in New York this gallant German, who in his active days had never sought any compensation, retired to Switzerland, where he lived on a CIA pension.

The evaluation of a new source offering fresh reports on critically important targets on which little or no hard data are on record remains a constant intelligence problem. If a spy is involved, his claimed access to the data and his motives for reporting it are closely examined. His reports are evaluated for possible internal contradictions. If the agent is active, he can be queried on areas in which his reporting can be tested against existing data known to be true. There are a score and more of such tests, but most take time and some require relatively easy access to the agent. In the Kolbe affair, the war was hot, time was precious, and communications between the isolated Bern station and OSS headquarters were clumsy and time-consuming. Given the obstinate British evaluation, it is a credit to Allen Dulles that he chose to march to his own drum and press ahead until the Kolbe reports were recognized for the treasure they were.

But as in so many incidents in secret intelligence there was an element in the Kolbe story that remained hidden from most of us who were involved while the case was running. Thanks to the extraordinary efforts

---

*An American writer and intelligence "expert" has described Kolbe as "bouncing back and forth from Berlin to Bern." Such an authority must have an unusual high-risk tolerance to describe an agent bouncing over the dangers involved in filching Top Secret documents from closely guarded Berlin offices, enduring air raids along the rail line, and slipping through a half dozen Gestapo checkpoints while carrying his death-by-torture warrant in a shabby briefcase.

of British cryptanalysts, and the cooperation of Polish, Czech, and French liaison colleagues and a lone German spy, the Nazi military and intelligence ciphers had been broken sometime before Kolbe became active. This success—code name ULTRA—rivaled only by the American triumph of breaking Japanese ciphers (code name MAGIC), was one of a handful of the great secrets of World War II. The ULTRA information made a vital contribution to the Allied victory in Europe and Africa. No secret was more tightly held or more rigidly compartmented within the services. Knowledge of the break was restricted to an absolute need-to-know basis.

The only element of OSS known to me to have had access to ULTRA on a continuing basis was the London office of X-2, the OSS counterespionage section in England. Although General Donovan was "indoctrinated"—the term for having been briefed and granted access to the ULTRA material—he was rarely in a position to follow it on a regular basis. To my knowledge James Murphy, chief of X-2, was the only OSS officer based in Washington who was indoctrinated and fully informed. It was his responsibility to keep General Donovan briefed on the most important ULTRA data.

At the time Kolbe appeared, the British were able to check his personal background and his reports against the ULTRA holdings. OSS could not have done so—those of us in OSS responsible for evaluating the Kolbe documents in Washington had no knowledge of ULTRA. It was nine months after the initial evaluation of the reports before the comparison of Kolbe's data to the ULTRA material carried the day in London, and his reports were given formal recognition. Called the "Boston Series" by OSS, Kolbe's information is now recognized as the very best produced by any Allied agent in World War II.

The limited dissemination of high-security intelligence reports and the rigorously compartmented knowledge of sensitive operational activity are essential security precautions. In practice, this means that even at relatively high levels of command, one senior officer may not have been briefed on a Top Secret Code Word operation being run in a nearby office. This imposes a heavy responsibility upon intelligence executives. The in-house dissemination of information must be organized so that those with the need to know are well enough informed to spot potential conflicts of purpose without spending every working hour staying abreast of everything that's going on everywhere. The answer is not a near-perfect flowchart, but a reasonable body of experience and seat-of-the-pants common sense.

My continuing effort to move closer to the action succeeded in January 1945, when I was assigned to the German Branch in London. Navy Lieutenant William Casey had just been named chief SI (secret intelligence collection) for OSS in Europe, and was supervising the effort to infiltrate agents into Germany. I may have come in through the side door, but it had opened on the serious world of secret operations.

Chapter 4

———

LONDON

When I left Washington my assignment was to prepare plans and ear-mark personnel for the OSS European headquarters that Allen Dulles was slated to establish in postwar Berlin. By the time I reached London in January 1945 it was obvious that it might be months before he would be establishing the OSS station in Berlin. The Battle of the Bulge and the furious fighting in the Ardennes were convincing proof that the Wehrmacht was far from collapse.

Without tipping his hand, Hitler had assembled a strike force of ten armored divisions, eighteen mechanized infantry divisions, with ample air support, and the necessary supplies and fuel. In forty hours the Germans had blown a hole twelve miles deep and at least six miles wide in the Allied lines. Tanks were within fifteen miles of Liège.

Plans for the Berlin station were set aside. In the meantime I was to make myself useful in London—that is, useful to Navy Lieutenant William J. Casey, the newly appointed chief for secret intelligence collection in Europe. I welcomed the new assignment.

Housing was in short supply, and I was lucky when Bill Casey invited me to share his quarters at 87 Harley House. The flat was a short walk from the OSS headquarters at 70 Grosvenor Street, and just around the corner from the American embassy on Grosvenor Square. Milton Katz, who would become dean of Harvard International Law School and serve as legal counsel for the Marshall Plan, was the third member of our brief ménage à trois. I had, of course, heard of Casey, whom General Donovan had brought into OSS from the Navy. By November 1944, when Casey was posted to London, he had gained a considerable reputation as one of General Donovan's protégés and troubleshooters.

General Donovan and Casey were birds of a feather—highly intelligent, aggressive, ambitious, and self-made. Both were lawyers descended from Irish Catholic immigrants. They were furiously hardworking, impatient, demanding of everyone about them, and with a keen sense of public service. And both were ardent conservative Republicans. Donovan was a born leader, capable of commanding intense respect and loyalty. He was brave, not to say reckless, and had a reputation as one of the most decorated American officers in World War I. Bill Casey took a bit more knowing.

In the hours we spent together, I pieced together Casey's background. After graduating cum laude from Fordham, Casey enrolled in the Catholic University School of Social Work in Washington. He was prepared to help the struggling poor, but had no interest in handing a dole to anyone who appeared to have no intention of ever going to work. He enrolled in a Brooklyn law school, and shaved twelve months from the three-year course while holding a full-time job. Before Casey's law practice was established, he began part-time work for the Research Institute of America drafting newsletters, books, and digests of the New Deal legislation. The business boomed, and Casey moved to RIA headquarters in Washington.

Casey's work at RIA and private practice were highly profitable, but he had a strong sense of public service. In September 1942 he became a consultant to the Board of Economic Warfare. Pinpointing and attacking choke points in Hitler's economy by preemptive buying and strategic blockades was interesting, but not enough so to satisfy Casey. In 1943 he put his career aside and was commissioned a lieutenant (JG) in the Navy. Even if Casey's poor eyesight had not ruled out sea duty, the Navy would not have submerged anyone with his economic savvy in a routine job on a headquarters staff. Casey found himself prodding shipbuilders into manufacturing more landing crafts—and earning only a fraction of his civilian income. This was not what Casey had in mind when he signed on with the Navy.

Casey knew little about OSS, but guessed that it would offer more action than his Navy desk job. When a friend tipped him to the OSS need for a more effective secretariat and registry, Casey presented himself to Lieutenant Colonel Otto Doering, the OSS executive officer, as a master of document control. In what General Donovan later referred to as "jig-time," Casey reorganized the secretariat and reduced the chaos involved in attempting to cope with the sixty thousand cables, dispatches, reports, studies, and other bits of paper that engulfed the OSS headquarters. He also established channels controlling the access that some thirty section chiefs had used to report directly to Donovan.

When Casey arrived at the London headquarters as a Navy lieutenant, a modest rank in a city bulging with senior officers, he carried orders from General Donovan to create a secretariat there similar to the one he had organized in Washington. Colonel David K.E. Bruce, OSS chief in Europe, had not asked for this bounty and was not immediately impressed by the rumpled, relatively junior officer Donovan had sent to do the job. But time was precious, and rather than argue the need for a reorganized secretariat, Bruce accepted Casey as a special assistant whose experience with the Board of Economic Warfare could be put to good use. This, plus Casey's ability to hone masses of material into succinct reports, complemented his reputation as one of General Donovan's protégés.

While on duty in Washington, I had developed a good picture of OSS activity in Europe. By June 1944, and the landings of the Allied troops in Normandy, OSS—in close coordination with the British—had successfully organized espionage and resistance operations in the occupied areas—France, Italy, Austria, Czechoslovakia, Hungary, and Yugoslavia. Individual Germans were recruited as agents in place in Germany and abroad. Aside from operations in the south, OSS activity in France was mounted from England and controlled by the OSS London headquarters. Operations in the south of France were staged from Algiers. All this activity was closely coordinated with the British, and OSS operations mounted from England were subject to approval by the British.

As OSS gained experience and developed its own resources, the British insistence on control began to chafe. General Donovan had for some time considered the possibility of infiltrating agents—by parachute or cross border—into Germany in the manner of the operations conducted in France and other Nazi-occupied areas. The British did not agree.

It was one thing, and difficult enough, Sir Stewart Menzies, chief of MI-6, the British secret intelligence service, informed OSS, to parachute agents into an area occupied by a hated foreign power. It was quite another matter to drop spies into a country policed by its own pervasive and highly efficient security forces, and where there was no organized resistance group that might offer the slightest support to an agent. If an agent was young and hardy enough to survive the drop, and to sustain life entirely on his own, the British asked, how could he also be expected to collect and report intelligence of any significance?

Here, an aside. Within the next decade, I would be embroiled in exactly the same issue—not with the British, but between CIA and the Washington foreign policy establishment.

In 1944, and as long as OSS operations were staged from England, the British position would stand. But General Donovan, as Casey assured me, was not one to take no, or even maybe, for an answer. After all, Allen Dulles had established "a few" agents in Germany, and this, as far as Donovan knew, was at least as much as the sophisticated Brits had achieved. In August, shortly after the Allied troops swept the Wehrmacht away from the Swiss border, Dulles was able to cross into France for his first meeting with General Donovan in twenty months. In Washington, I had picked up bits and pieces of this session. In London, Bill Casey gave me his more intimate view of the discussions.

Before the first session ended, General Donovan, with the thirty-one-year-old Casey at his side, had propositioned his star operative. Wasn't this the moment to begin parachute and line-crossing operations into the Nazi heartland, both to collect intelligence and to foster resistance activity?

Dulles disagreed. He had made his views known even before he left Washington. From the outset in Switzerland, he sought agents who had primary access to strategic information. It was technically possible, he admitted, to slip an occasional agent across the Swiss border into France, Italy, or Austria, but even this required a modicum of cooperation by the Swiss. As for crossings into Germany, Switzerland was not likely to risk becoming known as a staging area for clandestine warfare in the Third Reich. The Swiss were prepared to resist any German attack; Switzerland was not ready to incite a confrontation with the Wehrmacht.

More to the point, Dulles said, what access could any agent bold enough to cross into Germany hope to achieve? Was it not wiser to concentrate on Germans who in the course of their everyday activity had access to strategic information, and to approach them while they were abroad? Why not focus on recruiting agents—of any nationality— who had legitimate business or diplomatic responsibilities that allowed them legal access to Germany and to likely sources of important information?

The bits of these discussions that became known at my level in Washington were not sufficient to warrant a strong opinion. My feeling, however, was to a degree based on my experience as a reporter. One informed source was worth more than a dozen men in the street.

As for resistance activity, Dulles had assured Donovan, the returns were not all in, but Hitler had already put hundreds to death on the grounds they were somehow involved in the July 20 assassination attempt. The Gestapo was now running down the relatives of most of those only remotely involved in that plot. In the opinion of most Germans, Dulles averred, a successful anti-Nazi revolt would only hasten the much propagandized "unconditional surrender" of the German homeland. The prospect of such a surrender played into the hands of Hitler's propagandists. How could any resistance movement hope to sell Germans the notion of *unconditional* surrender to the Soviet horde?

General Donovan and Casey agreed with Dulles's approach, but were not convinced that there was no role for *inserting* agents behind the German lines. As the Allies pushed the Wehrmacht back to the German borders, military resistance would stiffen and there would be even more need for behind-the-lines support. Until that happened, Donovan would reluctantly postpone any intensive effort to infiltrate agents into Germany. He had not, however, abandoned the idea. I was not present at any of these discussions, but long after-hours sessions with Casey provided the details.

Bill Casey's observation that General Donovan was interested in establishing a permanent national intelligence service was the first time the thought occurred to me. Such a service, Donovan thought, should most logically evolve from OSS. He wanted to be sure that his vibrant, fully staffed and experienced organization survived the war intact and with a proven record of competence. He realized that when the fighting in France and the Lowlands slowed, a significant part of the OSS mission in Europe would wind down, with the most motivated warriors peeling off for assignments scattered throughout the Far East. He was concerned lest this cause some of the OSS European activity to be folded into existing military organizations.

When I left Washington the full impact of the near disaster on the Ardennes front had not fully registered. The Wehrmacht had been contained, but fighting still raged along the front. The German offensive demonstrated an Allied intelligence failure—in Casey's words, "a colossal failure."

The day following the attack, Casey cabled Donovan an urgent request for a more active role in Germany, underlining the need for military intelligence and suggesting that with the eventual breakdown of security in Germany, the opportunity for agent activity was much improved. He pointed out that Hitler's Reich was awash in foreigners, all of whom had ample reason to resist and fight against their German jailers. There were some two million Russian prisoners of war who might be stirred into revolt against their hellish imprisonment. The thousands of slave laborers and even volunteer workers—Poles, Belgians, French, and Dutch—scattered throughout Germany were another potential pool of activists. And who better to contact these people than survivors of the European labor movements—trade unionists, socialists, and even communists—who had managed to escape from Germany and find safe haven among the Allies? The OSS Labor Desk already had extensive contact with this group, and had found them responsive and enthusiastic collaborators. Their intimate knowledge of German industry had already proved invaluable.

General Donovan hastened to London. By the time he arrived a few days before Christmas, the reasons for the failure to detect German preparations for the attack were becoming clear. As the German forces retreated in Western Europe, the Wehrmacht turned increasingly to the use of landlines for communication; there were fewer radio transmissions subject to ULTRA coverage; a run of bad weather had severely impaired aerial reconnaissance; and the Allied commanders who were accustomed to the highest-level intelligence from London headquarters had grown complacent, and tended not to push tactical intelligence collection at the division and corps levels.

By the time I had arrived—by train from Scotland, where the naval plane had left me—General Donovan had named Casey chief of OSS/SI for Europe with carte blanche orders to penetrate Germany by any means. At the time, Casey had had a year's experience in OSS Washington, and less than six months in London as Colonel Bruce's special assistant. His new responsibilities paralleled those of the most senior and experienced British MI-6 German operations specialists and those of the German branch of SOE (Special Operations Executive), the sabotage and paramilitary element of British intelligence. On the assumption that these experienced senior officers might be more responsive to a young opposite number in mufti than to a two-stripe naval officer, Donovan arranged for Casey to be placed on inactive naval service and allowed to slip into civilian clothes. I was not expected to be dealing with any senior British officers, and was to remain in my Navy uniform throughout my tour in Europe.

Some OSS parachute operations were mounted directly from England, others from airfields in France. Airdrops into Germany were far more dangerous than those elsewhere on the Continent where some help from local resistance groups was available. There was no such support in the Third Reich, and OSS agents were on their own from the moment they were dropped. Only those with very recent experience within Germany had any chance of survival. These men—I knew of no women who were dropped into Germany—were not fearless, they were brave. They knew that the odds were heavily against them, and that capture meant death—probably torture and death. Among the German nationals, motives were mixed: many had been active in the German labor movement, others were simply opposed to Hitler and the Nazis. None of these agents were influenced by the prospect of any material reward, the standard $2400 death benefit notwithstanding.

A few days after my arrival, Casey assigned me to supervise the preparation and dispatch of an OSS-trained German agent that the British had cleared for a parachute mission into Germany. It was dark, and a light rain had begun to fall as we wedged ourselves into the staff car. My companion glanced anxiously at the windshield wipers. "At least the weather's clear over the target area," he muttered. "If it holds, the plane will leave." The driver eased away from the curb to thread a passage through the blackout and away from London.

Hours earlier, the young German, whose name and pseudonym I've long forgotten, had gone through the final briefing and a last oral run-through of his cover story. Not that it could matter much. The forged documents would support the cover legend and satisfy a preliminary police or military police examination. Despite the care lavished on the documents and in piecing together the cover, it was obviously impossible to backstop any documents in local German records. Even a perfunctory counterintelligence probe meant death for the agent. As the war ground on, and German administration began to fall apart, the military police were too hard pressed to bother with details involved in an extended interrogation. If for any reason the agent were to be referred to the secret field police, the military component of the Gestapo would simply assume he was a deserter and shoot him out of hand. To discourage others, the uniformed body, with a scrawled placard proclaiming the offense, would be left hanging from a lamppost.

In the rigidly enforced blackout the masked headlights of our staff car shed just enough light to alert imperiled pedestrians. Because all road signs had been removed early in the war, experienced drivers had learned to navigate by a self-taught form of dead reckoning, disciplined by highly developed survival instincts. From the rear seat it was impossible to know exactly where we were, but we reached Harrington Field in two hours, exactly on schedule. As we passed the officers' mess and reached a Nissen hut two hundred yards beyond, we could see the lonely black aircraft—as I recall it, a converted A-26 attack bomber.

The bleak staging area was quiet except for murmured comments in German as the webbed straps of the parachute were carefully adjusted. It may have been a myth, but we worked on the assumption that if the agent were apprehended and fortunate enough to be held for interrogation, it was important that there be no bruises about the shoulders or on the thighs that might indicate a parachute harness. The flight to the Ruhr area would be long and uncomfortable for the burdened young agent, but experience had shown that it was easier to adjust the chute on the ground rather than later when bouncing around in the blacked-out aircraft.

The young aircrew, whose lives were also on the line, ducked in and out of the staging area. Obviously preoccupied with the weather and flight plans, they barely glanced at their passenger. It took an extra measure of courage to volunteer to fly without fighter protection to a remote area which, unlike cities or industrial targets, would be difficult to find. Worse, the pilots were required to approach the drop zone at less than a very vulnerable thousand feet. In theory, agents were to jump at five hundred feet, a height which would best ensure that the drop area could be correctly identified, and which would get the agent on the ground quickly. "Fly low and slow" was an ironic bit of advice given tyro bomber pilots by their more seasoned comrades, but it was definitely not the recommended means of ensuring safe passage. It required iron self-discipline for the pilot and navigator, both anxious to scoot away, to be sure they had reached the target, and were low enough to signal the jump.

The bulky, one-piece coveralls zipped loosely over the well-worn, field gray Wehrmacht uniform, the padded parachute helmet, and heavy gauntlet gloves gave the impression that the agent was being fitted for a deep-sea dive rather than a parachute jump. Bits of equipment hung from the coveralls—a knife, flashlight, padded aviation goggles to protect the eyes if the landing was in a tree or brush, and an entrenching tool for digging the hole to bury the parachute. I wondered how much self-control it would take for the lone agent, who at best could only hope he had landed somewhere close to the chosen area, to dig a hole deep enough to bury the chute, the tangle of lines, and the coveralls. Then, in total darkness, he was to tarry long enough to camouflage the freshly dug dirt. Only then was he to leave the area with the heavy radio set—a death warrant—in a worn suitcase.

I knew that—briefings notwithstanding—my instinct would be to get far away from the landing site as soon as possible. I was in awe of the courageous agent, and I remain so.

After a handshake and final word with his case officer, the agent was guided to the plane. He turned, waved a token salute, and pulled himself up the narrow ladder into the belly of the aircraft. Six of us watched as the plane lurched across the field toward the takeoff area. No one mentioned it, but the knowledge that we would sit safely at the airfield while the flight crew and the young agent faced what could be the ultimate test kindled a long bout of intense reflection. The only consolation we had was that the agent had been given the best preparation we could contrive.

The aircraft was to maintain strict radio silence. It would be hours before it returned to base and could report that the drop had been made on target, and a great many more hours before the agent could set up his radio and signal a safe landing.

The odds were against the mission succeeding and the agent knew it. He had asked for and been issued a lethal tablet. Even in wartime, suicide devices are a snarled problem. The lethal OSS tablets were supplied only upon the request of the agent. From a security viewpoint, they were of some value. If the agent became convinced that he was about to be captured, he could of his own volition commit suicide and avoid the possibility of betraying comrades under the pressure of vicious torture. But there were many negatives. Despite the best testing possible, the tablets did not always work, and a botched suicide attempt would leave the agent even less able to protect himself. Worse, experience had shown that in the extreme anxiety of a dangerous mission, agents were rarely in a position to make desperate decisions, and might needlessly take their lives.

It was in London that I first heard the expression "hard target," a phrase which was to haunt me for thirty years. In time, I came to realize that the hard targets are the only objectives worth strategic intelligence attention. In the Europe of 1944, the hard targets were in Germany— Hitler, the High Command, the upper bracket of the Nazi Party, the foreign office, and the elite group of well-informed civilians who formed the Nazi establishment. By the time I retired, the hard targets included the USSR, the Soviet satellite countries, Communist China, North Korea, North Vietnam, Iraq, Iran, Syria, and the Near East terrorist groups. The less than strategic targets encompassed every potential flare-up anywhere on the globe that meant the President was to be closely informed.

OSS London was crowded with a remarkable congeries of men and women who were to make their mark in the postwar world. Under the command of Colonel David K.E. Bruce, later to be ambassador to France, Germany, and the Court of St. James, the London staff included Arthur Schlesinger, Jr., historian and presidential advisor; Milton Katz, of the Marshall Plan and Harvard Law School; Julia Child, who would forever change American cooking; Norman Pearson, professor of American literature at Yale; Richard Ellmann, scholar and biographer of Yeats,

Joyce, and Wilde, and dozens of other wildly assorted characters. OSS may have been the only organization in the European theater of operations in which ranks were relatively jumbled. In some offices, enlisted personnel—usually in civilian clothes—functioned on an equal level with uniformed officers.

One of the lessons of our efforts to penetrate Germany that should have been more thoroughly ingested in the immediate postwar years was the difference between the operations Allen Dulles had created in Switzerland and which, to a lesser degree, OSS had mounted from neutral Sweden, and those General Donovan and Bill Casey pushed from our London headquarters.

From the beginning of his work in Switzerland, Dulles had focused on recruiting sources who had near-primary access to the most needed intelligence. This is the category of source that in the years that followed was to become known as "agents in place." Dulles's operations were greatly facilitated by his location in Switzerland, surrounded by Germany and the various Nazi-occupied or -dominated countries. The diplomatic, business, and other cross-border travel to and from Germany and the occupied areas was as restricted as possible by German security controls. There were still enough legal travelers to provide a few potential sources with access to a high level of strategic intelligence.

One of the great strengths of the Swiss station was Dulles's range of contacts throughout Switzerland who were in a position to signal the presence of these travelers to the station. In some instances these contacts were able themselves to solicit the active cooperation of travelers, or to put a station officer or an intermediary in touch with the visitor. Many of Dulles's collaborators were well placed and sufficiently well informed to *elicit* significant intelligence from visitors who had no intention of cooperating with the Allies and no idea that their remarks would go straight to Washington and London.

Neutral Sweden also offered access to Germany and the occupied areas in Scandinavia, and along the Baltic. Bruce Hopper, the first OSS officer, arrived in Stockholm in March 1942. He came from London, skirting enemy-occupied territory in a fast-flying RAF light bomber. By December that year, the station—three men strong—was established. Although the State Department had reluctantly agreed to accept the OSS representatives as members of the legation, the minister in charge was less than welcoming. Within days of his arrival, the chief of station was informed that if anything resembling espionage was undertaken, the minister would insist that the State Department recall the OSS representatives. No matter that the most devastating conflict in history was raging—and that Sweden, like Switzerland, offered a unique location from which to collect information on the Third Reich and some of the Nazi-occupied areas—espionage was too naughty an activity to be sheltered on American diplomatic premises. It is much to Hopper's credit that within a year the OSS station had begun to function effectively.

In 1944 the Allied strategic bombing of German ball-bearing factories had cut production to the point that the Reich had to turn to Sweden for the vital supply. OSS agent reports on the tonnage of bearings and manufacturing equipment being shipped to Germany made it possible for the U.S. economic warfare authority to persuade Sweden to halt the shipments, which by then were accounting for a significant percentage of Germany's need.

By 1945, the station, then thirty-five strong, had recruited businessmen who were making regular trips to Germany and Scandinavia, opened liaison with representatives and intelligence officers of some of the governments in exile from the occupied countries, and made arrangements for the debriefing of refugees from the Baltic areas. It was a strong performance, deserving more public credit than it has received.

The operations organized by Casey and staged by the OSS field units attached to the Seventh Army in southern France were short-term tactical missions. As Germany's security forces disintegrated, these short-range operations—dubbed "tourist" missions, a euphemism if ever there was one—were able to report a minimum of tactical data of interest to the military. The agents we parachuted into Germany were brave men, dedicated patriots hoping for a new Germany and a better Austria.

By late August when Paris was liberated, the push was on for the various London-based headquarters to move forward, particularly toward the Paris area. OSS was no exception. My assignment to help organize the cadre of SI officers who would staff what had become known as the OSS German Mission was revived, and I was one of the early arrivals in Paris.

General Dwight Eisenhower had been in the Army long enough to know that if any units were allowed to establish rear area headquarters and support staffs in the Paris area, a significant portion of his forces would instantly find ironclad reasons to remain there. Despite the general's prescience and strict orders, Paris and its environs were soon engulfed by Allied forces. OSS was no exception, and our offices swarmed with officers and men in transit. Some were anxious for new assignments, and ready for transfer to the Pacific theater. Others were in a less discernible rush, content to catch their breath in the city of light before getting on with the war.

OSS headquarters were established on the Champs-Elysées in comfortable premises which had hastily been abandoned by a Nazi security unit. My billet in the Parc Monceau hotel was redundant proof of the U.S. Navy's reputation for taking care of its own. The hotel staff was not intact, but service had bounced back to a near-prewar standard. The various naval and military mess facilities remained under the thumb of the service cooks, and the hearty but tame GI rations soon began to appear in a new and welcome guise.

The most obvious traces of the German occupation had been erased, but Paris was still in some disarray. Black markets of every sort flourished. However happy the French were to have been freed of German occupation, and despite occasional flashes of exuberant black market chic, there remained a strong underlying sense of fatigue. The very visible and huge Allied military and civilian presence could only have been an added irritant as the Parisians struggled to reestablish their lives.

On May 8, the day the war ended in Europe, Colonel Russell Forgan, who had replaced David Bruce as OSS chief in London, and Allen Dulles, still slated to become OSS chief in Germany, had an appointment with General Eisenhower at SHAEF headquarters in Rheims. Because I had many questions for Dulles, who was still based in Switzerland, I was included in the ride from Paris.

It was immediately apparent that General Eisenhower's VE Day commitments made it impossible for him to keep his appointment. I was left in an outer office to muse on the defeat of the Wehrmacht, while my companions conducted their business with General Walter Bedell Smith, General Eisenhower's chief of staff. When they emerged from the meeting, I was introduced to General Smith. It was an odd quirk of history that three men of such wildly differing background, experience, and rank, but each destined eventually to become director of Central Intelligence in Washington, stood chatting in Rheims at the moment the Third Reich admitted total defeat.

In Paris, the roster for the move toward Germany took shape and an advance party pulled stakes to an interim location in Luxembourg, a picturesque medieval city. My hotel room window opened onto a view along a pastoral valley, with a single rail line etched along the horizon. In the distance, a lonely engine puffed toward Belgium and the remains of Hitler's Thousand Year Reich.

From Luxembourg we moved into Germany, to take up offices at the Henkel champagne factory on the outskirts of Wiesbaden in Hesse.

Chapter 5

———

WIEDER BERLIN

Whether the assignment of the OSS contingent to the Henkel champagne works in Biebrich on the outskirts of Wiesbaden was a sly bit of military humor—the OSS soubriquet Oh So Social had percolated from Washington—or simply the luck of the draw didn't much matter in 1945. The U.S. Army had taken over large chunks of the Hessen area, and because the Henkel premises were undamaged and the spa city of Wiesbaden had largely escaped destruction, we felt well served. The administrative offices of the champagne works served as headquarters, and a section of the wine-producing space was converted into a dining hall and kitchen.

The Henkel champagne works were closely associated with Joachim von Ribbentrop, who for seven years served as Nazi foreign minister. Joseph Goebbels, the Nazi propaganda chief and one of the brighter evil lights of Hitler's inner circle, described his colleague as having "bought his name . . . married his money, and . . . swindled his way into office." The Ribbentrop family tree had two branches, only one of which could sport the ennobling "von." Alas, poor Joachim was one of the plain vanilla Ribbentrops, a condition he remedied by bribing a *von* Ribbentrop aunt to adopt him. The rechristened Joachim *von* Ribbentrop acquired his money by marrying the daughter of the wealthy Henkel family. Although Hitler once described his foreign minister as a genius and compared him with Bismarck, von Ribbentrop's only diplomatic qualifications were a rich wife, fluent English acquired while peddling wine and spirits in Canada, and an affected posture of a deep thinker and man of the world. His diplomatic peers considered him an arrogant, bombastic fool—as ambassador to the Court of St. James, von Ribbentrop greeted George V with a Nazi salute. Goebbels and his wife poisoned their six young children before committing suicide in Hitler's bunker; von Ribbentrop was asleep in bed when arrested. By the time OSS occupied the champagne works, the bewildered but unrepentant former foreign minister was in a Nuremberg cell, awaiting trial and eventual hanging.

In memory, the atmosphere in Germany in the weeks after the unconditional surrender seems almost as unreal as it did at the time and is now difficult to re-create. The immense relief that the slaughter and destruction had ended was, of course, pervasive. Germany lay prostrate, its major cities reduced to rubble, its industry and transportation system largely in ruins, the central government nonexistent, and the interim local authorities scarcely up to their task. By summer it was already apparent that shortages of food, housing, medical care, and transportation would soon become critical. Black markets flourished, profiteering was rampant, workers and the middle class were reduced to selling valuables and making pathetic attempts at begging.

The inconvenience suffered by some of the Nazi elite when they were summarily ousted from their property to make room for the occupation forces was slight in comparison with the hardships the stricken population at large was beginning to endure. The shock that followed the revelation of the unimaginably appalling conditions in the concentration and extermination camps further hardened the Allied forces' reaction to the condition of the civilian population.

The Quartermaster Corps provided us with ample rations and quarters—ranging from make-do but comfortable billets and communal mess halls to handsome requisitioned villas staffed with servants. Detailed arrangements had been drafted for the occupation of Germany, but in the face of reality even the best plans required overhaul and considerable tinkering. An immediate problem was the intense pressure on the part of the noncareer military personnel to get home and out of uniform.

Priority for reassignment was based on length of service, combat time, decorations, and time served abroad. These factors could readily be determined, but when complicated by the legitimate hardship cases and the erratic availability of sea transport, this meant that an office fully staffed on Monday might find itself at half strength by Friday.

Despite the revolving personnel door, the planned organization of the OSS German Mission headquarters began to take shape. Offices and bases were opened in Berlin, Frankfurt, Munich, and other cities in the American zone of occupation. Although Allen Dulles had been appointed chief of the OSS German Mission with headquarters in Berlin, he was still closing out his activity in Switzerland, and dividing his remaining time between Wiesbaden and the small office that had been established for him in Berlin. The supervision of the day-to-day work was left to Dulles's deputy, Colonel William Suhling. AWD, as his senior staff referred to Dulles, paid careful attention to the well-being of his numerous anti-Nazi contacts in Germany and elsewhere throughout Europe. This collection of politicians, labor leaders, intellectuals, industrialists, and academics became known as the "Crown Jewels." The term stuck and lasted beyond Dulles's subsequent tenure as director of Central Intelligence.

For the German population and the tens of thousands of displaced persons and refugees, food was the most urgent requirement, but housing was a close second. Transport was another critical problem. Railways were barely functioning and jammed with refugees and displaced persons. Gasoline for private cars was all but nonexistent, and almost any form of motor transport beyond the reach of most. OSS operations officers who had made their mark operating in Nazi-occupied Europe, or recruiting and training agents to be parachuted into these areas and Germany, found themselves delivering food supplies, and acting as chauffeurs and all-around Ganymedes for the middle-aged men Dulles hoped would eventually play a role in rebuilding a democratic Germany. In the process some of these young Americans developed a sound understanding of Germany at a grassroots level.

Former agents like Fritz Kolbe, who survived the war and had remained in Berlin, were given special care. Modest pensions were established for the destitute and shunned families of the men and women executed after the July plot against Hitler.

It was in Biebrich that I met Navy Commander Frank Wisner, who arrived from Bucharest still shaken by his firsthand experience of the brutal Soviet occupation of Romania. I worked directly for Frank, who had taken over as intelligence collection chief in the American zone of occupation. Lieutenant Colonel Ides van der Gracht, the architect who had supervised the construction of the Pentagon, was chief of intelligence production, with responsibility for the evaluation and dissemination of intelligence reports. I recall Ides's exasperation when first reviewing some of our early intelligence disseminations. "In architecture," he said, "a foot is always precisely twelve inches; in these reports things often seem to be 'more or less a foot.' " While Ides was insisting on precision, I was sorting out priorities and pushing for more intelligence collection. Because of the fluid personnel situation, we both were involved in a version of musical chairs, attempting to fill the operations and administrative vacancies throughout the U.S. zone of occupation from an ever dwindling personnel supply.

A few of us were billeted in a well-staffed and comfortable—verging on plush—requisitioned villa on the outskirts of Wiesbaden. German houses of that period usually had a study or hallway garnished with mounted trophies of game presumably shot by the owner. Our lodgings were distinguished by a mounted rabbit head on which a taxidermist had affixed a miniature set of horns. The villa immediately became known as the Horned Rabbit Club.

There was more than enough work to go around, but there was also enough energy for an active social life. Hearty Army rations and liquor were plentiful, and odds and ends of the Sekt, the German version of champagne produced in the Henkel factory, became available on a daily basis. Some of this was so freshly bottled that we referred to it as the 1947 vintage, a beverage that could never have been confused with the most modest French champagne. Quartermaster purchasing agents in the United States appeared to have corralled the entire production of a notably harsh, blended American whiskey, a brand of which none of the OSS tipplers had ever heard and which, if it ever was offered on the American market, had mercifully disappeared by the time any of us got home. The Army PX had also contracted for an ocean of a particularly vile Spanish brandy. After some potentially lethal experimentation we came up with a relatively potable drink. A lavish jigger of brandy mixed with a tumbler of canned grapefruit juice became known as "Franco's Revenge."

With it all, the work got done and friendships were made that were to last a lifetime.

Among those quartered at the Horned Rabbit were Gordon Stewart, later to serve as chief of station in Germany; Stanley Baron, who left CIA to publish a number of well-received novels and become an editor at Thames & Hudson in London; and Rolfe Kingsley, one of the earliest OSS recruits and who remained with CIA until his retirement. Harry Rositzke, the Agency's first Soviet expert, also shared the premises. Robert Joyce, who replaced Dulles in Switzerland and later returned to senior posts in the Department of State, and Paul Blum, AWD's counterintelligence chief from Switzerland and an internationally known bookman and gourmet, were among our visitors.

In August, I left Biebrich to head the intelligence acquisition branch of the Berlin office.

———

When I boarded the train from Berlin in 1937, Hitler was near the height of his popularity. While taking credit for having ended inflation and beginning rearmament, he parlayed the reoccupation of the Rhineland and the international success of the Olympic Games into even broader support within Germany than he had enjoyed before becoming chancellor in 1933. In August 1945, Berlin was smashed almost beyond recognition. On my first flight over the acres of destroyed buildings it did not seem possible that the city would ever be rebuilt. As one of our young secretaries put it, "This Berlin's a *real mess.*"

It took a bit of doing—some streets were so nearly destroyed that they could not be recognized, but I located my former bed-sitter on the Wittenberg Platz. Looking out from the shattered building, I could see across the rubble for hundreds of yards in every direction. But those of us who doubted that the city would ever be rebuilt had not reckoned on the energy and determination of the German people in general and the hardy Berliners in particular.

Of my landlady and neighbors, I found no trace.

We established the OSS offices in a building on the Foehrenweg that had served as headquarters for General Ludwig Beck when he was chief of the German General Staff. General Beck was one of the earliest anti-Nazi plotters, and the highest-ranking Wehrmacht officer to resign his commission because of his intense dislike of Hitler. In deference to his age and distinguished military reputation, Beck was allowed to commit suicide twelve hours after the July 20 plot failed.

Our offices looked out on a dead-end street, an important security consideration in the early days when the occupying powers were still sorting out their sectors, and policing was haphazard. Desperadoes of every sort—discharged Wehrmacht personnel, Russian deserters, displaced persons, war criminals on the lam, desperate SS survivors—roamed the ruins.

One of the first problems to be settled in Berlin was personnel. It was soon apparent that the chief of one section of the Berlin office was spending more energy trading gasoline, coffee, and cigarettes for serious artwork, jewelry, and what might be called social favors than he was on operations. Much to his surprise, I sent him away with a personal file that ensured his days in intelligence were over. Circumstances were arranged so that he left Berlin with but a fraction of the loot he had amassed.

When Peter Sichel, a member of the Sichel wine family and early OSS recruit, arrived in Berlin to take over the unit, one of the incumbent section chiefs offered him a thousand dollars for his watch. Peter declined, and gave the man a choice between an investigation of his financial activity and immediate departure from Berlin and OSS.

"Turmoil" is a word that comes repeatedly to mind in reflecting on the early days of the occupation. Germany had collapsed, defeated, overwhelmed physically, politically, and socially. I doubt that many of us could understand the emotional carnage this caused. Corruption is contagious, and it was no surprise that it leaked into the occupation forces. This was my first experience of crime within the outfit, and I have not forgotten it.

It was in the small Foehrenweg offices and at meals taken every day at the house in which Allen Dulles was billeted that I got to know the man with whom I was to work for so many eventful years. My first impression, gained on our drive from Paris to Rheims on VE Day, was never to change. Parted gray hair, carefully trimmed mustache, tweeds, and his preferred rimless, oval glasses gave the impression of a boarding-school master, a virile Mr. Chips, rarely to be seen without a pipe in hand. Of course he didn't always wear tweeds, but as a colleague said, "It's just that AWD always looks as if he were wearing tweeds."

With his glasses pushed up onto his forehead, "Allen" had an easy laugh and a contagious sense of humor—for all of this, "Mr. Dulles" was a demanding boss. When he put down his pipe and leaned forward business was at hand and he meant it. His leadership quality required none of the trappings of authority; there were no bursts of temper or threats of discipline. Despite his seniority and reputation as an outstanding operative, he always exuded a welcoming manner. He was open to discussion until a decision was made; at that point unless additional data became available, the decision would stand. Dulles was a natural raconteur, and enjoyed talking shop and swapping anecdotes with the staff.

It was in Berlin that I first heard one of the stories he never tired of repeating. When Congress declared war on Germany on April 6, 1917, Dulles was a third secretary, the lowest man in the diplomatic pecking order at the U.S. embassy in Vienna. The evacuation train that hustled the embassy staff out of Austria arrived in the Swiss capital early Easter Sunday morning. As befitted his junior status, Dulles was detailed to the legation offices, sorting bundles of files and serving as de facto duty officer for the deposed Vienna staff. Not one to waste time bemoaning his bad luck—his twenty-fourth birthday had passed unnoticed on the trip to Bern—Dulles had found time to schedule an afternoon tennis session with a Swiss girl he had met on an earlier trip to Bern with his parents.

Mid-morning, the legation duty clerk handed Dulles the telephone. One of the many Russian émigré politicians was demanding to talk with an American official. Dulles identified himself. The Russian asked for an immediate meeting.

"On Easter Sunday?"

"Yes."

In his ten months in Vienna, Dulles had encountered several of the exiled Russian politicians. He was not impressed with the Russian's demand for an immediate meeting, but offered to make himself available on Monday.

"Too late, too late," the Russian spluttered. He was already booked to leave on Monday.

"Sorry," Dulles murmured, "but that's the best I can do." And so there was no meeting between Nikolai Lenin and the future director of Central Intelligence. The next day the train which would take Lenin and a handful of fellow Bolsheviks to the Finland Station in St. Petersburg left on schedule. Through the years the details sometimes varied, but Dulles rarely missed an opportunity to use the story to illustrate his deep-seated conviction that intelligence officers must keep the door open, and never miss the opportunity to meet someone new.

Dulles was occasionally stricken with gout, which, we learned, was as painful as a toothache and less easily managed. He never complained and the only warning that his foot was giving him hell was the sudden appearance of bedroom slippers and a rocky gait. Despite Dulles's self-control, I learned not to surface any proposal that was less than urgent, or which might seem rashly reasoned, when the slippers were in sight. Only a lighthearted sailor leaves port in view of a hurricane warning.

In the early days of the occupation the four national sectors (Soviet, British, French, and U.S.) had not been clearly defined and all one needed to move freely around in the ruins of Hitler's Thousand Year Reich was a uniform and four wheels. On one bit of personal reconnaissance I sneaked into Hitler's chancellery. This was in the Soviet sector, but the Russian guards took no notice of an officer in uniform who, in their eyes, was senior enough to rate a jeep. While poking around the banquet hall I picked a few pieces of intact crockery from the shoals of smashed porcelain that made navigation difficult in the huge room. Two pieces have disappeared, but one plate with "Kanzlei des Fuehrer" boldly stenciled in brown is in my study, a reminder of a war the Allies might well have lost had Hitler not hated the Soviets and admired the British.

The politics of Berlin and the developing problems of the four-power occupation of the Nazi capital were chaotic, and intelligence officers were constantly shifting from one target to another. My work ranged from tracking down die-hard Nazis suspected of organizing clandestine resistance to the occupation—in fact there was no such resistance—to searching for the hundreds of war criminals on our "automatic arrest" lists, seeking evidence of stolen treasure and looted artworks. Along with these responsibilities, we were to monitor Russian military depredation in the Soviet zone and trace any German scientists the Russians had not already seized.

One of the odd demands, possibly assigned by a historian on the Washington staff, was for details on the last days within Hitler's bunker. The score or more uniformed historians ferreting about in the shambles of the Third Reich had failed to uncover her, but Fred Stalder, one of our senior German-speaking case officers, unearthed Erna Flegel, a surgical nurse who had been on duty within Hitler's personal quarters in the Fuehrer Bunker. She had remained on the job until Hitler's suicide and the deaths of the Goebbels family. This wasn't a strategic intelligence coup, but Stalder's report was solid history.

There were so many, often conflicting, demands for information that it was almost impossible to sort out the priority objectives. The need for headquarters to establish a central authority through which all collection requirements were to be funneled and assigned a priority was one of the first postwar lessons I learned in Berlin.

Although the United States was still officially allied with the Soviet Union, pressure was building for my small section to learn exactly what the Russians were up to in the Soviet occupation zone and what political moves they might be planning. It was in these early days that the first traces of Cold War operations began to develop. Three of our staff maintained quiet relations with some of the Russian officers and officials who were more outspoken than Moscow was aware. Clandestine attempts were made to question Soviet defectors—called deserters at the time. Under the existing agreements with the Russians, our military were supposed to return all Soviet subjects immediately to Red Army authorities.

Allen Dulles was into everything, intelligence and otherwise. Rushing from city to city, from Crown Jewel to some new personal contact, he slowed down only to fire off scores of telegrams and letters barraging American authorities in Washington and across Europe with his views on everything from intelligence and political problems to economic and social matters. While scrupulously attending to the welfare of his former agents and contacts, AWD continued to spot new people he thought capable of helping to rebuild a democratic Germany.

However much General Donovan and his senior staff might have known or suspected in Washington, those of us in Germany were taken completely by surprise on September 20, 1945, when President Harry Truman abruptly issued the executive order terminating the Office of Strategic Services ten days hence. The order, which was not coordinated with OSS, the service chiefs in the Pentagon, or the Department of State, was to become effective on the opening of business October 1, 1945. The precise reason for the abrupt termination was not clear to us in Berlin at the time. We were left to assume that in striving to bring the government back to a peacetime footing and size, President Truman had made the closing of the many offices that had sprung up in response to the war a priority. Still, it seemed more punitive than rational to expect an organization that stretched from Washington across Europe, with elements in the Near East, Africa, China, Burma, India, and Vietnam to fold its many tents, abandon its properties, and rid itself of some 11,500 employees in ten days.

All that we in Germany knew was that for the moment we had been subsumed into a carryover organization known as the Strategic Services Unit (SSU), and that the OSS remains—personnel, property, and functions—had at least temporarily been divided between the War and State Departments. The SSU, nominally attached to the War Department, retained the operational remnants—intelligence collection and counterintelligence abroad. The Research and Analysis staff and responsibilities went to State. Brigadier General John Magruder, a regular Army officer and one of General Donovan's senior staff officers, was named chief of the Strategic Services Unit.

One of General Magruder's early messages to SSU Germany was to ask that Dulles, Frank Wisner, and I remain in place for the present. The plan to establish the OSS headquarters in Berlin had proved unrealistic, and was abandoned as the organization of the occupation armies and civilian governments began to take shape. The SSU headquarters were first established near Wiesbaden but soon moved to Karlsruhe, then Heidelberg, eventually to settle in Frankfurt am Main.

Dulles's reputation as OSS's most successful operative was already widely recognized. It was only later that I learned General Donovan was convinced that Dulles had too little interest in the administrative side of secret intelligence to be an effective chief of an organization as complex as the OSS German Mission was certain to become. It was not until Dulles came back to intelligence work in CIA that it became apparent to others of us that the talents he brought to his personal operational activity never quite equated with his reluctance to concern himself with the administrative burdens of secret intelligence. His skill in exploiting and expanding his range of personal relationships remained unsurpassed.

We never discussed this at the time, but it was clear that the abrupt and essentially unplanned-for dissolution of OSS, and transfer to the transparently jerry-built and transient SSU organization, hastened a decision that AWD knew he had to make. It had been apparent for some weeks that his personal objectives went well beyond managing an organization scattered across occupied Germany, under the thumb, if not fist, of the military occupation authorities, and with a most uncertain line of command in Washington. There could be no question that Dulles felt most comfortable running things on his own with a minimum of supervision from above.

Another fact bearing on AWD's problem was his 1926 decision to resign from the State Department and abandon a promising diplomatic career. Without a personal fortune, he was not prepared to live on the then modest civil service pay scale. In 1945, with three children to support, and a well-honed taste for comfortable living, he faced the same problem. His older brother, John Foster Dulles, had remained with the Sullivan and Cromwell law firm throughout the war, and was now pocketing several times more than Allen could ever hope to earn in government.

These personal considerations were only part of the problem. Allen Dulles had an intense interest in making sure that the United States would come out of the war with a national intelligence service that would serve it effectively in the future. Would the new service be an independent civilian outfit or merely another obscure unit soon to disappear among the various military intelligence organizations? Or was it possible that the Department of State might tuck secret intelligence away as a hidden component of its other responsibilities? One thing was certain: Allen Dulles wanted to be in on the decision making and doubted very much that his voice could be heard from as far away as Germany.

I was disappointed but not surprised in October when with very short notice Allen turned the Berlin base over to me and left Berlin for Washington.

Chapter 6

GETTING IN

By December 1945 the postwar organization of the former OSS offices (Strategic Services Mission to Germany) had taken shape. The Berlin detachment was coming up to speed, and Peter Sichel was well prepared to act as chief of the operations component until my replacement arrived from Washington. I'd been away from my family for a year; there was my son to get to know and serious decisions to be made. It was time for me to leave Berlin.

Transatlantic flights were long in those days, and as luck had it, Frank Wisner and I traveled together in a Navy aircraft. Frank was my boss, but his offices were in the mission headquarters in Biebrich, and we had spent little time together. The eighteen-hour flight gave me the opportunity to begin to know the man from Laurel, Mississippi. While an honor student at the University of Virginia, Frank had developed enough of a reputation as a runner to be invited to the Olympic track and field trials in 1936. This did not square with Frank's father's idea of how a young man should spend his summer vacation. Wisner senior thought that a job in a bottling works would do more for his son's character than a few weeks of track competition. The family philosophy—that from those to whom much is given, much is expected—was not wasted on young Wisner.

After law school, Frank joined the Carter Ledyard law firm in New York. Six months before Pearl Harbor, he volunteered for naval service. The outbreak of war and a stretch of naval intelligence office jobs prompted Frank to seek something more active. An introduction by a former professor paved the way for transfer to OSS. After assignments in Cairo and Istanbul, Frank arrived in Bucharest in August 1944 as the last Wehrmacht units were retreating from Romania. He was one of the first OSS officers to come face-to-face with the Russians, and the experience was to shape the rest of his life.

We were an hour out over the Atlantic when I noticed a *Time* magazine review of *The Age of Jackson* by Arthur Schlesinger, Jr. I nudged Frank, and asked if by any chance Schlesinger, the historian, might be related to the Corporal Schlesinger who worked with us in Wiesbaden. Frank grimaced, then laughed and said, "Damn it, if I'd had anything to do with it, he would have been promoted." No doubt about it, OSS had talent to spare.

Frank and I were convinced that an intelligence service along the lines of General Donovan's OSS would be essential in the years to come, but neither of us had a clear picture of the progress being made in Washington, or even what the prospects for such a service might be. In the process of resigning my Navy commission as a lieutenant commander, I began to assemble the bits and pieces of what had transpired since September 1945, when President Truman had given OSS ten days to close shop.

Like most landmark events, the impact of President Truman's sudden directive had a light side. The morning the termination order was announced at General Donovan's staff meeting, Rudyard Bolton, a soft-spoken, internationally known ornithologist specializing in Africa, shot up from his chair. Thrusting both arms toward Heaven, he shouted, "Jesus H. Christ, I suppose this means that it's back to those goddamned birds," and stumbled from the room. In those days Africa specialists were hard to come by and the professor was to remain with CIA until his retirement.

When OSS was officially terminated, the White House staff, the Bureau of the Budget, and OSS had not completed any postwar liquidation plans. The resulting confusion triggered a fierce bureaucratic battle for the OSS remains and the eventual responsibility for a national intelligence service. The Department of State saw itself as the logical niche for a civilian intelligence function, while the War Department assumed it would run all military intelligence activity and report such political intelligence as it deemed worth collecting. The FBI was determined to cling to its intelligence responsibilities in Latin America and dreamed of extending its authority around the globe. In the White House a few staffers actually thought an intelligence czar might be able to direct, coordinate, and discipline all the existing intelligence components from a perch on the President's shoulder.

Scattered among these contesting entities was a handful of civilian and military personnel who could not forget that in the weeks before December 7, 1941, the United States had collected enough information to have shown that the Japanese were planning an attack that might most plausibly fall upon Pearl Harbor. Because there was no central office responsible for collecting and evaluating information, these bits and pieces of intelligence were strewn among codebreakers, the Department of State, War Department, Navy Department, and the White House. Coherent analysis and dissemination was impossible. This fired the determination of these men to create an independent, unified intelligence agency.

One thing is certain. The notion that CIA was created in response to the Cold War is totally false. The need for a central intelligence authority was clearly perceived long before the postwar ambitions and hostility of the Soviet Union were recognized. Even before the Japanese surrender, the advent of the atomic bomb sharpened the insiders' conviction that the United States could never again risk another Pearl Harbor.

Two members of the Truman administration, Assistant Secretary of War John J. McCloy and Donald Stone of the Bureau of the Budget, cooperated quietly and with great foresight to preserve the most important functions of OSS. Stone transferred the vital OSS Research and Analysis (R & A) branch to the State Department. John McCloy contrived to place the intelligence collection (SI) and counterintelligence (X-2) components in the hastily assembled Strategic Services Unit (SSU), temporarily attached to the War Department, and commanded by Brigadier General John Magruder. Although the War Department would simply have merged the OSS personnel and files with the existing G-2 organizations, McCloy ordered General Magruder to preserve SI and X-2 as "a going operation." However jerry-built a structure, SSU served to keep the OSS headquarters intact and the remaining OSS field stations in place, to serve as cornerstones of the nation's first peacetime national intelligence service. American intelligence owes a considerable debt to John McCloy, Donald Stone, and General Magruder for putting the national interest above the parochial ambitions of their parent services.

Tucked away in SSU, I was spared much of the bruising bureaucratic wear and tear of the struggle for primacy in the intelligence field. By late January 1946, when I resigned my commission as lieutenant commander and doffed the naval uniform I had worn throughout my OSS service, I knew I could no longer postpone a career decision.* Before my return to the United States, and as much as I hated to admit it, my long-held ambition to have my own newspaper had faded. Even the smallest dailies were now beyond any financial means I might be able to raise. The job offered me by the *Indianapolis Times* did not appeal. More to the point, I now realized that I was hooked on intelligence. The need for an effective intelligence service in the turbulent and anything but benign postwar world seemed obvious. The work was exciting; the prospect of participating in building a new and unique peacetime organization was at the least challenging. The fact that none of us really knew what the career prospects might be added a tingle to the decision. In its bureaucratic limbo, SSU scarcely qualified as a safe career bet, but it was the only game in town that appeared to encompass the best of the OSS legacy— an unmistakable élan, experienced personnel, files, liaison relationships, and an overseas establishment.

Coincidentally with my as yet unspoken decision, Stephen Penrose, a

---

*The OSS personnel roster encompassed four categories. Officers and enlisted men and women from the Army, Navy, and Marine Corps were interspersed with civilians serving at various civil service grade and pay scales. In London, the enlisted personnel who bore responsibilities customarily reserved for commissioned officers were fitted out with civilian clothes. Although denied access to both officer and enlisted clubs and messes, these pseudo-civilians were provided per diem expenses which more than covered housing and subsistence on the economy. Most of those in this category considered it a good deal. They had considerable responsibility and ample compensation. As junior officers in rank-ridden London, they would have the same job, but with the added responsibility of shining their boots and saluting just about every passerby.

civilian in charge of espionage and counterintelligence in SSU, and later president of the American University in Beirut, called me to his office. He came straight to the point. Responsibility for Central Europe would be mine for the taking.

"*Central* Europe?" I asked.

"Germany, Austria, Switzerland, Poland, Czechoslovakia, and Hungary," he said. Then, with a lingering glance at the map on the wall beside his desk, he added, "And a real handful it's likely to be."

I agreed with his assessment and accepted the job.

Chapter 7

GETTING UNDER WAY

By the time I had hung my hat in the bare-bones office on the second floor of Q building at the SSU headquarters in the former OSS complex at 2230 E Street, the search for war criminals, former intelligence officers, and hidden Nazi funds had wound down. By February 1946, the accounts with our wartime activists were settled, decorations had been awarded, and agent bonuses and pensions arranged. Most of the OSS training areas—ranging from the torn-up grounds of the Congressional Country Club in Washington to a chunk of Catalina Island in California—had been returned to their well-reimbursed owners. Various cover businesses were liquidated and safehouse rentals relinquished. In comparison with our other problems this had been the easy part.

The expression "hit the ground running" came to mind when, an hour after I had mastered the combination to my office safe, Stephen Penrose summoned me for a more detailed briefing on my new responsibilities. Along with preserving the essential functions and assets of OSS in Central Europe, reducing personnel and building a cadre of well-qualified staff, reporting on Soviet activity and policies in the Soviet-occupied zones in Germany and Austria, monitoring and penetrating Soviet intelligence in the Allied-occupied areas of Germany and Austria, and reporting on Soviet policy and activity in Poland, Hungary, and Czechoslovakia, my branch was also to maintain liaison with Allied security and intelligence services throughout Central Europe. Penrose paused for a moment before adding softly that the Central European branch should also be prepared occasionally "to cope with other, more nearly ad hoc, requirements."

There were moments in the months to come when I felt like an apprentice juggler trying to keep an inflated beachball, an open milk bottle, and a loaded submachine gun in the air. The hours were long, but we were all younger in those years.

A few days after my commitment to SSU, President Truman established the Central Intelligence Group (CIG). Under a director of Central Intelligence, a presidential appointee, the CIG would be responsible to the National Intelligence Authority (NIA), a committee consisting of the secretaries of state, war, and Navy, and chaired by Admiral William Leahy, chief of staff to President Truman. The CIG would correlate and evaluate foreign intelligence reports and prepare daily briefs of the most important material for the President. Rear Admiral Sidney Souers, a Missouri businessman and friend of President Truman's, was named the first director of Central Intelligence on January 23, 1946. His staff consisted of some eighty officers and clerks on loan from the War and State Departments. With no funds of his own, and dependent upon money from the budgets of its foster parents, CIG appeared to be a disembodied headquarters completely dependent upon the kindness of others.

Throughout Admiral Souers's tenure as chief of the Central Intelligence Group, SSU, with responsibility for espionage and counterintelligence abroad, remained lightly tethered to the War Department and under the direction of General John Magruder and his deputy, Colonel William Quinn.

The reaction of those of us at the SSU work level, and far removed from the struggles between the contesting departments, was guarded. So far, so good—a national peacetime intelligence organization had been established and its director appointed. But how effectively, we wondered, could CIG function while reporting to a committee (NIA), each member of which was determined that his own agency be given primary responsibility for the future "independent" service? Not the least problem was J. Edgar Hoover—in the wings, but scarcely offstage, and still positioning himself to shanghai CIG and its functions.

Because OSS was an executive agency, responsible to the Joint

Chiefs of Staff, it had been possible to effect informal relationships with the entrenched line bureaucracies—the Bureau of the Budget, Department of State, the Pentagon, FBI, Treasury, and such. In the postwar period these well-established offices were under pressure to cut personnel and budgets, and to get back to handling the nation's business as usual. Although cover and budget agreements with the Pentagon, State, and the Bureau of the Budget had to be effected, and formal liaison channels established with the FBI and the military intelligence agencies, there was little enthusiasm in the traditional bureaucracies for making ad hoc adjustments to the needs of an organization as nebulous as the Strategic Services Unit.

An important problem, and not the least of our difficulties, was personnel. At peak strength OSS numbered a few more than 12,000 members, divided between some 9000 in the operational components, 1300 in the research and analysis field, and the remainder in administrative and security support work. These figures included civilian employees and assigned military personnel ranging from private soldiers to general officers. Most of the OSS personnel had no intention of staying in government service. The older members would return to established careers in civilian life; the younger people had college to finish and careers to undertake. Only a few saw the country's need for our "peculiar service" and were hooked on the challenge it offered. Colonel Quinn referred to the precipitate loss of some 87 percent of our staff as "the mad exodus." Six months after OSS closed shop, only some 1600 SSU employees remained.

My outfit, Foreign Branch M (FBM), one of the several SSU geographical branches, had 228 personnel abroad and a headquarters staff of thirty-five. The other branches covered the Far East, the Near East, Africa, Western Europe, and the USSR and Baltic states. It quickly became apparent that FBM had fallen heir to a rich share of the operations personnel in SSU. With the collapse of the Third Reich, experienced OSS operatives, as well as technical and support people, surged into Germany and Austria with the occupation forces. Throughout these areas and in the Eastern European capitals, those who thought it might be possible to make a career in intelligence, or who were in no rush to get home, had hung on. One young officer remained in Switzerland for no more profound reason than to spend his weekends skiing. During the war Allen Dulles had outlawed skiing—there was no time for sport, and absolutely no excuse for a broken leg. The winter's experience of post-war intelligence work was just enough to hook the skier: he retired from a senior CIA position twenty-five years later.

Pleased as I was by the legacy, my fellow branch chiefs were already foraging for exactly the type of experienced people FBM had inherited, and I had no choice but to fend them off at every turn.

One bit of fortune was a chance encounter with Elizabeth Dunlevy, one of the first employees enlisted by General Donovan when he began to assemble the Office of the Coordinator of Information (COI), the OSS predecessor organization in 1941. Elizabeth, who had married one of the two survivors of an OSS team parachuted into Czechoslovakia late in World War II, agreed to come to FBM as my secretary and administrative assistant, beginning a working relationship which lasted until my final day in office. Elizabeth was unique. She took dictation as fast and as accurately as a tape recorder, could spell every word in the dictionary, and punctuate as deftly as H. W. Fowler himself. Elizabeth was a canny judge of people, and her knack of treating everyone, irrespective of his position, with absolute equality was exceptional. For the first year and more of our work together, she also functioned as the branch administrative officer. When a new table of organization was established, and Foreign Branch M was reorganized as Foreign *Division* M, Elizabeth surrendered her administrative duties to an office of seven employees. Her tenure stretched from the COI in 1941 through OSS, SSU, CIG to CIA—and from an entrance-level clerical job to the director of Central Intelligence's executive secretary. Elizabeth's performance speaks for itself.

One vexing aspect of my responsibilities was greeting employees returning to Washington from the FBM field stations. After sorting out the most likely prospects—ranging from station chiefs to clerks—it was necessary to urge them to stay on with SSU, an apparently bastard organization with an unpredictable life expectancy. The path between attempting to retain the best people without giving too sanguine a picture of what they might be getting into was indeed narrow.

Recruiting new personnel was a different problem. The moment of truth came with the inevitable question, "Just what job is it that you're offering?"

At that point I had no choice but to say that nothing could be offered before a background investigation had been completed, and that this would take at least three months. If the prospective recruit appeared flummoxed by the prospect of gambling a few months' unemployment against an unspecified position in an outfit that might vanish before any job materialized, I was authorized to say that we would try to put him or her on a temporary payroll doing odd jobs—that is, unclassified work— until the clearance problem was solved.

"Odd jobs, unclassified work?"

"There's a lot of research to be done at the Library of Congress . . . all that sort of thing," I'd say cheerfully. As well as being a useful *pis-aller,* this was perfectly true. It seems unbelievable these days, when the foreign policy establishment is in danger of being smothered with information, that in 1946 the government-wide dearth of data on the USSR and the Eastern European countries mandated hundreds of hours to be spent ransacking the Library of Congress and other open sources for essential background material.

The former OSS premises—four masonry and two temporary wooden structures—that CIG and SSU had taken over were atop a slight knoll in the Foggy Bottom area. Our neighbors were a local brewery, a faded roller rink, an abandoned gasworks, and, just beyond walking distance, the new State Department premises. My office was in Q building, one of the wooden structures built early during World War II. When the building had to be given up, we moved to a string of temporary buildings ranged along the Reflecting Pool in front of the Lincoln Memorial. In some ways these shabby, essentially inconspicuous but centrally located buildings seemed appropriate for a secret intelligence organization. There was one problem. When President Franklin Roosevelt authorized construction of the buildings, he underlined the provision that they were *not* to be built to last. He had no intention of destroying the handsome vista stretching from Lincoln's brooding figure to the Reflecting Pool and along to the Washington Monument. Roosevelt's wishes had certainly been respected. The construction work was rough and manifestly not meant for the ages. The buildings were cold in winter, wet in rain, soggy and stifling in summer. The heat absorbed by the tin roof of my second-floor office taught me the difference between perspiration and sweat. When the temperature and humidity reached a certain point—we called it "fission"—civil service regulations required us to send the staff home. Though we worked in shirtsleeves, carbon copies seemed to melt in our hands. Without air conditioning, the soggy summer in Foggy Bottom meant that like the Dead Sea Scrolls, some files had to be peeled apart.

There were other, more substantive problems. In the pressure of the hot war, OSS personnel security clearances had often been rushed to completion. The urgent need for qualified linguists and good area knowledge was such that recently arrived refugees offered one of the best and most readily available sources of supply. Because few refugees had been in the United States long enough to have established any sort of record, the usual background and neighborhood investigations were almost meaningless. For the same reason, the customary interviews with the candidate's listed references were of little use. Few of the refugees had friends or even acquaintances who had not themselves recently arrived and were also without checkable backgrounds.

Nazi Germany, its European allies, and Japan were the most obvious wartime security threats, but none of these intelligence services had been able to organize anything resembling penetration operations in this country. Attempts to foster sabotage and political activism had been readily detected and rolled up. The German efforts to land hopelessly ill prepared agents by submarine were doomed from the start.

Ironically, the situation with our ally—more accurately co-belligerent—the USSR was entirely different. Despite the desperate pressure the Soviet Union was under during World War II, GRU (Soviet military intelligence) and NKVD activity against the Western Allies and the United States in particular was, if anything, intensified. OSS security screening presumably eliminated any *known* Communist Party members from sensitive government positions, but allegations and rumors of communist activity were less intensely pursued. The result was that some Communist Party members and many dedicated fellow travelers were taken into the armed services, civilian agencies, and OSS. In the months after the war when the chasm between Soviet objectives and those of the Western powers became more obvious, the problem of communist penetration of the government was recognized as serious. As the postwar turf battles smoldered and raged in Washington, self-serving leaks about SSU's alleged security problems continued to surface.

Early in Colonel Quinn's tenure, an SSU operative had procured an impressive bundle of intelligence on the Soviet Baltic Fleet—the design, armaments, and characteristics of the important ships, and diagrams showing in detail the fleet's organization and command structure. Quinn took the package directly to the Office of Naval Intelligence. The admiral in charge glanced at the documents and handed them back to Quinn with the comment that "the community" knew that the SSU, like OSS before it, was riddled with communists, and that ONI could not possibly have any association with SSU. For good measure, the admiral added that the reports were most likely deception material straight from Moscow.

A few weeks later, an SSU operation netted a foreign diplomatic code. Colonel Quinn tucked the code into his briefcase and arranged an urgent appointment with Colonel Carter Clarke of the Army Security Agency, a forerunner of the National Security Agency (NSA). After a long wait, he was admitted into the colonel's office. He handed the package to Clarke and explained the contents. The ASA man refused it, saying in effect, "Surely, you know what everybody in town thinks about SSU."

Quinn acknowledged that he knew exactly what some people were saying, but suggested that the colonel have an expert take ten minutes to check out the data. The analysis took a bit longer, but the material was authentic.

In 1946 there seemed to be as many colonels as there were lieutenants on the loose in the Washington bureaucracy, and J. Edgar Hoover's carefully nurtured reputation was at its peak. It was common knowledge that Hoover had resented General Donovan and his relationship with President Roosevelt, and considered OSS a collection of amateur interlopers in the intelligence world. Although the FBI was responsible for domestic security and counterintelligence activity, odds seemed against Hoover's agreeing to deal personally with SSU, and the more so with a mere colonel. To his surprise, Quinn was granted an interview.

When he took over SSU, Quinn explained, there were some 12,000 employees. Now there were about 1600, scattered from Washington to Vietnam. Half the Washington establishment seemed to assume most of the SSU staff were fellow travelers, if not outright communist spies. This was nonsense, Quinn said, but it had to be proved. If the FBI agreed to check the political and criminal backgrounds of the SSU staff, Quinn would provide complete background data on all employees.

Hoover, who was convinced that throughout the war he had been both ignored and upstaged by General Donovan, was obviously surprised by Quinn's straightforward request for help, but immediately agreed to begin the investigations.

Sensing that he was on a roll, Quinn suggested that if Director Hoover were to name one of his officers as liaison to SSU things might be speeded up. This was the beginning of what became the postwar relationship between the FBI and CIA. Despite occasional setbacks and interagency collisions, this essential relationship has continued to serve the country well.

The FBI's initial sorting out of the SSU staff background data revealed only one potentially serious security case. Shades of Martha Dodd in Berlin, a young supply clerk was discovered to be romantically involved with a Soviet diplomat. She was fired. There was, of course, more Soviet intelligence involvement with OSS than that, but the intensive security reviews had not ripened at this juncture. (It was at about this time that U.S. cryptologists began to break into Soviet intelligence cable traffic—code name VENONA—passing between Washington, New York, and Moscow. These often fragmented messages would eventually give a revealing picture of the strenuous efforts the NKVD and Soviet military intelligence made to break into OSS.)

The tangled backgrounds of some of the anti-fascist refugees who served OSS well and bravely were at the least murky and at the best might have taken a long time to clarify. In fairness it seemed wiser to refuse the applications of those who were unlikely ever to receive full security-clearance status rather than risk having to dismiss them after they had invested months or more in their intelligence career. With the help of SSU's security officer, Peer de Silva, a West Pointer who had served in personnel security with the Manhattan Project, we dropped those whom we were certain would have subsequent problems. To avoid any possibly unwarranted black mark in anyone's record, we found non-security reasons for failing to continue to employ them.

Throughout the civil service there was a common practice against employing homosexuals. This reflected the prevailing practice in state and local governments, but was most rigidly enforced in agencies involved with classified information.* This prohibition was based primarily on the assumption that homosexuals were more subject to blackmail than their straight colleagues. Whatever truth there may have been in this, the world's security services had been highly sensitized to homosexual security problems by an agent who had been uncovered a year before World War I.

The Redl case is so bald an example of a successful spy that even a century later it is worth a moment's reflection. Alfred Redl, the son of a railway clerk, grew up in Galicia, an impoverished Austro-Hungarian province. Redl chose the army as an escape from poverty, and qualified for military cadet school. In time, he was admitted to the Imperial War College—an accomplishment for an officer with none of the social credentials and financial support typical of the Austro-Hungarian officer corps. After a sabbatical year in Russia, with no responsibility other than to keep his eyes open and to learn the language, Captain Redl was appointed to the elite, four hundred–man General Staff Corps. He had fashioned an exemplary career in the caste-ridden Austro-Hungarian army, but was a less perfect soldier than his role-playing suggested.

Redl had spun hopelessly into debt keeping up with the swank that came easily to the well-funded aristocrats with whom he served. The costs involved in supporting his hidden homosexual life added to the financial burden.

The young officer's first General Staff assignment was to the intelligence bureau, the Kundschafts Stelle. In 1900 most ambitious officers would have considered it a ticket to oblivion. Redl reasoned that he could rouse the somnolent office and exploit it for his own advancement.

In Russia, the chief of intelligence regarded the young captain's assignment as a gift. Redl had attracted the attention of Russian intelligence during his sabbatical year. His homosexual activity was monitored, and his debts were uncovered. On form, there could be no better recruitment target than the officer with de facto responsibility for all espionage and counterintelligence activity of the Imperial General

---

*In 1950, Senator Kenneth Wherry, GOP floor leader, found "homosexuals and other sex perverts" were "not proper persons" for government jobs. Wherry was equally known for his malaprops—"Chief Joints of Staff," "Indigo China," "my unanimous opinion," etc.

Staff. And who might be more likely to succumb to an approach than a closeted but aggressive homosexual whose combined salary and allowances for three years would not cover his current debts?

The Russians were blunt. Redl would be well paid for military and political information. If he refused, the General Staff would be alerted to the extent of his debt, and shown that the underlying reason was the blackmail payments, the consequence of his hidden sex life. Along with the military data, Redl would also identify Austrian agents operating in Russia and, more important, report on German and Italian military and political relations with the Dual Monarchy. To bolster Redl's reputation, the Russian case officer would feed him information on expendable Russian agents operating against Austria-Hungary.

After five successful and well-publicized years in the intelligence bureau, Redl was appointed chief of staff of a military corps, a step toward further promotion. In 1911 he received his last decoration, the "Expression of Supreme Satisfaction"—an award of such distinction that it could only be presented by Emperor Franz Josef.

In May 1913 a glitch in the communications system—perhaps the most common weakness in espionage operations—closed the Redl case. Caught in a trap set for an unidentified agent, Redl asked permission to commit suicide. In the manner of a penny dreadful—and perhaps an effort to protect Franz Josef's government from scandal—Redl was obliged with a pistol and a single bullet. One of the most productive spies in history died without any interrogation.

The inventory of Redl's effects gives a measure of his motivation. A hundred sixty cases of champagne were cellared at his posh Vienna quarters. His wardrobe contained more than a hundred dress shirts, a score of uniforms, and a dozen fur-trimmed greatcoats. A locked closet held ball gowns, lingerie, makeup, and other transvestite fixings.

Critics who dispute the value of spies should remember Redl. During his years as a Russian spy, he disclosed every detail of the Austro-Hungarian military forces, he blinded the General Staff—and to a degree the German military as well—to the existence of some seventy-five Russian divisions. In the months before the outbreak of war, it would have been impossible to revise the mass of these plans, or to create an entirely new family of codes and ciphers. Redl's treason gave the empire's enemies every military and political advantage. With good reason, the Austrian press referred to Redl as "the hangman of the Austro-Hungarian Empire."

Homosexual activity was a criminal offense in the Austro-Hungarian Empire, but it was not necessarily at the root of his recruitment. Redl's career-long record shows a voracious appetite for money and suggests that even without the threat of blackmail, the Russians might simply have bought him.

When first on the General Staff, Redl worked with another young officer, Theodor Koerner. Fifty years later, Koerner, then president of the Austrian Republic, told a young American writer that he remembered Redl well. They often met for coffee. "Like everyone else who knew him, I liked Alfred very much. He was always dignified—entirely the gentleman—but in a very friendly way. . . . He knew a great deal about military and international affairs, but more than that, his knowledge of human behavior was startling."* And so it must have been for this prototypical penetration agent.

—

In June 1946, Admiral Souers completed a final bit of business before retiring almost as quietly as he had arrived as the first director of CIG. He recommended Lieutenant General Hoyt S. Vandenberg, a nephew of the powerful Republican Senator Arthur Vandenberg, as his replacement. With prescience, and probably advice from Admiral Leahy and General Eisenhower, President Truman agreed.

Hoyt Vandenberg was the personification of an Air Force general. Forty-seven years old, lean and handsome to the point of glamour, he was fresh from a brilliant wartime record in the Army Air Force, and commander of the Ninth Air Force. His ambition to be chief of staff of the independent Air Force was temporarily on hold. Pending the passage of the Reorganization Act, which would establish the Air Force as a separate branch of service, the honor of being the first Air Force commanding general was being held for General Carl A. Spaatz, the Eighth Air Force commander in World War II. On his return from France, General Vandenberg was named assistant chief of staff, G-2 in the Pentagon. This five-month assignment was enough for Vandenberg to confirm his

*Quoted in Robert Asprey, *The Panther's Feast* (New York: Putnam's, 1959).

wartime impression of the need to revamp the intelligence structure, to eliminate overlapping responsibilities, and to create an administratively and financially independent agency that could effectively collect and evaluate the political, economic, technological, and social aspects, as well as the military strengths, of world powers.

With the sense of urgency of a pilot anxious to get his aircraft off the ground and on the way, and with the self-confidence of a man who in wartime had run an organization of 18,000 employees and 4000 aircraft, Vandenberg zipped through a series of briefings and a quick *tour d'horizon* of the European stations. It was only a few days after the new director of Central Intelligence had slipped out of uniform that one of our more sartorially perceptive observers noticed that the general had so many decorations he was always able to choose a buttonhole rosette that complemented his tie and shirt.

Those of us in SSU soon learned that when General Vandenberg took over CIG, he was determined to turn what many insiders still considered to be a fragile bureaucratic curiosity, manned by a hotchpotch of civilian and military personnel, into a national intelligence service. In July he created an Office of Research and Estimates (ORE) to provide the White House and other agencies with daily and weekly current intelligence summaries and analysis. The thunder of the State Department's furious objections was still shaking the walls when, without apparently pausing to catch his breath, Vandenberg simply absorbed the SSU, its responsibility for intelligence and counterintelligence abroad, its cadre of experienced personnel, foreign stations, and files into CIG. He also won access to the cryptographic product of the National Security Agency.

The orphan Strategic Services Unit was then reborn as the Office of Special Operations (OSO), and Colonel Quinn was replaced by Colonel Donald Galloway, who assumed the title assistant director of special operations (ADSO). Coincidentally, Vandenberg convinced President Truman to pry responsibility for secret intelligence operations in Mexico and Central and South America from the iron grasp of J. Edgar Hoover.

Along with others at my level, several rungs below the general, I was fascinated to watch our new boss tuck these accomplishments under his belt. Vandenberg was influential in convincing President Truman that CIG, as presently organized and staffed, was unworkable and that only a fully funded, formally established, independent intelligence service would suffice. It was a bravura performance, and one for which General Vandenberg has not been given enough credit. He served eleven months before returning to the Air Force in May 1947. His premature death in 1954 was a sad loss.

In May 1947, President Truman appointed Rear Admiral Roscoe Hillenkoetter as the third director of Central Intelligence. "Hilly," as he was known to his friends, had considerable intelligence experience. He had been a staff officer for intelligence under Admiral Nimitz in the Pacific theater during World War II and was serving as the naval attaché in Paris when he was appointed director of Central Intelligence. When the National Security Act was passed in July 1947, the Central Intelligence Group was made an independent department of the executive branch and renamed the Central Intelligence Agency, with Hillenkoetter as its first director. CIA's mission was defined as advising the National Security Council on national security; making recommendations to the NSC on the coordination of intelligence activities of the various departments; correlating, evaluating, and providing for the dissemination of intelligence; and "perform[ing] such other functions and duties related to intelligence affecting national security as the NSC will from time to time direct." The act was deliberately loosely written to avoid the dread words "espionage" and "counterintelligence."

Vandenberg's concept of CIA as an executive agency controlling all other intelligence components of the government was fiercely opposed by the Department of Defense intelligence services, the Department of State, and the FBI. As a rear admiral and a relative newcomer in Washington, Hillenkoetter was in no position to force the issue, which President Truman ignored. During his three-year tenure, Hillenkoetter concentrated on establishing the young Agency as senior to the military services and the FBI. In this he was successful.

It was in these years that the period of intense reorganization, personnel problems, and turf struggles ended, and postwar operations began to take shape. Some of these remain of interest, not merely because of the role they played as we learned our trade.

Chapter 8

—

THE GEHLEN
ORGANIZATION

The day after Allen Dulles signed his OSS discharge documents in December 1945 and returned to civilian life, he reminded a meeting of the Council on Foreign Relations that a too rigidly enforced denazification policy in Germany would mean that many of the people essential to getting Germany running again would be barred from any such activity. By definition more than 500,000 Germans might legally be classified as war criminals. It was obviously essential, he said, to bring leading Nazis and war criminals to trial. It would, however, be quite another matter to imprison half a million people for months while attempting to sift the criminals from the run-of-the-mill Nazi Party members whose experience and skills were needed. He added, "We've already found that you can't run the railroads without taking in some Nazi Party members."

Dulles's appearance at the council meeting was a signal that his work as a partner in the New York law firm of Sullivan and Cromwell did not mean that he was stepping out of foreign affairs. Within six months, Dulles was beckoned back into the intelligence world. When General Vandenberg replaced Admiral Souers as director of Central Intelligence, he asked Dulles to form a board of consultants to advise him personally on the problems of "central intelligence." Dulles did not delay in forming a distinguished group—Kingman Douglass, William H. Jackson,

Robert Lovett, Paul Nitze, Frank Wisner, and Admiral Souers. Along with his Sullivan and Cromwell responsibilities, his work with the Foreign Relations Council, drafting several articles on Germany, and writing a book-length manuscript,* Dulles found ample time to consult with General Vandenberg and to draft proposals for the shape and organization of what was to become the Central Intelligence Agency in 1947.

It was with Dulles that my first official brush with Pentagon operation, code name RUSTY, came in 1946. Dulles invited Colonel Donald Galloway, my boss in the operations element of CIG, and me to a New York town house, where General Edwin L. Sibert, chief of staff, G-2, the senior G-2 officer in the American occupation zone in West Germany, briefed us on Operation RUSTY. At the time, it was one of the most ambitious and complex G-2 operations.

Several U.S. military officers played important roles in establishing the RUSTY operation, but the project was essentially the responsibility of General Sibert and the creation of Major General Reinhard Gehlen, a German General Staff Corps officer, who for the last three years of the war served as Hitler's intelligence chief on the Russian front. As commanding officer of Fremde Heere Ost (FHO, Foreign Armies East), Gehlen was the equivalent of chief of staff, G-2, on the eastern front. In April 1945, Hitler had had enough of what he called Gehlen's "defeatist" estimates of Soviet strength and intentions. He ordered Gehlen's retirement, and replaced him with a presumably more optimistic officer.

Within a month Hitler committed suicide, the Thousand Year Reich had collapsed, and General Gehlen was holed up in the Bavarian Alps.

Gehlen had reasoned as early as 1943 that when the democracies finally became aware of Stalin's expansionist intentions, the Allied coalition would fall apart. More significantly, he assumed that the need to defend the West would eventually "force the Western allies to make common cause with [Germany] against communism."† Several high-ranking Nazis had the same notion, but Gehlen's view was somewhat more realistic. Unlike the others, he accepted as fact the probability that the Allies would insist on Germany's unconditional surrender. Gehlen

Germany's Underground (New York: Macmillan, 1947).
†General Reinhard Gehlen, *The Service* (New York: World, 1972).

was prepared to wait until the post-surrender dust had settled before making his move.

Because Hitler considered any planning based on Germany's possible defeat to be a capital crime, Gehlen took care to keep his post-retirement plans to a handful of his closest associates. In preparation for leaving his command, Gehlen supervised the transfer of some fifty steel containers of the FHO files from the eastern combat area to safety in Germany. His plan was to offer American intelligence a unique body of research and order-of-battle data, and a ready-made, thoroughly experienced organization—in effect a reconstructed FHO—prepared to provide a wide spectrum of intelligence on the USSR and its activity in Eastern Europe.

Two weeks after the surrender, an American lieutenant took Gehlen into custody. The former general was astonished to find that he was just another POW. American intelligence had extensive knowledge of the German forces it faced, but had paid scant attention to German intelligence activity on the Russian front. Gehlen remained an unknown quantity until Soviet officers working on a joint commission sorting out German POWs approached a British officer and expressed a strong interest in finding the former FHO chief and some of his staff. When G-2 was informed, they realized that if the Russians were so keen to locate a mere one-star general among the hundreds of high-ranking officers and war criminals in the POW cages, Gehlen might be worth a close look.

A few days later a group of G-2 officers listened as an interpreter translated Gehlen's glowing account of the FHO's competence, its files, and the experience and ability of the officers, analysts, and operatives. When he was sure of G-2 interest, Gehlen added a bit more bait: if the Americans acted promptly, the German network of agents in the USSR could be reactivated.

General Sibert knew that by allowing his staff even to listen to Gehlen's views on the USSR he was running well ahead of General Eisenhower's policy of not soliciting help or advice from former Nazi authorities. He decided that an exception should be made, and that Gehlen's proposition be given a closer examination. It was soon clear that the FHO had been a competent military intelligence organization. From prisoner interrogation, low-level, across front-line agent activity, analysis of aerial photography and radio intercept, to the study of captured documents and soldiers' letters from home, German efficiency, record-keeping, and analytical skills were of a high order. As Sibert saw it, Gehlen's initial proposal seemed tailored to help fill a near vacuum in the American military intelligence establishment.

When Gehlen expanded his offer to collect tactical intelligence with the suggestion that he might also "reactivate" some of the Nazi agents allegedly active within the USSR, the American listeners might have drawn a deep breath. Tactical military intelligence is a far stretch from strategic intelligence collection. Gehlen's FHO operated on a tactical level, along the eastern military fronts. Strategic intelligence was handled by the Abwehr, with responsibility for intelligence collection abroad. The RSHA (Reichssicherheitshauptamt, Reich Main Security Office) encompassed the Gestapo, the Sicherheitsdienst, the SS security service, and the criminal police. Under the command of Heinrich Himmler and Walter Schellenberg, the RSHA also collected foreign intelligence. Aside from occasional cryptographic breakthroughs, telephone intercepts, and a well-placed agent (code name CICERO) in Turkey, none of these organizations was effective. Senior British and American counterintelligence officers knew that every one of Germany's wartime agents in England—and many of those active in other areas—had operated under Allied control throughout most of the war. The false information these agents reported had convincingly deceived Hitler as to Allied invasion plans and strength in Europe. Moreover, as postwar study of the NKVD and GRU took shape, it began to look as if the Russians had also been highly effective in deceiving German intelligence on the eastern front. If this proved to be true (and it was) German strategic intelligence—east and west—had been duped. Tactical military intelligence is important; strategic intelligence is vital.

In August 1945 the War Department brought Gehlen and four colleagues to Fort Hunt near Washington for a closer look. After weeks of debriefing and discussions, they were returned to Germany. No one in Washington appeared anxious to make any decisions about the future of Fremde Heere Ost, or with the possible building of a future German intelligence service. The Pentagon was content to leave the specifics to G-2 in Germany. Pending final Pentagon approval, it was informally agreed that under G-2 sponsorship, Gehlen was to establish a clandestine intelligence organization that would collect information in East Germany and elsewhere in Eastern Europe. The organization would be financed by G-2, and work "jointly" *with* but not *for* American authorities. When a sovereign German government was established, that government would decide whether the organization should remain in being or not. Although RUSTY would receive its directives from the Americans, and would furnish G-2 with its reports, the American officers working with Gehlen in Washington neglected to insist upon being given the names of and biographic data on the RUSTY staff personnel. Nor did G-2 demand this information on the agents and sources employed by RUSTY and paid by G-2. Even in the confusion of the immediate postwar intelligence picture, this oversight violated one of the fundamental rules of secret intelligence, and helped to set the stage for the security disasters that in time all but destroyed the entire effort.

There is no principle in the espionage canon more important than that an intelligence service must know—or at the least continuously strive to know—exactly with whom it is dealing. In fairness, we must remember that in the months after Germany's defeat the United States was removing its forces from Western Europe and, in effect, disarming at the moment the USSR was reinforcing its troops and consolidating its strength behind what was rapidly becoming the Iron Curtain. In the early months of the occupation, the military, political, and social conditions in Germany verged on the chaotic. As the Soviet position became clear and its intentions began to clarify, the Pentagon, the State Department, the intelligence services, and the White House realized that the United States was ill prepared to deal with its new antagonist. In comparison with the depth and mass of the political, military, and economic data that had been collected on Germany and Japan, the intelligence files on the USSR were all but empty. The demand for military and political intelligence increased exponentially and on what sometimes seemed to be a daily basis. For the moment RUSTY seemed to offer a quick fix.

It was in this atmosphere that G-2 authorized RUSTY to begin operations on an ad hoc basis. In occupied Germany's distressed condition, RUSTY's ample budget and access to commissary supplies were a powerful beacon to potential recruits. Although Gehlen agreed with the G-2 rule that no former SS, Gestapo, or Sicherheitsdienst personnel would be employed in RUSTY, the fact that the German staff did not disclose the names of its personnel or agents meant G-2 could not check its own files or the captured Nazi Party, SS, Gestapo, Sicherheitsdienst, and

Wehrmacht records for war criminals or other compromised Nazis. As a result, RUSTY's own security and background checks on new employees were minimal; an oral recommendation by a staff employee would often suffice. Former German intelligence officers were recruited, and they in turn promptly hired old colleagues, former agents and informers, relatives and friends. To my knowledge none of the Gestapo, SS, or Sicherheitsdienst veterans were taken into senior positions, but some who wriggled in at lower levels would in time make their way ahead.

The RUSTY intelligence product on the Soviet forces in East Germany was soon recognized as valuable. Other solid reporting came from the effective interrogation of POWs returning from the USSR and the numerous refugees from Eastern Europe. One of the most valuable activities was a radio intercept station operated from Schloss Kransberg near Frankfurt. The radios were handled by experienced operators who had learned their trade in months of around-the-clock service on the eastern front. During the Berlin airlift, these reports—taken from intercepted voice traffic of the Soviet Air Force—supplied General Curtis LeMay, the Air Force commander in Germany, with a running account of which MiG-17s were up, which were down, and the airfields from which they were operating. General LeMay considered this "real time" reporting an essential element in the success of the airlift.

Within a few months it became apparent that the cost and the problems of managing the ever-burgeoning effort were more than G-2 had expected. There was intense rivalry within the organization as members jostled for position. Worse, the political aspects of intelligence cooperation remained explosive. There was no public enthusiasm and even less official tolerance for anything smacking of Germany's military revival. The black shadow of the Gestapo and the SS hung heavily on any whisper of renewed German intelligence or security work. The British and French, each interested in developing independent activity with Germany's former intelligence operatives, were not above suggesting that Gehlen's organization was a nest of Nazis mothered by otherwise unemployable former General Staff officers.

As RUSTY's East German reporting became more useful, the Pentagon clamored for even more intelligence. Gehlen expanded his efforts to oblige, but adamantly resisted anything resembling close control by his American "partners." By rough count some four thousand people had been helped to survive the most difficult postwar months by becoming affiliated one way or another with RUSTY. Costs soared and the problems of supervising such a vast supposedly secret organization were staggering. G-2 realized it had an outsized and ravenous bear by the tail.

CIA officers in Germany were uniformly dismayed by the noisy and insecure activity of the RUSTY operatives. The intelligence, particularly on East Germany, was valuable, but as seen by our German station, it hardly offset the poor security and discipline of the RUSTY operatives.

The security and control problems continued to worsen in Germany until in 1947, the year CIA came into existence, the Pentagon asked the Agency to take over the RUSTY operation.

The decision to accept responsibility for the operation was made by the DCI; the ongoing responsibility was very much mine. At my level this meant establishing a headquarters section and then selecting the personnel who would begin work in Germany with what was becoming publicly known as the "Gehlen organization." It always struck me as odd that as much as Gehlen professed to admire the British approach to official secrets—and to envy the fact that the identity of the British intelligence chief was never publicly acknowledged or mentioned in the press—he was the only intelligence chief I can recall who had never troubled to discourage the public linking of his own name to that of his service.

Staffing the Washington headquarters unit was relatively easy. Donald Huefner, levelheaded, fluent in German, sensitive to policy considerations, and detail-oriented, was an obvious choice to head the Washington office. Finding a man with these qualities senior enough to cope with Gehlen in Germany was a greater problem. The former general was more than a handful, and we had no illusions about his probable reaction to the inevitable changes our new management would introduce. To begin, we would insist on having the names and biographic data of everyone on the organization's staff. Moreover, we would screen the political backgrounds of all the staff personnel.

The perceived Nazi flavor of the Gehlen organization had not yet become a favorite East German and Soviet propaganda target. It was not until 1950 that this charge developed considerable resonance in the Western press and political circles. Although he played no role in the German resistance and his memoirs reflect little criticism of Hitler,

Gehlen was never a Nazi Party member. His failure to keep all former Nazi security and intelligence officials out of RUSTY was a costly mistake. It provided East German and Soviet propagandists with a long-lasting and potent propaganda source. The threat to expose a RUSTY member's unsavory Nazi background also offered the various communist espionage services a potentially useful blackmail tool.

When it became apparent that none of the CIA officers in Germany were interested in picking up this hot potato, there occurred one of the bits of luck that sometimes—if too rarely—save the day. At the moment I was most desperate, Colonel James Critchfield's file crossed my desk. A regular Army officer from the North Dakota plain, with extensive combat experience in Italy, France, and Germany, and a recent military intelligence assignment in Vienna, Colonel Critchfield had become so convinced of the importance of intelligence in the postwar world that he decided to abandon his promising military career—he was one of the youngest ground-force colonels in the Army—and join CIA. When Colonel Galloway, a loyal West Pointer, failed to talk Critchfield into remaining in the Army, he got up from his desk, clapped Jim on the shoulder, and said, "I think you're a damned fool, but I'm sure glad to have you join CIA."

If ever I hit upon the right man for the right job, the choice of Jim Critchfield for the Gehlen organization was among the best. Although he had but recently arrived in Germany to take over an important Soviet assignment, Jim's military background and experience suggested he might be the man to make an on-the-ground assessment of RUSTY. Five weeks later, Critchfield filed a long cable to Washington. He emphasized that an organization employing some four thousand people, with offices scattered across Germany, and unknown agents operating at various posts in Western Europe, controlling—to some degree—scores of other agents, and feeding the Pentagon intelligence it badly wanted, could scarcely, as had once been suggested in Washington, be broken up and allotted at random to various American offices. Critchfield made the point that Germany would eventually become sovereign, it would surely have an intelligence service of its own, and in time would again figure prominently in any European equation. Current American interests and future German concerns would both be served by continuing a joint endeavor under stricter management. Failing such a decision, Critchfield felt the RUSTY project should be terminated.

Within days the field responsibility for this rambunctious and unloved baby was deposited on Critchfield's doorstep. For the ensuing seven years he turned in a remarkable performance managing our relations with the German organization. By nature cool and soft-spoken, Jim came quickly to understand his German military associates, some of whom he had actually faced on the battlefield as he led his task force across France and into southern Germany. With a minimum of guidance from Washington, he effected the necessary changes in policy and practice, and weathered the inevitable arguments and conflicts, while also managing to win the confidence and respect of Gehlen's group.

It was perhaps typical of Critchfield's approach to his job, and his ability to establish rapport with the difficult general, that, in his first meeting with Gehlen, Jim asked for a list of German staff employees. Gehlen balked, but a day later he handed the data to his new colleague. Assembling the details on the widespread Gehlen operations took more time.

One of the serious operational problems was Gehlen's continued support of individuals and groups of intelligence entrepreneurs which CIA had begun to identify as fabricators devoted to creating and peddling information, allegedly coming from Eastern Europe and the USSR, which was often both false and deceptive. Ironically, some of the agents involved had been employed by German intelligence during World War II.

It was not long after we had accepted responsibility for the Gehlen organization that Critchfield realized that along with Gehlen's intention eventually to shape an independent German intelligence service, he had a second, less obvious objective. This was to help preserve, pending an eventual German government position on "remilitarization"—a real buzzword in those days—a handful of former senior Wehrmacht officers well qualified to lead such a development. To this end he employed, among others, Lieutenant General Adolf Heusinger, who had served as chief of the Operations Division of the Wehrmacht until he was arrested and imprisoned by Hitler after the July 20 assassination attempt. Heusinger, who sympathized with the plotters but was not involved in the attempted coup, was briefing Hitler and was wounded when the bomb went off. In the investigations that followed, Heusinger's anti-Nazi opinions were uncovered. After the war he was a witness for the prosecution at the Nuremberg trials.

Under Heusinger's direction, the former Wehrmacht officers worked nominally in the evaluations and estimates component of Gehlen's staff. They scrupulously avoided responsibility for anything smacking of espionage, their primary concern being to develop plans for what would become the armed forces of a new German federal republic. With the 1950 outbreak of war in Korea, Chancellor Konrad Adenauer moved to ease Germany into the treaty organization that was to become NATO. Despite what seemed to be irreconcilable views within our government, and with the British and French, a common policy was achieved and Germany was admitted to the treaty organization in 1955. General Heusinger went on to play an important role in the new Germany until his retirement as chairman of the Federal Republic's Supreme Military Council.

The German Federal Republic became sovereign in May 1955. A year later, when the Gehlen organization became the Bundesnachrichtendienst (BND), the German Federal Intelligence Service, Jim Critchfield's job in Germany came to term.

In the years that followed, the BND suffered its share of difficulty. Gehlen's sometimes eccentric security practices, based in part on his notion of the "honor" of the German officer corps, could not cope with the exposed and very difficult situation he faced. The Soviet, East German, and other communist services effected penetrations of Gehlen's organization that laid bare secrets which might have destroyed any other intelligence service. Gehlen's proclivity for involving himself in domestic political matters harmed the service and in time damaged his relationship with Chancellor Adenauer. His efforts to assume responsibility for domestic counterintelligence as well as foreign operations were seriously mistaken but wisely ignored by his government. In a democracy these two activities should remain separate.

In the end, Gehlen achieved his objective. An independent German intelligence service had been formed. The BND survived its many difficulties and today enjoys a respected partnership with the NATO community.

Chapter 9

—

FABRICATION
FACTORIES

By 1949 the Cold War was an established fact of life. The civil war in Greece, Stalin's heavy-handed occupation of most of Eastern Europe, his repeated observation that the communist and capitalist worlds could not indefinitely coexist, and his manipulation of the European Communist Parties had erased most remaining notions of any East-West cooperation.

In February 1946 the news that a few months earlier Igor Gouzenko, a Soviet military intelligence code clerk in the Ottawa embassy, had defected and brought with him a bundle of documents detailing Russian intelligence activity in Canada—scarcely a threat to the USSR—and against the United States focused official and public attention on Stalin's aggressive espionage operations. The scope of the Canada-based espionage net was not publicly disclosed, but as the investigation continued it was apparent that the Soviet intelligence operations against the American atomic weapons programs were well advanced and highly productive. We didn't know it at the time, but these operations had begun in 1942.

The certainty that the American monopoly on atomic weapons could not endure for as long as our policymakers had assumed added an urgent dimension to the Pearl Harbor syndrome. How long, Washington policymakers asked, *would* it take the USSR to develop its own atomic weapon? CIA was established to prevent the risk of another sneak attack. It was the Agency's responsibility to answer the question. No matter that the USSR had been a target for less than three years, or that no Western intelligence service had established sources that might conceivably have answered this question. We had failed. The fact that CIA's experienced officers amounted to little more than a cadre, none of whom had any experience in Soviet operations, was pertinent but less than consoling.

There was no easy fix. The missing ingredients—an adequate operational data base and a body of experienced personnel—could not be purchased. It was up to the Agency to create both and at flank speed.

The answer to Soviet atomic developments came in September 1949 when a long-range weather detection aircraft identified radioactive elements in a weather system over the North Pacific. Intensive analysis proved beyond doubt that the USSR had exploded an atomic device in late August. This was well ahead of the conventional estimate which had been prepared before the extent of the Soviet penetration of the Manhattan Project had been determined. The Los Alamos spies had given the Soviet scientists a considerable leg up.

It is impossible to understand the role and activity of the Western intelligence services in the early postwar years without an appreciation of the intensity of the demand for information on the USSR and Eastern Europe, and the way in which urgent requirements expanded and accelerated. From mid-1946 onwards every political and military development fueled the demand for intelligence. Budgets were increased, eased upwards, and then increased again. If there are more graphic illustrations of the predictable result of throwing money at a problem that hasn't been thought through, none comes to mind.

One of the forgotten phases of the postwar years in Europe was the cottage industry that sprang up in response to the urgent need for solid information on the USSR and Soviet-occupied areas of Eastern Europe. By January 1947 the demand for intelligence had increased to the point that a legion of political exiles, former intelligence officers, ex-agents, and sundry entrepreneurs were turning themselves into intelligence moguls, brokering the sale of fabricated-to-order information to the various official intelligence services. For months after the end of hostilities, it was still possible for the émigré groups beginning to gather west of the Soviet-occupied areas to maintain contact with their compatriots and political sympathizers in the homeland and to receive some firsthand information. As the Soviet occupation settled down, these clumsy cross-border communications were destroyed or brought under Soviet control. By the time Western services had focused their sights on the new targets, none of the existing communications remained viable.

In a textbook example of the supply-and-demand equation, a harvest of fabricated "intelligence" blossomed, with shares of the crop available to anyone with an open pocketbook. The faked reports were usually tacked onto a frame of overt material lifted from the press, and the debriefing of market-fresh refugees. Once assembled, the authentic and easily verified material was spiced and inflated with outright fabrication attributed to various—but always "high-level" and "in-place"—sources whose identities could be known only to the intelligence peddler.

If an intelligence service was hard pressed for data on the production of uranium in East Germany—and we all were—fabricators would respond appropriately. I recall a sample of "radioactive uranium"—allegedly and improbably pinched from an East German shipment en route to Moscow—that arrived in a cocoon of tinfoil the girth of a softball. The enclosed walnut-size chunk of lead was less valuable than the wrapping.

This is not to suggest that we were complete fools. Communications between field stations and headquarters were slow, there was less air travel, and the postwar espionage world was young. At that time the demand for a bit of East German or Czech uranium was so intense that the whiff of a breakthrough seemed reason enough to move quickly. Instead of taking the time to look into the agent's background, examine the means by which the sample was obtained, and consult atomic energy experts on the likelihood of any outsider being able to identify and make off with a bit of uranium, the sample was purchased—albeit at a fraction of the asking price. At the time the few dollars involved in such cart-before-the-horse nonsense was of less moment than the remote possibility of missing a significant opportunity and, perhaps not incidentally, of losing a chance to show our clients that the young Agency was not sitting on its bureaucratic backside.

I long ago came to suspect that the temptation to abandon well-proven operational procedures in hot pursuit of an allegedly fleeting opportunity has throughout espionage history been responsible for more painful pratfalls than any other professional lapse. In practice, one of the bits of evidence pointing to a possible provocation by an opposing service, or perhaps the presence of a fabricator, is the admonition to respond immediately lest a once-in-a-lifetime opportunity to win all the marbles be lost forever. It may be that an occasional windfall has been lost because of too long a look before leaping. If so, the molehill of losses must be measured against the mountain of haste-makes-waste disasters.

Even in the early days, detecting fraud involving material that could be laboratory tested was relatively simple—the bit of ore was uranium or not; the stoppered and wrapped test tube of "nerve gas" was lethal or benign. Unfortunately, offers involving intangible and ephemeral data on political schemes, military planning, or intelligence activity were more difficult to evaluate.

The fabricators soon learned that a single basic report could be tailored to appeal to various American and other Western buyers. Throughout the American occupation zones in Germany and Austria, the Army, Air Force, and Navy each maintained diverse, more or less independent, intelligence offices, each striving to make its reputation. Similar situations existed in the British and French intelligence establishments. Although efforts were made to effect coordination and stamp out duplicated effort, more often than not the situation appeared to be beyond the ability of the bureaucracy to solve. The sellers' intelligence market soared.

The proliferation of reports ostensibly from widely different sources but presenting roughly similar fabricated data made false confirmations a constant threat. At one point it was estimated that some 50 percent of the information on file in the West on the USSR and Eastern Europe had come from such sources. The notion that pitched battles were being fought by Russian or Ukrainian resistance forces and the Red Army, and other such apparently sensational scoops, was smothering our modest reports showing how the USSR was consolidating its grip on the occupied areas. Until sound data bases could be established, evaluation and analysis of nonscientific data were all but impossible.

We soon found that the study of the operational mechanism that allegedly produced the reports was far more effective than attempting to evaluate the actual intelligence product. Case officers with wartime operations and interrogation experience readily adapted these skills to postwar activity. Unfortunately these experienced officers and equally practiced operations analysts and desk officers—usually women in those days—were scarce.

Along with the budget increases, personnel ceilings were raised to a level that threatened to engulf our training facilities. This suggested a corollary to the American inclination to find a dollar solution to difficult problems. In secret intelligence the addition of more staff does not necessarily guarantee increased production. In many instances, a lean outfit will outperform its plump neighbor. Any reasonably intelligent person can be taught the fundamentals of secret operations in a few months, and a student's grasp of these principles is not difficult to test. The application of classroom knowledge to operations in the field is not as easily taught. The best, if not only, solution is at least two years' field experience under a competent boss. In my division in the late forties, the twoscore operatives with this much practical experience were literally veterans, and our handful of experienced managers were in even greater demand. In those formative years we were creating our own postwar operational doctrine day by day.

As we examined the entrepreneurs' wares it became possible to sort them into two categories. First came individuals operating alone, often former intelligence operatives or agents, most of them survivors of the loosely supervised Nazi intelligence efforts in Eastern Europe and the USSR. These people tended to create their product from scratch—memory and the world press. No motive was more basic than patching together a livelihood in the desperate postwar economy.

A more serious problem was the intelligence offices created in the various émigré groups, and usually staffed by former intelligence personnel and senior military officers. These people came with more intellectual heft, personal presence, and a better sense of the market than the less prepossessing lone operators.

The minor scams ran to form. An alleged middleman represented a Russian or Eastern European official who wanted to sell information to cover his debts, support a mistress, or finance his eventual defection and life in the West. To protect himself, the alleged source would in no circumstance reveal his name or position in the Communist Party hierarchy. He—I recall no women being cited as mysterious sources in those macho days—trusted only his intermediary, in itself evidence of shaky judgment. The go-betweens had most often bubbled up from the bottom of the local black market. In practice, an operations officer would purchase an initial report or two. If the material showed any promise, an effort would be launched to identify the alleged source, and to determine the bona fides of the middleman. This might involve surveillance, telephone taps, extensive name tracing, and an unconscionable amount of time. There were as many variations on this theme as there were wine taverns in Vienna and beer halls in Berlin, but each had to be sifted for a possible treasure. The fact that on occasion a few nuggets of value were uncovered meant that we had to continue struggling against the impossible odds.

Some junior officers learned their trade chasing these phantoms, but the time involved took our attention away from developing the techniques that in the future were to produce significant results.

More serious than the individual fabricator was the industry that evolved into a string of what a perceptive analyst dubbed "paper mills." The leadership of the various émigré organizations that had formed in the West usually comprised a handful of formerly prominent political figures. The fact that effective contact between the exiles and their real or imagined constituency in the homeland had effectively ceased did not, of course, reduce the need for funds to nourish the émigré groups and, incidentally, to maintain the lifestyle of the leadership. The exiles soon learned that the best way to serve both purposes was to enlist the support of the intelligence-hungry Western services. While émigré leaders chatted politics, intelligence matters were left to former professionals—sometimes self-styled "professionals." In the absence of live sources, the temptation to fabricate plausible data was often overpowering.

The efforts of the fabrication factories to milk Western intelligence and to influence U.S. policy approached its peak in 1952. As late as 1951, a third of the CIA operational effort in occupied Austria was devoted to tracking down fabrication. It was at this time that Walter Jessel, then chief of the Austria-Hungary branch at headquarters, undertook an intensive study of the problem. He had served as reports chief in Germany in 1946 when we were shifting from the wartime concentration on

German targets to the USSR. Walter had effectively spiked the continuing flood of such reports as the number of rapes committed by Soviet
troops in Silesia, dreams of a Wittelsbach restoration, and the occasional
flash details of Hitler's submarine voyage to Argentina, in favor of the
more solid information on Soviet activity and intentions in East Germany.

On his return to Washington, Jessel studied the "intelligence" we
were beginning to identify as wishful thinking, refugee hearsay, and fabrication. He confirmed our suspicion that the fabricators were selling
slightly altered versions of the same report to three or four of their customers. It was soon possible to trace the movement of cloned reports
through various consumer channels. Given the proprietary interests of
some of the American agencies involved, this was a sensitive bit of business. The impressive political backgrounds of some of the leading exile
political figures gave them access to—and a measure of influence on—
prominent businessmen, members of Congress, and others with ties to
ethnic communities in the United States.

Jessel began with a study of a prolific Hungarian paper mill run by
General Andras Zako, who in 1944 was chief of VKF-2, the intelligence
component of the General Staff of the Hungarian fascist premier Ferenc
Szálasi. Keeping a prudent step ahead of the Red Army, Zako and some
of his Iron Cross colleagues made their way to Austria, where the general became a founding member of the right-wing MHBK, the League of
Hungarian Veterans. It was not long before Zako's reports from the usual
variety of "high-level" sources found their way to market. By 1952,
Zako was the very model of an intelligence entrepreneur.

The obvious solution to the fabrication problems was coordination
between the various intelligence services. This was less easily achieved
than reason would suggest. No intelligence service will lightly disclose
the identity of any agent or contact; competition between the several services was fierce, and some services and a few well-entrenched senior officers had built reputations on intelligence that Jessel's analysis showed
to have been fabricated. General Zako's enthusiastic customers were not
easily convinced that they had been hoodwinked, and some high-
ranking officers were suspicious of CIA's motives for even suggesting it.

General Bedell Smith was director of Central Intelligence when Walter Jessel and I brought the Zako study to his attention. Smith directed us

to brief the United States Intelligence Board—made up of the chiefs of all the U.S. military and civilian intelligence services—on our findings. As the briefing unfolded, and the charts and supporting data to substantiate Jessel's claims of fabrication were presented, General Charles Pearre Cabell, then chief of Air Force intelligence and later deputy director of CIA, asked, "Who in the Air Force could be buying this crap?" Jessel quietly pointed out that not only the Air Force, but every member of the board were major clients of the Zako paper mill. Jessel's hard work broke the back of the fabrication industry. The cleanup—which included similar but less extensive fabrication activity in the Far East—took time and feelings were bruised, but coordination was achieved. Basic files were winnowed, doubtful information was replaced with solid data, and the basis for the sound analysis of incoming intelligence was established. The fabrication factories were slowly boarded up.

As part of the cleansing process the names, operational characteristics, and photographs of identified fabricators were circulated among the Western services in documents we called "Burn" lists. In time, I suppose a bit of secret paper will surface in which someone will be found to have recommended that secret agent "Willy Piefke" be "burned." However tempting that punishment might have been, let it forever be understood that in our jargon, "to burn" meant nothing more than adding a villain's name to the circulating lists of culprits known to fabricate intelligence reporting.

—

In fall 1948, President Truman named Allen Dulles chairman of a committee to investigate how CIA was functioning and to recommend appropriate changes. Dulles appointed William H. Jackson, who had served as General Omar Bradley's intelligence officer before joining OSS, and Mathias Corea, a former New York attorney general, as committee members. All three were New York lawyers. Jackson and Corea had both been active in the informal intelligence support group Dulles had organized shortly after his return to practice law in 1946.

The committee report was presented to the National Security Council in January 1949. It recommended that the Agency be organized in five divisions: Estimates, Research, and reports; Operations, Administration, and Coordination. The last division was to coordinate U.S. intelligence activity and synthesize intelligence information. After noting the some-what scattered aspect of CIA operations during its first year, the report recommended that the Agency's directives be specified by the National Security Council. Because the President chaired the NSC, this arrange-ment would ensure CIA's direct link to him.

General Walter Bedell Smith replaced Admiral Hillenkoetter as direc-tor of Central Intelligence in October 1950. In January 1951, Allen Dulles was appointed deputy director for the Office of Special Operations and the Office of Policy Coordination—effectively chief of intelligence, counter-intelligence, and covert action operations. William Jackson was named General Smith's deputy.

From my position below the salt, it was almost immediately apparent that as much as Dulles enjoyed being back in operations, there was no reason to believe that he would linger long this far from the summit. As I recall, my best guess was twelve months—close, but wrong by two months. AWD replaced William Jackson as Bedell Smith's deputy in August 1951. In February 1953, when President Eisenhower named Be-dell Smith under secretary of state, Dulles was named director of Cen-tral Intelligence.

Chapter 10

—

MR. DULLES
TAKES OVER

From the moment General Bedell Smith brought Allen Dulles into CIA, it was obvious to us all that the general and Allen were as different as two men their age in the same work might ever be. Smith was the Army prototype of what used to be called a mustang, an officer who had made his way through the enlisted ranks without the benefit of a service academy or even a college degree with its by-product, a reserve commission. General Smith had earned his stars by furiously hard work, an iron self-discipline, and relentless attention to business. He expected no less from his subordinates and was not reluctant to point out any short-fall in terms that even the least gifted private soldier would understand and take to heart.

In contrast, Allen Dulles had lived a life of comparative ease. Although he had no private fortune, Dulles had always moved comfortably in the company of those who had. He worked hard for two degrees at Princeton, earned a law degree at George Washington University, and was welcomed into a prominent law firm. Dulles's manner—that of a self-confident Ivy League gentleman, at ease in his work and secure in his position in life—masked his own strong ambition and devotion to duty. It is safe to say that Dulles understood Bedell Smith a bit better than the general ever fathomed the wellborn intellectual that his deputy seemed to be.

Dulles was sometimes offended by Smith's occasional drill-sergeant manner of dealing with all his subordinates, but there was only one serious discomfort in his relationship with the general. Bedell Smith was director of Central Intelligence and Allen Dulles was not.

More than that, Dulles was not shaped to be anyone's deputy, particularly in the one job that he was determined to have as his own. Fortunately for all concerned it was reasonably clear that Smith did not regard his post as DCI as the apex of his career; it was at the most a milestone. In the meanwhile, Dulles put up with the general's abrasive behavior, and concerned himself with the aspects of secret intelligence that mattered most to him. He respected Smith's talent for recognizing the decisions that needed to be made and his ability to push lesser matters to the side. When the time for decision came, the general was able to ignore the nuances that often plagued and compromised the solutions proposed by less confident executives. Invariably, Smith's decisions dealt with the heart of the matter. Once the decision was made, the details—no matter how complex—were left to be dealt with at lower levels.

At the time, the DCI and his senior staff officers still occupied the buildings General Donovan and the OSS staff had used throughout World War II. These were a short distance from the new State Department building, but at least a fifteen-minute trip from the offices of the operational components, ranged along the Reflecting Pool in front of the Lincoln Memorial.

A few months after Allen Dulles replaced Smith, I went to his office with an outgoing cable for his release. On the chance that the director might have a question, any cable important enough for his signature was hand-carried to him by the officer who had drafted it. I no longer remember the cable—in a busy week there might be several such messages—but it was in early 1954, sometime after I had received two promotions.

Here a bit of background. The first promotion, in March 1951, lifted me from the Central European Division to chief of the Foreign Intelligence (FI) Staff with responsibility for intelligence collection operations worldwide. This was a welcome assignment because for the first time it gave me detailed insight into the FI activity of the stations beyond the European area and the opportunity to get to know the personnel involved in the many far-flung posts.

In January 1953, I replaced Lyman Kirkpatrick in the job we called COPS—chief of operations. This gave me responsibility for both intelligence collection and covert action operations. The job also meant that I was deputy to my old friend Frank Wisner, who was deputy director for plans (DDP). Kirkpatrick had fallen ill with polio, and it had become apparent that his health would not permit him to carry the double duty as chief of operations and deputy to the DDP.

The new job was demanding and required my quickly coming to grips with a wide variety of covert action operations, some areas of which were new to me. The reason we called this job chief of operations rather than deputy deputy director for plans is obscure, but I was satisfied not to be known as a deputy's deputy. Title notwithstanding, when Wisner was out of town I acted in his place and I did so for seven years. It was a testing job, but it was a pleasure to work with Frank.

The "plans" element of the DDP title was, of course, a fig leaf presumably chosen to shield fainthearted members of Congress and other such sensitive souls from a too revealing glimpse of Wisner's job, which some years later would be more forthrightly titled deputy director for operations (DDO). Despite the change in name, the DDP and DDO were the same job.

That morning, Dulles fiddled a bit with the cable I had brought in before signing it. As I edged out of my seat to leave, Allen motioned me to stay. It was mid-morning, and definitely not the time the DCI would pick for any business-as-usual or even an encouraging personal chat. In the few seconds before he began to speak, I ran through a list of topics he might have on his mind. Nothing registered, but then we had worked closely together in Germany and I was used to these surprise encounters.

"A word about the future," Dulles said. There was a weighted pause before he added, "The *Agency's* future."

I may have nodded apprehensively because he gave me a reassuring smile before saying, "You remember the conniving and blood spilling that went on when we were trying to sort things out in 1946? What would Central Intelligence be responsible for? Would there even be a service?"

I hadn't played much role in the battle, but everyone in the outfit at the time remembered the bureaucratic furor.

"It was perfectly clear then," Dulles said, "and it's all down in black and white that the fundamental purpose of Central Intelligence is to prevent anything resembling another Pearl Harbor." Another brief pause. "And as of 1948 it's been equally clear that we have full responsibility— all of it specified in NSC 10/2, documented and legal—for most aspects of *covert action* operations."

I was, of course, aware of the covert action history from the moment in 1947 when President Truman's National Security Council issued a directive (NSCD 4/A) charging the Agency with responsibility for covert *psychological* operations. Within a week, CIA had established the Special Procedures Group and began to plan propaganda operations in Eastern Europe. In 1948 the communist coup in Czechoslovakia and a cable from General Lucius Clay, the U.S. military commander in Germany, warning that war with the USSR "may come with dramatic suddenness" roused the National Security Council to issue NSC Directive 10/2. This "Nonskid"—as we referred orally to National Security directives— abolished NSCD 4/A, defined the broad range of covert action operations, and established the policy that all such activity be "planned and executed [so] that any U.S. Government responsibility for them is not evident . . . and that if uncovered the U.S. Government can plausibly disclaim any responsibility for them." Responsibility for covert action was lodged with CIA.

Still not sure where Dulles was headed, I must have nodded my understanding.

"Although the press and the public never seem to remember it, you know as well as I do that operations are at best only a fraction of our responsibility. Right now, the Directorate for Intelligence [DI] is doing its job, and is on top of all the intelligence coming into the government. Our estimates are sound and the analysis is getting a good response from the consumers."

He seemed to ruminate for a moment before coming bluntly to his message for me. "It's the operations directorate that concerns me, and I want to be absolutely sure you understand how important covert action operations are right now." Dulles must have caught my surprise for he quickly added, "Intelligence collection has its place—no question, no doubt about it. And by and large I'm satisfied with the progress we're making. But I want you to be sure that everyone in operations has it firmly in mind that the White House and this administration have an *intense interest* in every aspect of *covert action.*" He paused again, silently to underline his emphasis.

For some time I had sensed that Dulles considered me a specialist in FI—foreign intelligence collection—and I suspected that he thought I lacked a full measure of his own deep interest in political action, Radio Free Europe, Radio Liberty, black propaganda, economic warfare, paramilitary operations, and all the other aspects of clandestine subversive activity.

"Mind," he said, "I know full well that intelligence collection can be vital."

For a moment I suspected that he was preparing to serve me a second helping of the same bone, something along the line, "Bully for FI... *but*..." with the important part of the message coming after the conjunction. Whatever might follow, Dulles was right in assuming that I considered intelligence collection the bedrock operational activity.

"What I'm getting down to, Dick, is that no matter how important collection is, in the short and even the long run, it just doesn't *cost* very much."

This really was a surprise. In what I was now beginning to perceive as my innocence, I'd always thought that the nickel-and-dime costs involved in running spies were a very large plus. The Pentagon had recently informed CIA that the recruitment and exploitation of Soviet military intelligence officer Major Pyotr Popov in Austria had already saved the Department of Defense an estimated half-billion dollars in research funds. Popov was costing us less than $4000 a year. Even in those early days, it was electronic operations, support to various liaison services, global radio intercept systems, and other monitoring activity that consumed the bulk of the intelligence budgets. Half a decade of spy wages and the combined expense of all the associated espionage paraphernalia would easily be covered by the cost of a single up-to-snuff Air Force bomber.

"Let me make this clear," Dulles continued. "We have to face the fact that because espionage is relatively cheap it will probably always seem inconsequential to some of our less informed friends on the Hill—in both houses of Congress. They're accustomed to dealing in billions. What kind of impression can it make when I come along and ask for a few hundred thousand dollars and a bag of pennies? Believe me, I know the way they think up there. If there's no real money involved, it can't be important, and they just won't pay much attention to us."

I let this pass as a rhetorical observation, but my expression must have struck Dulles.

"For all the responsibility we've been given, we're still living on a shoestring. Just look at our real estate. You operations people are working in those shacks down by the Reflecting Pool." Dulles was right about that—the buildings were in such rotten shape that the repairs needed repairing.

"And if that's not enough," Dulles continued, "you operations people spend more time getting to and from my office than it takes to deal with the problems you've come to discuss."

It was easy to agree. The DCI, his immediate staff, and various administrative offices were still housed in the former OSS premises at 2230 E Street, a fifteen-minute trip from the Directorate for Plans offices stretched out along the Reflecting Pool in front of the Lincoln Memorial. As our responsibilities increased, the distance between the DCI and the operations offices became more of a problem every week.

"Make no mistake," Dulles said. "The way we're going, our responsibilities are running way ahead of our budget, and there's a legitimate and growing market for covert action."

This observation came at what I have come to consider the high tide of covert action. In August 1953, Mohammed Mossadegh, who had undercut the authority of Shah Mohammed Reza Pahlavi, was ousted in a deft covert action. The following year in Guatemala, Jacobo Arbenz, the leftist president, opted to abandon his post rather than risk what we had led him to believe would be an armed invasion by opposing Guatemalan dissidents. This transpired a few weeks after Czechoslovakia had delivered some 2000 tons of arms Arbenz had solicited. U.S. operations, both authorized and initiated by President Eisenhower, were conducted with relatively little cost and a minimum of violence. Although the Eisenhower administration was in a position to deny its role in these actions, it could scarcely have done so in a convincing manner. At the time the USSR was so clearly recognized as an aggressive and dangerous antagonist, the plausibility of such a denial did not seem to matter.

I did not need Allen Dulles to convince me of the emphasis being placed on the Agency's covert action capability. It was obvious to me that the impact of the back-to-back operations in Iran and Guatemala—and another earlier and relatively unsung success in thwarting communist influence in the 1948 election in Italy—had registered heavily in the White House and with John Foster Dulles, the secretary of state. Our extensive support of the non-communist labor movements in France and Italy, and quiet underwriting of the non-communist, intellectual left were also impressive. In a very short time, and in my view with perhaps too little reflection, covert action had become a favored instrument. Diplomacy had its uses, but in those years the impatient Eisenhower administration had convinced itself that even the most effective diplomacy took too much time and the result was often uncertain.

I had little quarrel with the scores of proposed covert action activities that I had approved as they crossed my desk. Some of the published total numbers of CA operations the Agency ran in those years are misleading. Most were inconsequential: a few dollars to a democratic political party outfunded by a local communist front; an editor on an influential newspaper cultivated by a respected left-wing but anti-communist intellectual he might otherwise never have met; enough money to permit a feminist group to finance a campaign to increase the women's vote in a close upcoming election; and relatively small funds allocated to encourage editorial and news coverage of issues that some of the foreign press might have ignored. In many small countries without extensive foreign intelligence services, this level of activity is quietly conducted by diplomats stationed in embassies and consulates. This is low-key, unexceptionable stuff in comparison with a handful of heavier, more nearly strategic CA operations.

All the same, on the way back to my office I had much to think about. However important as an activity standing between effective diplomatic pressure and open intervention, strategic CA operations were high-risk ventures, not to be lightly undertaken. I was convinced that as long as Frank Wisner was deputy director for plans, and the senior covert action operations authority, the two of us could maintain the right balance between espionage and covert action. Irrespective of any possible White House pressure, Frank was not likely to be stampeded into unwise CA activity. Dulles's rather cynical approach to the Agency's budget would soon vanish as the costs of developing the U-2 aircraft and other outerspace surveillance capabilities would in a sense go right through the roof. His concern for what he perceived as my failure to recognize strategic CA operations as a foreign policy panacea would remain throughout his tenure as DCI.

Chapter 11

THE NOISY SIDE
OF THE STREET

However long it took the staff car to thread its way back to my office, it got there before I had fully digested Dulles's briefing. In the years since AWD's expression of his enthusiasm for covert action operations, I've had time, and certainly occasion enough, to reflect on it. One thing is certain. No aspect of CIA operations has attracted as much public comment or as many screams of outrage as the operations now categorized as covert action. In the years since the early Dulles era, my own views have matured and hardened.

The term "covert action (CA)" slipped into the CIA intelligence lexicon sometime after the Agency was established in 1947. Although the various activities now encompassed by that coinage have been part of secret intelligence activity throughout history, the term was not used by OSS, nor do I recall seeing it in any of the wartime British documents. The genesis probably came in December 1947 when the National Security Council made CIA responsible for "Covert Psychological Operations." The difference between "covert" (which my desk dictionary defines as "hidden") and "secret" (defined as "kept from knowledge . . . or hidden") is a nuance too subtle for me. A subsequent National Security Council document dropped "Psychological" from the expression, and simply authorized CIA to carry out "Covert Operations." Because this term can be construed to embrace all manner of secret intelligence activity, it quickly evolved into the more accurate and restrictive expression "Covert *Action* (CA)." The word "action" is meant to distinguish CA from espionage. A colleague describes espionage as the "theft of secrets." Most of the results of successful CA operations are clearly to be seen—an election won or lost, a shift in the editorial position of a newspaper, the increased activity of an opposition party. In contrast, successful espionage goes unnoticed, with the victim unaware that a secret has been compromised.

In OSS, General Donovan had made a useful distinction between paramilitary operations and political and psychological activity. Paramilitary operations were conducted by small units of *uniformed* troops infiltrated into strategic areas to train and operate with armed indigenous resistance forces. In contrast to the uniformed personnel, subject by treaty to treatment as POWs if captured, the other OSS branches infiltrated *agents* into enemy territory to collect intelligence, conduct sabotage, and support clandestine resistance activity. If detected, agents disguised as civilians were subject to execution as spies. The aptly named OSS unit Morale Operations (MO) was responsible for clandestine political, psychological, propaganda, and economic warfare activities. In the field, these operations were conducted by agents.

The 1948 National Security Council decision to bundle such diverse endeavors as paramilitary campaigns and the overthrow of foreign governments with more modest activities—many of which might accurately be described as clandestine public relations—under this new and ambiguous name may have created the impression that CA activity was an invention of CIA. Not so.

—

Covert action is as old as secret intelligence. George Washington was the first American president to make use of it, and he occasionally enlisted Benjamin Franklin's help. Congress established the Committee of Secret Correspondence for "the sole purpose of corresponding with our friends in Great Britain" and elsewhere abroad in 1775. Funds were allocated to pay "such agents" as the committee might dispatch. The committee collected intelligence, initiated covert actions, devised ciphers, opened mail, and acquired foreign publications for use in analysis. In

1790, Congress granted the President a "Contingency Fund for Foreign Intercourse"—perhaps then a less ambiguous expression. The expenditures were neither accounted for nor audited by Congress. Money from this fund was used in a secret attempt to ransom the American seamen held hostage by "Arab terrorists" on the Barbary Coast.

One of Ben Franklin's CA operations, concocted in 1777, has always appealed to me. A letter purportedly from Frederick II of Hesse Kassel to King George III urging the British to make more aggressive use of the German mercenaries in battling the American insurgents was forged. The prince reminded King George that in addition to the fee he was being paid for the use of his troops, he was also due a comforting bonus for each soldier killed. As of the moment, the prince complained, too few of his troops were being killed to make the venture as profitable as he had been led to expect. He also suggested that it might be more humane to allow the German wounded to die rather than keep them alive to live wretchedly as cripples.

The forgery added a wallop to the various open offers of amnesty and free farmland available to Hessian deserters. It was a well-targeted, inexpensive, self-contained covert action. Of the 30,000 German mercenaries employed by the British, more than 5000 are known to have deserted.

———

In 1946 when we were struggling to keep SSU up and running, no one gave a thought to the fact that most of the operations people who had opted to stay in the service were specialists in espionage or counterintelligence. The OSS political and psychological warfare operatives seemed spontaneously to have scattered at the end of the war. The fact that covert action had not figured in the discussions on how secret intelligence was to be organized and who would control it may have convinced the OSS Morale Operations specialists that there would be no role for them in the new organization. When Steve Penrose briefed me on my responsibilities in Central Europe, he made no reference to any covert action.

This was unfortunate. The political and psychological warfare veterans were well qualified for peacetime secret intelligence work. Those I knew were intellectually oriented and might have provided a useful counterweight to some of the enthusiastic young activists who did remain. I suspect that another reason so few of the MO veterans chose to remain with the outfit was that many were older and had more of a stake in resuming their established careers than risking a commitment to something as chancy as SSU seemed to be.

Lothar Metzl, an Austrian who had emigrated to the United States sometime after Hitler's Anschluss, was an exception to the exodus of OSS Morale Operations veterans. From the day I met him until his retirement, Lothar looked as if he had just stepped out of a Vienna coffeehouse—rumpled, quizzical, and slightly preoccupied. He had begun his career in musical theater in Vienna, and in this country worked on the Broadway production *Vienna Sings.* In OSS, Lothar wrote and recorded a series of songs by Marlene Dietrich that were used to spice the OSS broadcasts to the Wehrmacht. Dietrich's OSS records were never put on the open market. Years later, Ernest Hemingway, a friend of the singer, rashly offered a considerable price for a set of the recordings. Lothar wrote Hemingway's publisher offering to swap a collection for the manuscript of a Hemingway short story. There was no response.

Lothar weathered the CIA growing pains and turned his lifelong study of the Comintern and various national Communist Party organizations to professional use. For some twenty-five years, he served as the Counterintelligence Staff's expert on international communist activity. Lothar monitored every slight shift in Communist Party policy or doctrine as accurately as a seismograph. He also could retain the attention of congressional committees while enlightening them on what he slyly referred to as the "broader aspects of the movement."

———

If Stalin had intended to force the United States and its allies to rearm and rally to contain Soviet expansionism, he could not have created policies more calculated to achieve that end than those he implemented. While the Allies were disarming, Stalin's three-million-man army had hunkered down and then began rapidly to embed itself in Germany, Austria, Hungary, Poland, Czechoslovakia, Romania, and Bulgaria. The USSR's 1940 annexation of the Baltic countries—Latvia, Estonia, and Lithuania—was scarcely subject for further discussion. The prospects for open elections in most of Eastern Europe were nil. Rather than aid in the economic reconstruction of the Soviet-occupied areas, Stalin's policy was one of outright exploitation. His support of guerrilla activities in Greece and China was masked but was as blatantly obvious as the Soviet support to subversive elements throughout Western Europe.

In February 1946 an eight-thousand-word cable from George F. Kennan, U.S. chargé d'affaires in the USSR, jolted Washington policymakers into recognizing the Soviet Union as a tangible enemy and an aggressive threat to this country and the Western democracies. This resulted in the Truman Doctrine—a defense line, this far and no farther, drawn on the political landscape—and the Marshall Plan, a uniquely generous offer to fund the reconstruction of the European economies of both victors and vanquished.

By July 1947, Frank Wisner had had enough of sitting on the sidelines. He left his law firm to accept a post as number two in the State Department's Office of Occupied Territories. His immediate responsibility was to serve as State's representative on an interagency group studying the role of psychological warfare in combating the USSR's global political aggression. It was soon apparent to the White House, Department of State, and Pentagon that a more active response to the subversive aspects of Soviet foreign policy than could be made by the overt agencies was required. A choice had to be made between giving the responsibility for clandestine political, psychological, and paramilitary warfare to a new agency or to a component of an existing department. Secretary of State George Marshall insisted on controlling policy, but did not want to encumber, let alone stain, American diplomacy with secret activity. He would leave the covert response to Soviet subversion to another agency.

CIA's role in covert action actually began before the government had recognized a continuing need for such activity. In 1947 it was apparent that the impending elections in Italy and France might well deliver the governments of those countries into the hands of the Communist Party and thus Stalin. On a broad front, U.S. government and private support was organized to help the non-communist labor unions and democratic political parties in both countries. CIA slipped funds to the non-communist organizations, developed press campaigns, and helped rally public support abroad. This support and the electorate's common sense carried the day: the communist parties lost the elections in Italy and France.

In one important sense the success of these efforts was a mixed blessing—it alerted policymakers to the existence of an all-but-forgotten tool. It was thought that covert action, properly executed, meant never having to wait in the hope that diplomatic activity might resolve a snarled foreign-policy problem. A CA operation might solve the problem in weeks. There was another important consideration: if, as unlikely as it seemed, an operation were ever to go awry, the failed effort could be plausibly denied. It was in this sanguine atmosphere that the new covert action organization and programs were established.

In June 1948 the National Security Council made a compromise decision. It established the innocently named Office of Policy Coordination (OPC), and assigned it to CIA for what the Army traditionally called "rations and quarters." This meant that Admiral Roscoe Hillenkoetter, then director of Central Intelligence, would house, administer, and pay the OPC staff, but would have no substantive control of OPC policy or activity. OPC would report directly to the National Security Council and to the secretaries of state and defense, and would receive its directives and marching orders from these offices. This lame compromise between establishing yet another secret organization and giving CIA full responsibility for covert action operations seemed to have been most heavily influenced by the reluctance of the State and Defense Departments to give the upstart CIA any more responsibility than it already had. Granted the understanding that many in Washington were convinced that the United States was headed for war with the USSR, it is difficult to see how anyone might have thought this compromise could have worked.

Those of us in the Office of Special Operations were more curious than concerned about these decisions. It was not that we were all so blasé we couldn't be bothered, but that we were running hard to keep abreast of our daily responsibilities. Moreover, the fact that the outfit was still in a teething mode, and without a sufficiently broad base of experience, left us little time for strategic reflection. The benefit of a few back-to-back months of organizational peace might have aroused more comment and speculation on the advent of OPC. Little did we know.

The National Security Council first listed OPC's responsibilities in a blunt secret charter that directed it to engage in "propaganda, economic warfare; preventive direct action, including sabotage, antisabotage, demolition and evacuation measures; subversion of hostile states, including assistance to underground resistance and support of indigenous anti-Communist elements in threatened countries of the free world."

If this were not handful enough, these activities were to be planned and conducted so that if ever exposed, the American government could "plausibly disclaim any responsibility." It seems impossible to believe that the paramilitary activity authorized in the OPC charter could be carried out in a manner that could plausibly be denied by the President, but I do not recall any serious challenges to this instruction at the time.

In an unclassified document published in 1995, CIA presented a delicately phrased but significantly new definition of covert action: "An operation designed to influence governments, events, organizations, or persons in support of foreign policy in a manner that is not *necessarily* attributable to the sponsoring power; it may include political, economic, propaganda, or paramilitary activities" (emphasis added).*

In my opinion, a covert action operation that is not *necessarily* attributable to its sponsor does not qualify as a covert activity.

Before signing on with the State Department, Frank Wisner had worked with Allen Dulles and a handful of private enthusiasts who served as volunteer intelligence lobbyists. Frank had led the agitation for a new secret agency specifically authorized to engage in all forms of secret political, psychological, paramilitary, and economic warfare. In 1948, Frank slipped quietly aside from his State Department assignment and was appointed chief of OPC. Highly intelligent, experienced, energetic, and impeccably well connected, he was uniquely well qualified for the job.

By the time President Truman's nomination of General Bedell Smith to replace Admiral Hillenkoetter as DCI had been confirmed by the Senate in August 1950, it did not take any marked insight to realize that General Smith was not likely to allow any element of his new command to report to and receive orders directly from the secretary of state or anyone else in Washington. One of the general's first acts was to tell Wisner that as of the next morning, OPC was part and parcel of CIA, and that it would report to and receive its directives from the director of Central Intelligence. Frank was realist enough to know that the change was bound to come. The fact that it came this quickly did not make it any more welcome.

A Consumer's Guide to Intelligence (Washington, D.C.: U.S. Government Printing Office).

The most serious remaining problem was an internal one, the merging of OSO and OPC facilities, administration, and personnel. OSO personnel had paid little attention to OPC in its inception. From the moment OPC moved into the OSO quarters alongside the Reflecting Pool and began to undertake field operations, antagonism between the two disciplines developed. Two areas of conflict evolved, one operational, the other administrative.

Operational tradecraft was the fundamental problem. The first person I heard use "tradecraft" to describe the mechanics of secret intelligence was Allen Dulles. I doubt that he coined the expression, but he obviously liked the homespun sound of it. A colleague has pointed out that the Russian term for the arts and practices of espionage is "conspiracy," and that while American operatives learned tradecraft, their Russian antagonists were boning up on conspiracy. My friend thought that the slightly sinister overtone of the Russian term was more fitting a secret intelligence organization. Each to his own.

The first OPC operatives had not been in the field for long before it became obvious that in the rush to get operations under way, the OPC supervisors had paid too little attention to tradecraft and cover, and were failing to coordinate with the local OSO staff. In the pursuit of the overly ambitious OPC objectives, OSO equities were ignored, and security discipline was often poor.

Administratively, one of the earliest gripes was pay. Wisner had convinced the National Security Council that to make OPC work, he would need the very best personnel possible. From the outset and within the confines of the civil service pay scale, OPC sometimes based a new employee's pay on his salary in private life. Previous secret intelligence or diplomatic experience, language skills, and area knowledge were treasured, but the pickings were slim, and many recruits were accepted without any of these qualifications. This was exactly opposite of OSO practice. OSO recruits who did not have pertinent intelligence experience, language skills, and area knowledge came aboard at entry-level pay levels adjusted in part to their educational backgrounds and ages. Subsequent promotions were based on experience, languages, area knowledge, and proven operational competence. In practice, many inexperienced OPC officers were at least one pay grade above OSO personnel, with equal responsibility.

Within a year of its inception, OPC opened five foreign stations and hired more than three hundred employees. Three years later, forty-seven foreign posts had been established,* and the domestic and overseas staff had grown to some three thousand people. Even in the "the-Russians-are-coming" atmosphere prevailing in Washington and the Western European capitals, it was not possible to recruit, security-clear, and train this many officers and clerks in anything as complex as the responsibilities that had so optimistically been loaded upon the Office of Policy Coordination.

At the time, background security checks for staff employees took a minimum of three months. Training for staff officers involved another three months—and might profitably have been expanded to twice that time. Existing training facilities were swamped by the new arrivals. As a result, some employees were sent to the field with little training, and sometimes after only a familiarization period on one of the headquarters desks. Once in the field, fledgling operatives, no matter how well trained, require close guidance by experienced supervisors. In some OPC offices, the supervisors had little more experience than their staff.

In the months following the merger of OPC and OSO in 1952 it sometimes seemed unlikely that we would ever effect the coordination Bedell Smith assumed would follow his decision to form a unified organization. It took some doing, but the merger of the two functions—intelligence and covert action—was achieved. In sketching this period, I was reminded of how much there is to be said for the way some OPC officers achieved so many of their objectives while hammering their service into shape. Some of the most effective and longest-running covert action projects—Radio Free Europe and the Congress for Cultural Freedom—were established in this early period.

—

In 1951, Mohammad Mossadegh, the contentious nationalist prime minister of Iran, began systematically to undercut the authority and policy of the youthful Shah, Mohammed Reza Pahlavi. Mossadegh also national-

---

*In almost all instances, the OPC operatives shared office premises with the established OSO installations. This was easily done in the still-occupied areas in Germany and Austria. It was more of a problem in other areas.

ized the Anglo-Iranian Oil Company and effectively resisted British diplomatic pressure and a partial naval blockade meant to force a change in his policy. American interests in Iran were not felt challenged until it became apparent that the prime minister might turn away from the traditional British-Iranian alliance and accept a hefty loan and other accommodations with the USSR. At this point, Secretary of State Dulles agreed to support the British position. A joint British-American plan to remove Mossadegh and restore the Shah's authority was agreed upon.

CIA's point man in the operation was Kermit Roosevelt, a grandson of Theodore Roosevelt. Kim, as he was known, was an OSS veteran and an early CA enthusiast. He was assisted by a handful of CIA officers. In two months, and at a cost of two hundred thousand dollars, the joint coup d'état tumbled Mossadegh from office and brought the Shah back from a prudent sojourn in Rome to the Iranian throne.

For insiders, the effort was an incredible success. But when the Eisenhower administration's faith in covert action as a foreign policy panacea soared, Kim Roosevelt was moved to sound a thoughtful warning.

As he describes it in his book,* Kim tried to convince a high-level meeting, chaired by John Foster Dulles, that the coup had succeeded because CIA's study of the Iranian situation convincingly showed that the Iranian people and most of the military "wanted exactly" the results the Eisenhower administration was seeking. When Kim noticed that Foster Dulles was paying no attention, he added a most significant caveat. "If we [CIA] are ever going to try something like this again, we must be absolutely sure that [the] people and army want what we want. If not, you had better give the job to the Marines!" As Kim noted, "Foster Dulles did not want to hear what I was saying. He was still leaning back in his chair with a catlike grin on his face."

At the time the covert action enthusiasts were celebrating their success and pondering further ventures, I never heard any discussion of Kim Roosevelt's advice, or even a reference to it.

A few weeks after Kim briefed Foster Dulles, the Eisenhower administration directed CIA to undertake another operation, code-named PBSUCCESS. Allen Dulles turned to Kim Roosevelt, an obvious candi-

---

*Kermit Roosevelt, *Countercoup: The Struggle for Control of Iran* (New York: McGraw-Hill, 1979, p. 210).

date to oversee the ousting of the democratically elected government of Guatemala. Kim looked into what we used to call the "facts bearing on the problem" and politely refused the assignment.

The 1950 presidential election in Guatemala was expected to be a slam-bang contest between Francisco Arana, the chief of the Guatemalan armed forces, and Jacobo Arbenz, the minister of defense. Although both served in the administration of President Juan Arévalo, whose effort to effect changes in land management and to introduce social reforms, including the right of workers to organize unions, had infuriated the wealthy oligarchy, Arana had become increasingly conservative. Arbenz remained loyal to Arévalo's policies and, like his mentor, had sought left-wing support, including support from people who sympathized with the outlawed Communist Party. A few weeks before the election, Arana was lured into an ambush and killed by a posse of gunmen. A contest that would have given the Guatemalan electorate a clear choice between a conservative candidate and a leftist became an easy victory for Jacobo Arbenz.

In 1952 a CIA national estimate showed that Guatemala's numerically small Communist Party was exercising a political influence far out of proportion to its voter strength. The following year, the State Department recognized the influence of the Communist Party as an increasingly serious problem. Diplomatic efforts to change President Arbenz's political slant were ineffective. By 1954, Arbenz had expropriated thousands of acres of the United Fruit Company's plantations, legalized the Guatemalan Communist Party, and invited its participation in the government. President Eisenhower and Secretary of State Foster Dulles had reluctantly, if quietly, accepted the probability that there could be little "rollback of communism" in Eastern Europe, but there was no chance that they would tolerate Arbenz's apparent level of communist enthusiasm in our national front yard.

Diplomatic suasion had failed, and the days of open military intervention in our hemisphere seemed to have passed. An ambitious covert action operation was the obvious answer. This decision was underlined when an intelligence report showed that a Swedish-owned ship had landed in Guatemala bearing some two thousand tons of Czech arms.

President Eisenhower authorized a $20 million budget, and an operations plan was drafted. A Guatemalan exile, Colonel Carlos Castillo

Armas, was the central figure and commander of the rebel forces, the main components of which were an army of several hundred men and a small air force training in Honduras. An extensive propaganda campaign was launched in May 1954, and the Voice of Liberation, a clandestine radio station ostensibly operating from secret bases in Guatemala, began broadcasting news of battles within Guatemala and transmitting "orders" to notional resistance groups. On June 18, 1954, Colonel Armas and his ragtag force crossed the Guatemalan border unopposed. Air raids were faked—the planes dropped improvised bombs that were loud but harmless. The alleged results were widely publicized in exaggerated accounts broadcast by the "rebel" radio. Arbenz and his advisors were confused but held fast, and the Guatemalan military commanders remained quiet.

On June 20, Allen Dulles informed President Eisenhower that the operation had stalled and success was "very much in doubt." Unless the Guatemalan army moved against Arbenz, there was little probability that the coup would succeed. What was needed, Dulles told the President, was three aircraft to replace the vintage planes lost to ground fire and mechanical failures. Eisenhower agreed, and the "sale" of aircraft by the Air Force was negotiated. The lightly disguised planes were delivered by CIA pilots and momentum was restored to the rebel forces.

At this moment the relentless radio propaganda and deception moved Arbenz to make a final mistake. Convinced that he was facing an all-out attack, Arbenz panicked and ordered weapons be given to the "people's organizations and political parties." This was too much for the conservative army commanders. Arbenz was convincingly told that the army would no longer support him and that he should resign. He did so and slipped across the border into exile.

It was a near thing, but another ambitious covert action had succeeded.

PBSUCCESS introduced Richard M. Bissell, Jr., to covert action operations. After a brilliant scholastic record at Groton and Yale and a hitch at the London School of Economics, Bissell had entered government service in World War II as a key figure in directing the most efficient use of vital merchant shipping. After the war he taught economics at MIT and engaged in private consulting work. In 1948, he was summoned to Washington, where he wrote the first draft of the Marshall Plan. In 1952, he joined the Ford Foundation, a job that led to his exploring the ways in which CIA might promote resistance to the Soviets in Eastern Europe and gave him the opportunity to work with various old friends—Frank Wisner, Frank Lindsay, Tracy Barnes, and Max Milliken, then all with CIA. In 1953, Allen Dulles, also a friend, persuaded Bissell to join the Agency. His first brush with operations came as a staff officer involved in the complex political and logistical support of PBSUCCESS, at the time the Agency's largest CA project.

Chapter 12

—

BREAKING THE ICE

$\mathbf{A}$s the Agency gained its growth and settled down, the operations command channel remained much as it was initially conceived. In 1953 it went from Allen Dulles, director of Central Intelligence (DCI), to the deputy director for plans (DDP), Frank Wisner. As DDP, Wisner also shared responsibility with Dulles for the high-level contacts with the White House, Department of State, and Pentagon. In my role as Wisner's deputy and chief of operations, I supervised all operational activity except the work handled directly by Dulles or Wisner. I was also responsible for headquarters and overseas personnel assignments. Next in the line of command were the chiefs of the various area divisions. As in the Department of State, day-to-day activity was supervised by the country desk officers in each of the area divisions.

The rapid growth of CIA from its inception in 1947 to the mid-1950s and the merger of the covert action and espionage elements in 1953 meant there was more than enough work to keep Wisner and me busy. Although fully informed of all covert action operations, I concentrated—*pace* Mr. Dulles—on intelligence collection, counterintelligence, and foreign liaison activity. Frank was primarily concerned with covert action and policy matters, but was also abreast of my work, and participated in all the important personnel decisions. At no time was either of us excluded from oversight of the other's activity. This was particularly important in my case, because when Frank was out of town I took over. We had an easy and, I think, very effective working relationship.

There was always more than could be done in anything resembling a normal workday. I made it a practice to leave the office when I felt I had coped with what had to be done that day. To attempt to deal with everything that reached one's desk was to encourage a constantly increasing burden, with ever more problems being presented daily. The solution—to take a page from General Smith's practice—was to effect a sort of in-box triage, and to refuse to consider any problem that could be solved at a lower level. Day in and out I probably averaged a fifty-hour workweek. This sounds tame enough, and rightly so had all the hours been spent at my desk.

But international secret intelligence is a twenty-four-hour-a-day activity. It may be 3 a.m. in Washington, but somewhere on earth it is high noon and a crisis may be on the boil. Some of the late-night problems were resolved in cryptic telephone calls to a watch officer; others required a return to the office. In the days before electronic beepers, this meant being tied night and day to a telephone. It also put a premium on having the right people serving as watch officers. To be avoided were both the bold souls and the nervous nellies. The first were all too prone to make important decisions on their own; the nervous nellies were unwilling to resolve—or even to postpone until dawn—the least significant problems.

There is an element involved in secret intelligence management that writers have neglected. I doubt very much that there is any government activity encompassing the mix of personnel as that in OSS and CIA. As a division chief I might in an average week deal substantively with a high school graduate who had learned two languages while working on a Mediterranean tramp steamer, a history major too bored to remain an academic until given tenure, a young newsman who insisted on interesting work but whose family needed the security of a civil service job, a professional ballplayer with an M.A. and a bad knee, a clutch of bright graduates of state universities and a few from the Ivy League. I doubt that any manager can come to know and evaluate such a variegated collection of people by studying personnel records and doing business across an office desk. In my case it took a measure of after-hours association to develop the necessary understanding of my colleagues. In retrospect, these relationships remain some of my most valued career memories.

Frank Wisner routinely worked somewhat longer office hours and devoted more of his private time to work-related social activity than I did. In saying this, I neither boast nor complain. We were younger in those days, we were fascinated with our work, and we recognized its importance. Frank knew the Agency people with whom he worked personally very well, but much of his after-hours social life involved key people in other agencies. Dinner *chez* Wisner was always an intellectual workout with the brightest Washington had to offer. Sadly, Frank was to pay dearly for his deep dedication to his responsibilities.

By the mid-fifties our postwar operations had taken shape. Aggressive personnel recruitment netted an excellent crop of young officers. The training courses, which were initially based on the wartime curriculum, improved radically as our early postwar efforts were studied and brought into the classrooms. At all levels, in the field and at headquarters, our supervisors profited from their increasing experience.

The postwar operating rules were much the same as those established during the war. The difference was improved communication, the easing of travel, and a less frantic peacetime pace. This meant that our Washington headquarters was kept informed in detail, and was in position to approve and supervise every significant operational activity. In most cases senior and mid-level headquarters personnel had served in the field, and many of those in the field had done time in Washington. This helped dampen the generic conflict between the field operatives—who considered themselves front-line, twenty-four-hour-a-day activists, making do from foxholes, and who pictured the headquarters staff as forty-hour-a-week second-guessing bureaucrats. For their part, the headquarters personnel enjoyed imagining themselves fighting endless bureaucratic battles in defense of the field operatives who were battening on their overseas cost-of-living allowances while not handling agents *exactly* as the desk officers would have done if they were in the field.

In the early days, balancing the equation between stifling initiative by attempting to micromanage operations from the headquarters desk and allowing field operatives a free hand in making high-risk decisions required constant monitoring. The possible consequences—intended and otherwise—of most operations are best judged by senior headquarters personnel who have a broader and more current view of policy and security implications.

Our initial approaches to intelligence collection in the USSR and Eastern Europe were heavily freighted with the high-priority requirement to provide what was called early warning. This was another manifestation of the Pearl Harbor syndrome—never again. The simple solution—seen ever so clearly by the intelligence consumers in Washington—was for CIA to establish agents in Moscow and in position to uncover any Politburo plan for the Red Army to march to the English Channel. This was a logical requirement, but at the time the possibility of recruiting and running any such sources was as improbable as placing resident spies on the planet Mars. Throughout this period the urgent demand for intelligence—not to say information—on the USSR and its satellites was intense and relentless. All of our most ambitious operations were undertaken on the assumption of the policymakers that war might come at any time. The pressure for results ranged from repeated instructions to do "something" to exasperated demands to try "anything."

The most practical, if least dramatic, response to this requirement was radio intercept, aerial reconnaissance along the periphery of the communist states, and the *de visu* activity of CIA personnel and military attachés under official cover in the target areas. There were two exceptions. Because travel was relatively free from Vienna and Berlin we were able to recruit and run agents throughout the Soviet zones of occupation in Austria and Germany.

The first two decades of the Cold War were marked by an intense concern about Soviet policy on Berlin. Were the Russians going to provoke a crisis and attempt to oust the British, French, and American occupying forces from their legal positions in West Berlin? In March 1948, General Lucius D. Clay, the senior American official in Berlin, sent an alarming cable to Washington stating that war might "come with dramatic suddenness." The Agency was more reserved: our estimate said there was no "reliable evidence" that the USSR would resort to military action within the next sixty days. So far, so good, but the Soviets continued to harass Western access to and from Berlin by road and the railway. On June 20 the Soviets took the final step and closed the rail and road connections between Berlin and the Western-occupied areas of Germany. Electrical power was cut off, and food supplies from East Germany were stopped. The blockade was complete. President Truman responded with an airlift that supplied the necessities for the West Berliners to sustain life and was designed to convince the USSR that we had every intention of remaining in Berlin.

Stalin lifted the blockade in May 1949, but throughout my tenure it seemed that every foreign policy issue, from the establishment of NATO to the outbreak of hostilities in Korea, was to resonate in Berlin. The Berlin base, subordinate to the Agency chief in West Germany, was to prove itself again and again by the intelligence reporting it garnered in East Berlin and the Soviet-occupied areas of East Germany.

In Washington, our intelligence consumers became fixed upon a second-best solution to the early warning problem. CIA was to infiltrate agents into the western border areas of Poland, Czechoslovakia, and Hungary. The notion was that when the agents we called line crossers— either professional smugglers, or émigrés and refugees familiar with the target area—had transited the Soviet-occupied areas in Germany and Austria, the problem was half solved. All that remained was to nip across the eastern border into Poland, Czechoslovakia, or Hungary. Which is to say that all the agent had to do was skip through the mine-fields, dodge the electronic detection devices, and vault the electrified wire fences while avoiding the patrols and observation towers.

Once beyond the sparsely populated and heavily policed border areas, the agent was to make his way to a village where he would recruit a relative or friend who, with eyes peeled for alarming troop movements, might serve as a resident agent. Except for the facts that without the motivation fueled by the hot war, and that any agent intelligent enough to function efficiently once across the border would be far too well informed to undertake any such mission, these notions were a replay of the Allen Dulles and General Donovan wartime positions.

In peacetime, professional smugglers, usually simple souls at the lower edge of the criminal world, were accustomed to working with the connivance of the border guards. By the late forties, an activity based on bribing communist border guards offered no future whatsoever for any entrepreneur. In Europe, we were saddled with this cross-border responsibility until the mid-1950s. There may have been exceptions, but I do not recall any significant results from any of these time-consuming operations. We squandered hundreds of man-hours proving the truth of this.

Our most dramatic approach involved inserting agents—recent refugees, or deserters, usually Red Army enlisted men—into the USSR by parachute or small boat landings along the Baltic coast. As one cynical case officer expressed it, parachute operations into the USSR proved two things. Because no aircraft were lost, the USSR's defense of its airspace was but a fraction as effective as its near 100 percent control of its borders and its pervasive internal security measures. The second proof, he said, was that the law of gravity was as strong in the Ukraine as it was in our parachute training areas. Some brief radio contact was maintained with a handful of the inserted agents, but the effort was as much a failure as the cross-border operations.

None of the cross-border operations produced any significant intelligence, but the backup programs which involved us in an intensive study of life in the Soviet Union and Eastern Europe were highly profitable. Documents of all varieties were collected, and refugees were extensively questioned on local conditions and daily life. A wealth of current political and economic information flowed from the refugees making their way west through the relatively open doors in Vienna and Berlin into the refugee reception centers. As useful as this was, it did not provide the strategic intelligence it was our responsibility to uncover. It did, however, give us an up-to-date understanding of the communist world's internal security controls and everyday life in our target areas. Those of us who were familiar with the Nazi Gestapo soon learned that Hitler's secret police had not been in the same league as Stalin's. This should not have come as a surprise—the Soviet secret police had the advantage of some two decades' more experience than the Gestapo. In time, we were to learn that Stalin envied Hitler's security services, and prodded his own secret police to ape them. This was but one of Stalin's many dead-wrong judgments. There was nothing the KGB could have learned from the Nazis.

By far the most ambitious, and in the end successful, of our operational efforts was the recruitment of Soviet and Eastern European officials stationed abroad. This activity ran alongside a campaign to encourage and solicit the defection of communist officials who for security reasons were unable to remain in place, or who simply were not willing to run the risk of staying on the job as an agent.

As a division chief in the early fifties, I always budgeted time for a final interview with operations officers leaving for field assignments. It was my last chance to underline our priorities, and to insist that we risked becoming complacent running agents who at best were only in position to peek over the security fences the Communist countries had constructed around their policymaking and military headquarters at home, and the embassies and other installations abroad. There was no way the Agency could provide the White House and other intelligence consumers with the strategic intelligence they demanded as long as our sources were on the outside, looking in. The only way to fulfill our mission was to develop inside sources—spies who could sit beside the policymakers, listen to their debates, and read their mail.

I would point out that defectors were important—certainly the next best thing to penetration. But defector information was finite: it ceased the moment the defector stepped out of his office and crossed to our side. Because many of our officers had been briefed by defectors, it was not necessary to stress the fact that even after months of interrogation and resettlement, defectors were still valuable—to be consulted like a shelf of fine reference books.

Supervisor by supervisor, officer by officer, this approach began to take hold. There remained problems aplenty. As in headquarters, so it was in the field—there was always more than enough work to go around. Abroad, it was essential that everyone maintain some level of cover. As long as Austria and Germany remained under military occupation, relatively large offices could be maintained inexpensively under nominal military cover. Elsewhere, cover came more dearly and demanded some percentage of each officer's working day. In high-risk areas, operatives working under "deep cover" were sometimes required to spend more than forty hours a week at the cover job. In some areas this meant that the time spent on operations was no more than what might otherwise have been spent on a weekend hobby.

There was also the operational support structure—we called it "plumbing"—to be dealt with. In the occupied areas of Germany and Austria, the operational plumbing was comprehensive, and included safe meeting places, surveillance agents, operational vehicles, letter drops, and technicians trained to make quick audio installations, handle clandestine photography, fashion short-range electronic communications, cope with secret inks, and rig simple versions of some of the gadgets James Bond always had at hand. Incidentally, it sometimes seemed that the more impressive a device appeared in the workshop, the more fragile it was and the more likely it was to fail in the field. It took some on-the-job experience before case officers learned not to fling these prima donna utensils into the back seat of an automobile, but to treat them with the delicate hand they required.

Field offices were often saddled with a variety of peripheral responsibilities. In his persistent effort to prove the Agency's value, Allen Dulles too often welcomed responsibility that belonged elsewhere. This "can do" attitude (Dulles would have hated this expression) was to plague us. In the early days, some complex visa applications had to be investigated. Illegal East-West trade was of some importance, but could often be as well covered by embassies as by CIA. Some national Communist Parties were valid targets, but only in areas where there were close ties to the USSR. The foreign policies of allied and neutral countries were of interest, but were the proper responsibility of embassy political officers who maintained the traditionally open relations with their foreign office opposite numbers.

In NATO and neutral countries, an important CIA responsibility was to maintain effective liaison with the local intelligence and security organizations. With the exception of the obvious world powers, very few smaller nations maintained foreign intelligence services. Most were primarily concerned with internal security. Throughout the Cold War in Europe, these domestic security services were the front line of defense against Soviet espionage and political subversion. The ability of the indigenous services to maintain effective surveillance of illegal Soviet activity within their borders was critical. To varying degrees, the allied services were happy to provide local information in return for a steady supply of the intelligence and security data we collected worldwide. When, for example, a Soviet "diplomat" was transferred from Latin America to a European post, it might take months of surveillance before the local security service could determine whether the Russian was a diplomat or an intelligence officer. If the Agency had made a positive identification of the Russian in an earlier posting, hundreds of hours of street work might be saved or redirected. Today there is a similar identity of interest in the activity of the various terrorist organizations.

It was tempting for our field offices to make a flashy showing against the peripheral objectives rather than continue to flail away at the hard targets that often seemed beyond our grasp, but we kept at it. The first break came in Vienna in 1952.

Pyotr Semyonovich Popov, then a major in the Soviet military intelligence service (GRU), was born a peasant in an impoverished village along the Volga, far to the northeast of Moscow. He was thirteen and proudly wearing his first pair of leather shoes when his older brother insisted that at least one member of the peasant family have a bare-bones education at one of the special schools being established in the peasant areas throughout the USSR. Three years later, young Pyotr won acceptance at a middle school. In 1940, after the USSR invaded Finland, and the Red Army was still desperately trying to replace the 35,000 officers eliminated in Stalin's purges, Popov's school was abruptly transformed into a military academy.

Weeks after the German tanks rolled across the Soviet border in 1941, Popov, with six years of formal education and twelve months' military training, was commissioned a lieutenant. In March 1945, Popov, by then a twenty-three-year-old battle-seasoned captain, was selected for the Frunze Military Academy. Assignment to this school was the first step in the education of promising Red Army officers. Popov, who never overestimated his abilities, would point out that this was less an honor than it seemed. Wily combat commanders preferred to keep their best officers at hand, and would select less promising candidates to fill any quota— no matter what honor might be involved—that included transfer out of the combat areas.

A few weeks before his graduation, Popov's dogged struggle to keep up with his classmates won him another opportunity. He was offered assignment to Glavnoe Razvedovatel'noe Upravlenie (GRU), the military intelligence directorate of the Soviet General Staff. This was another fluke. Popov's most obvious qualification for assignment to the GRU was a manifestly clean security file—his peasant background was proof that he had never been exposed to unsuitable political influences or foreign entanglements of any kind. His combat career was undistinguished other than showing clearly that he followed orders and, like the qualities traditionally attributed to peasants, was able to take things as they came. Moreover, the GRU was desperate to replace the losses it had suffered during the war.

If Popov accepted, he would face another three years of schooling at the Military Diplomatic Academy, the highest-level and most prestigious school in the Soviet system. The last thing he wanted was another round of academic work, and though he doubted his ability to complete it, he recognized the opportunity, and had recently married and was expecting a child. Once again Popov squeaked through to graduate in 1951. The Soviet Union had literally given this peasant the best it had to offer.

Popov's first assignment was to the GRU *rezidentura* in Vienna. In November 1952 he took the incredible risk of dropping an envelope into the automobile of an American diplomat. In Russian, his letter contained an anonymous offer to sell the table of organization of a Soviet armored division, and specified the street corner on which he could be met if American intelligence authorities were interested in the proposition.

The Vienna plumbing was in place. Because there were obvious risks in meeting an anonymous, alleged Russian at a place of his choosing in the international sector of Vienna, the meeting area was staked out with a protective surveillance—a pair of officers in two radio-equipped vehicles. A shabby Volkswagen stood by, ready to whisk the alleged Russian and Alex, a recently naturalized Russian-speaking contact man, to a safe house in the U.S. district of Vienna. The meeting was recorded and monitored by a case officer and a technician.

The Russian's document was obviously authentic, and neither Alex nor our backroom auditors had any doubt that our guest was a Soviet officer. Even better, the Russian's civilian clothes were strong evidence that he was an intelligence officer. Alex followed his brief perfectly. He convinced the apprehensive Russian that he would have to return to the safe house a week hence. By that time, Alex said, the document would have been evaluated by experts and the requested payment of 3000 Austrian schillings (then $280) approved. Although the Russian gave every indication that he was interested only in a one-time deal, Alex stood firm.

Within hours after the cable reporting the development reached my office, George Kisevalter, a fluent Russian-speaking case officer, was en route to Vienna. In Washington, we effected a maximum security hold-down on the case, and at the work level knowledge of the operation was literally restricted to a handful of officers. Allen Dulles and Frank Wisner were the only senior officers not directly concerned with the case who had any knowledge of it. I handled every aspect of the operation in Washington.

It was weeks before Kisevalter was able to gain Popov's confidence and much longer before he could confidently reconstruct the Russian's motive for approaching us. It was not, as Popov first insisted, because he needed 3000 Austrian schillings to cover the official funds he had spent carousing. One way or another he could have replaced the money. It was the process of thinking his way through the problem that triggered his bold approach to us.

Popov was a peasant, and would forever see the world through a peasant's eyes. Despite the repeated promises of the communist authorities and Stalin to improve peasant life, as far as Popov was concerned nothing had been done. Life in the villages would remain at subsistence level as long as Stalin and the communists retained power. As he moved about in the Soviet-occupied zone of Austria it was immediately apparent—Stalin's propaganda notwithstanding—that even the poorest Austrian farmer enjoyed a standard of living beyond what any Russian peasant could ever hope to achieve. Popov loathed Stalin, his henchmen, and what he was convinced would be their political legacy. It was because of his conviction that the United States was the only power fully capable of resisting Stalin that Popov came to us.

The Popov operation ran for some six years, enduring his transfers from Vienna to Moscow, to East Germany, and finally to the GRU headquarters office in East Berlin. By 1958, Popov's security had eroded. Under deep suspicion, he was recalled from Berlin in 1959 and arrested in November. After a series of counterintelligence moves the KGB brought the Popov operation to term in October when a Moscow CIA contact was seized at a brush meeting with Popov. When a furious attempt to recruit the CIA officer failed, the KGB loosed a blast of publicity, and the case officer was expelled from the USSR. After a secret trial, Popov was executed by a firing squad in June 1960.

Popov could have escaped with his family at various times after he began his work with us. We never urged him to remain in place, never understated the dangers he was running or the threats to his security, and we frequently reaffirmed our offers of safe haven. Popov was fully cognizant of the dangers he risked. His final reply to an offer of escape is a measure of the man. "I was born a Russian and I will die a Russian. This is one thing those bastards will never take away from this peasant."

Pyotr Popov was an outstanding example of the value of an agent in place. For years, he was the best U.S. source of early-warning intelligence. Until he fell under suspicion, Popov single-handedly provided the most valuable intelligence on Soviet military matters of any source available to the United States. His reporting had a "direct and significant influence on the military organization of the United States—its doctrine and tactics—and permitted the Pentagon to save at least 500 million dollars in its scientific research program."* He identified more than six hundred Soviet intelligence officers, and provided information on hundreds of Soviet agents. As I recall, we budgeted some $400 a month for his wages. Rarely did he accept payment for anything but expenses, nor in a given year was his Agency income as much as $3500.

As one of my colleagues wrote, "Popov was an imperfect man. He drank too much. He was forgetful. He was bored by what he considered political nuances and he saw the world in black and white. Given the opportunity, he ran breathtaking—in retrospect, almost insane—risks. Although he loved his wife and children, he was hopelessly devoted to a . . . mistress. But for six years he trundled bales of Top Secret information out of the secret centers of Soviet power. In the process he shattered the Soviet military intelligence service, caused the transfer of the KGB chief (a four-star general and one of the most powerful men in the USSR)."

Pyotr Semyonovich Popov, the Russian peasant, was an authentic hero.†

---

*David E. Murphy, Sergei A. Kondrashev, and George Bailey, *Battleground Berlin* (New Haven: Yale University Press, 1997), p. 281.

†The Popov operation is described in detail in William Hood, *Mole* (Washington, D.C.: Brassey's, 1993).

Chapter 13

—

DIGGING IN

Agent operations were not the only means of penetrating the security defenses of the Soviet Union. There were also technical operations ranging from broken ciphers, which were so important in the defeat of Germany and Japan, to sophisticated electronic eavesdropping, high-altitude aerial reconnaissance, and telephone and mail intercept.

The spark that kindled one of our most ambitious technical efforts was detected in late 1948, when we noted that the Soviet military, intelligence, and diplomatic headquarters in Germany and Austria were beginning to change from using ultra-high-frequency (UHF) radio transmissions to existing telephone landlines for communication with Moscow. The UHF traffic between Moscow and the Soviet-occupied areas was subject to interception—a passive but relatively inexpensive activity. The intelligence yield was not great, but it did contribute to the order of battle and early warning data we were under pressure to produce. As the UHF traffic dwindled, demand for early warning and other data on the USSR skyrocketed. Our interest in the Soviet landlines intensified.

By 1951 our research showed that the landlines followed the original conduits established for telephonic traffic before World War I in Austria and Germany. The proximity of these lines to areas in which we might work suggested a long-shot possibility of breaking into the mass of communications between Moscow and the Soviet occupation headquarters in Austria, Germany, and the Central Group of Forces in Hungary. However slight our chances, the potential product of a successful operation appeared to justify an all-out effort.

Landlines can be intercepted only by tapping the telephone cables. Breaking into the lines—most of which were tucked underground—would be a considerable undertaking, but would have one advantage over radio monitoring. Aside from the enciphered classified messages, there would be a flood of clear text communications transmitted by Teletype and, we hoped, a bounty of telephone chatter from which substantial nuggets might be mined.

Within the Agency, knowledge of the operations—known as SILVER in Vienna and GOLD in Berlin—was restricted to the officers directly involved. In Washington, Allen Dulles and Frank Wisner were fully informed. As Frank's deputy and chief of operations, I was, in effect, the action officer, and at times dealt with routine matters which in other operations would have been the lot of an officer with a year's experience under his belt.

At the time we were getting under way, William K. Harvey was chief of the Counterintelligence Staff. Until his transfer to Berlin, Bill did much of the spadework on the intercept program. He worked closely with Frank Rowlett, an outstanding cryptographic specialist who had transferred to the Agency from the National Security Agency. An early step was the assignment of a communications specialist to Vienna and another to Berlin. The operation was so closely held that in Vienna only the office chief and his deputy were informed. When Bill Harvey took over the Berlin base in 1952 only he and the specialist had full knowledge of the activity.

Within the Agency offices, cover stories within cover stories had to be invented to explain the presence of the specialists and the various closed doors to their fellow officers.

Allen Dulles briefed the President, the secretaries of state and defense, and the general commanding the Joint Chiefs of Staff. Before the first on-the-ground action was taken, the ambassador in Bonn and the general commanding the occupation force were briefed. The cooperation at these levels was outstanding.

The first steps were to identify and recruit agents in East Germany and Austria with access to the telephone routing diagrams showing the lines carrying the important traffic. This is easily said, but it required months to recruit the agents able to produce the data we needed. Had the Russians got a cogent whiff of our interest in the landlines, we would have had no choice but to bring the effort to an end. When the circuits carrying the bulk of Soviet military, diplomatic, and intelligence traffic between the various headquarters in Berlin, Vienna, Budapest, and Moscow were identified, inviting targets were uncovered in Vienna and Berlin. Both cities were under Allied and Soviet military occupation at the time.

We were well along with this research in Austria when our Vienna office learned that the British had independently come upon the same idea and had made considerable progress in tapping into the underground cables. The potential value of the intercept product in Austria and Germany meant there was too much at stake to risk any overlapping effort in such a narrow field. The British agreed, and we each cooperated to the hilt at all times.

Underground telephone lines are considerably more difficult to break into than those above ground. Landlines are highly vulnerable to moisture, and are routinely monitored with sophisticated devices that immediately pinpoint the slightest break in the cables' protective conduits. Like firemen responding to a blaze, repair crews dash directly to the spot where trouble is detected. The lines can be intercepted only by cutting into the protective sheath through which the cables run. In the seconds available before the alarm sounds, it takes a highly developed mix of physical dexterity and applied science to fool the sensitive monitoring devices.

The months of research indicated that the best site for a tap in Berlin lay less than two feet underground, alongside a heavily traveled highway, some three hundred yards within the Soviet-occupied area of Berlin. The highway was regularly patrolled by Soviet military police.

By 1953, Harvey had settled into Berlin as chief of base. In Berlin, as in Vienna, the necessary plumbing was in place and functioning. By August, Bill had the Berlin plan well in hand. A tunnel, with about 6 feet of head room and 1800 feet long, would be dug from the U.S. sector in Berlin to the buried cables some 900 feet within the Soviet-occupied sector. A spacious building, ostensibly a military warehouse, was constructed to serve as an on-site headquarters and cover the entrance to the tunnel. It would also explain the to and fro of our personnel, and mask the movement of engineering equipment. Before the digging began, experiments in tunnel construction were conducted in New Mexico and in Surrey, England. The disposal of 3200 tons of earth was dealt with in daily increments.

Ventilation is one of the difficult engineering problems in a long tunnel. Air had to be circulated in and out of the lengthy tunnel. The ventilation problem was compounded by the need to ensure that no noise leak from the tunnel or from the 6-by-8-foot space where taps were close to the surface on the Soviet-patrolled highway.

Technically, the tap itself represented the greatest security threat to the operation. It was a tribute to the competence of the British technicians that the lines were opened, the taps installed, and everything returned to normal before the Russians noticed any fluctuation in the closely monitored landlines. The tapping was completed in August 1955.

At the time, this was the most elaborate and costly secret operation ever undertaken within Soviet-occupied territory. Some of the tunnel anecdotes are true. From the outset American personnel, hidden in the apparent "warehouse" and armed with binoculars, maintained a twenty-four-hour-a-day watch of the area stretching from the warehouse to the tap site into the Soviet sector. As dawn broke one morning, the watcher dropped his binoculars, pushed the panic button, and shouted that a dusting of snow was melting on the warm ground above the tunnel. The melted snow marked the tunnel path from the warehouse to the tap site as precisely as if it had been laid by a surveyor's transit. The crisis was eased when the first half hour of early-morning sunlight melted all of the light snowfall. A few hours later, Harvey had contrived a temporary solution to the problem: in mid-winter and without any explanation, squads of Quartermaster soldiers stripped every available air conditioner from Army premises throughout Berlin.

There is less that need be said about the cesspool inadvertently breached as the tunnel engineers navigated beneath a bombed-out farm, or the laundry that had to be established in the warehouse to cope daily with the inexplicably soiled clothing of those working underground.

Despite the number of personnel directly involved in the operation—translators, analysts, case officers, clerical staff, security guards, and consumers—security was maintained within the Agency. At the time, I thought that this number of personnel—each having knowledge of some aspect of the complex activity—was about as extensive as was feasible from a security viewpoint. The difference in this staff—who were security vetted, indoctrinated, and trained in security practices—and those who were later involved in some of the most ambitious covert action operations was profound. There was, for example, no possibility of thoroughly indoctrinating and closely monitoring the security of the hundreds of people involved in the Bay of Pigs paramilitary action.

The cooperation of senior military personnel in the field and in Washington was impeccable, as it was at the highest levels of the State Department in Washington and abroad. In retrospect, the tunnel was an operational triumph. Bill Harvey, who pushed the operation through its innumerable, and sometimes apparently unsolvable, problems, deserves great credit.

The operation ran for eleven months and eleven days. On April 22, 1956, the Soviet authorities decided that its exposure would no longer imperil George Blake, a KGB agent in place in one of the most secret sections of the British intelligence service. The fact that Blake was involved in the tunnel operation from the time the first shovel was put to earth has caused a number of writers to believe that the entire intelligence product was tainted with deception, and of trivial value. I disagree.

By the time the operation was in full swing, the 600 tape recording machines functioning in the "warehouse" were consuming 800 rolls of tape daily—some 1200 hours of recording. In Washington, fifty translators fluent in German, Russian, and sometimes both were employed full-time. This was in addition to the on-site teams in Berlin and those functioning in the UK. The fact that only three landline cables were tapped is misleading. These three cables contained 172 circuits, each of which was capable of simultaneously carrying eighteen separate channels. At full blast, 3214 lines could be recorded.

The value of the intelligence that poured out of the tunnel was such that for two years after the site was closed, analysts and reports officers were still involved in processing the take. Trivial it was not.

Our most optimistic estimates were fulfilled twenty times over. A valuable by-product of the torrent of clear text, routine administrative communications, was floods of chitchat. At the lowest level, some lonely communications clerks were gossips, regularly swapping small talk with their distant colleagues. Even more rewarding were the man-to-man exchanges between senior Soviet officers who were convinced that they were far too intelligent and disciplined ever to disclose anything of possible interest to any potential eavesdropper. Little did they know. Their unvarnished comments on the quality of Soviet military equipment, the intellectual capacity of fellow officers, and the wisdom of Moscow's military policies were in more than one sense priceless. SILVER and GOLD proved to be apt cryptonyms.

The tunnel data provided detailed information on the Soviet army and air force, weapons, equipment, plans, combat readiness, personnel, and administration. Information on KGB and GRU officers and assignments was regularly sifted from the mass of recorded material. The tapped lines gave uniquely candid glimpses of the opinions, character, and professional inclinations of many of the most senior officers in the Soviet military establishment. This one project fulfilled intelligence requirements that could not possibly have otherwise been satisfied. Because the bulk of the data was fundamental to any assessment of the Soviet military establishment, it remained valuable for a decade and more.

One of the significant values of inside data, whether documentary or provided by an agent in place, is that it permits the further evaluation of the information collected from other sources, and of the conclusions based on the analysis of all the previously existing data. The possibility that the product of any operation is contaminated with deception must be factored into the evaluation of every intelligence collection effort. Because deception operations are complex and sensitive, most intelligence services restrict deception to strategic objectives. There was no evidence of deception in the vast product of either the tunnels in Vienna or the more comprehensive Berlin project. When Blake was arrested in 1961 a retrospective examination of the tunnel material was initiated. Obviously the entire tunnel product could not be reevaluated, but a study was made of the strategic data. Again, no indication of deception was found.

Within the KGB, knowledge of the Blake operation was restricted to the senior officers directly involved. Former KGB officers who handled the Blake operation have denied that any knowledge of the Berlin tunnel, or the security threat it posed, was ever transmitted by the KGB to the Soviet military. These counterintelligence officers are equally convinced that knowledge of the Berlin and Vienna tunnels was also withheld from the ultra-secret KGB office responsible for strategic deception operations. This is a vivid example of the value Russian intelligence has always placed on protecting agents in place.

If there is evidence of deception in the GOLD material, it has not surfaced as of this writing.

Given the vast amount of valuable data we took from the tunnel, it is fair to ask how KGB counterintelligence officers could allow the operation to continue as long as it did before finding a plausible way of closing it down without compromising George Blake. The only explanation for this apparent trade-off is that Blake had moved from the assignment he had at the time the tunnel was being planned, and the KGB officers had no idea of the amount or value of traffic we were handling. I doubt that anyone in Moscow imagined that the tunnel routinely consumed so many hundred rolls of tape a day, or that a total of 368,000 Soviet conversations were recorded.

Before he was exposed, George Blake was apparently a competent intelligence officer, with average career prospects. As an SIS officer under diplomatic cover, Blake was taken prisoner in South Korea when the North Korean forces occupied Seoul in June 1950. He remained in North Korean and Russian hands until the prisoners were repatriated via the USSR in April 1953. After what appears to have been a routine questioning about his captivity, Blake's security clearances were restored and he was assigned a job that gave him full access to the planning of the Berlin tunnel.

Blake's interest in communism as an adult was ironically tweaked when he studied a handbook written by the SIS senior expert on Marxist theory and communist practices. While he was in captivity, one of the very few books available to Blake was Karl Marx's *Das Kapital.* This book and Blake's dislike of a competitive society, contempt for the British class system* and for American foreign policy, and a deep reli-

---

*In a personal letter to me, Sir Dick White, a former chief of MI-5 and SIS, observed that he thought Blake was partially motivated by his feeling that he would never be accepted as a social equal by his British colleagues because he was foreign born.

gious conviction, combined with the severe hardship of POW life, were apparently enough to convince him that Marx's theory "from each according to his abilities, to each according to his need" as interpreted by Stalin was the way to go.

In autumn 1951, Blake asked his Korean captors to arrange a meeting with a Russian officer. This was done, and Blake volunteered his services to the USSR. He was interviewed at some length by a KGB officer who recruited him as an agent in place in the British service. Like so many other important agents, Blake was literally a walk-in.*

Blake's history illustrates a security dilemma. Should an intelligence service continue to employ staff members or agents who are known to have been in hostile hands for any length of time? If they are to remain employed, should they be granted full security clearances? The easiest answer is that of an oncologist: if tissue is *possibly* malignant, the safe solution is to remove it. In security practice, this has a marked downside. The problems any captured staff employee or agent faces in maintaining morale and a measure of security discipline under hostile interrogation and brutal treatment are obvious. The fact that no matter how bravely and securely a captive responds, the knowledge that even if he survives the ordeal his career is at an end is not calculated to stiffen resistance.

In my opinion the only reasonably fair solution is a policy that guarantees former prisoners a career-long employment in nonsensitive work, with the promise of promotion parallel to others of his grade and relative competence. This compromise is not likely to satisfy every prisoner who planned a career in secret intelligence, but it can be made more tolerable by a system of bonuses based on the severity and length of imprisonment.

Compassion notwithstanding, George Blake should not have been returned to duty with a full security clearance.

---

*George Blake, *No Other Choice* (New York: Simon & Schuster, 1990), p. 286.

Chapter 14

—

WITHIN THE GATE

Sometime after I left the Agency, David Frost convinced me to sit down with him for what turned out to be an extended interview. David is a master of his craft, and along with allowing me to get a few things off my chest, he prompted me into an observation I had not thought to make. We were deep in our conversation when David asked what, as DCI, had worried me most. He appeared to be as surprised by my instant response as by my answer.

A recurring nightmare, I said, was that I would come into the office one morning and learn that someone in the Agency had been recruited by the KGB.* What's more, I continued, rarely a day passed that I got to the bottom of my in-box without some reflection on the *apparent* fact that the Agency was the only major intelligence service in the non-communist world that had not suffered a damaging penetration by the KGB or its subordinate communist services.

By "penetration," I meant that no staff member of the Agency was *known* to have been recruited as an agent by any hostile intelligence service. On the operational level we encountered our share of foreign

---

*This interview occurred several years before security cases such as those of Aldrich Ames and Edward L. Howard were uncovered.

agents ostensibly loyal to the Agency who had been doubled against us, and who were in the employ of, and loyal to, adversary services. Double agents of this sort are a constant operational concern, but most can be detected, and sometimes exploited, by routine tradecraft procedures. Penetration at the staff level—the traitor within the gate—is a security problem of the utmost importance.

From the end of World War II to the time I retired from the Agency, the long and continuing string of espionage arrests and prosecutions in this country and abroad was ample evidence of how successfully the KGB and GRU had penetrated their foreign targets. Soviet counterintelligence was no less effective in penetrating the Western intelligence and security services. Among the European agencies publicly known to have been penetrated by the KGB or GRU were the British, West German, Italian, Swedish, and French. These counterintelligence operations ran parallel to the agents the Russians had established in the United States— in the Army, Navy, Air Force, and State Department—and in the military, foreign offices, industries, and research laboratories of the other countries of significant interest to the Politburo. Beneath the well-publicized spy trials, there existed a mass of classified data that amply reinforced my conviction that Soviet intelligence was indeed a formidable threat.

There is an equally substantial body of evidence that the Soviet services had instructed, honed, and polished the intelligence and security organizations of their Eastern European allies. As had the KGB, these smaller services capitalized on the prewar experience of Communist Party underground activists and the surviving veterans of wartime intelligence and resistance operations. The espionage skills, area knowledge, language facility, and security acumen of the veteran operatives were immense assets. The experience gained in life-and-death field operations cannot be replicated in any training school. While directing and monitoring the work of its satellite cohort, Soviet intelligence protected its investment by recruiting agents within each of the Eastern European services, and in position to ensure that nothing—good or bad—was withheld from Moscow.

By 1950, the KGB, GRU, and Eastern European espionage and security services had combined to form the most experienced, and the largest, peacetime intelligence apparatus in modern history.

In the United States, data provided by defectors from the various communist intelligence services, information gathered in CIA penetration operations, FBI security activity, and that of other agencies and the military had over the years exposed penetrations of the Army, Navy, Air Force, State Department, and National Security Agency. In my time, as far as we could determine, only CIA had remained invulnerable. Our security procedures were sound and as effective as we could make them. But were they good enough?

As a colleague has reminded me, "Any intelligence chief who tells his president, prime minister, or politburo that his service is not penetrated either is a fool or has not read the literature. The most any chief can say is that 'at the time I left my desk, I knew of no such penetration.' "

There is only one sure answer to the question of penetration and that rests in the files of the opposing intelligence services.

As we studied the KGB and its history, it became apparent that for all of its experience and competence, there were serious weaknesses in the Soviet intelligence services. Some of the failings were endemic, the sort that can be found in the secret police of any dictatorship—notably the political rigidity and the harsh internal discipline that lead to dishonest reporting, and sometimes to defection. Other weaknesses reflected the economic, political, and social shortcomings of the Soviet system. From the early days of the Russian Revolution and the Cheka to the collapse of the USSR and the revamping of the KGB and GRU, dropouts and defectors have characterized Russian intelligence. And small wonder. The service was built on a brutal heritage.

The Great Terror, as the purges Stalin unleashed in 1934 and which had subsided by 1940 have come to be known, hit the intelligence services as hard as it struck the military, the Communist Party, and all of Soviet society. Along with liquidating or sending some 50 percent of the Red Army officer corps, including three field marshals and thirteen three-star generals, to the gulag, Stalin played no favorites. The NKVD itself fell victim. Stalin struck hardest at the domestic and headquarters elements of his intelligence and security forces trapped within the USSR. Between 1934 and 1938, two NKVD chiefs, Genrikh Yagoda and his successor, Nikolai Yezhov, were removed and liquidated. In 1937 alone the NKVD executed over three thousand of its own officers.* (This figure includes a large number of NKVD domestic security personnel who had little or nothing to do with the espionage apparatus.)

Most of the operatives stationed abroad must have had some idea of what was happening to their comrades at home, but station chiefs, case officers, and some deeply covered agents accepted the "routine orders" to return to Moscow. This pruning of the organization might have suggested to the rank and file that although there were likely to be frequent openings at the top, the overall career prospects in the NKVD were pretty grim. Not so. The wonder is that in the face of the evidence of what was going on in Moscow, so very few of the operatives abroad could bring themselves to flee or strike back at the system that seemed so determined to destroy them.

By the time the bloodletting ended, Stalin had done more damage to his foreign intelligence and security apparat than the combined counterintelligence forces of his enemies, antagonists, and sometime allies had been able to accomplish up to the end of World War II.

Among the defectors were Ignace Reiss, Walter Krivitsky, Alexander Barmine, Lieutenant General Alexander Orlov, Lieutenant General G. S. Lyushkov, Whittaker Chambers, Hedda Massing, and Elizabeth Bentley. Had Reiss and Krivitsky been thoroughly interrogated, and if General Orlov had agreed to disclose what he knew, Western counterintelligence would certainly have identified most of the cadre of spies who were to number among the KGB's most precious sources—Kim Philby, Donald Maclean, Anthony Blunt, Guy Burgess, Duncan Lee, Alger Hiss, and the score of others who have remained unknown. But this was not to happen.

Reiss was gunned down in Switzerland before he could begin his planned fight against Stalin. After initial contact with French, British, and American officials, Krivitsky was found dead in a Washington, D.C., hotel room. His death was declared a suicide, but most probably was an artfully contrived murder. General Lyushkov, an NKVD communications specialist, defected to the Japanese in the Far East and was interrogated jointly with German representatives. General Orlov lived anonymously in the United States until Stalin's death. Although fiercely

---

*Ronald Hingley, *The Russian Secret Police* (New York: Simon & Schuster, 1970), p. 166.

opposed to Stalin, Orlov had offered the dictator a deal. As long as Orlov's family in the USSR was not persecuted, the general would remain silent. After Stalin's death, Orlov remained loyal to the agents he had dealt with while in the NKVD. Unfortunately, Orlov was so badly handled by his first FBI contacts that in the end he provided only a superficial glimpse of the data he might have been persuaded to offer.

With the German invasion of the USSR, many of the officers and operatives who had survived were released from the gulag, tidied up, and reemployed. But the problems that faced this older generation of operatives had not been erased. From 1945 throughout my career in the Agency, defectors from the Soviet and satellite intelligence services continued to give us intimate pictures of the Soviet espionage methods and of some of its successful operations. The inside data provided by the defectors helped us develop the means to handle the Soviet and Eastern European walk-ins as agents in place within their own service. These agents—notably Lieutenant Colonel Popov and Colonel Penkovsky, and more than a score of others—provided a wealth of intelligence, with much of the most important data ranging far beyond the counterintelligence information that lay within their immediate reach. We could not, however, uncover hard evidence of any significant penetration of the Agency. In a narrow sense, this was reassuring—apparently our security procedures were working. But "apparently" is not a word that many counterintelligence officers find comforting.

Counterintelligence (CI) is probably the most misunderstood secret intelligence function. The work itself has suffered as many definitions as there are intelligence services. A recent CIA publication offers a useful but limited definition of counterintelligence: "Information gathered and activities conducted to protect against espionage, other intelligence activities, sabotage, or assassinations conducted for, or on behalf of, foreign powers, organizations, persons, or terrorist activities."* This covers the important *defensive* security responsibilities of CI, but does not specifically mention *counterespionage* (CE).

During World War II, a distinction was usually made between counterintelligence and counterespionage. The term "counterespionage" has

*A *Consumer's Guide to Intelligence* (Washington, D.C.: U.S. Government Printing Office, 1995); PAS 95-00010, p. 52.

slipped out of the Agency vocabulary, but I recall it as useful. If we define "counterespionage" as "the *penetration* of foreign intelligence services, the exploitation of double agents, and support to strategic deception activity," it separates the essentially *defensive* aspects of counterintelligence from the *aggressive* exploitation of hostile intelligence services. This is something I might well have sorted out while still in office. It escaped me, and I must now bow to progress and use the broader term.

George Washington had as keen an appreciation of counterintelligence as he had of other intelligence disciplines. Aside from its hasty revival during wartime and some periods of political stress, General Washington's counterintelligence legacy had seriously faded by the outbreak of World War II and the advent of OSS. When OSS was organized, counterintelligence was a component of the foreign intelligence branch. It was only when the British service unveiled ULTRA, one of its great secrets, to OSS and the upper bracket of the American military command that the most aggressive elements of CI came fully back to life.

It was with the advice of the British that a separate OSS CI branch was formed in 1943, and, at the suggestion of a British liaison officer, christened "X-2." The term was a sly, English sort of wordplay based on the high-level British Twenty Committee, the group which planned and oversaw the strategic deception operations that protected every important Allied military initiative in Europe and the Near East. Two Xs can equal twenty, but, as German intelligence was never to learn, may also symbolize a double cross. (When the Top Secret deception operations were taking final form in London, an OSS officer, exasperated by the security surrounding counterespionage, posed a question: "If X-2 is so damned secret, why does it call attention to itself by picking a code name straight out of a dime novel?" A security-minded X-2 officer whispered that the term had been lifted from the Washington, D.C., public transportation service. The bus line that ran close to the OSS headquarters in Washington was labeled "X-2.")

Of the several OSS components that worked with the British in the European theater, none were more closely tied than X-2 and the MI-6 counterintelligence staff in London. Within OSS, no component was more strictly compartmented from other elements than X-2. And of the OSS officers who remained in service with CIA, none were more influenced by their wartime experience and training than the X-2 veterans. Some knowledge of X-2 is necessary to an understanding of how CI developed in the Agency.

Until 1974, when a memoir was published,* one of the last great secrets of World War II remained classified. The fact that the ULTRA secret was so tightly held governed every aspect of X-2. Top Secret ULTRA was originally a security classification covering deciphered German radio traffic. A handful of British, Polish, Czech, and French cryptanalysts had begun work on German ciphers in the early 1930s. Soon after the outbreak of war in 1939, the British rallied some of these experts and, one step ahead of the Gestapo, slipped them into the UK as an adjunct of the British codebreakers.

By 1940 the first breaks were being made in messages encrypted on a cipher machine the Germans named ENIGMA. With increasing success, the British continued throughout the war to intercept and decipher the classified radio transmissions of the Wehrmacht, Luftwaffe, Kriegsmarine, and the intelligence services, the Abwehr and Sicherheitsdienst. To my knowledge, X-2 was the only OSS unit that had daily access to the ULTRA product, and even this was restricted to the German intelligence communications.

The importance of this cipher breakthrough can scarcely be overvalued. The collapse of Hitler's Reich and the unconditional surrender of the German forces in 1945 has overshadowed the memory of just how convincingly the British were defeated in France in 1940, and that the remnants of the army evacuated from Dunkirk and the relatively weak RAF were all that stood between a cross-Channel invasion by the powerful Wehrmacht and the well-equipped Luftwaffe. The plight of British forces in the Mediterranean and Far East was no less desperate.

In the course of the intensive security briefing and indoctrination of X-2 personnel, Churchill was quoted as saying that in 1941, when the British forces were stressed to the breakpoint, he would have sacrificed an entire, fully equipped army corps to preserve the secrecy of the ULTRA data. The ability to unbutton the most secret communications from the German high command, and Hitler personally, to the distant Wehrmacht and Kriegsmarine commanders was without question a key

*F. W. Winterbotham, *The Ultra Secret* (London: Weidenfeld & Nicolson, 1974).

element in the Allied victory over Germany. In the more narrow CI and security field, access to the German intelligence traffic was of equal importance. Without ULTRA it might have been a different war.

No one has caught the essence of counterespionage better than Churchill, when in 1943 he remarked, "In wartime, truth is so precious that she should always be attended by a bodyguard of lies." The extremely sensitive exploitation of captured German agents who were turned, and continued to operate under British (and later joint British-American) control, rendered essential support to the deception operations protecting every important military initiative in Europe and the Near East.

Because of ULTRA the British were able to neutralize and control *all* German intelligence sources in England, and many of the German agents in other areas. In the final preparation for Operation Overlord, when the estimate of German preparedness to face the cross-Channel invasion was critical, General Eisenhower's G-2 was able to report that the German General Staff had no independent intelligence sources in the UK, and that the deception operations had not been compromised.

Hours after the Allies landed on the Normandy beaches, the German high command delayed reinforcing the Normandy defense force, while dithering as to whether the landing was the real thing or a deception intended to cover an all-out attack in another area. When the V-1 buzz bombs and V-2 rockets were harassing London, the UK-based double agents reported that the bombs were falling some distance from the intended target. Berlin obligingly shifted the range, with the result that the weapons fell on sparsely inhabited and less strategic areas some distance from the intended London targets.

It was one thing to protect ULTRA, and to blind and then deceive the enemy. It proved more of a problem to keep the ULTRA secret from an ally, even from an ally that had but recently cooperated with and signed a nonaggression treaty with Hitler. From very early on, Soviet intelligence had knowledge of the ULTRA breakthrough, and continuing access to as much of the deciphered traffic as its agents could slip to their Soviet masters. One agent in place in MI-6 had access to the deciphered German intelligence traffic. Others were securely situated at Bletchley Park, where the codebreakers, translators, editors, and clerical staffs worked on the deciphered material.

Breaking into the ULTRA secret was not the only significant success of the Soviet intelligence services whose staff and senior agents had barely survived Stalin's purges. Another chapter of operational success was disclosed in September 1945 when Igor Gouzenko, a GRU cipher clerk, walked out of the military intelligence offices in the Ottawa embassy with scores of highly classified GRU messages strapped to his midriff. His escape and desperate approach to Canadian authorities was a near thing, but successful. The documents he carried exposed a network of Soviet spies ranging from Canada to the United States and Britain.

In Canada, twenty-two people were arrested and a trail uncovered that in the ensuing years would lead to the Rosenbergs in New York, to Klaus Fuchs and Allan Nunn May, the British nuclear scientists, and provide positive proof that the Soviets had thoroughly penetrated the Top Secret Manhattan Project. This evidence of the extent and depth of Soviet espionage would finally unleash an overdue American and British counterintelligence attack.

From the late 1920s the Soviet intelligence services had operated in the United States as if our open society were a well-stocked hunting preserve. As Hedda Massing remarked to a friend, "I could have walked into most of the government offices in Washington wearing a sandwich board saying 'Soviet spy on the prowl,' without attracting the least attention." The hunting was so effortless that the Russian operatives failed to compartment many of their operations. By the time the FBI finished questioning Elizabeth Bentley, a Soviet operational *bonne à tout faire* who bolted out of the apparat in 1945, she had named more than one hundred agents and sympathizers of the two Soviet services. Whittaker Chambers was even more closely informed. The photograph of Alger Hiss standing a few feet behind President Roosevelt, who is seated across the conference table from Stalin at Yalta, catches the essence of the early CI problem.

An exception to the sloppy handling of many of the American agents was the highly professional exploitation of Donald Maclean, who for much of World War II was first secretary in the British embassy in Washington. Maclean had a "Q" clearance and was responsible for liaison on atomic matters. He was one of the most important Soviet agents in the atomic field, and was in a position to keep Moscow thoroughly informed on British and American policy developments. He was unearthed through a break in the Soviet cipher system.

Soviet intelligence did not limit its targets to officials; high-ranking, well-informed establishment figures were equally sought out as agents. The KGB's peacetime effort to recruit Joseph Alsop, then one of the most prominent and respected American journalists, is a sour example of the techniques the Soviets had perfected over decades. When Alsop decided to make his first trip to the Soviet Union, he applied to the Soviet ambassador in Washington for a visa that would allow him to spend two or three weeks moving freely in the post-Stalin USSR. The visa was granted, and Joe arrived in Moscow in January 1957. He was well received and more favorably impressed by the intellectual and political climate than he had expected to be. Along with an extended session with Nikita Khrushchev, interviews with factory managers, and a trip to Siberia, Alsop participated in the social mixing of the diplomatic, journalistic, and artistic worlds in Moscow.

In the course of a late-night gathering of Moscow bohemians, Alsop, a scrupulously closeted homosexual, responded to the advances of one of the guests. When the party broke up, the young man accompanied Joe to his hotel room. The next day, two of Alsop's Russian partying companions took him aside and told him politely that he was in a serious jam. In the Soviet Union, homosexual relations were a serious criminal offense. After showing Alsop the photographs of his tryst which the police would use in court, the Russians said they might be able to square things if, once back in Washington, Joe would agree to help in the Soviet effort to develop better working relations with the United States. He would, of course, be well compensated for the time involved in this cooperation. If Alsop did not agree, the Russian police would have no alternative but to advise U.S. officials of Alsop's criminal activity while a guest of the USSR and to proceed with court action.

For all of their experience in rigging such incidents—a spiked drink being part of the setup—the KGB had chosen the wrong target. Shaken by his own stupidity, Alsop refused any semblance of cooperation with the KGB.

The following morning, Alsop went to the U.S. embassy. Ambassador Chip Bohlen, an old friend, was not in. Joe handed a sealed envelope to Bohlen's secretary and left for a scheduled trip to Leningrad. When

Bohlen read Alsop's account of the incident, he summoned Joe back to Moscow, hustled him onto a plane and out of the USSR.

In Washington, Alsop told his story to Frank Wisner, another old friend. Frank advised Alsop that there was no practical alternative but to report the incident to J. Edgar Hoover. Alsop agreed. The FBI director had long considered Alsop a troublesome reporter, and according to his custom in such incidents, made sure that the secretary of state, the attorney general, the secretary of defense, and President Eisenhower were fully informed.

As threatened, the KGB mailed the photographs to various journalists, officials, and friends of Alsop. Joe's friends and colleagues stood firm, the photographs were destroyed, and no public reference was made to the incident.

Sometime later the KGB attempted to revive the operation and once again circulated the photographs. At this point, Joe had had enough and was prepared to make the story public. When he asked me about it, I advised him to remain silent rather than burden his family and friends with this long-ago embarrassment. Joe agreed with my suggestion that I quietly tell the KGB to knock it off. An Agency man whose cover job brought him into frequent diplomatic contact with a high-ranking KGB officer carried the message. On my behalf our man told the KGB that unless it stopped attempting to peddle this sordid story, the Agency would respond in kind, and with enough data to compromise several KGB officers.

This episode ended with a net loss to the KGB. The impact of the photographs on those who saw them was more convincing than any of the security briefings routinely offered to officials and others visiting the USSR. Security personnel were again reminded of how aggressively hostile intelligence agencies work on their home terrain. Joe Alsop's well-known hostility to police states—communist or otherwise—was intensified, and he remained a staunchly independent political commentator until he retired from journalism in 1974.

—

The Agency's counterintelligence effort was established and shaped by two men as different from one another as seemed possible. Bill Harvey collected guns. Jim Angleton bred orchids.

William K. Harvey graduated from Indiana University with a law degree in 1937 and joined the FBI in 1940. After a falling-out with J. Edgar Hoover, Harvey left the FBI in 1947 and joined the Agency a few weeks later—a move that infuriated Hoover. Harvey was a conspicuous exception to the profile of many CIA senior officers. He had never been abroad, and had no foreign language or professional experience in foreign affairs or intelligence collection. Although there was a fair sprinkling of Ivy League graduates in OSS and among those who stayed on with the Agency, there was among most of the senior postwar staff an unmistakable patina not so much of Ivy, but of some experience abroad. Harvey made no accommodation to the office climate entirely new to him. If anything, he appeared deliberately to intensify the aspect and solid attitudes of his midwestern background.

The first writer who characterized Bill as "CIA's James Bond" had either never read Ian Fleming's books, seen a Bond movie, or caught a glimpse of Harvey. It was always obvious that Bill would never win the battle with his waistline—he was much more than heavyset. A more pertinent description would have concentrated on his phenomenal memory, aggressive approach to business, and knowledge of Soviet espionage in the United States. I learned to have time at hand before asking him a question on any aspect of it.

One of Bill's most marked eccentricities was his enthusiasm for guns. No matter that his colleagues who had parachuted into Nazi-occupied Europe or worked with guerrillas in the Far East would never again willingly choose to carry a weapon, Bill was rarely seen without a pistol stuffed into his belt. The professional persona he appeared to favor was that of a senior police officer, a master of the terrain assigned to him, wily, informed, perceptive, and deeply patriotic. He was also deliberately blunt and loudly outspoken, qualities that, with his heavy drinking, were eventually to catch up with him. Bill was not, and never pretended to be, a man for all seasons. But what he did best, he did very well.

James Angleton projected an entirely different image. Although he was born in Boise, Idaho, in 1917, he lived with his family some years in Italy, where his father represented an American firm. Angleton attended Malvern, a British public school, and had worked in France on a summer vacation. After graduation from Yale, he spent a year at Harvard Law School before entering the Army as a private soldier in 1943. After twelve weeks of basic training, Angleton was offered a choice of adjutant general officer cadet school or assignment to OSS. The freshly minted corporal opted for OSS. Jim's father, Lieutenant Colonel James H. Angleton, an early OSS recruit, was serving on General Donovan's staff pending an assignment to Italy.

Jim was assigned to the Italian desk in X-2 London and commissioned in 1944. He was transferred to X-2 Italy when an OSS station was established in Rome in 1944. A year later, he was named chief of X-2 Italy in 1945, and in 1946 became chief of station. Jim remained in Italy until 1947 and the signing of the peace treaty that ended the military occupation of that country.

As a young man, Jim was bone thin, gaunt, and aggressively intellectual in aspect. His not entirely coincidental resemblance to T. S. Eliot was intensified by a European wardrobe, studious manner, heavy glasses, and lifelong interest in poetry. Jim's eccentricities were as pronounced as Harvey's. To the degree possible in a bureaucracy, he kept his own hours, was not often in his office before nine-thirty, and even more rarely did he leave before 7 p.m. He loathed staff meetings and seldom spoke up. I suppose he must sometime have had lunch at his desk or conceivably in the senior officers' mess, but I recall no such event. Good restaurants were his venue of choice. His lunch "hour" was a lengthy extension of his office time—devoted to liaison meetings with foreign colleagues, operational contacts, his office staff, other Agency officers, or someone selected from the incredible hotchpotch of friends that one of his colleagues described as being from "real life." Like Frank Wisner's, Jim's professional responsibilities extended deeply into his after-hours time, with frequent late-night, work-related dinners.

Harvey always seemed to me to be all of a piece—he was what he was, no bones about it, and with no apparent contradictions in his personality. Angleton was as many-faceted a man as anyone I've ever known. Along with his passion for orchids, Jim made gold jewelry, collected antique fly rods and reels, was a passionate fisherman, enthusiastic poker player, skilled investor, prizefight fan, and literary scholar. His range of friends who had no relation to his work was extraordinary. In contrast to Harvey, Jim affected an entirely romantic persona, preoccupied, mysterious, and not above implying that "if only you knew just one of the secrets I hold, you would know all you ever need to know about me." It seemed to amuse Jim to present himself in the manner of the familiar caricature of a secret agent—floppy black hat and an outsized black overcoat, which, all in fun, presumably concealed a stiletto. Sadly, like Harvey's, Jim's heavy drinking worsened late in his life. In retirement, he was able to stop drinking overnight. He could not erase a lifetime of heavy smoking, and this contributed to his death.

—

Sometime after my retirement, and the day before I was slated for a session with the Counterintelligence (CI) Staff at the Agency, I was having lunch with a retired colleague, an OSS X-2 veteran. "Remind them that no intelligence service can for very long be any better than its counterintelligence component," he said. "And recommend that they chisel the words into the granite entrance out there."

He had a point. A quick glance in the rearview mirror shows that the most notorious traitors and successful spies in this century would have been barred from sensitive government work, or exposed early in their careers, had basic counterintelligence precautions been taken. Throughout his career Colonel Redl, of the Austro-Hungarian General Staff, lived ostentatiously beyond his means, was heavily in debt, and deeply involved in legally proscribed, and blackmail-prone homosexual activity. Some twenty-five years later, Kim Philby, the prototype of a KGB-sponsored penetration agent, was active in communist circles while at Cambridge University, and subsequently engaged in an ostensible flirtation with Nazi sympathizers. Philby's first wife and Austrian in-laws were Communist Party members. His close friend Guy Burgess, a brilliant if drunken tosspot, was well known as a leftist.

Of all the Western Allied leaders, Prime Minister Churchill had the keenest interest and most sophisticated grasp of intelligence operations. Yet, when Churchill arrived at the Big Three conference in Yalta in February 1945 for the discussion of postwar Germany and Eastern Europe, his secret negotiating positions had been plucked clean by Soviet agents in the British Foreign Office and intelligence services.

President Roosevelt fared little better. It was not until Alger Hiss was chosen to accompany Roosevelt to Yalta that the promising young State Department officer came fully into his own as a Soviet GRU spy. From the time preparations for the conference began until Hiss returned to Washington via Moscow, he was astride every secret aspect of the U.S. negotiating tactics. In the United States, a thorough background check would have exposed Hiss as having been flagged as a Soviet agent in 1939 by French Premier Edouard Daladier to Ambassador William C. Bullitt. This information probably came to the French intelligence service from Walter Krivitsky, who defected from the Soviet NKVD in 1937. In September 1939, Whittaker Chambers informed an assistant secretary of state that Hiss, among others, was a GRU agent. Although the NKVD attempted to wrest Hiss from the GRU stable of agents, he remained a creature of the GRU throughout his active service.

If Stalin's self-confidence needed bolstering, the knowledge that he would arrive at the conference table almost as well briefed on the American and British negotiating positions as were Churchill and Roosevelt should have done the trick. If not, Stalin might have been encouraged by the fact that he was also well informed on the progress the Manhattan Project was making on the development of the atomic bomb.

Heinz Felfe's documented position in the Nazi intelligence/security organs should have barred him from sensitive postwar employment in West Germany. Instead, his record was set aside and Felfe, while using his KGB wages for luxuries beyond the limit of his earned income, burrowed into the heart of the BND, General Gehlen's postwar intelligence service.

More recently, Aldrich Ames's record as an undisciplined, drunken, and indifferent CIA officer did not interfere with his continued access to highly classified data until shortly before his arrest. While on duty in Washington, Ames lived handsomely beyond the constraints of his civil service salary.

Routine counterintelligence and security housekeeping, conducted with reasonable diligence, would have felled these and other less well-known traitors long before they touched any real treasure.

It was in Washington when we were putting our postwar house in order that we fully grasped the fact that throughout the war, the intelligence services of our co-belligerent, the USSR, had actually intensified espionage against the United States. In the Western world, the widespread respect for the Red Army's resistance to the Nazi invasion and the tremendous sacrifices of the civilian population reinforced the motives of Communist Party members and their fellow travelers, and created an optimum operational atmosphere for Soviet espionage.

By wartime standards, OSS background checks on native-born citizens and immigrants of a few years' standing were adequate to rule out possible Axis sympathizers, criminals, and most undesirables. Recently arrived immigrants—refugees from around the globe and with no track record in the United States—and persons hired abroad were more of a problem. The urgent need for area knowledge and language competence meant that many such qualified recruits were taken on at face value. Ironically, the most serious known breaches in OSS security were made by native-born citizens. Although OSS avoided Communist Party members, a few slipped through the security barricade. By the war's end, the NKVD and GRU had established a baker's dozen agents and a fistful of enthusiastic contacts in the OSS Washington offices. As viewed from the NKVD headquarters in Moscow, Duncan Lee was the best-placed agent.

With a Rhodes scholarship and a Yale Law School diploma in his briefcase, Lee, a descendant of the Civil War general Robert E. Lee, joined the Donovan & Leisure law firm in 1939. General Donovan took a shine to Lee and brought him along as a personal assistant when OSS was established. However admirably placed to service his NKVD masters, Lee was not among the bravest of OSS men. He valued his own safety to the point that he refused to deliver documents, and insisted on reporting orally to his NKVD controllers. When pressed to deliver, Lee—delicately—advised his Soviet controller that he considered it "inexpedient" to remove documents from Donovan's office.

Granted our mutual intention to defeat Nazi Germany, and the brief tenure of the known Soviet spies within OSS, these penetration agents caused marginal damage to the United States. To my knowledge, all were ousted in the OSS closedown.

By late 1945, a thorough security reevaluation of the OSS carryover staff was under way. While striving to keep valuable employees on the roster, I worked closely with the Office of Security in weeding out the relatively few people who wished to stay on but whose background might not have passed the new security rules. Within the Agency the most dramatic incident, and one that forever should have convinced us all of the absolute necessity of a strong counterintelligence capability, occurred in 1949 when Harold Adrian Russell Philby, universally known as Kim, was posted to the British embassy in Washington. As a career SIS* officer, he was responsible for both SIS and MI-5 (the British internal security service, roughly the equivalent of the FBI) liaison with CIA and the FBI. At the time, the Washington assignment was the most important foreign post in the British intelligence services.

Philby was more qualified for an intelligence assignment than SIS realized when he was recruited in 1940. Having signed on with the NKVD in 1934, Philby came to SIS with some six years' experience as a Soviet spy tucked beneath his résumé. As an undergraduate at Cambridge University, Philby became an enthusiastic Marxist, a political orientation he shared with many of his wellborn classmates who were anti-Nazi, pro-labor, and opposed to the conservative British foreign policies. The NKVD harvested a remarkable crop of agents at Cambridge. Among them were Donald Maclean, who was to become a successful British diplomat; Guy Burgess, a gadfly on the fringes of wartime intelligence in London, and first secretary at the Washington embassy when he decamped for Moscow with his friend Maclean; and Sir Anthony Blunt, a wartime MI-5 officer, subsequently "Keeper of the Queen's Pictures" at Buckingham Palace. The tangled social relations of this foursome were eventually to prove an element in their exposure.

Several histories of Kim Philby's treason have been published, as well as his own skillfully poisoned autobiography.[†] He was born in 1912, graduated from Cambridge University in 1933, and recruited by Soviet intelligence in 1934, at the time Stalin's purges were at full blast. After a brief hitch as a foreign correspondent for the London *Times* in Spain with Franco's forces, and with the British army in France, Philby was recruited by SIS after the Dunkirk evacuation. His career flourished, and by 1944 he was recognized as one of the most promising young SIS officers.

In late 1944 when the defeat of the Axis powers in Europe appeared certain, SIS—presumably prompted by Churchill—quietly began to turn some of its attention to the USSR. After engineering a series of office in-

---

*The British Secret Intelligence Service (SIS) was for decades known as MI-6, a World War I term that has been slow to die. The specific date of the change in terminology from MI-6 to SIS must be one of the best-kept secrets in British intelligence—I've yet to find a consensus on the date of the change.

[†]Kim Philby, *My Secret War* (London: MacGibbon & Kee, 1968).

trigues, Philby was appointed chief of Section IX with responsibility for *all* SIS operations against the USSR. As in Colonel Redl's day in Vienna, the henhouse was once again in the trust of a Russian fox. By 1946, Philby was so well established that he was named a Commander of the Most Excellent Order of the British Empire—steps short of a knighthood, but an ironic prize for a Soviet spy.*

When Philby was named SIS chief in Washington in 1949, his reputation as an outstanding officer preceded him. Bill Harvey, who professed a dim view of almost everything British, was moved to tell a colleague, "At last the Limeys have sent someone over here that I can talk business with." Angleton, who had met Philby in London, also welcomed him.

Several writers have assumed that Philby and Angleton had become close friends in London before Jim's posting to Italy. Philby has even been described as "one of Angleton's instructors, his prime tutor in counter-intelligence."† In fact, no such tutorial relationships existed in London at that time. Moreover, Philby worked in the SIS offices some distance from the Ryder Street premises occupied by X-2. Although they met a few times, Philby was very much senior to Angleton, who arrived in London as a recently commissioned second lieutenant, in civilian clothes, but a junior member of X-2 nevertheless. Those were busy days, and Philby was occupied with the double task of nurturing his reputation within SIS while also servicing the NKVD. The hours he could spend cultivating the OSS staff might most profitably have been devoted to the senior X-2 officers rather than the most recent junior newcomers. It was in Washington that the Angleton-Philby relationship developed, and was to sour.

It can only have been a fluke, but as it happened I had no reason to have any professional contact with Philby in Washington. I did see him socially, usually at a reception or dinner party. He was an amiable host and a personable guest: his liaison colleagues recognized him as a brilliant and indefatigable intelligence officer. Philby had a well-developed

---

*Sir Anthony Blunt's knighthood was revoked after his role as a Soviet agent became public knowledge.

†Phillip Knightley, *The Master Spy: The Story of Kim Philby* (New York: Knopf, 1989), p. 118.

knack for getting on with Americans. He tried to come across as a "typical Englishman," Hollywood style. Kim moved easily in most situations but was not entirely able to conceal the fact that he was always on the prowl. I was never sure whether his occasional stammer was an affected version of the false diffidence of his upper-class pals or simply a tool to give him an extra moment to frame a response. There is no doubt that he served his British and Soviet masters to great effect.

Philby's cover, which provided the best possible access to the high-level secrets that most interested Moscow, began to unravel when American cryptographers broke into a series of Soviet intelligence cables between Moscow and the NKVD posts in Washington and New York. The VENONA intercepts, as they were known, allowed American and British CI officers enough of a glimpse at a Soviet spy, code name HOMER, to identify him as Donald Maclean, wartime first secretary at the British embassy in Washington. Philby, who had represented the British in these investigations, allegedly used Guy Burgess to warn Maclean, by then chief of the American desk at the British Foreign Office, that he was about to be exposed. It now appears that the KGB asked Burgess, who had been living with Philby and his wife in Washington, to accompany Maclean on at least part of his escape to the USSR. Burgess made the mistake of going all the way to Moscow, where he would reluctantly remain for the rest of his life.

This hand-in-hand escape prompted Harvey, whose opinion of Philby had thoroughly eroded, and Jim Angleton to begin, independently I believe, to examine Philby's background. Harvey forwarded a memorandum to General Bedell Smith, then DCI, analyzing Philby's background and activity, and concluding that he was undoubtedly a Soviet agent. A bit later, Jim Angleton, whose staff responsibilities included supervision of foreign liaison, came to a similar if more guarded conclusion. At General Smith's request, Philby was recalled.

In London, Philby weathered the security storm and was allowed politely to resign from SIS. It was not until 1963, after a confrontation with a senior SIS colleague in Beirut, Lebanon, that Philby realized he had come to the end of the road. He signaled his KGB controller and was smuggled aboard a Soviet ship. He died in Moscow in 1988.

When CIA reorganized its operational headquarters in 1954, Frank Wisner, the director for operations, established three operational staffs to provide oversight of the principal operational activity: Foreign Intelligence Collection (FI), Covert Action (CA), and Counterintelligence (CI). Bill Harvey moved along to assignments that would lead him to Berlin and the tunnel project. Jim Angleton became chief of the CI Staff, the only Agency assignment he ever wanted. He remained in that post until his forced retirement in December 1974.

Chapter 15

—

SOLDIERING ON

The events that led to a crisis in my career began in 1956, a time of relentless pressure on Frank Wisner and the rest of us. The year got off to a rolling start in February, when Nikita Khrushchev made his landmark secret speech to a closed session of the Twentieth Party Congress in Moscow. As soon as rumors spread that Khrushchev had signaled the end of the collective leadership that had existed since Stalin's death, and given the party congress a candid view of the late dictator's policy and practices, there was an international scramble to obtain the actual text. While we were groping through a shower of alleged bits and pieces of the speech, Jim Angleton picked up a copy of the text and we soon found another.

By April, the KGB decided that George Blake would no longer be threatened if they exposed our Berlin tunnel and phone taps. As a byproduct the Russians planned to make a propaganda profit by inviting the entire Berlin press corps to inspect and photograph the installation. Rather than being "shocked, repeat shocked" to learn that espionage was going on in Berlin, the news media were thoroughly impressed by the scope of the operation and the technical wizardry involved. The Soviet spin-tyros scuttled back to Moscow with considerable egg on their faces.

In June, labor unrest and riots in Poland brought the return of Wladyslaw Gomulka to office and a confrontation with Khrushchev. When Khrushchev backed off, ripples of discontent and hope for a loosening of the controls the USSR had imposed spread through much of Eastern Europe. At about this time it became apparent that Frank Wisner's commitment to his work had begun seriously to affect his health. Frank was obviously tired when he left Washington on a long-planned visit to the key European offices. By coincidence the trip began on October 23, the day Budapest street demonstrations against the Soviet presence in Hungary flared into open revolt. Six days later Israeli forces unleashed an attack on Egypt and began the occupation of the Sinai Peninsula.

The British and French presented Cairo with an ultimatum the Egyptians obviously could not accept. Within hours, the Anglo-French allies bombed Egyptian airfields and occupied both sides of the Suez Canal. In Budapest, Hungarians had seized Soviet small arms and were battling the local Red Army units to a standstill. On November 3, Secretary of State John Foster Dulles underwent surgery in Washington. Three days later, President Eisenhower, still recovering from a heart attack, won his second election.

After a series of around-the-clock discussions in London, Paris, and Germany, Wisner reached Vienna on November 7, three days after elite, battle-ready Red Army combat units, 200,000 strong, crossed the border into Hungary. It had been an extraordinary confluence of events.

Isolated from the Washington policymakers and without access to his customary flow of informed comment, Wisner felt intense frustration. It was soon apparent that the Hungarian people had won their revolution and bested the Soviet occupation forces. But without artillery and tanks, the gutsy Hungarians could not hope to win a war—or even hold their own—against the invading Red Army. Despite the Eisenhower and Foster Dulles election campaign enthusiasm for rolling back the Iron Curtain, nothing short of armed intervention by NATO could hope to repel the Soviet forces as they swept across Hungary. As Eisenhower pointed out, it would be as difficult to move a fully equipped army to Hungary as it might be to transport such a force cross-country to Tibet. There was no significant NATO support for what would at best be a desperate military venture. Nothing could be done except to offer safe haven for the more than 200,000 Hungarians who were forced to flee.

Rather than return to Washington, Wisner continued the trip, his nervous fatigue becoming more obvious each day. After stopping in Rome and Athens, where he ate a serving of spoiled clams, Wisner returned to Washington. He was exhausted, infected with hepatitis, and running a high fever. After a hospital stay, Frank returned to the office and resumed his heavy schedule. It was apparent to those of us closest to him that he was again demanding too much of himself, and that his conduct in the office was becoming erratic. Once again he went into the hospital. Frank suffered manic depression, a grim sickness now more readily diagnosed and treated than was possible in his day.

Throughout the period of his absences, I acted in Wisner's place as deputy director for plans.

It was not until Frank formally left the job in the fall of 1958 that Allen Dulles invited me to his office for a sandwich lunch. Although I routinely saw Dulles several times a week, the luncheon invitation was out of the ordinary. To the extent I thought about it at all, I assumed that I knew what Allen had on his mind. As it turned out, I was half right. Dulles did use the occasion to announce that he had chosen a replacement for Wisner.

Dulles began with a long review of Richard Bissell's distinguished career in government. Almost without a pause, he recounted Bissell's outstanding performance in bringing home the U-2 overhead reconnaissance program, short of the deadline, and $3 million under budget. He then reminded me of OXCART, the exotic refinement of the U-2 aircraft, and CORONA, the first earth-orbiting photographic satellite, projects which Bissell had rammed through.

After this recitation Dulles informed me that he had selected Richard Bissell to replace Frank Wisner and that I was to soldier on as Bissell's deputy.

That I was surprised and disappointed is to put it mildly. After seven years as Wisner's deputy, and many months of acting in his place, I felt I had earned my spurs. Because Frank was never keen on organizational or personnel matters that did not impinge directly on activities in which he had a strong personal interest, I had had full sway over operational and other concerns fundamental to the clandestine services. In those seven years I accompanied Frank to the DCI's senior staff meetings every morning, and had developed an understanding of activities and problems beyond the immediate concerns of the DDP. My disappointment and surprise were indeed genuine.

No matter how gracefully Dulles presented his decision, this apparent vote of no confidence was reason enough to consider leaving the Agency. My reaction to the DCI's decision was further soured by the fact that although Bissell succeeded brilliantly in every task he had taken on, he had almost no experience in operations, and a somewhat less than comprehensive grasp of our worldwide activity. Moreover, he had encountered and worked with no more than a score of the DDP personnel. In the next few days I put this obvious solution to my problem to one side. There was no rush; resignation could come at any time.

As an alternative to leaving, I could have accepted an overseas assignment as chief of station. Such a post would have been much less stressful than my Washington job, and would have brought me closer to operations than was possible at headquarters. There was one serious professional problem inherent in this solution. Both Dulles and Bissell were known within the Agency—and in many quarters of the government as well as to our more informed foreign liaison contacts—as covert action enthusiasts. In thinking about Dulles's decision, I concluded that my guarded reaction to some of the more ambitious covert action schemes was at the root of the decision against me. If I were to step down—and any foreign assignment would be seen within the Agency and by others in Washington and abroad as just such a move—it would almost certainly be read as an Agency decision to emphasize covert action over the traditional responsibility for espionage and counterintelligence abroad. Officers who planned to make their careers in these disciplines might be expected to feel that their work had been downgraded in importance, and that covert action was to be the flavor of choice for the next decade.

A third possibility would be to smother my pride and stay put— "soldiering on," as Dulles delicately put it.

My decision came down to a few facts. First, and certainly foremost, I was, and still am, fascinated by every aspect of intelligence activity. It is not for everybody, but for me it was the best possible work. Moreover, I felt that I could continue to make a useful contribution to the Agency for several more years. Aside from these personal feelings, I was, and still am, convinced that there is no greater threat to world peace than poorly informed or misinformed leaders and governments. The "Pearl Harbor factor" has by now been beaten into the heads of our policymakers. But even in the world of 1958, it seemed to me that the likelihood of an armed attack by a major power was slight. The wiggle room between a diplomatic standoff and military confrontation seemed most likely to be dominated by the nation with the wisest foreign policy and the best intelligence service. Today, the more likely perils—anthrax spilled in the subway or tucked into letters, car bombs cozied up to undefended targets—are as much a threat as any likely attack by a world power. And, as in the past, the first line of defense remains a competent intelligence service.

My decision to remain in place was difficult but, for me at least, correct.

Looking back at that time in my life I realize that my reaction to Dulles's decision was more that of surprise than any lasting bitterness. I also thought that aside from the obvious personal qualities, the minimal necessary professional background for whoever might have taken Wisner's place would have included some reasonably close-in experience with intelligence collection, counterintelligence, covert action operations, and some experience and knowledge of liaison with foreign intelligence services. I was also convinced that an understanding of the qualifications and training necessary for operations officers and a reasonable familiarity with the hundred or more professionals who held the key positions in the directorate would have been essential. Measured against these criteria, and despite his outstanding personal record, I could only regard Dick Bissell as a peculiar choice for the job.

I assumed that Bissell would, early on, take me aside and give me an understanding of just what he expected and how he wanted our two offices to function. This was never to happen. Bissell settled down in his office, and for want of any other instruction, I carried on. This meant that I dealt with everything that crossed my desk which I assumed would not require Bissell's direct attention. The only significant change in our offices was Bissell's appointment of Tracy Barnes as a special assistant. When planning for the effort to unseat Castro began, Bissell named Barnes as his deputy for ZAPATA, the operation which ended at the Bay of Pigs. At the time Barnes settled in, the ZAPATA traffic no longer crossed my desk.

Frank Wisner and I had worked as a team. We received simultaneous distribution of significant cable and dispatch traffic, and other communications, and we consulted on all the more important operations and senior personnel appointments. Our communication was always fluent and candid. Dick Bissell never discussed with me any activity or related personnel assignments involving activity which he personally directed. Nor do I recall his ever soliciting my advice. Bissell appeared to have little interest in espionage as such, and none whatsoever in counterintelligence. His lack of concern with what has become known as HUMINT— a barbarism encompassing secret intelligence collected by human beings—was obviously influenced by the scope and quality of the material flowing from his technical operations—particularly CORONA, the orbiting photographic satellite program.

Although the superbly detailed photographs taken from what I call outer space could not show what foreign policymakers were thinking or discussing among themselves, the data on foreign *capabilities* were outstanding. A good agent in the right place can be expected to produce intelligence that cannot be duplicated by any amount of overhead photography, but no spy can hope to reveal the mass of data that were such easy pickings for the unmanned satellites. The fact that this material could be produced without any compelling diplomatic or political bothers is also a significant advantage. Outer space and other technical legerdemain costs millions. Espionage was—at least in those days—dirt cheap. Both activities are essential, and the one can be counted upon to nourish the other. There remains an obvious management problem in maintaining a balance between the two.

From early in his Agency career, Bissell's attention—partially conditioned by his work with the U-2 and CORONA—was fixed on the USSR and its satellite communist dependencies. A parallel concern involved high-level covert action operations, the potential importance of which had been driven home to him by the overthrow of Arbenz in Guatemala, and Allen Dulles's abiding enthusiasm for that activity. But by 1960, Bissell's attention and that of the White House and the National Security Council were increasingly focused on sub-Saharan Africa. Belgium's hasty decision to grant independence to the Congo in June 1960 brought the developing confrontation of Soviet and Western interests to the forefront.

At the time, the Congo seemed to be compounded of elements destined to fuse into an explosion at the slightest misstep by any of the interested parties—the impoverished and inflamed local population, the USSR, the United States, other Western democracies, and the United

Nations. The country was rich in cobalt, tantalum, bauxite, and fistfuls of other strategic material. It was surrounded by states, some of which had yet to be blessed with experienced or stable governments.

Belgium had surrendered the Congo without having educated and trained a body of Congolese who were prepared to take over from the colonial masters. This policy was not so much the product of neglect as it was to ensure that for some time to come the Congo would have no choice but to depend upon the cadre of Belgian officials who would remain behind to administer the government, staff the army officer corps, and man the sizeable security force. And perhaps not incidentally, to continue to exploit the country.

With independence came Patrice Lumumba, a prime minister whose political wisdom and ability to govern were more apparent to some of his constituency at home than could be seen from abroad. After weeks of growing strife, the country erupted. The Congolese troops rebelled against their Belgian officers and Belgian military forces intervened to protect the considerable Belgian holdings. The richly endowed Katanga Province declared its independence from the Congo. The UN asked Belgium to withdraw, and prepared to deploy its own peacekeeping forces. Lumumba enplaned for Washington to plea for economic aid. After winning some support, he blithely admitted that he was considering inviting Soviet troops to help the Congo rid itself of the despised Belgian forces.

At this time, Agency officers in the Congo cabled Washington to the effect that the country was about to succumb to a classic communist takeover, with strong Soviet support. Prime Minister Lumumba was seen as incompetent to run the country, let alone to preserve its independence from the USSR. A few days later, Allen Dulles met with President Eisenhower and the Special Group, the White House body that approved covert action operations. Eisenhower expressed his strong view on the need for very straightforward action in the Congo. The minutes of this meeting stated that the Special Group "agreed that planning for Congo would not necessarily rule out consideration of any particular kind of activity which might contribute to getting rid of Lumumba."

The following day, Allen Dulles drafted a cable to the Congo station saying in part, "In high quarters here, it is the clear-cut conclusion that if [Lumumba] continues to hold high office, the inevitable result will at best be chaos, and at the worst would pave the way for a Communist takeover of the Congo, with disastrous consequences for the prestige of the UN and for the interests of the free world generally. Consequently, we conclude that his removal must be an urgent and prime objective and that under existing conditions this should be a high priority of our covert action."*

In those days, whenever Allen Dulles drafted an operations cable, he invariably sent it to Bissell or me for coordination before releasing it to the field. As it happened, Bissell was on vacation when this cable was prepared and I simply signed for the DDP. The phrase "In high quarters" would have been understood by any senior Agency officer to be a reference to the President. The intent of the cable seemed as clear to me at the time as it does today. As a former commander of the Allied Expeditionary Forces in Europe, President Eisenhower had extensive experience in life-and-death decisions, and can only have known exactly what he was saying. In this context, I vividly recall the newsreel coverage of *General* Eisenhower on June 5, the eve of D day 1944. As he moved slowly along a file of heavily burdened and fully armed Rangers, he looked each in the face, and stopped to shake hands and encourage the young men who were to lead the landing assault in Normandy. No one could have known more certainly than General Eisenhower exactly what these men would face in the next few hours, or could have calculated their chance of survival more accurately. The decision to plan moves against Lumumba was President Eisenhower's.

The first brush that I had with a problem of this sort came early in 1947 when Elizabeth Dunlevy caught me at the door as I was leaving my office. She thrust an incoming cable into my hand. "Colonel Galloway wants to see you on the double." In those days, we were still in the crumbling temporary buildings alongside the Lincoln Memorial Reflecting Pool. I managed to glance at the cable as I made my way down the stairs, the only stable element in the decaying building.

Colonel Donald Galloway, a regular Army cavalry officer, was a recent arrival, having been brought into the outfit by General Vandenberg. Given the title assistant director for special operations (ADSO), the colonel headed the espionage and counterintelligence components of the

---

*U.S. Senate, *Alleged Assassination Plots Involving Foreign Leaders* (Washington, D.C.: U.S. Government Printing Office, 1975), pp. 14–15.

Central Intelligence Group. Galloway had a commanding presence: tall and square-jawed, he had big hands, long fingers, and a seldom modulated parade-ground voice. He was rarely known to issue an oral order without the coda, "And on the double, *please.*" He may also have been the last officer at West Point to have instructed the cadets in equestrian etiquette.

Galloway fixed me with a frozen glare before I got through the door and into his office. "Just what are you going to do with that damned agent who's been playing games with us in Germany." It was less a question than a demand to know why I had not already done something about the cable that I had still not finished reading. I cannot remember the agent in question, nor do I recall exactly how I tried to temporize long enough to find out where Galloway was headed. I needn't have bothered.

"Why don't you just have the bastard eliminated?"

"You mean, have him killed?"

"Yes, Helms. That's exactly what I mean."

For a moment I considered reading the colonel a sermon on the propriety and the perils of any such peacetime action. Fortunately for our relationship as it was to develop, I realized that as an experienced front-line commander, Galloway might not need any such moralizing from me. I took a deep breath and settled for something along the line of "I . . . er . . . don't think that would be wise."

"Why not?" Patience was not one of the colonel's virtues.

With this, I got down to business. "In the first place," I said, "we want to make damned certain that we're not creating a bigger problem than the one we're trying to solve. Down deep, even the toughest-talking Americans are raised in the Boy Scout tradition. Under battlefield pressure, almost anything goes. Now that the shooting's stopped, there's no telling what immediate impact this sort of action may have on a person, or what he might come to think of it a few months later. It's afterwards, when the pressure is off, the urgency has vanished, and the emotions have quieted, that there'll be time to think it through again. But by then it will be impossible to re-create the pressure and the circumstances that led to the decision, and everything will look different. That's when things begin to fall apart, and someone may think that an anonymous note to the local newspaper will put everything straight again."

"The NKVD does it," Galloway said, and mentioned two of the Western services that in peacetime were known to lapse into what they called "executive action."

"They're welcome to it—but in peacetime there are simpler solutions."

Having got across this much thin ice, I eased up. Colonel Galloway growled a few words and dismissed me.

As Dean Acheson once commented, the writer of a memorandum of conversation does not come off second best. Nonetheless, I've recounted this incident as I remember it. I have a fond memory of Colonel Galloway and great respect for his combat record, but at the time it seemed to me that the veteran soldier had spoken too quickly and rashly. The fact that we never discussed this topic again makes me think that he came to agree with me.

When Bissell returned from vacation, I dropped out of the command channel on the Lumumba matter. At one point, an officer Bissell had detailed to go to the Congo to direct the operation came to me to say that he had refused the mission. He asked if I agreed. I said that I did. Dick Bissell accepted the officer's decision, and no more was said about it.

At about this time, Lumumba was placed in protective custody—more accurately house arrest—by the UN authorities in the Congo. He escaped in November 1960 and attempted to lead his followers against his political rival, Joseph Mobuto, and the UN forces. He was captured by Mobuto a few days later, and in January 1961 was flown to Katanga, the secessionist province. Sometime after his arrival in Katanga, Lumumba was murdered, probably by Mobuto followers.

Time had solved the problem. The Agency had no influence in the action whatsoever.

There is no easy answer to the question of assassination. Clearly, boundless misery would have been avoided if Hitler had been struck down after he assumed absolute power in Germany, and his plans for the future had become clear. At least as much might be said had Stalin been eliminated before he established himself as the sole authority in the USSR. Lumumba was scarcely such a threat, but he was by any standard unfit to rule the Congo. This said, in peacetime the assassination of troublesome persons is morally and operationally indefensible. There are invariably other solutions, not the least of which is time—time for the immediate and sometimes fierce tactical pressure to subside or for the problem to be reevaluated and another solution found.

As far as the United States is concerned, the issue was closed when in February 1976, Executive Order 11905 was issued. Section 5, Restrictions on Intelligence Activities, subparagraph "g," states: "No employee of the United States shall engage in, or conspire to engage in, political assassination." I have no quarrel with this order other than to say that in wartime, when air raids are coincidentally killing hundreds of noncombatants, I see no reason the assassination of enemy leaders such as Hitler and his immediate staff should be forbidden.

Chapter 16

—

CALL IT HUBRIS

For some time before Fulgencio Batista, the president and resident dictator of Cuba, decided enough was enough and decamped for Miami on New Year's Day 1959, the prevailing opinion of Washington's Latin American experts was that although Raúl Castro was a fully frocked communist, his older brother Fidel was perhaps no such thing. Because Batista had long since outworn his welcome, Fidel Castro appeared to many to be a reasonably plausible change. He was surely a leftist, but he had parlayed a shoestring invasion into a full-fledged takeover in Cuba. Even in the quick-change atmosphere of Caribbean and Latin American politics, this was an accomplishment. What's more, Castro achieved this after having failed to overthrow Batista in an earlier invasion effort, and had as a result served two years in Batista's prison on the Isle of Pines.

Castro was from the Cuban middle class and had a law degree. His well-propagandized enthusiasm for land reform, universal education, and social change had a significant appeal to Cuban peasants and the urban working class. He was young, energetic, forceful, and without question possessed a considerable romantic charisma.

The Agency had long maintained a presence in Cuba and had monitored Castro's activity for months before Batista chose to decamp. Despite Cuba's proximity to the United States, and the fact that the country was at least as vulnerable to radical political change and subversion as many others, it did not rank high on the White House list of priority concerns.

In April 1959, four months after he had stepped into Batista's vacated offices in Havana, Castro was invited to the United States by the American Society of Newspaper Editors. He was cautiously received by official Washington, but was welcomed by some of the media as a promising replacement for the thoroughly discredited Batista. Castro arrived well briefed. He dropped wreaths at the Lincoln and Jefferson Memorials, told the Senate Foreign Relations Committee that he had no intention of expropriating American property, and assured TV audiences that he was opposed to communism and was an enthusiastic champion of a free press and open elections. But Castro had no luck at all with Vice President Richard Nixon. After spending three hours of a Sunday afternoon listening to Castro in the Vice President's quiet office in the Senate Office Building, Nixon drafted a secret memorandum of conversation that left little doubt that he considered the Cuban a loose cannon and probably a communist.

In a remarkably short time after his return to Cuba, Castro managed to convince Washington's policymakers and other Western observers that he was indeed a communist and that his freely chosen political and military ally was the Soviet Union. It was also soon apparent that Castro intended to use Cuba as a base from which to mount political and paramilitary activities in the Caribbean and Latin America wherever the prospects seemed favorable. The notion of tolerating a dictatorship openly dedicated to these objectives and located a ninety-mile hop and skip from the Florida coast was not acceptable to President Eisenhower.

In January 1960 the Special Group—the National Security Council element responsible for authorizing covert action—formally instructed CIA to develop an operational plan. Some three months later, President Eisenhower approved the Agency plan involving propaganda, the creation of a unified Cuban opposition to Castro, and the formation of a cadre of some twenty Cuban exiles trained in guerrilla tactics—infiltration, sabotage, and communications. This group was, in turn, to develop a hundred or more Cuban agents who were to be infiltrated into Cuba where they would "be placed" within "various dissident groups" and in enclaves in the Escambray Mountains. By any standard, this would have been an ambitious—and most probably impossible—assignment for a secret intelligence service.

As Richard Bissell expresses it in his book: "Our immediate goal . . . was to model the guerrilla organization along the lines of the underground organizations of World War II."* The assumption—unknown to me at the time—that the operation was to resemble the World War II organizations cannot have been made on the basis of even a rudimentary knowledge of their activity. Without exception, the European resistance was primarily directed against a brutal, foreign—and, in many cases, traditional—enemy. There were quisling governments of varying strengths in each of the German-occupied countries, but the root enemy was Nazi Germany. Whatever else may be said about Castro, his government—though not elected—was Cuban.

The first step in the initial covert action plan was to be the creation of a command and control net on the island with the mission to establish safe houses, receive supplies, and accommodate infiltrated agents. This considerable task was seen to require upwards to "200 highly disciplined members . . . rigidly trained . . . compartmented in such a way that they would not know one another." There was, Bissell writes, "*a firm belief* [emphasis added] within the agency that it would be possible to build up this kind of underground mechanism in Cuba."†

Here I must say that insofar as any such firm opinion may have existed within the Agency, it could have been held only by those who had little knowledge of the underground work in Europe during World War II, and perhaps even less understanding of CIA's more recent resistance efforts in Eastern Europe and the USSR. The romantic notion that some two hundred agents could be "rigidly trained" and compartmented so that "they would not know one another" would have been beyond the resources of any intelligence service known to me. Indeed, the security and logistics problems involved in training and handling a score of agents in this fashion would have strained the Agency's facilities. The only venue for a plan of this scope is a Hollywood motion picture studio.

Allen Dulles had as good a grasp of underground resistance operations as anyone at his level in Washington. I cannot understand Dick Bis-

---

Reflections of a Cold Warrior (New Haven: Yale University Press, 1996), p. 154.
†Ibid.

sell's and Dulles's failure to look more deeply into the facts bearing on this proposed plan. The best I can suggest is that Bissell's great success with the U-2 and CORONA projects, and Dulles's determination to prove the Agency's capability, resulted in a collective suspension of judgment.

I saw some of the initial cable traffic but was not consulted on any aspect of the planning or the personnel staffing of the project, nor did the ever-increasing daily operational traffic cross my desk. The command channel for the Cuban undertaking, code name ZAPATA, ran from the DCI, Allen Dulles, to the deputy director for plans, Richard Bissell, and Tracy Barnes, Bissell's special assistant for the operation. At the lower level, staff, branch, and section chiefs were assigned operational and administrative responsibility.

I am, of course, acutely aware that I write this some four decades after the fact, and that errors are always most clearly to be seen in the rearview mirror. There is no need here to rehash the complex émigré political aspects of the operation; all of the appropriate documents are available for study. The most I can contribute is an explanation of my role and a comment on the operation itself.

In concept, Operation ZAPATA was the outgrowth of what were perceived by some to have been the successful tactics involved in the ousting of Mossadegh in Iran and the overthrow of Arbenz and his government in Guatemala. To a lesser degree, the romantic view of the wartime resistance activity in much of Europe appears also to have contributed to the notion that covert action could be used as an all-purpose foreign policy tool. It seemed to me and to many others—notably Kermit "Kim" Roosevelt, who engineered the operation in Iran—that while covert political action was useful, it should not necessarily be applied to foreign policy problems that might plausibly be handled through diplomatic channels or, in extreme situations, by military intervention. Kim's observation, made after he had ousted Mossadegh, had been forgotten.*

The Iranian operation was a squeaker. The situation was much in our favor, but even a bit of bad luck might have undone the intended result. At least as much can be said for the operation in Guatemala, where the prevailing conditions were less favorable. It, too, was a near thing. In

*See Chapter 11, p. 117.

planning secret operations, it cannot be assumed that any move will go unchallenged, that no misstep will occur, and that luck will always be on our side. In operations of a high level—and the ousting of Castro certainly qualified—contingency planning must take the possibility of failure, bad luck, or otherwise fully into account.

As I saw it at the time, the Agency's most appropriate role was to penetrate the Castro government, and to contain, and in time destroy, its capacity to export the Cuban revolution, and the ability to engage in paramilitary activity in our hemisphere. This was within our competence, and in fact we were subsequently to break Castro's paramilitary sword at the hilt by seizing his weapons caches in Venezuela and elsewhere, and by quietly penetrating and exposing Cuba's inimical political and intelligence activity.

As Bissell puts it in his book: "By late 1960 the agency had received a thorough education in the difficulty of establishing an effective guerrilla organization."* Sadly, this was one of the lessons that many of us had already learned and not forgotten. Insofar as the learning might not have been universal, there were many in the Agency who between them could surely have foreseen the nearly insuperable problems the operation faced. There was no way that a paramilitary force a thousand strong could be *secretly* recruited, trained, and armed with an air force and the naval support necessary to ensure a successful landing. Aside from that, the island's geography did not lend itself to a broad scale of guerrilla activity. Equally to the point, the likely response of the Cuban people had not been thoroughly explored.

Allen Dulles had more than enough professional experience and operational judgment to have refused rather than encouraged Washington policymakers to assume the obvious risks of such an ambitious effort. Bissell did not have the experience to know this, or to select the Agency staff best suited to work with him.

Tracy Barnes might by a stretch have been assumed to have the requisite background to serve as Bissell's deputy for the operation. In fact, Tracy was, to some degree, a man of Allen Dulles's imagination. If one were to create a colleague who would appeal to Dulles's every enthusiasm, Barnes would have been a perfect construct. He was a wellborn

*Reflections of a Cold Warrior, p. 154.

product of the eastern establishment—graceful, well educated, fearless, patriotic, and engaging. Unfortunately, like those who no matter how great their effort seem doomed never to master a foreign language, Barnes proved unable to get the hang of secret operations. Even worse, thanks to Allen Dulles's constant praise and pushing, Tracy apparently remained unaware of his problem.

Dulles met Tracy in Switzerland when he was assigned to the OSS station after his parachute mission in France. After the war, Dulles recruited Tracy for CIA and sponsored and furthered his career from that point to his assignment as Agency chief in Germany—where he left no identifiable footprint—and subsequently to a parallel post in the United Kingdom, a job for which he was equally unqualified. Had it not been for Dulles's continuing sponsorship, no matter how hard Tracy worked at each of these assignments, he might have moved laterally and effectively into more suitable Agency work of a nonoperational nature.

As DCI, Dulles was in a position to insist that the ZAPATA operation have the best possible support from within the Agency. But in an effort to protect security, Allen kept the operation compartmented from other CIA elements which could have been useful to him. He made this decision despite the fact that more than a thousand Cubans and dozens of American contract personnel had knowledge of the plan.

Cuban intelligence was not world class, but it had the significant advantages of area knowledge, a level of domestic political support, the latent ethnic loyalty of some Cubans living abroad, and the excellent help offered by the KGB and GRU officers on assignment in Havana. There could be little doubt that Castro and his Soviet advisors were kept reasonably informed on the ZAPATA project as it developed. On our side, a single CIA officer was assigned the vast counterintelligence responsibility for the project. At no time was Jim Angleton's CI staff asked for support in coping with the obvious security problems.

Because the limited invasion force could succeed only if the Cuban military failed to resist the invasion, and if the Cuban population rallied to the *Brigadistas,* an estimate of the level of support Castro enjoyed within Cuba, and the likelihood of the population rising to join forces against Castro, was of critical importance. The preparation of such estimates was a primary responsibility and daily activity of the Directorate for Intelligence (DI). These essential estimates were well within the DI's ability to provide. High-level scuttlebutt being what it is, Robert Amory, the deputy director for intelligence, was certainly aware that Dulles and Bissell were heavily occupied with a high-security operation and that the target was Cuba. Given the fact that knowledge of the operation was also scattered throughout the Cuban émigré communities, there seemed no reason Dulles should not have consulted Amory and his staff under whatever security restrictions the DCI might have mandated. No such consultation occurred and no estimates were requested.

It was Dulles's intention to staff the task force with competent personnel, and instructions were issued for the various divisions to supply competent officers at the various grade levels. CIA was a well-disciplined organization, but it takes little bureaucratic experience to suspect that while some well-qualified personnel would be made available by the various division chiefs, there was the chance that some officers less well qualified for such a high-risk operation might also be transferred. Within the Agency, personnel are annually ranked in order of perceived competence at their respective grade levels. Even if one had no hands-on knowledge of various officers, it would have been possible to use the personnel ranking charts as a guide. In this fashion a requirement might have been leveled on a division chief to make "two GS-15 officers within the high 20% bracket of the ranking profile immediately available for reassignment." Draconian perhaps, but a reasonable substitute for personal knowledge of the employees. This was not done.

More important was the fact that the constant high-level nibbling at the Agency's original assumptions and plans for logistic and military support had so altered the final plan that the original concept had all but disappeared.

Even though I was not directly involved in or consulted on any aspect of the activity, I had by osmosis gained a reasonable idea of what was going on. My impression that the project was entirely too ambitious to be considered a secret activity was partially offset by my assumption that if the *Brigadistas* appeared about to be overwhelmed, President Eisenhower, the old soldier who had initiated the operation, would think—in for a dime, in for a dollar—and provide sufficient U.S. military muscle to carry the day. After all, Eisenhower had reversed his policy in Guatemala when it appeared that Operation PBSUCCESS would fail, and at the critical moment had provided the military aircraft needed to ensure victory.

In clinging to this assumption, I failed to consider the important fact that the Kennedy administration was very new to the game. Coincidentally, I also neglected to consider the possibility that the new administration might not have been sufficiently alerted to the need for an agreed plan of action in the event that the *Brigadistas* might be overwhelmed before they could be reinforced by an American military force. No matter how well qualified the individual members of a new administration may be—and President Kennedy took office with a very strong staff—the first few weeks before any incoming administration settles down are not the most propitious time to risk radical foreign policy undertakings.

In the early morning of April 17, 1961, the ZAPATA Brigade force seized a beachhead along the Bay of Pigs—the original and more feasible landing area having been vetoed by President Kennedy. Two days and some hours later, the surviving 1189 members of the attack force were still contained within the beachhead. After President Kennedy refused to provide the desperately needed additional air support and their ammunition was almost exhausted, the men had no choice but to surrender. Although strenuous and gallant individual efforts were made to pick up the few *Brigadistas* escaping from the beachhead, an organized evacuation of the survivors was impossible.

In December 1962 the prisoners were ransomed at the cost of $53 million worth of medical and food supplies.

The specific tactical reasons for the military failure of the operation have been thoroughly and publicly explored, and there is no need to detail them here. Except for the bravery of the Brigade and the beyond-the-call-of-duty dedication of the Americans who were involved, Operation ZAPATA as it developed was in most of its aspects much as one writer describes it, "the perfect failure."*

---

*Trumbull Higgins, *The Perfect Failure* (New York: Norton, 1987).

Chapter 17

FALLOUT

It was twenty-four hours before the full impact of the surrender at the Bay of Pigs, and the collapse of the ZAPATA operation registered with President Kennedy and the new administration. When it did, the effect was no less than stunning. With the apt quotation, "Victory has a hundred fathers, and defeat is an orphan," President Kennedy rallied and gamely took the blame for the failed operation.

No matter that President Eisenhower had directed the Agency to prepare a plan for Castro's overthrow, or that the Pentagon had failed accurately, and loudly enough, to assess the possibility of a failed invasion, or that President Kennedy had at the last moment denied the planned aerial support. ZAPATA was a CIA operation, a foreign policy disaster, and a humiliating experience for the country.

At the Department of State the whispered reaction was, "We told you so." In the inner circle at the Pentagon, senior officers sniffed and reminded one another that it takes more than an Ivy League diploma to execute a successful military action. At the White House, President Kennedy asked rhetorically how he could have been so stupid, and speculated on how he might correct things at the Agency.

Allen Dulles had planned to remain as DCI for another two years, but this was clearly not to be. He offered his resignation to the President.

Kennedy accepted it but asked Dulles to remain in place for some time to come. There would be no public reference to the resignation until the President appointed a replacement. The President's decision was based on a genuine regard for Dulles and respect for his achievements, as well as a desire to avoid anything resembling an after-action scalding of scapegoats.

Kennedy then called Dick Bissell to the White House and informed him that he could not continue as deputy director for plans. He explained—perhaps a bit gratuitously—that in a parliamentary government, the prime minister would have had to resign, while the senior civil servant would have remained in place. In our government, Kennedy said, the President is elected for four years and is expected to complete his full term. He then asked Bissell to remain in place until another CIA assignment could be found for him. Bissell was later offered another deputy directorship—in the scientific field—but he declined and left the Agency in February 1962 to become president of the Institute for Defense Analyses.

President Kennedy was not accustomed to defeat. He had no intention of allowing the likes of Castro to hand him his hat, and did not hesitate to move ahead without waiting for the after-action studies. On May 5, the National Security Council, as always precisely reflecting the President's position, noted that there would be no change in the administration's position on Cuba, and that U.S. policy would continue to "aim at the downfall of Castro." The council also stated that although "the U.S. would not undertake military intervention in Cuba now," it would not "foreclose the possibility of military intervention in the future."

Kennedy had climbed back into the ring swinging.

—

While Bissell remained in place, he was heavily occupied with the political fallout and operational problems left in the wake of the surrender at the Bay of Pigs. This left me to cope with much of the responsibility Bissell had previously allocated to himself. These were a variety of sensitive, often ambitious, covert action operations which required careful monitoring from my desk. This was not the time for any operational blunders. Even the most routine intelligence collection operations, recruitment attempts, and counterintelligence activity required the closest headquarters scrutiny. More than once I reflected on Dulles's comment that I was to "soldier on" when Bissell became deputy director for plans. The weeks following the ZAPATA debacle more nearly resembled an Iron Man marathon than any moments of mere soldiering.

In the Agency corridors the speculation that Mr. Dulles would be asked to resign was temporarily stilled when, within three days of the surrender at the Bay of Pigs, President Kennedy appointed General Maxwell Taylor, who had retired in 1959 as Army chief of staff, to head a presidential inquiry on what had gone wrong in the ZAPATA effort. Assisting General Taylor were Robert Kennedy, the attorney general; Admiral Arleigh Burke, chief of naval operations; and Allen Dulles, DCI. At this time, Dulles instructed Lyman B. Kirkpatrick, then CIA inspector general, to conduct an in-house CIA study of the failed operation.

Before the invasion, Robert Kennedy was known to have expressed doubt that Operation ZAPATA could succeed. By the time Castro had rounded up the surviving *Brigadistas,* young Kennedy was making no effort to conceal his determination to find those whose bad judgment had so harmed his brother. At the Agency, the impression was that Robert Kennedy, whom none of us knew well enough to judge, would serve as his brother's vengeful hatchet man. In that depressed atmosphere, it was easy to imagine the probable result—an upending of the Agency, with the espionage and intelligence production elements blistered in the heat generated by the failed covert action.

When he joined the investigation, Robert Kennedy's criticisms were loud and persistent. Whether it was the result of General Taylor's perceptive and levelheaded approach, the influence of Admiral Burke and Allen Dulles, or his own findings, Kennedy was to develop a more balanced view of the Agency than he had in the days after the collapse of the ZAPATA operation. In the weeks that followed, we were relieved to learn that he was a quick study. The two months of back-to-back interviews and briefings with the committee left Kennedy with an abiding interest in covert action and a measure of respect for the Agency. He remembered AJAX, which restored the Shah to the Peacock Throne, and PBSUCCESS, which rid Guatemala of Jacobo Arbenz, and had time to reflect on the assistance provided to the Tibetan guerrillas. That operation had only a slight positive effect, but it had, he discovered, remained secret.

As we got to know one another, I incidentally learned that Robert

Kennedy preferred to be called "Bob" rather than "Bobby," a name he reserved for family use.

One odd aspect of the painful incident was the trouble General Taylor's committee had in finding a name for itself. First it was General Taylor's Board of Inquiry on Cuban Operations Conducted by CIA. Soon after, it designated itself The Green Study Group. In the end, it became known as the Paramilitary Study Group, a term that, as the investigation progressed, came to make good sense.

General Taylor's instructions were to "study our governmental practices and programs in the area of military and paramilitary, guerrilla and anti-guerrilla activity which fell short of outright war with a view to strengthening our work in this area . . . and to direct special attention to the lessons which can be learned from the recent events in Cuba." The study that resulted was broader in scope and more balanced than Kirkpatrick's inspector general report, which concerned only the Agency's role in the operation.

The Taylor investigation proceeded with something akin—at least in a bureaucracy—to the speed of light. The group's first gathering occurred on the Saturday the President told General Taylor that he was to lead the inquiry, four hours later. The second assembly occupied all of the following Monday, with some twenty sessions following hard on the heels of these initial meetings. General Taylor's conclusions made it clear that there was more than enough blame to go around—the Agency, the Department of Defense, the Department of State, and the White House staffs all came in for a share. In reading the report, I confirmed my conviction that ZAPATA was such a complex venture that by the time it had developed its own fatal momentum, the breakdown of almost any element in the plan might have doomed the entire effort. Despite General Bedell Smith's salty recommendation that the covert action "bucket of slops" be provided its own cover and separated from the espionage and intelligence production elements of the Agency, no such action was seriously considered.

Because I had nothing to do with the planning or execution of ZAPATA, there is little I can add to the data and existing analysis of the undertaking. I do, however, have some views on covert action operations. Allen Dulles and those who conceived Operation ZAPATA can be given credit for maintaining a semblance of secrecy while recruiting, training, arming, and convoying a paramilitary force of more than a thousand exiles to the Cuban coast. This was an achievement, but scarcely a blueprint for future activity. Today, there is little reason to assume that even these preliminary operational steps could be realized without risking a crippling media reaction.

Covert action has been referred to as the "third choice"—an activity more aggressive than conventional diplomatic maneuvering and less drastic than military intervention. This is true, and the best possible reason for our government to retain a covert action capability. In seeking to maintain such a means, we must realize that today's world is far too sophisticated to permit covert action to be wielded about like an all-purpose political chain saw. At its best, covert action should be used like a well-honed scalpel, infrequently, and with discretion lest the blade lose its edge.

"Plausible denial" has become an outmoded concept and is likely to remain so. From the outset in 1947, at the direction of the President, CIA had briefed selected members of congressional oversight committees on Agency activities. The arrangements were ad hoc as specified by each President. This never sat well with the Congress at large, and many members continued to insist that Congress be kept informed in a "timely fashion" of the start of any covert action operation. In 1974, Congress passed the Hughes-Ryan amendment to the Foreign Assistance Act, requiring CIA to inform eight (now two) separate congressional committees in advance of any CIA operation other than intelligence collection.

The new rule states: "The President may not authorize the conduct of a covert action . . . unless the President determines such an action is necessary to support identifiable foreign policy objectives of the United States and is important to the national security of the United States, which determination shall be set forth in a finding." Freely translated, this means that the President must sign and present to the intelligence oversight committees of Congress a document known as a presidential finding. In addition to describing each planned covert action operation in detail, each finding is to include a certification that the President has determined that the operation was necessary. At this point, "plausible denial" went straight out the window. Today, only the boldest chief executive would deny knowledge of a document which he has signed and presented to both houses of Congress.

In the secret operations canon it is axiomatic that the probability of leaks escalates exponentially each time a classified document is exposed to another person—be it an Agency employee, a member of Congress, a senior official, a typist, or a file clerk. Effective compartmentation is fundamental to all secret activity. These days, the daily press and the electronic media have contacts in the executive branch and in Congress to a degree never imagined in 1961. The potential for leaks—deliberate or accidental—is vast.

Compare these conditions with a quotation from a paper Allen Dulles wrote but never published. Dulles was a firm advocate of covert action and at one time actually believed covert action to be the prime function of CIA. The following is quoted from Dick Bissell's memoirs:

> Allen Dulles wrote a paper on the Bay of Pigs, never published, that is very revealing. There is one particular sentence that he re- works over and over in draft form: "Great actions require great de- termination. In these difficult types of operations, so many of which I have been associated with over the years, one never suc- ceeds unless there is a determination to succeed, a willingness to risk some unpleasant political repercussions, and a willingness to provide the basic military necessities. At the decisive moment of the Bay of Pigs operation, all three of these were lacking."*

Sometime after Dulles retired, it was suggested that Lyman Kirkpatrick had given an erroneous impression as to the extent CIA was responsible for the failure of the ZAPATA operation. Kirkpatrick responded with a memorandum dated December 1, 1961, saying that he thought the fail- ure of the operation should be charged in order of importance to the fol- lowing factors:

> a) An overall lack of recognition on the part of the U.S. Govern- ment as to the magnitude of the operation required to overthrow the Fidel Castro regime.
> b) The failure on the part of the U.S. Government to plan for all contingencies at the time of the Cuban operation including the ne-

Reflections of a Cold Warrior (New Haven: Yale University Press, 1996), p. 191.

cessity for using regular U.S. military forces in the event that the exiled Cubans could not do the job themselves.

c) The failure on the part of the U.S. Government to be willing to commit to the Cuban operation as planned and executed those necessary resources required for its success.

Kirkpatrick's references are to President Kennedy's cancellation of air cover at the critical moment, the unwillingness to use U.S. Navy support for the landing, and other controversial possibilities of help from governmental entities other than CIA.

I would add to these considerations a factor which has never received much attention. The plan for the Bay of Pigs operation originated in the Eisenhower administration, and had built into it President Eisenhower's concept of its needs and possibilities and plans. By the time the Cuban exile troops were trained and ready to fight, a new administration had taken over. I recall running into Dick Bissell and McGeorge Bundy in the corridor adjoining our former offices alongside the Reflecting Pool at the Lincoln Memorial. I sensed an almost conspiratorial air in their head-to-head conversation. It was my guess at the time, which has subsequently proved to be correct, that Dick was "selling" the new special assistant to the President for national security affairs on the operation to unseat Castro and change the nature of the Cuban government.

There were several discussions at the director's morning staff meetings in which Dulles expressed his concern that the new Kennedy team be thoroughly briefed on all CIA components. But here lay a problem. In briefing Bundy, the President, and others on ZAPATA, Dulles's and Bissell's emphasis was obviously placed on the prospect for success, with little attention paid to what might be seen as the weaknesses of the plan. To be specific, did President Kennedy understand from the beginning that air cover would be essential at the time of the landings, and that a lack of this cover might likely doom the entire enterprise? I doubt that this was ever stressed. At the critical moment it was President Kennedy who, with the prodding of Dean Rusk, the new secretary of state, canceled the essential air cover.

In the early weeks of any new administration extra care must be observed in any new foreign affairs undertakings, and even in modifications of existing programs. In their haste to rid Washington of the old and to substitute a shiny new penny, the transition teams tend to concentrate on personnel appointments and new organizational concepts. This is particularly true in the "black world" of clandestine operations and secret weapons developments. The new players have much to learn about how things in this strange new universe actually work. It is also important to remember that the new team is invariably less than a "team." The key members have not had time to work together, to get to know one another, or to uncover the shortcuts that facilitate interoffice communication. This is a distinct liability, particularly in a crisis situation.

The fact that plausible denial is an outmoded concept does not necessarily mean that all forms of covert action have gone by the board. U.S. support for the Afghan guerrillas during the Soviet Union's occupation of Afghanistan was undoubtedly an important factor in the eventual withdrawal of the Soviet troops. The sentient world knew that the United States was providing essential weapons and other support. Nevertheless the means by which this was done were regarded as sufficiently cloaked to keep the Soviets from raising hob in the United Nations or seeking other revenge on Washington.

There is an aspect of covert political action that touches on the newly modish "law of unintended consequences." Some observers consider Operation AJAX to have been an Agency mistake. Had Mossadegh remained in office, they reason, he *might* have created an Iranian political system which would have headed off the revolution against the monarchy without bringing about the oppressive rule of the mullahs. PBSUCCESS is now thought by some to have fathered a Guatemalan regime which produced years of military brutality.

However one may evaluate these speculations, it must be remembered that the Agency's role in Operation AJAX, as directed by the President, was to depose Mossadegh. The order to oust the Arbenz government also came from the White House. After any such successful operation, the continuing responsibility for establishing and nurturing a sound new government is not, and should never be, the ongoing task of an intelligence agency. This sort of nation building is the proper province of the State Department and other governmental and aid agencies. In some situations, the Department of Defense must lend a hand. Insofar as there is any continuing role for the Agency, it would best be to support the various overt activities by helping to keep inimical local or hostile foreign political elements from penetrating or taking over the new government, and to lend a hand in any ancillary operations which would support the basic mission.

General Taylor completed his 154-page report on the ZAPATA operation in June 1961, almost exactly two months after the surrender at the Bay of Pigs, and three months before Kirkpatrick had finished the inspector general's report.

—

To the best of my knowledge, the term "Special Group" came into use with the advent of the Eisenhower administration. The origin of the term, and the reasons to affix the Special Group to the Office of the National Security Advisor as a subcommittee, can be left to historians. The important fact is that the root purpose of the Special Group as it was initially conceived was to provide authorization for every significant CIA covert action operation as specified by the National Security Directive 5412/2.

An important secondary purpose of the Special Group was to establish a screen, protecting the President from having to assume personal responsibility for every risky covert action operation. In the event a secret undertaking were to go wrong, it would thus be possible for the President "plausibly to deny" any knowledge of the infamous activity that had been approved by his overzealous administration. (The likelihood that as soon as the Special Group approved a given operation, the national security advisor would have scuttled into the Executive Mansion to brief the boss would remain one of the administration's secrets.) Unfortunately, even this minimal cover was to be whisked away when Congress won the right to insist that the President sign a finding stating once and forever that he had formally approved the international skulduggery his subordinates had undertaken. Today, the spoiled detritus of every failed covert action initiative is flushed directly onto the President's lap.

Under President Kennedy, members of the Special Group were the deputy secretary of defense; the under secretary of state for political affairs; General Maxwell Taylor, the President's military advisor; the national security advisor, and the director of Central Intelligence. When this group became the center for all activity in respect to Cuba, Robert

Kennedy, the attorney general, added himself to the roster. The group then became known as the Special Group (Augmented).

One of the recommendations made by General Taylor's Study Group was that President Kennedy establish a subcommittee on counterinsurgency. Thus was born the Special Group Counterinsurgency (CI). A relatively new term, "counterinsurgency" was defined as the "use of all available resources . . . in preventing and resisting subversive insurgency and related forms of indirect aggression in friendly countries." The Special Group (CI) was responsible for coordinating U.S. efforts to assist foreign governments—at the time, Laos, South Vietnam, and Thailand—which were threatened by guerrilla insurrection. General Taylor chaired the group, which included General Lyman Lemnitzer, chairman of the Joint Chiefs of Staff; the directors of the United States Information Agency and Aid for International Development; the deputy secretary of defense; the under secretary of state for political affairs, and Robert Kennedy. On an ad hoc basis, this high-level group was often joined by the deputies of various other U.S. agencies involved in the operations.

These innovations were accomplished by the Kennedy administration in less time than it might take the civil service to sort out a change in the roster of officially designated parking places. Even veterans with a fluent knowledge of government structure and practice had trouble keeping pace with the new administration. For decades, the acronym "CI" had served as shorthand for "counterintelligence." By the time some of the old hands had learned that the same letters as appended to the Special Group (CI) had a secondary meaning, counterinsurgency as an activity had all but slipped off the President's blip screen.

By summer 1961, our reports showed Castro rapidly consolidating power and his military forces steadily gaining strength. In an estimate— of the sort sadly lacking before the Bay of Pigs—the United States Intelligence Board (USIB) stated that the combined strengths of the Cuban army and militia were now such that there was no chance that any invasion by Cuban exile forces could overthrow Castro's government. Nor could any guerrilla force be expected to succeed in gaining and maintaining a substantial foothold anywhere on the island. As USIB saw it, only a modern, fully equipped military force would have the strength to oust Castro and his *Fidelistas*.

This did not please the White House. In early July, as directed by the President, CIA came up with a new proposal on Cuba. Once again, the President was not impressed. First ZAPATA—strike one! And now this? The CIA plan to increase intelligence collection and propaganda was entirely too passive—strike two! Later that July, Admiral Arleigh Burke handed the President a memorandum echoing the Agency's earlier judgment that any real change in Cuba would require the use of U.S. military forces and that the longer we waited, the more difficult the operation would be. A few days later, on the occasion of his retirement, Admiral Burke went to the White House to receive a Distinguished Service Medal. The admiral got the well-earned medal, but his memorandum was strike three and out!

It was three months before President Kennedy came up with his own plan.

I remember the spring and summer of 1961 as a busy interregnum marked with flashes of abrupt change, dampened by the anxiety most of us shared about the shape and the future of the Agency. The press repeatedly jumped the gun in naming any number of persons who were surely to replace Allen Dulles. (I recall no such public speculation on Dick Bissell's likely replacement.) It was not until late September that President Kennedy named John Alex McCone as Allen Dulles's replacement as director of Central Intelligence.

As much as I was to value my subsequent promotion to replace Dick Bissell, it was with deep sadness that I watched the untangling of events that led to the resignation of Allen Dulles. He had served the Republic well, was a fine leader and an innovative master of his craft. I will remember him for his lifelong achievements and remarkable personality rather than the blunder which was as much the result of the era in which we worked as it was of that final, sad chapter of operational lapses.

Chapter 18

—

A NEW MAN

Unlike the often contradictory range of comments that journalists, historians, and former colleagues offer on high-level presidential appointees, there was an unmistakable consistency in the descriptions and evaluations of the new director of Central Intelligence. None of us realized it at the time, but John McCone turned out to have been exactly the right man to replace Allen Dulles.

The new DCI was little known in the intelligence community, but McCone was not a Washington newcomer. His government service began in 1947 with a brief hitch as a special deputy to the secretary of defense, James V. Forrestal. His next post was as under secretary of the Air Force from 1950 to 1951. From 1958 to 1961 he served as chairman of the Atomic Energy Commission. McCone, a conservative Republican and Catholic convert, was fifty-nine years old when he replaced Dulles. Unlike his predecessors, McCone had no formal intelligence experience. He was a successful businessman, an executive who made his fortune in private industry, much of it as a wartime shipbuilder in California.

In November 1961, a few weeks before his retirement became effective, Dulles, with McCone in tow, undertook what became a whirlwind farewell tour of the European capitals. In addition to meetings with senior Agency personnel, Dulles introduced McCone to many of his personal contacts. McCone, who also had a wide variety of well-placed friends and business associates in Europe, was impressed by the depth and scope of Dulles's connections. The trip also gave McCone a view of Allen in action, and an occasional glimpse of some of the contradictions in his approach to what Kipling called "the great game."

No one in the Washington headquarters knew McCone personally, and we were all eager to get a firsthand impression of the new boss. As luck had it, one of the senior officers in a station the pair had visited was called to Washington on routine business. It happened that he was the only DDP officer to have spent a few hours alone with McCone. Dulles stayed with the local station chief, and had arranged for McCone to stay as a houseguest of this other officer for three nights.

After a day of introductions, briefings, elaborate liaison lunches, and dinners, a somewhat the worse-for-wear McCone liked to relax over a noggin of bourbon and the opportunity for an informal chat with his host. At one point, McCone rather plaintively asked why Dulles insisted that McCone impose himself as a houseguest rather than stop at the local four-star hotel.

McCone was not impressed when his host loyally mumbled, "I suppose it was for security reasons."

"I've been in and out of that hotel for ten years," McCone said. "I've spent the last five days racing around the Continent, being entertained and examined by the chiefs of a half dozen intelligence and security services. I've met two prime ministers, half the foreign ministers in Western Europe, and a score of politicians, émigrés, and otherwise. As far as I can see, there can't be many people on the Continent who don't know I'm here. Who is Mr. Dulles hiding me from by insisting that I impose myself on you and your wife?"

McCone's host had known Dulles from OSS days. "It may be a security reflex, dating back a few years," he suggested loyally. "Mr. Dulles sometimes has two ways of looking at things. He has his own habits of operating, and rather likes showing the flag. Obviously, this works very well for him. The difference is, that with one or two exceptions, Mr. Dulles expects the rest of us to keep cover. Along with that, he damn well insists that we know our way around town and have a line on exactly who's who in our part of the world. Mr. Dulles never seems to have had any trouble riding both horses, but it can be a stretch for the rest of us."

McCone took another sip of bourbon.

On the eve of the visitors' departure, McCone's host had arranged for an in-house cocktail party for his two guests and a mix of senior and junior Agency staff. McCone was particularly interested in meeting as many of the overseas officers and families as possible. The reception came a few days after Heinz Felfe, a senior officer on General Gehlen's West German intelligence staff, had been exposed as a longtime KGB agent. Under close interrogation in a German prison, Felfe had begun to talk freely, if not entirely candidly. Because of the Agency's close relationship with Gehlen's service, we had a considerable stake in the damage Felfe had caused. In view of Dulles's intense interest in the case, I had prepared a long message covering some of Felfe's confession and addressed it to Dulles. My cable arrived in the local signal center at precisely the time the guests were assembling for the reception. At Allen's request the report—more than a dozen uncut pages, on a scroll of perforated paper just as it was torn from the Teletype machine—was brought directly to him.

As his host told us, Dulles pushed his glasses up onto his forehead, took a chair beside a fireplace, and began to study the incoming message. After a few moments he summoned two of the senior officers most concerned with the implications of Felfe's treason to read over his shoulder. A question arose, and one of the junior staff was beckoned to provide an explanation. After a page or two more had been read, there was another question and a second young officer was summoned into the circle.

McCone, who at the time could have had only the slightest knowledge of what was involved, remained at a distance, chatting with the other guests but clearly fascinated by the goings-on.

It was a sentimental vignette. Dulles, surrounded by two generations of operatives, savoring a final glimpse of field operations a few days before his retirement.

—

By the time Dulles and McCone returned from Europe, Lyman Kirkpatrick, the Agency inspector general, had finished the in-house study of the ZAPATA operation that Dulles had requested. Kirkpatrick—"Kirk" as we knew him—had been recruited for OSS by General Donovan.

After a hitch in London as an order-of-battle specialist, he ended the war as General Omar Bradley's intelligence briefing officer. Kirk joined CIA in 1947, and played an important role in the merging of the covert action and espionage elements of the Agency early in General Bedell Smith's term as DCI. He was a bright, aggressive, and well-organized staff intelligence officer. He preceded me quite briefly as Frank Wisner's deputy and chief of operations.

When Kirk contracted polio on a tour of our overseas posts in 1952 and suffered a long hospitalization, I was moved from chief of the Foreign Intelligence Staff to replace him on a temporary basis. Despite Kirk's partial recovery, it became apparent to Allen Dulles that even though Kirk had bravely undertaken another long trip at the end of his convalescence, his confinement to a wheelchair meant that he would never be sufficiently mobile to cope with the activities and stress associated with the chief of operations job. When Dulles confirmed me as Wisner's deputy, he appointed Kirk as the Agency's inspector general. This was an important position, but a bitter disappointment for Kirkpatrick, an ambitious man whose goal had been to become DCI after serving as deputy director for plans. As IG, Kirk felt that he had been removed from the command line.

Kirkpatrick's critique of the ZAPATA project covered much the same ground as General Taylor's report, but was harshly outspoken and severely critical. The report and thirteen attachments were printed in time for Kirk to hand a copy to John McCone on November 21, 1961. This came a week before McCone was to be officially sworn into office. With the document in hand, McCone boarded an airplane headed for the West Coast. Upon landing, he telephoned Kirkpatrick and instructed him to hand all copies of the report to Dulles. He then said in effect that he regarded Kirk's handling of the report that Dulles had commissioned as a self-serving breach of command channels and a lapse of courtesy. Furthermore, he added, he did not agree with all of the analysis nor the manner in which Kirkpatrick had expressed it.

Twenty copies of the report were printed. Three were circulated to the senior staff. One copy was sealed and placed in the DCI's personal safe. The remaining copies were destroyed. Some writers' assertions notwithstanding, the report was never "circulated" within the Agency. Aside from Dick Bissell, Tracy Barnes, and three of their senior operations officers, who collectively prepared a rebuttal to the report, only a handful of the most senior executives in CIA read it in 1961.

Under the terms of the Freedom of Information Act, the report was declassified in 1997, and presumably required reading in the study halls of the world's intelligence services. The report does not add anything significant to what was widely known at the time. Kirk's sweeping criticisms of the individuals involved in the operation—many of whom had worked themselves to the point of exhaustion—ranged from the White House staff to the lowest-ranking Agency and military personnel. Having known Kirkpatrick for a number of years, I can only assume that when he realized his career was stymied, he unconsciously allowed some of his personal disappointment to impinge on his judgment. Nevertheless, Kirk was to stand by his conclusions in subsequent correspondence with McCone.

In 1962, McCone recognized Kirk's experience and competence by naming him executive director of the Agency. Still in a wheelchair, Kirk retired three years later to accept an academic appointment at Brown University.

—

In aspect, McCone was another example of a man who might have stepped straight from central casting in Hollywood. His white hair, ruddy cheeks, brisk gait, impeccable dark suits, rimless glasses, aloof manner, and unmistakable self-confidence were the profile of a modern executive. He had an extraordinary memory and the ability to pick the essence from any document no matter how long or complex, and to reduce it to a few sentences. He grudgingly accepted the notion that any existing routines were useful—at least until they had been thoroughly tested. For McCone, deadlines were deadlines, and no matter if sometimes unrealistic, were to be met to the minute. He also knew that all manner of devils dwelt in the details.

McCone was a superb administrator. There were times when I suspected he may have felt that he had met his match in coping with some of the Agency's administrative procedures. Until he learned why some of our homegrown practices seemed less than business-like—they had to be bent around the demands of operational security—he was prepared to make a clean sweep. Efficiency and security are diametrically opposed concepts. One of the marks of a competent chief of operations is his ability to fine-tune the balance between efficiency and security in respect to the local operational climate.

One of my first meetings with the new DCI came in November 1961, sometime before the President's new approach to the Cuba problem surfaced. I was still Dick Bissell's deputy, but because it was widely known that he would soon be leaving, I acted in his place until my appointment as DDP in February 1962.

McCone began by reminding me forcefully of President Kennedy's intense concern with Cuba, and his determination "to be rid of Castro and the Castro regime." Then, without so much as an oral comma, he said that as of that moment I was the DCI's "man for Cuba." I said, "Yes, sir."

McCone offered no further elucidation, and I asked for none. In the preceding weeks, I had seen enough of the new boss to realize that it would have been a mistake to ask for further guidance. The existing command channel for our Cuba activity was, at best, improvised, and throughout the months of intense activity, had been subjected to innumerable ad hoc tinkerings. McCone assumed that having shown me that he was aware of the situation, I would know how to correct it and would do so without requiring any further discussion or direction. A meeting with Dulles on a problem like this would have been much more comfortable. After discussing the problem at some length, I would have been asked to suggest alternative command structures, and to recommend two or three officers capable of taking charge. McCone expected each of us to handle our own responsibilities, and it only took one occasion for the survivors to realize this.

That afternoon I removed the Cuba responsibility from the Cuba desk—a component of the Caribbean Islands branch of the Western Hemisphere Division, reporting through the chief of that division to Tracy Barnes of Dick Bissell's staff, and thence to Bissell himself—and established a task force directly under my command.

Bill Harvey, recently back from Berlin, had no experience in Latin America or the Caribbean when I named him chief of the Cuba task force. He was, however, an aggressive officer and a demanding and conscientious executive, and he had a good knowledge of the operations personnel he could count on. His first move was to christen his unit

"Task Force W." It was only later that I learned that the "W" stood for William Walker, an American adventurer who had been active in Nicaragua in the 1850s.

—

The code names for most Agency operations are picked in sequence from a sterile list, with care taken not to use any word that might give a clue to the activity it covers. On some large projects, code names are occasionally specially chosen—GOLD, SILVER, PBSUCCESS, CORONA. When Bob Kennedy requested a code name for the government-wide plan that Richard Goodwin was drafting, an exception was made. Goodwin was on the White House staff, and the plan concerned Cuba. Occasionally the special code names come close to the nerve, as did MONGOOSE.

Chapter 19

—

AN AGILE MAMMAL

From the moment John McCone told me I was to be his man on Cuba until the death of President Kennedy, not a day passed but that I spent some time—ranging from a dozen telephone calls and thirty-minute conferences in my office to half-day sessions in the executive offices at the White House—discussing Castro and his government. Dick Bissell was still DDP, but had stepped aside from most activity.

Richard Goodwin's plan for MONGOOSE established a "command operation" headed by Attorney General Robert Kennedy and General Taylor, with General Edward G. Lansdale as chief of operations. Given the intense White House pressure for action against Castro, the concept that the activity was to be government-wide was correct. On its own, the Agency could not possibly have handled the whole of MONGOOSE as conceived by the Kennedy administration. The proposed actions—a conventional list of almost every variety of intelligence and covert operation—were to be parceled out to the Pentagon, State Department, and various other agencies, some of which were not normally concerned with covert action or foreign policy.

I first heard of General Lansdale, then an Air Force lieutenant colonel, in 1950 when he was seconded to CIA and posted to a senior OPC position in the Philippines. Using his cover as an advisor to the

Philippine army, Lansdale helped the Philippine government put down the Huk guerrilla forces which had already brought significant areas of the country under their control. The Huk movement, a direct descendant of the Hukbalahap guerrillas who had fought the Japanese invaders, was under strong communist direction. Colonel Lansdale identified Ramon Magsaysay, a congressman, as a potential leader who with some guidance and support might be able to find a path between the established but corrupt right-wing politicians and the increasingly powerful left. With Lansdale's help, Magsaysay became secretary of defense, and was able to launch a series of military moves and political initiatives, including an important land reform program, which by 1953 had tamed the Huk movement and contributed directly to Magsaysay's eventual election as president.

In Washington, President Eisenhower recognized Lansdale's operation as a prime example of sophisticated political action. Not only had a guerrilla insurrection been put down, but Lansdale's behind-the-scenes activity had maneuvered Philippine political, military, and establishment figures into doing the job themselves. A corrupt government had been turned into a working democracy. It was a tour de force. Just about everything worked right.

Sometime after the Magsaysay election, Lansdale moved along to Vietnam. There things did not go as well. The linguistic, cultural, and political differences between the Philippines and Vietnam were, of course, profound. It was not surprising that Lansdale was never able to establish the intimacy with Ngo Dinh Diem that he had with Magsaysay.

This raises an interesting point. The affinity that Colonel Lansdale effected with Magsaysay was not unique. In some areas, in developed countries and otherwise, a few of our people were also able to create equally rewarding relationships with senior political or military figures. It was my experience that no matter how successful these few operatives were in one assignment, when transferred to another country, they were never able to repeat their success. Obviously a fluent language, depth of area knowledge, and a natural affinity for the local cultures played roles. But even in situations where our officer had the necessary language and reasonable area knowledge, it proved impossible to duplicate the close ties which existed in the earlier assignment.

Logic notwithstanding, at least two of the closest relationships flourished without the benefit of a truly common language. One senior foreign official was reduced to pleading with our man to forget about any more lessons in the local language and simply speak English. Despite months spent in intensive language study, our officer was another of the unfortunates who regardless of effort can never communicate in anything but their mother tongue. The depth to which this level of rapport can be developed often seems more the result of some indefinable social, political—conceivably even biological—chemistries than operational wizardry.

General Lansdale's appointment as chief of operations for MONGOOSE immediately raised jurisdictional problems. The notion that the various agencies were simply to detail men, money, and matériel to Lansdale was dead on arrival. Despite the attorney general's expectations and his persistent exhortations, none of the cabinet secretaries or department chiefs were able to skip lightly over the existing rules and practices of their own organizations.

The custom of appointing a "czar" to command an urgent, government-wide program can be counted on to comfort the less discerning members and supporters of a new administration and to play well at the call-in, talk-show level. In practice, I've noticed that the freshly ennobled czars are likely to find themselves entangled in the same administrative and fiscal procedures that confront the existing agencies. Worse, few newcomers have the experience to maneuver around the snarls which the old-timers have learned to avoid. As it happened in MONGOOSE, most department and agency chiefs were to learn that they had little choice but to make their contribution to the project according to prescribed procedures and, as a rule, at a tempo only marginally accelerated. The time lost in this process was one of the least problems the Kennedy administration faced in its struggle with Castro.

On January 18, 1962, General Lansdale assigned thirty-two tasks to the Departments of State, Defense, Commerce, and Treasury, as well as to CIA, USIA, the FBI, and the Immigration and Naturalization Service—the last being a newcomer in the covert action field.

The following morning, senior representatives of the various agencies and I were summoned to the attorney general's office for an initial discussion of the Lansdale directive. None of us had had time to respond to the specified activities—an entirely conventional listing of almost every variety of espionage and covert action technique.

As McCone's man for everything Cuban, the load landed right in my lap.

Despite the fanfare, the marching orders bore a discouraging resemblance to Dick Bissell's and Tracy Barnes's initial proposal to re-create their version of a European, World War II resistance movement in Cuba. The directive appeared no less of a pipe dream the second time around. The meeting did provide Bob Kennedy the opportunity to underline the President's position. With all of the customary Kennedy "vigor," and in the most forceful language, Bob informed us that Castro's removal from office and a change in government in Cuba were then the prime foreign policy objectives of the Kennedy administration.

The repeated blunt references to "eliminating" Castro brought us once again to the moral aberration of political assassination in peacetime. The details are to be found in the Senate Report No. 94-465, *Alleged Assassination Plots Involving Foreign Leaders,* dated November 20, 1975. This is not an easy document to fathom, but the basic data can be winnowed out. None of these efforts, which were first considered under the Eisenhower administration, offered anything but the slightest promise and, predictably, none went more than a step beyond the initial proposals.

The first approach of any consequence to eliminating Castro occurred in 1960, when the chief of the CIA Security Staff, who served in a separate CIA directorate, was authorized to contact Mafia members with the proposition that they arrange Castro's removal. The syndicate's presumed motive for engaging in this operation was to regain their properties in Cuba and, perhaps not incidentally, to gain some goodwill from the federal authorities who otherwise were intent on breaking up the Mafia and convicting its leadership. Although many promises were made, and planning went on for some time, the effort came to naught. As might have been predicted, none of the criminals ever got around to taking any action.

There is little to be said for intelligence agencies attempting to work clandestinely with organized crime—that is, all manner of racketeering and *any* aspect of the narcotics trade. Nor is there any reason to attempt to involve lower-level individual criminals in secret activity. Without exception in my experience, the criminals, organized or otherwise, who offer their services—or when solicited, agree to cooperate—have their own overriding agendas and motives. Aside from a romantic, if transient, glow of patriotism, the underworld invariably expects to be rewarded with an unwritten hunting license—in effect, an informal federal tolerance for some level of ongoing criminal activity. If this doesn't suffice, a bundle of $100 notes might be expected to seal the bargain.

The legends that OSS went about learning its business by employing second-story men to teach otherwise innocent college graduates the trade are nonsense. Professional criminals tend to spend their salad days in jail and their sunset years mousing about at the bottom of the employment market. There is nothing any of them might be able to accomplish in a foreign environment, and no "street smarts" they can pass along—except perhaps to suggest that low-level crime doesn't pay. When exposed to daylight, the so-called professional hit man is most often a thug who can only practice his trade at point blank, has never spent any time on a firing range, or even learned how to clean his weapons.

The approach to the Mafia began before I became DDP, and I was unaware of it until I replaced Bissell. After checking into it, I told Bill Harvey—who agreed entirely—to close it down.

Under relentless pressure from Bob Kennedy, we went to work. Before MONGOOSE had run its course, some 600 CIA staff employees and between 4000 and 5000 contract personnel were involved. Our activity ranged from establishing a refugee interrogation center—based on the model of the highly productive center we had earlier established in Germany—to a variety of sabotage and collection operations. Agents were established in Cuba; operations against Cuban installations abroad and efforts to recruit or defect Cuban officials were undertaken. Extensive propaganda operations were also initiated, but our attempts to create a unified émigré political movement were only marginally successful. The support structure for a nominally clandestine activity of this size was as complex as it was huge. At one point, the secret CIA navy was the third largest in the area. Yachts, fishing craft, speedboats, and supply vessels were modified for our purposes.

The steady flow of intelligence data and National Estimates showing that Castro's military and the internal security and foreign intelligence services were continuing to gain strength did not lessen the Kennedys' determination to even the score with Castro. However ambitious, our sabotage efforts never amounted to more than pinpricks. The notion that an underground resistance organization might be created on the island remained a remote, romantic myth.

Within a few weeks of Bob Kennedy's hammering us for results, I realized that he had but a slight idea of what was involved in organizing a secret intelligence operation. He appeared to equate the director of Central Intelligence position with that of the chief of the General Staff. If the President were to telephone the Pentagon and explain that he had urgent need for a hundred military officers—three generals, and an assortment of colonels and captains—chances are that a roster of professionally well qualified officers, unquestionably loyal to this country and prepared for immediate assignment anywhere in the world, would reach the White House by the close of business. I tried several times to convince the attorney general that the DCI would have rather more of a problem attempting to assemble a half dozen operationally and linguistically qualified, highly mobile secret agents.

Spies do not have any shelf life; they cannot be warehoused. Ninety-nine times out of a hundred, a spy is recruited for a specific assignment, usually to steal secret data, or to report on activity in which he is involved, or may observe. Other agents may be used to take some clandestine action. As a rule, a spy who has lost the insights for which he was hired is soon to become an ex-spy. He may be retained briefly while he tries to uncover access to something else of importance, but there is no way in which he can be held in readiness for a different assignment. One of the benchmarks of a well-run station is that it does not cling to spent spies. For deserving ex-agents—and as appropriate—a pension, severance pay, a Christmas gift, and a sterile, distant letter drop in the unlikely event something does come up are all to the good. Loyal and effective collaborators deserve to be left with a smile. Time spent attempting to retool a spy is better used in finding new sources.

A second category of agents is engaged in operational support. These activists may be used for surveillance—on the street, manning a photographic facility, planting and maintaining audio devices. Others might troll for new sources, or serve as a letter drop, a front for a safe meeting place—there are scores of clandestine support tasks that these agents perform. The most important strength of support agents is their knowledge of *exactly* how things work in their neighborhood, and their ability to slip quietly about their business without attracting so much as a glance. This ingrained area knowledge cannot easily be shifted to another city, and is quite impossible to export across a border. The little old ladies who may be convinced that they are serving as a drop for love letters or neighborhood busybodies who may think they are helping a private detective keep an eye on a straying husband obviously cannot be transplanted.

The point I repeatedly tried to make with Bob was that few shortcuts can be taken in recruiting agents. If even a reasonable level of security is to be maintained, recruitment can be a long process. The prospective agent has to be identified, and his apparent access to the information we are after must be determined before security checking can begin. In the sabotage and paramilitary operations which the President was most urgently pressing, agent selection was less complex. A politically motivated and physically fit young man able to undertake a paramilitary assignment did not need to be examined as carefully as someone involved in the penetration of a sensitive office. Even in MONGOOSE we had to collect enough personal data to permit records searches and background checks to be made before the candidate could be made aware of our interest. With luck and extra effort, these procedures might be pushed through in a ballpark average of about a month.

If this initial checking is satisfactory, a contact man has to be chosen and provided with cover. Cover was a persistent problem. These activists could not be grouped under a common cover—if one were blown, all would be compromised. Dozens of separate covers had to be devised and monitored. If the candidate accepted our initial proposal, he would then prepare a lengthy personal history statement that would be balanced against the data we had already assembled. The Cuban émigré community in Florida is closely knit, and at times seemed more nearly to be an extended family with long-standing interest in knowing how everyone is getting along.

If everything, or almost everything, checked out, only then could we begin recruitment discussions.

The six hundred Agency personnel we rallied in the course of Operation MONGOOSE were not spies as such, but operations officers and contract employees with varying stakes in career employment. Agency people can be moved on relatively short notice. This often creates serious problems for families with children in school, but it is a fact of life in our trade. The remaining people were agents or paramilitary activists of one sort or another—and had nothing but a passing, and usually part-time, relationship with the Agency. They could not be moved about or relocated without a commitment to future employment.

Bob Kennedy and I must have gone through this dialogue a dozen times. His consistent response was, "Yes, Dick, I do understand." A short pause would follow, and then, "But let's get the hell on with it. The President wants some action, right now."

And back to my office I would hustle.

For all the White House pressure, and the combined efforts of every-one involved, Operation MONGOOSE never quite lived up to the dic-tionary definition, "an agile mammal."

—

However shortsighted it now seems, there can be no denying that from the late 1940s until the advent of Castro, the Agency had neglected Latin and Central America and the Caribbean area. The fact that in World War II the area had been an FBI responsibility was only a small part of the problem. The root causes were the lingering momentum of the war in Europe and Asia, and the Cold War consensus that the basic national se-curity threat was the USSR, China, Southeast Asia, and international communism. The Agency's relatively belated attention to the Western Hemisphere also reflected Washington's long-standing on-again, off-again concern for our southern neighbors. Only when the Soviet Union began to exploit the situation did things change. At the time Castro seized Cuba, the Agency was adequately, if thinly, represented through-out the area. As Castro's impact became apparent, it was clear that im-mediate buildup was necessary. Even before Operation ZAPATA began to take shape, we also realized that we had too slight a reserve of deep area knowledge. After the Bay of Pigs, reinforcements came rapidly throughout the hemisphere.

—

After almost a year of intense effort, Bob Kennedy, as always speaking for his brother, scheduled the first annual review of the MONGOOSE operations. The timing could scarcely have been less fortunate.

CIA had within the previous twenty-four hours found the undeniable

facts against which we could test all of our previous reports and estimates. A flight of a CIA U-2 high-altitude photoreconnaissance aircraft
over Cuba had shown beyond doubt that Khrushchev had established,
and was probably in the process of arming, a number of intermediate-
range ballistic missiles in Cuba.

This opinion was based on the first interpretation of the U-2 films at
about 7 p.m. on October 15, 1962. McGeorge Bundy, the national security advisor, was alerted, and informed that it would be impossible to
prepare a detailed briefing—with enlarged photographs, maps, and
backup data—for President Kennedy before breakfast time. Kennedy
was in New York, engaged in whirlwind political campaigning, and was
not expected to be back at the White House until after midnight. Bundy
decided to wait until morning to brief the President.

Kennedy was bedside, reading the *New York Times,* when McGeorge
gave him the news.

Until President Kennedy and his closest advisors could be fully
briefed and the congressional leaders informed, the knowledge was
rigidly confined to the handful of persons with an absolute need to know.
Of those who would attend the MONGOOSE meeting, only Bob
Kennedy, General Lansdale, and I met that definition. We decided that
the abrupt cancellation of the annual review would tip too many people
to the looming crisis.

The other participants, all painfully aware of how far short of the
President's directives the MONGOOSE operation had fallen, were probably further depressed by what seemed to me to be the transparently nervous preoccupation of Bob Kennedy and General Lansdale. I suspect
that my own appearance was also less than reassuring. Aside from my
having to wrestle with the political and operational implications of the
situation in Cuba, my wife, Julia, was being readied for a bout of serious
and extremely delicate surgery in a New York hospital. There was one
final irony: John McCone, the only senior member of the Kennedy administration who was convinced that Khrushchev had been lying in his
teeth, was in California attending the funeral of his stepson, killed in a
motor racing accident. An Agency plane was dispatched to bring
McCone back to Washington. General Marshall Carter, his deputy, represented him.

Bob Kennedy opened the MONGOOSE annual review by expressing

the President's general dissatisfaction with the operation. He pointed out that although the project had been under way for a year, the results were very discouraging. There had been no successful acts of sabotage, and one such effort had failed twice. The President had acknowledged that there had been "a noticeable improvement . . . in the collection of intelligence but that other action had failed to influence significantly the course of events in Cuba." The attorney general went on to point out that despite the fact that Secretaries Rusk and McNamara, Director of Central Intelligence John McCone, General Taylor, McGeorge Bundy, and he *personally* had been charged by President Kennedy with finding a solution, only small accomplishments had been made.

Bob Kennedy then announced that henceforth he would meet at nine-thirty every morning with senior representatives of each agency involved in MONGOOSE. Given the travel time involved in getting about in Washington at that hour, and the impossibility of measuring progress on such a broad range of operations on a twenty-four-hour basis, there seemed to be more than a whiff of a disciplinary flavor in this decision.

It was almost three hours before the meeting disbanded and I could get back to the Agency for a reprise of the program with my own staff.

Despite my suspicion that rumors of the red-hot Cuban situation might have leaked, no indiscreet questions were raised, and no reference was made to what I knew would within hours become a gut-wrenching doomsday confrontation.

Chapter 20

—

FACING OFF

Is it true, Dick?" Bob Kennedy had asked. He spoke before I had got halfway across his expansive office.

"Yes, Bob, it surer than hell is absolutely true," I said. It was a quarter past nine o'clock on Tuesday, October 16, 1962, when I came into the attorney general's office. Kennedy was in shirtsleeves, his suit jacket draped over the back of a leather chair. A new collection of his children's watercolor paintings was posted along the wall at the side of Bob's document-littered desk.

Kennedy got up from the desk and stood for a moment staring out the window. He turned to face me. "Shit," he said loudly, raising both fists to his chest as if he were about to begin shadow boxing. "Damn it all to hell and back."

These were my sentiments exactly. The fact that late on October 15 we had established positive proof that Khrushchev, despite his earlier assurances to President Kennedy, was installing and probably arming medium-range ballistic missiles (MRBM) in Cuba spoke for itself. The essence of this proof was photographs taken by a U-2 aircraft and confirmed by agent observations on the ground. Within the Directorate for Plans, knowledge of the U-2 product was restricted to me, my deputy, Tom Karamessines, and a handful of senior officers.

Bob and I spent a few minutes sorting out a legal problem that Anatoli Golitsyn, a recent KGB defector, had encountered before Bob had to leave for a meeting of the Executive Committee and briefing on the U-2 data at the White House. EXCOM, as it was called, was the highest-level committee in Washington. Only the President, Secretary of State Dean Rusk, Secretary of Defense Robert McNamara, and National Security Advisor McGeorge Bundy were regular members. At the meeting that morning, Bob told me, the roster would read like a who's who in the Kennedy administration—Vice President Lyndon Johnson, General Maxwell Taylor, Douglas Dillon, George Ball, U. Alexis Johnson, Chip Bohlen, Ted Sorensen, Roswell Gilpatric, and Paul Nitze. General Carter would represent McCone, who was on his way back from California.

My immediate business with the attorney general finished, I hurried back to the Agency for an update on the gathering Cuba crisis, and to prepare for the meeting of the Special Group (Augmented) that afternoon. Bob had decided to go ahead with the session rather than risk alerting any outsiders to the likelihood that a crisis was on the boil before the President made a public statement. The only topic on the SPGA agenda was a review of the year's progress on Operation MONGOOSE. Aside from my preoccupation with the U-2 data and concern for Julia in the New York hospital, there was reason enough not to look forward to the meeting.

—

We had been busting our britches on the MONGOOSE operation, but aside from a marked improvement in intelligence collection—which was a considerable achievement—there was damn-all to show for it. Despite our maximum effort we had not inspired any resistance activity worth the name in Cuba; the—in my opinion, ill-advised—sabotage operations were but pinpricks. The political emigration was less than unified. Propaganda was, at the least, ongoing. It was the ouster of Castro and his unelected government that interested the President; the increase in intelligence was a by-product, no matter how helpful it was to the all-important production of sound National Intelligence Estimates.

The Agency's operational arm was stretched taut and thin. Our response to President Kennedy's demands had already resulted in what must have been the largest peacetime secret intelligence operation in history—some four to five thousand staff and contract personnel, acres of real estate, and a flotilla-size private navy.

Tales of Soviet weapons being seen on the island were crowding the press and electronic media. Senator Kenneth Keating of New York fueled the President's blazing frustration by repeatedly asserting on the Senate floor that offensive missiles were arriving in Cuba. Despite direct questions, the senator refused to disclose his alleged sources.

We had for some time been receiving reports that army personnel, heavy military equipment, and—at least allegedly—missiles of one variety or another were being off-loaded from Soviet ships. Other data indicated military installations were under construction in Cuba. There were so many reports that it was all but impossible to sort the imagined or fabricated information from the valid material. A mass of information came from debriefing refugees at our interrogation center in Opa-locka, northwest of Miami. Some of the data came from observers who had legal and plausible reason to visit the island; other reports originated with agents in place in Cuba. Literally thousands of these reports continued to flash and flicker across the horizon. Were they harmless like heat lightning or high-voltage, potentially lethal lightning bolts? We needed hard, checkable data against which we could test our product.

As always, agents resident in a denied area present difficult handling problems. Snags that would easily be resolved in an occasional face-to-face meeting were vastly more difficult to untangle in the brief radio messages or even in secret writing communications. In rural areas near the military bases and airfields we were attempting to keep under surveillance, the local people had little daily occasion to write anything, least of all something as taxing as an intelligence report. If we asked too detailed questions in following up on reports from agents in the field or even refugees at the interrogation center, we risked leading our sources, and inadvertently convincing them that they had seen the things we expected them to view. We also chanced the possibility that if our questions were too urgent, a source's imagination might be roused and his judgment dampened. Others might be moved to tell us what they thought we wanted to hear and, to enhance their reputation—in some cases perhaps income—be moved to fake a few observations. Incoming data had to be checked against every fact at our command.

I recall a report claiming that underground submarine pens had been constructed at Matanzas. Our analysts checked the geological structure of the shoreline and the crucial depths of the bay. There was water aplenty for an outboard-powered launch, but it was too shallow for even the smallest submarine. Another report alleged that light bombers were being stored in a cave. The analysts pulled our comprehensive speleological surveys of Cuba off the shelf and were able precisely to locate the cave in question. The survey showed that the cave curved sharply a few yards inside the entrance. There was room enough for a Jeep to maneuver, but no way an aircraft might negotiate even the first bend.

A merchant seaman provided a detailed description of what he thought might be a rounded concrete dome covering missiles. His report came with complete range and compass bearings taken from the pier at which his ship was docked. The analysts checked the sailor's data. The facts were perfect; the sailor's attention to detail was an unexpected treasure. It took a map of Havana and a recent city directory to establish the fact that the suspect dome covered a relatively new movie theater.

John McCone was increasingly sure that unless the President acted promptly, communist control of Cuba would soon reach a level that nothing short of a full-fledged military invasion would remove Castro from office. This was not a view that the President wanted to hear. As far as Kennedy was concerned, it was up to the CIA-sponsored sabotage and propaganda operations, and the indigenous Cuban resistance forces, to inspire open revolt. Dean Rusk and Robert McNamara were uneasy about any dramatic moves against Cuba; both were concerned about possibly dramatic Soviet initiatives in West Berlin, or against the Jupiter medium-range ballistic missiles the United States had earlier installed in Turkey.

Meanwhile our reports continued to show ships unloading military personnel, crated cargoes, and civilians, said to be "technicians," at Cuban ports. It was now without question that the Russians had installed surface-to-air missiles in Cuba. Despite this evidence, the consensus of the Soviet specialists in every pertinent Washington office was that the buildup was defensive—the surface-to-air missiles were merely anti-aircraft weapons. In the experts' opinion, Khrushchev had not violated his promise to Kennedy that only defensive weapons would be provided to Castro. There was only one dissenting voice.

All of the expert opinion notwithstanding, John McCone simply did not believe that Khrushchev would commit the newest version of his highly successful surface-to-air missiles, the SA-2, to Castro unless there was something vital to be protected. As McCone saw it, only the need to protect the medium-range ballistic missile sites would balance this equation. McCone's deductive logic was one thing, proof positive was another.

For some time the Agency had been authorized to fly occasional, relatively low-level photoreconnaissance missions as long as the aircraft remained a relatively safe fifteen miles off the Cuban shore. The rationale for this near-crippling caution was that if an aircraft were to be shot down, it could be said that the plane was a bit off course, but still over international waters. At best, the resolution of oblique photographs was far less productive—important targets were often hidden behind mountains or other structures—and much more difficult to interpret than direct, overhead pictures.

The high-altitude U-2 photography presented no such problems. But each U-2 mission over Cuba had to be authorized by the President. We tried to keep to a monthly schedule for these flights, but cloud cover and occasional equipment problems meant that some flights had to stand down. When this happened, President Kennedy insisted that we wait for the next scheduled mission. We were also enjoined to stay well away from what we called the business end of the island—the western area where the SA-2 surface-to-air missiles were most heavily concentrated.

After making another strong representation to President Kennedy to remove some of the restraints on operations over Cuba, and to review actions that might be taken before Khrushchev installed missiles in Cuba, McCone left for California. In his absence, General Marshall Carter was in charge.

Short of an operational windfall in the nature of an extraordinarily well placed agent, our best means of testing the flood of reports was high-altitude photography. As late as September 10, CIA flights were restricted to international waters and the relatively unrewarding Cuban areas less heavily protected by well-emplaced SA-2s.

From early September our various sources and U.S. Navy observation of the numerous Soviet ships en route to Cuba continued to show military buildup. With strong Pentagon support, General Carter pressed

McCone's request for permission to conduct overflights of the most heavily protected areas of the island. In the White House, the recent loss in China of a U-2 plane flown by Chinese Nationalists and the inadvertent straying of an Air Force manned U-2 over the USSR added a measure of sensitivity to the possible flights over Cuba. To my considerable satisfaction, it was a report from a spy that triggered permission for the U-2 to undertake its history-making mission.

On September 12 an observer agent, the lowest man in the secret intelligence hierarchy, reported that missiles were being moved into a roughly sketched trapezoid area reaching from San Cristóbal in the southeast to San Diego de los Baños in the southwest, and from Consolacíon del Norte in the northwest and Las Pozas in the northeast. At first the report seemed like another well-meant but not very closely observed collection of bits and pieces. After extensive examination, the agent's information proved to square with other reports from the area—notably considerable military traffic, and long, canvas-cloaked trucks moving like scythes, toppling telegraph poles along narrow village street corners before disappearing into restricted areas in the nearby countryside. Cuban country roads and the Red Army's seventy-foot trailer trucks were highly incompatible.

This was the spur the White House needed, and U-2 overflights of the San Cristóbal area were authorized. It was four days before the weather cooperated, but minutes before midnight, on October 13, a U-2 took off from Edwards Air Force Base in California and headed for San Cristóbal, Cuba. If everything went according to the flight plan, and it was the hurricane season, Major Richard S. Heyser, the pilot, would be some 70,000 feet—roughly fourteen miles—above his target by 7:30 a.m. on October 14. At that altitude, the remarkably high-definition film permitted resolution to some thirty inches—not quite enough to limn a football, as some press accounts have suggested, but quite good enough to spot a Soviet soldier perched on an open privy a discreet two hundred yards from an MRBM site in Cuba.

For all of its technical marvels, the U-2 was an extremely delicate aircraft—"an eggshell with wings"—and at its best, very difficult to fly. Before qualifying for six months of special U-2 training, a pilot had to have had at least a thousand hours' flight time in single-engine jet aircraft. Despite its altitude capability, the U-2 was vulnerable, as we had learned over the USSR, to the Soviet SA-2 surface-to-air missile. Turbulence, through which a conventional photoreconnaissance aircraft might pass while merely jostling the pilot, was known to have snapped the wing from a U-2.

Major Heyser reached the Isle of Pines at 7:31 a.m. EST, a few seconds off schedule. Twelve minutes later, he switched off the cameras and headed for McCoy Air Base in Orlando, Florida. It was, as he put it, a "milk run." Given the developing crisis, it might also be counted as one of the most significant reconnaissance missions in history.

In the tradition of a tired pony express rider flinging saddlebags to a colleague on a fresh horse, the film—an entire roll being five thousand feet long—was rushed to a waiting aircraft and hustled to the Naval Photographic Intelligence Center in Suitland, Maryland.

While the highest level of foreign policy, defense, and intelligence officials—and a relative handful of their most senior staff officers who were cleared for U-2 product—waited for the results of this mission, others continued to deal with the more routine aspects of the developing crisis.

It was mid-morning on the sixteenth before President Kennedy had his first glimpse of the U-2 photographs. What most of us might have identified as the early digging of a cellar for a private home was in the view of the photo-analysts a part of the unmistakable footprint of an SS-4, medium-range ballistic missile (MRBM) launching site. Later, when the Russians had further developed the launching area, Bob Kennedy remarked that it looked "like a football field badly in need of new turf."

Arthur C. Lundahl, whom Dick Bissell had brought into the Agency in 1953 to organize a photographic intelligence center, had begun his work in aerial photography in Alaska during World War II. Art was not only an outstanding scientist, but also had great skill in presenting vastly complicated scientific data to nonspecialists. Standing to one side as the President bent over to study the photographic evidence—prepared in some forty-eight hours of around-the-clock work by the photo center staff—Art answered the President's first question.

"Are you sure these are MRBM sites?"

"Yes, Mr. President," Lundahl said. "I am as sure of this as a photo-interpreter can be of anything."

As the briefing continued, Lundahl was able to answer each of the President's questions. How long will it be before the rockets are ready to fire? (Three days.) This answer gave the President a good idea of how much time he had left to negotiate before possibly taking military action to neutralize the weapons. What is the range of the SS-4? (About one thousand nautical miles.) How accurate are they? (The CEP—circular error of probability—is from a mile to a mile and a half.) Can more than one missile be fired from the same platform? (Two and perhaps three can be fired from one launcher. Refire time is five hours.) How many sites are there? (As of this morning, three sites with four launchers on each have been identified. We think more will be found.) What is the throw weight of the SS-4? (From twenty-five kilotons to two megatons.)

There was one final glum observation. The U-2 photographs revealed two SS-5 intermediate-range missile sites under construction. These weapons had a range of over two thousand miles, sufficient to reach many major cities in the continental United States, and much of eastern Canada and northern South America.

Lundahl's answers were based on the entire spectrum of information available to the Agency—the debriefing of defectors and refugees, communications intercepts, analysis of press and scientific literature, diplomatic reports, overhead photographic reconnaissance, and agents in place in Cuba and the USSR. A more telling example of the interplay between analysis and human and technical sources could hardly be found.

I am scarcely an impartial observer, but in looking back at the exhausting thirteen days when a single misstep might have led to a nuclear confrontation and possibly war, I confess to a certain pride in the CIA's operational role. From the Cuban farmer's first signal to the Agency, to the revolutionary U-2 aircraft and fabulous photographic equipment that Dick Bissell had brought to life, to the CIA agent in Moscow who had access to the innermost secrets of the Soviet nuclear arms and missile programs, CIA had served its purpose.

The intense intelligence, diplomatic, political, and military activity that followed the briefing of the President have been dissected and analyzed to a fare-thee-well, and the results published in scores of books and articles. Still, it seems to me that one important element in the face-off between the two nuclear powers has been slighted in the retelling. McGeorge Bundy, President Kennedy's national security advisor, and the one person in the White House who was most directly concerned with the intelligence services, is a case in point.

Sometime after the October 16 briefing of President Kennedy, Ray Cline (later the CIA deputy director for intelligence) became convinced that the U-2 photographs of the surface-to-surface missiles (SS-4s) at San Cristóbal were the key to the successful resolution of the crisis.

When the crisis subsided, Ray asked both Bob Kennedy and McGeorge Bundy if they would tell him "how much that single evaluated piece of photographic evidence [the San Cristóbal SS-4 sites] was worth . . . they each said it fully justified all that CIA had cost the country in all its preceding years."* The key word in the question Ray posed is "evaluated." Without the data supplied by Colonel Oleg Penkovsky, code name HERO, an agent in place in Moscow, the photographs could not have been evaluated in detail, and the precise capability of the SS-4 MRBM and other missiles could not have been made known to the President. Nor would the President have known how much time he might have to negotiate before taking military action to destroy the missiles.[†]

McGeorge Bundy had apparently forgotten his comment when, in an interview with Michael R. Beschloss, he remarked in effect that he thought Penkovsky's importance had been exaggerated in the literature of the period.[‡] Bundy then noted that in the text of his own book he had managed to avoid even a single reference to the spy.[§] This will pass for a gratuitous comment on a man who of his free will, and at the cost of his life and the well-being of his wife and family, had volunteered his ser-

---

*Ray Cline, *Secrets, Spies and Scholars* (Washington, D.C.: Acropolis, 1978), p. 197.

[†]Dino A. Brugioni, a longtime CIA officer, supervised all of the Agency's aerial photography and briefing material during the missile crisis. His book *Eyeball to Eyeball* (New York: Random House, 1991) is an excellent inside account of the crisis.

[‡]*The Crisis Years: Kennedy and Khrushchev, 1960–1963* (New York: HarperCollins/Burlingame, 1991), p. 768.

[§]*Danger and Survival: Choices About the Bomb in the First Fifty Years* (New York: Random House, 1988).

vices to the United States, the United Kingdom, and the free world. While pondering Bundy's views I was reminded of a comment made by Richard Wilmer Rowan in 1937. In remarking on what he called "the Great-Man treatment of history," Rowan writes that "the great men themselves, when composing memoirs or correcting the grade of their eminence, have been disposed to protect their spies . . . even those safely deceased—by preserving their anonymity and resisting the temptation to divide with them the credit which otherwise must burden the narrator alone. Concern for the ultimate security of the spy is never so acute . . . as when the time comes to save him from his . . . share in the public acclaim."*

In the two years before his execution, Penkovsky supplied CIA and the British Secret Intelligence Service more than five thousand pages of highly classified Soviet missile data, war plans, and military and political intelligence. This information was without question a fundamental part of the data that permitted President Kennedy to make the decisions that avoided the possibility of a nuclear showdown and perhaps war.

Unlike Lieutenant Colonel Popov, the first GRU officer to offer his services to CIA, Colonel Penkovsky moved in the upper bracket of Soviet society. Popov was born a peasant. Only a series of extraordinary coincidences allowed him to fight his way from the dirt floor of his peasant home to a commission in the Red Army and assignment to the intelligence service. In contrast, Penkovsky came from the upper-middle class, and could plausibly have claimed fringe membership in the lesser nobility in Russia. His father was a mining engineer who died in the 1920s as an officer in the White Army, fighting the Bolsheviks. From the time he was accepted into the Young Communist League (Komsomol) and commissioned as an artillery officer, Penkovsky was able to fudge the details of his father's past sufficiently to allow himself to become recognized as a promising officer. He married the daughter of a lieutenant general, and as a result of his wartime service attracted the attention of another senior officer. General Sergei Varentsov, who was

*Richard Wilmer Rowan with Robert G. Deindorfer, *Secret Service: 33 Centuries of Espionage* (New York: Hawthorn, 1967), p. 1. First published in 1937 as *The Story of the Secret Service.*

subsequently appointed chief marshal of artillery, came to regard Penkovsky as a surrogate son.

After his graduation from the Frunze Military Academy and the Military Diplomatic Academy, Penkovsky was assigned to the GRU, Soviet military intelligence service.* By 1960, and his promotion to colonel, Penkovsky feared that because of his father's background, he might never be cleared by the KGB for promotion to general. In the eyes of the security service, it did not matter that Penkovsky was only four months old when his father died.

Like most volunteer agents, Penkovsky's motives were complex. The faults, weaknesses, and corruption that Lenin and Stalin had inflicted on Russia were all too obvious. Through no fault of his own, Penkovsky felt that his career was frustrated. From what he had seen of the West, he admired the political system and envied the comfortable life and personal freedom offered by the capitalist democracies. Penkovsky was acutely aware of the threat the USSR posed to the West, and was convinced that the easygoing democracies seriously underestimated the peril they faced. He had a taste for the good life, and took risks to enjoy it. But this danger was a remote second to the ultimate peril he faced in his role as a penetration agent.

From the moment Penkovsky passed a letter to two young American tourists in Moscow in August 1960 to the scores of hours spent in London and Paris with his case officers, the brush meetings and the servicing of

---

*The GRU collected military and political intelligence abroad and was responsible for the security of the armed services. The KGB had both internal security and foreign counterintelligence responsibilities, and also collected intelligence abroad. Although the missions of the two services overlapped and caused continuous bickering, neither the KGB nor the GRU had the slightest compunction about engaging in operations theoretically the province of the other. In the early days and through World War II, the GRU was the stronger intelligence collection service, and its personnel and methods were more sophisticated than those of the KGB predecessor organizations—the Cheka, OGPU, NKVD, and NKGB. The parallel activity of the services permitted Alger Hiss to deny that he worked for the KGB, and for his supporters to come up empty-handed after a cursory glance at selected KGB files. The GRU files will reflect a different history. By the mid-1950s, the espionage element of the KGB had shaken much of its secret police mentality and had begun the recruitment of educated and linguistically competent young officers, well qualified to work abroad. The KGB continued to flourish and was to become the more powerful and senior of the Soviet intelligence organs.

dead drops in Moscow, and the anxious time snapping some five thousand photographs—and incidentally exhausting two Minox cameras—his life was on the line. The dust of the missile crisis was still very much in the air when the operation came to term. On November 2, 1962, a signal from Penkovsky informed us that he had placed an urgent message in a Moscow dead drop. A few hours later, our young embassy employee was arrested while attempting to service Penkovsky's dead drop. Penkovsky's arrest had come some weeks earlier, after a long and sophisticated surveillance. Our after-action assessment of the operation showed no indication of deception until the time of his arrest.

As always with a "walk-in," as we irreverently referred to volunteer agents, the first consideration is the possibility of provocation. Was the chap sent to us by an opposing intelligence or security service interested in eventually deceiving us, or was he merely to provoke a glimpse of our personnel and clandestine facilities? The next step is quickly to determine if the volunteer is the person he says he is, and thus has plausible access to the information he is offering—that is, might he be a self-serving fraud, intent on improving his fortune? These protective procedures are practiced around the globe, from the quietest diplomatic and intelligence backwaters to the most exposed and sensitive posts in hostile police states. In the USSR, we had, of course, long since learned that the KGB and its sister intelligence and security services were masters of provocation and deception operations. The Russians did not invent these operations—although the czars' various police organs left a rich heritage for the KGB to build on—but they may claim to have developed the techniques to a near art form.

The details of how we determined Penkovsky's bona fides—and verified his position in Soviet intelligence, traced his career from his field assignment in Turkey, and learned of his persistent, friendly approaches to American, Canadian, and British officials—are spelled out in *The Spy Who Saved the World.** The extreme sensitivity of our limited facilities in the USSR mandated a most cautious response to Penkovsky's approach in Moscow. In 1960 an important part of Ambassador Llewellyn "Tommy" Thompson's mission was to improve relations with the

---

*Jerrold L. Schecter and Peter S. Deriabin (New York: Scribner's, 1992). This excellent book gives an informed, inside view of the entire Penkovsky operation.

USSR. Thompson was an accomplished diplomat and expert on the Soviet Union. Understandably, he did not want to risk giving the impression that the Moscow embassy was a nest of spies. In view of the repeated, and often successful, KGB efforts to compromise and blackmail Western diplomats with just such provocations as Penkovsky seemed to offer, Ambassador Thompson insisted that Penkovsky be kept far away from any official American installation in the USSR. In the ensuing weeks, as we struggled to rig a secure response to Penkovsky's offer, there were moments when I thought it might remain just beyond our reach. As it turned out, it was Penkovsky who, with almost unbelievable luck, solved the problem.

After waiting four months to hear from us, Penkovsky undertook a series of bold—all but foolhardy—approaches to British and Canadian businessmen and diplomats. Today, when diplomats, businessmen, and tourists move around in Moscow as casually as they might in downtown Dubuque, Iowa, it is difficult to comprehend the extent to which the Soviet security organs monitored the movement and activity of foreigners in the USSR. This level of surveillance made it possible for the KGB to launch provocations and blackmail operations on a uniquely sophisticated level. I recall at least two foreign ambassadors, various high-ranking embassy and military personnel, and numerous clerks who fell victim to these operations. Tourists and others without diplomatic immunity were also at risk of arrest and blackmail.

These provocations and blackmail operations served another important KGB purpose. For the Western powers, the best defense against these operations was to advertise this KGB practice and to warn officials and private persons against accepting any documents or letters proffered by apparently well-meaning Russians. To the degree these warnings were effective, we will never know what legitimate offerings and opportunities we may have missed.

In view of the tight surveillance the KGB maintained over all foreigners, it was nothing short of a miracle that Penkovsky's repeated attempts to contact us escaped KGB notice. This was such an exception to the rule that it was not until Penkovsky's initial reports were evaluated and proved to be of such great sensitivity and value, we felt reasonably sure the bold approach was not the first step in some high-level deception effort. On my staff, even Jim Angleton, the ultra-cautious counterintelligence chief, agreed that Penkovsky's reports were entirely too revealing ever to have been used to authenticate a deception operation.

Because Penkovsky eventually succeeded in reaching British officials with his request for contact with us, and in respect to our long-standing relationship, we agreed to join forces in handling the Penkovsky operation. Joint operations are usually to be avoided for reasons ranging from petty to profound—methods are different, egos clash, routine procedures tangle. The Penkovsky operation was an exception. Harnessed in tandem, our combined facilities were much enhanced. The extraordinary value of Penkovsky's reporting smoothed the few kinks that developed.

The Cuban missile crisis ended on November 2, 1962, when the Soviets began dismantling the missiles and destroying the launching sites.

Colonel Penkovsky was brought to trial in May 1963 with Greville Wynne, a British businessman who had served as a contact man. Wynne was sentenced to eight years' "deprivation of liberty."* Penkovsky was found "guilty of treason to the Motherland" and sentenced to be shot to death. On May 17, *Pravda* announced that "O. V. Penkovsky had been executed."

Here I want to put two often cited notions about the Penkovsky operation to rest. From the outset, every bit of operational and intelligence reporting on this activity went across my desk. I received all the incoming traffic and released all the outgoing messages. For reasons not clear to me, Greville Wynne, who performed bravely throughout the operation, has alleged that he had accompanied Penkovsky to Washington for a secret meeting with President Kennedy. Penkovsky would surely have enjoyed such a trip, and President Kennedy, who would probably have thought I was mad to ask, might conceivably have agreed to meet the spy. More to the point, had the opportunity for any such visit been remotely possible, neither I nor my British colleague would have agreed to run any such lunatic risk. Even if the weather and aircraft involved promised to cooperate perfectly, we could not possibly have permitted Penkovsky to drop from the sight of his Soviet colleagues for the two days likely to be involved in such an undertaking.

---

*In April 1964, Wynne was exchanged for Gordon Lonsdale, a Soviet agent who had been imprisoned in England.

It has also been alleged that Penkovsky (and before him, Lieutenant Colonel Popov) were not shot but were burned alive in the presence of some of their colleagues. However sensational, there is no evidence to support this grisly notion. It may have sprung from the fact that in the aftermath of an execution, an officer must be present to certify that the cremation was performed.

Colonel Oleg Vladimirovich Penkovsky and Lieutenant Colonel Pyotr Popov deserve the respect and gratitude of us all. Their story needs no imagined embroidery. The truth is drama enough.

Chapter 21

—

KHRUSHCHEV
BLINKS

As the crisis with the Soviet Union in Cuba developed and ran its course, I was fully occupied with focusing the Agency's espionage operations on every possible aspect of the confrontation. This kept me a step away from those at the EXCOM level who had the lonely responsibility for dealing firsthand with the very real possibility of nuclear war. From October 16, when President Kennedy was shown proof that nuclear weapons were being installed and armed in Cuba, to October 28, when Khrushchev informed Kennedy that the "Soviet Government has ordered the dismantling of bases and the return of [the] equipment to the USSR," the U.S. government and the country at large had functioned admirably. In the face of a possible nuclear war, there was no panic in the streets, and the President presided over his administration with what today strikes me as considerable wisdom. He marshaled his forces prudently, balanced sage advice against various hotheaded or weak-kneed proposals, and navigated a steady course to the best possible result.

It is commonplace to note that we will never know how good a president Kennedy might have become. Maybe so. But there is evidence enough to support plausible speculation.

In the weeks leading up to the missile crisis, Bill Harvey and Robert Kennedy had crossed swords several times, and I had more than once advised Bill to remember that in arguing with Robert Kennedy he was also taking on his older brother. Unfortunately, my counsel had little effect.

If one were to cast about for someone positively calculated to rub against every grain of Bill Harvey's being, the chance of finding anyone who might fit the measure more closely than Robert Kennedy would have been zero. To say that Bill was paunchy would have been a mistake—he was much more than hefty. Robert was lithe. Bill was Indiana and University of Kentucky. From his underpants to button-down shirt, Bob was East Coast and Ivy League. Bill had earned his way in life without the benefit of family influence. Bob was born to the manor, and as a young man he took the best of everything for granted. In office, Bob spoke with the full backing of his brother. Harvey had the DCI's confidence and mine, but when he spoke with Bob it was as a lieutenant dealing with a general. Harvey was never to see it that way.

I doubt that anyone could have done a better job of attempting to run our part of the MONGOOSE project than Harvey did. He was a compulsive worker, and had all but exhausted himself attempting to draft plans and create operations that would win Bob's approval and that of General Lansdale. Viewed from our side of the fence, the oral directives of both these men were often inconsistent, and too frequently subject to abrupt changes. A few weeks before the missile crisis, Bill's frustration with trying to carry out a string of next-to-impossible missions while satisfying the two totally different senior people, neither of whom had more than a slight notion of what was involved in agent operations, became impossible for him to hide. I no longer remember what it was that fired the explosion, but in early September, Harvey and Robert Kennedy tangled in an all-out oral donnybrook. No matter that the incident which ended their relationship came as the result of honest misunderstandings on both sides: Bill Harvey was persona non grata with Robert Kennedy and the White House.

This was not the moment I would have chosen to make any such serious a personnel change, but things had gone too far for any attempt to restore the relationship. As an interim solution, I assigned responsibility for liaison with Robert Kennedy and his staff to Harvey's deputy, Bruce Cheever, who had come back from Europe to join Task Force W. Although relieved of the responsibility for personal liaison with Robert Kennedy, Harvey would continue in place until a replacement could be found. The job required an experienced senior officer who was aggressive, fast on his feet, wise in the ways of Washington, socially adroit, and quick to learn.

By the time the missile crisis had subsided, I had chosen Desmond FitzGerald as Harvey's replacement.

"Des," as he was known, was never in OSS but he might well have been—he was a prototype of the score or so top-drawer, impeccably well connected New Yorkers who populated the earliest OSS cadre. Unlike many of his coevals, he marched to his own drum. A few days after Pearl Harbor, Des enlisted as a private soldier. He was thirty years old, with a wife—Marietta Peabody, a New England socialite, who later married a British diplomat, Ronald Tree—and a daughter, Frances, and a son to whom he was devoted. After a severe dose of rugged combat service with General Joseph Stilwell and Chinese troops in the China-Burma theater, Major FitzGerald returned to New York. Despite a flirtation with New York politics and a promising future with his law firm (Hotchkiss Spence), Des welcomed the CIA job that his friend Frank Wisner offered him. This time, he did not start out as a buck private—his first assignment was as executive officer in the Office of Policy Coordination element of the Agency's Far East Division. It was in covert action that Des found his Agency métier.

One might have expected—or so it seems given this passage of time—a moment of relaxation after Khrushchev directed the destruction of the missile sites. This was not to be. Although as part of the negotiation President Kennedy had forsworn attempting any invasion of Cuba, he and his brother remained absolutely determined to trounce Castro once and forever. Having been relieved of the manifest impossibility of raising and transporting an indigenous invasion force, the MONGOOSE operation came slowly back to reality. Along with penetrating Castro's government at home and his installations abroad, I was also directed to contain Castro's effort to export his revolution, blunt his efforts to inflame political disaffection throughout the hemisphere, and negate any Cuban attempt to support the overthrow of possibly vulnerable governments. This was a full basket, but more nearly within the grasp of the Agency than the original MONGOOSE conception.

From the months that followed the crisis, one incident remains in mind. President Kennedy placed a high priority on uncovering "hard evidence" of any violation of Khrushchev's commitment that Castro might be tempted to make. In short order, "hard evidence" became the hot expression of the day. Without this level of data, I learned, accurate secret intelligence from a merely reliable source was not thought good enough. It seemed that everyone within earshot of the President had developed such a penchant for mentioning hard evidence when discussing any aspect of our reporting that the expression became one word, "hardevidence."

Robert Kennedy was still the President's man for all things Cuban. As before, the intensity of Bob's interest reflected, and sometimes seemed to magnify, the President's preoccupation with Cuba. Bob's persistent demand for irrefutable proof of Castro's violation of any of Khrushchev's post–missile crisis agreements also came directly from the President.

We had for some time been quietly monitoring Castro's relations with a fringe revolutionary group in Venezuela. In November 1963 an agent informed us that Castro's operatives were about to land some three tons of small arms, ammunition, and mortars on the Venezuelan coast. The plan, as concocted in Havana and slipped to us by our agent, was to use the weapons to paralyze the Venezuelan government in time to halt the national election slated for December 1. Castro's notion was that two or three terrorist bombs in the vehicular tunnel in Caracas and a few rounds of mortar fire would cause enough panic and confusion to allow the revolutionaries to seize the government and overthrow President Rómulo Betancourt, "a bourgeois liberal" and one of Castro's many bêtes noires.

The boldness of this undertaking was more an earnest of Castro's ambition than a tribute to his assessment of the revolutionary potential in Venezuela. Conditions in some areas of Central America would have provided a more fertile ground for armed revolution than Venezuela.

Castro's scheme was a clear violation of the policy agreement that followed the missile crisis, and came almost exactly a year after the press conference in which President Kennedy had pledged peace in the Caribbean if all offensive weapons were removed from Cuba, *and* if Cuba ceased attempting to export its aggressive communist objectives.

With the desk officer for the operation alongside to answer technical questions, I called on Robert Kennedy late in the afternoon on November 19, 1963, with one of the Belgian-made submachine guns we had filched from the arms cache. In an effort to conceal the origin of the weapons, the Cubans had attempted to scrape away the Cuban army shield and serial numbers the guns had originally borne. Fortunately, one of our technicians* had developed an acid which, when applied to the filed area, rendered the original markings legible. There was one hitch—the restored markings faded from the blue steel barrel in a matter of seconds. Worse, our acid treatment could be applied only twice before the markings faded permanently away. A complex bit of photography solved the problem.

The attorney general heard us out, and studied the photographs. After rather reluctantly surrendering the gun, he picked up the telephone. Half an hour later we were in the White House, answering the President's questions as he studied the photographs spread out on a coffee table in the Oval Office and examined the submachine gun. How, the President asked, did the Cubans get three tons of ordnance to the beach? Fortunately, Castro's *Fidelistas* had in effect answered the President's question. In the process of getting smartly away from the scene of the crime, the Cubans had overlooked one of their outboard-powered launches. It had been left where they beached it, two hundred yards from the weapons cache.

When the meeting ended, the President arose from his rocking chair and stood beside the coffee table looking toward the Rose Garden. I leaned over and took the submachine gun from the coffee table and slipped it back into the canvas airline travel bag in which we carried it— unchallenged—from the parking lot to the President's office. As the President turned to shake hands, I said, "I'm sure glad the Secret Service didn't catch us bringing this gun in here."

The President's expression brightened. He grinned, shook his head slightly, and said, "Yes, it gives me a feeling of confidence."

My colleague and I then went out one of the French doors opening onto the portico. As we walked away, we could see the President again signing mail. He had interrupted work on his correspondence to take us into his office for the briefing.

That afternoon, it occurred to me that I did not have one of the customary autographed photographs of President Kennedy. I called Kenneth O'Donnell at the White House. "Of course," he said, "I'll take care of it."

Three days later, President Kennedy was murdered.

*Lee Vagnini, a forensic chemist.

—

John McCone and I had spent the morning of November 22 with PFIAB (the President's Foreign Intelligence Advisory Board) and on our return to the Agency were having lunch in a small room adjoining the DCI's offices. On the remote chance that some DCI might inadvertently have to deal with back-to-back visitors, neither of whom would want the other to see him on these premises, Allen Dulles had designed this space as a holding area. For reasons unknown to me—but certainly not as some writers have suggested as a tribute to a foreign intelligence service—the chamber became known as the "French Room."

We had not finished our sandwiches when the door flew open, and one of McCone's aides who had been following the President's trip to Texas on live TV in a nearby office brought the news of the shooting in Dallas. McCone picked up the phone to check with the Agency Crisis Watch Committee. A few moments later, he clapped on his hat and left to meet Robert Kennedy at his home at Hickory Hill, not far from the Agency headquarters. Despite occasional head banging over MONGOOSE and their age difference, Bob Kennedy and John McCone had become friendly.

As I rushed for the elevator to my office I had a few moments to phrase the book message I would send to all of our overseas offices. Despite the time-zone differences around the world, there was clearly no need to inform any overseas post of the assassination. The most obvious message would be a flash instruction to everyone everywhere to forward every scrap of information possibly dealing with the actual assassination and any bit of information conceivably pointing to a plot involving any foreign power. I was satisfied that in responding to any such message, the more senior of our office chiefs would have the judgment to screen out any manifestly lunatic rumors or allegations. I was less sure that some of our more junior people in isolated posts would be in a position to make such a judgment and—better safe than sorry—might upend the barrel for any allegations, no matter how wild. Once transmitted, any urgent message on such a sensitive subject would perforce be immediately disseminated in Washington and would forever remain a part of the permanent record. If sent by priority cable precedence, such a message would be evaluated and disseminated with appropriate comment on the possible validity of the content. This would avoid creating any unnecessary alarm, but would, of course, also be part of the permanent record.

By the time I reached my office, Elizabeth Dunlevy had notebook and pencil in hand. Within a few minutes we had prepared a priority book message: "Tragic death of President Kennedy requires all of us to look sharp for any unusual intelligence developments. Although we have no reason to expect anything of a particular military nature, all hands should be on the quick alert at least for the next few days while new president takes over reins."

The events concerning that ever-so-sad day have all been laid bare and documented. I have only a few observations to make. First, all of the speculation and conspiratology notwithstanding, I have not seen anything, no matter how far-fetched or grossly imagined, that in any way changes my conviction that Lee Harvey Oswald assassinated Kennedy, and that there were no co-conspirators. Furthermore, I know of no information whatsoever that might have any bearing on the assassination that has been concealed from the public.

Two incidents involving the Agency bear mention here. In mid-October 1963, Des FitzGerald came to my office. For some time, Task Force W had been in contact with a Cuban we referred to as AMLASH. He was both a medical doctor and a Cuban army colonel. He had also known the Castro brothers from his early days in the student movement. From the outset of his contact with us, AMLASH had repeatedly expressed his intention to overthrow Castro by means of a military coup, and had identified a number of ranking officers whom he assured us shared his view. Although we were satisfied that AMLASH was pretty much as he presented himself to us—he really was on friendly terms with Fidel Castro and even closer to Raúl—he remained something of an unknown quantity. His intelligence reports were of interest, but considering his personal relations with Castro, not very revealing. Given the relentless, blistering heat from the White House, I was scarcely of a mind to drop anyone whom we were satisfied had a reasonable access to Castro, and who was apparently determined to turn him out of office.

AMLASH had strong views on how such a coup might succeed. He was opposed to any scheme involving the creation of a network of kindred activists, and was convinced that any carefully worked-out operational plan would be compromised long before action might be taken.

His idea, and it struck me as plausible, was that in time some incident might suddenly offer the opportunity for spontaneous action by the like-thinking senior officers who were secretly opposed to Castro. AMLASH did not plan to assassinate Castro, but he repeatedly made it clear that any coup would likely fail unless, in the process, Castro and the strongest of his followers were, as he put it, "taken out" before they could regroup and retaliate against the coup leaders.

As presented by AMLASH, his plan seemed to fit the White House conception—a revolution in Cuba, by Cubans, with a minimum of support from abroad.

Our contacts with AMLASH were necessarily restricted to his occasional trips abroad with athletic teams or as a member of some visiting Cuban delegation. He was now in Paris, and once again sketching the possibility of a military coup. Before taking any further action, AMLASH had informed our contact man that he would not move without some face-to-face, high-level assurance that he could count on the political backing of the United States. To no one's surprise, Robert Kennedy was AMLASH's contact of choice.

In my experience, most politically oriented émigrés and a few of the more senior agents in place yearn for contact with a recognizable public figure. Agents can usually, and very legitimately, be talked out of any such meeting on the obvious security grounds. Political activists are another matter. They want reassurance that their work is appreciated by those at the top, and many welcome the status—and perhaps the "bragging right"—of being able to say, "The last time I spoke with my friend, [X], he said. . . ." No matter how obvious the morale-building effect of such a meeting would be, I can think of only one or two instances in which I thought that the risk could be justified.

Des agreed with me that although Bob Kennedy might agree to meet AMLASH, no good could come of it. One obvious purpose of an intelligence service is to serve as a secret screen between overt officialdom and some of the more dubious, or self-serving, denizens of the nether depths. One of the many problems that had bedeviled Bill Harvey was Bob Kennedy's frequent, and invariably uncoordinated, meetings with agents or contacts that were being run by task force case officers. However rewarding this may have seemed to Kennedy, it was a gross violation of security, and played hob with operational discipline.

I agreed that Des go to Paris and meet the Cuban under whatever "high-level" guise Des might contrive. As it turned out Des did not trouble to affect any more high-level credentials than his appearance and manifest self-confidence suggested.

Despite what some writers have put forth, the objective of FitzGerald's meeting was to explore the possibility that AMLASH's scheme might work. It was at this meeting that AMLASH made it clear that in discussing coup plans with his potential confederates and meeting our contact man, he knew that he was running lethal risks. He explained that although officers in Havana customarily carried loaded pistols, the prescribed form was to leave such weapons in an outer office when visiting Fidel Castro. In the event he might be arrested in Castro's presence, AMLASH assumed he would eventually be executed. With this in mind, AMLASH fashioned a grim but not necessarily unrealistic plan. If he were to be seized, it was AMLASH's intention to put up a fight and to take one or more of his enemies with him to the grave. Against this possibility, AMLASH asked FitzGerald for a weapon he could conceal upon his person.

Des returned to headquarters, and I agreed that AMLASH be given some such device.

At a meeting with his contact man in Paris on November 22, AMLASH was given a ballpoint pen concealing an injection device loaded with a more or less readily available but lethal chemical. In a struggle, AMLASH would presumably take the pen from his pocket, stab an assailant, and automatically trigger the injection. AMLASH considered the device useless and handed it back to the contact man. (Had it been shown to me, I would have refused to offer it to AMLASH.) At no time, and by no one involved, was this clumsy device intended to be an assassination weapon.

This meeting did not involve any plan to assassinate Castro. The fact that the session occurred on the day President Kennedy was murdered adds another sour note to that sad history.

AMLASH was arrested in Havana in March 1966, brought to trial, and found guilty of treason. His death sentence was commuted by Castro. Thirteen years later AMLASH was released and permitted to leave Cuba.

Chapter 22

———

THE HEART
OF THE MATTER

When I succeeded Dick Bissell in 1962, I began to focus more than I had previously on the work of the Directorate for Intelligence (DI). The directorate was responsible for CIA's intelligence production—the prime responsibility assigned to the Agency by Congress in 1947. Ray Cline, an OSS veteran, had joined CIA in 1949, and later replaced Robert Amory as deputy director for intelligence. Ray was always anxious to make his presence felt in intra-agency discussions and in competitions for the President's attention. He was intensely aware that the Directorate for Plans, thanks to the public's apparently endless fascination with espionage and all its trappings—as portrayed by Hollywood—was the only element of the Agency that caught the public eye. This undercut Ray's desire for the prominence to which he felt entitled.

It is difficult to describe the sometimes subtle maneuvers in relations with a colleague, but in time I became aware of what I can best define as Ray's hand in my pocket. More specifically, he wanted my job.

It was not long after Admiral William Raborn replaced John McCone as DCI that Ray decided he needed a change. He had effected an excellent relationship with McCone, and enjoyed their frequent give-and-take on foreign policy problems. But there was none of that with the admiral, who had almost no experience in foreign matters and even less enthusiasm for being upstaged by an expert. Ray took a deep breath and asked for a post in Germany.

—

In beginning this memoir, I was determined to try to give the DI at least a fraction of the credit it has earned. I first thought to check on how a few of the scores of writers have given the work of intelligence agencies its grossly distorted reputation. No luck.

Best-sellers from William Le Queux, early in the century, to Ian Fleming, Len Deighton, and their less talented followers ignore the fact that the purpose behind the imagined hugger-mugger involved in secret intelligence collection is to keep national policymakers well enough informed to make sound decisions and to avoid catastrophic mistakes. Nor could I find help from the writers who had varying degrees of actual intelligence experience. Their firsthand knowledge ranges from the espionage efforts of Somerset Maugham in Switzerland and Russia in the First World War, Graham Greene's MI-6 service, and Eric Ambler's military staff work in World War II. John le Carré's considerable professional background in Cold War activity brought things up to date. Like most of the better spy novels, le Carré's early books most often involve some aspect of counterintelligence—spies against spies—rather than intelligence collection.

No matter how perceptive and skilled, none of these writers have fashioned an informed, intriguing or, Heaven forfend, dramatic account of the platoons of skilled scholars, analysts, and scientists who are at the heart of the matter—the production of intelligence reports and National Estimates for the nation's top command.

—

It was General Walter Bedell Smith who, as DCI, shaped the Directorate for Intelligence. When he replaced Rear Admiral Hillenkoetter, the Agency was under fire for its failure clearly to signal the communist takeover in Czechoslovakia, Tito's exit from the Soviet bloc, and the collapse of the Nationalist government in China. The criticism was further inflamed when North Korea launched its attack on South Korea.

General Smith determined that the available but scattered data had contained more than a whiff of the probability that North Korea would attack South Korea. The Agency mandate to centralize intelligence evaluation and dissemination had not yet been achieved. Admiral Hillenkoetter's single star did not glow brightly enough for him to force the Pentagon's three-star generals and admirals to comply with CIA's legislative charter.

In winning his three stars as General Eisenhower's chief of staff in the critical phase of World War II, Smith had earned the reputation, and sufficient political clout, to enforce the cooperation of the other U.S. intelligence agencies at all levels. He also had the organizational savvy to recognize the Agency's problem.

One of General Smith's first steps was to establish the Office of National Estimates (ONE), reporting directly to himself. His purpose was to provide national leaders with a coordinated analysis of *all* the information available to the U.S. government on national security issues. The sources encompass ultra-secret signals intelligence, State and Defense Department reports, imagery, overhead reconnaissance, data from CIA agents, and such open sources as the world media—press, radio, and TV.

Another of Smith's initial moves was to summon Professor William Langer from his post in the Harvard history department. Langer's experience—he had organized and run the OSS Reports and Analysis office (R&A) during World War II—made him the right choice to set up the new office. The professor promptly established a board of some twelve persons with the sole responsibility to produce coordinated national intelligence estimates. The impressive group was a deliberately mixed assembly including academics, retired diplomats, senior military officers, business executives, and lawyers. Some had World War II intelligence experience.

The board was to be supported by a small staff of area specialists. These usually younger experts did the heavy lifting involved in preparing initial draft estimates by integrating and supplementing a wide range of contributions. The wear and tear involved in achieving consensus between younger staff and the senior board served to boil down any flabby prose or possibly muffled judgments in the final product.

One of the more cogent pleasures of the scientists and scholars staffing the DI is knowing that along with the important world newspapers and clips from Associated Press and foreign news agencies, their in-boxes will be filled with the most sensitive State and Defense Department reports and documents, highly classified espionage reports, intercepted communications of all sorts, and think pieces from even the most obscure sources.

At DCI Smith's insistence, the board had no responsibility—administrative or executive—other than to produce National Intelligence Estimates (NIEs) coordinated with the other U.S. intelligence agencies. The process of establishing ONE is easily recounted, but in action it was a fundamental step in thrusting CIA into position to discharge one of its primary missions—the production of National Intelligence Estimates based on all information available to the government.

From the inception of CIA, the director has worn two hats. He is both the director of Central Intelligence and the director of the Central Intelligence *Agency*. As DCI, he is the President's senior intelligence officer, with overview of all other government intelligence components. As the director of the Central Intelligence Agency, he runs the Agency. Thus, when the ONE completed a National Estimate, the director of Central Intelligence submitted it to the intelligence components of the State and Defense Departments. When the estimate was approved by the DCI and forwarded to the chiefs of other agencies it was returned to the DCI for his final signature and dissemination to the White House and National Security Council. Some estimates are produced on an annual basis; others are more nearly ad hoc. The process can take months; in a crisis, a few hours will suffice.

CIA is not the only agency doing this analysis; both the State and Defense Departments indulge in it. The critically important difference in the CIA analysis and that of other institutions is that the Agency product is independent of the occasional parochial interests of other government offices—including the various departments, notably State and Defense—and the executive agencies.

There is another vital distinction: the director of Central Intelligence reports directly to the President. Although National Estimates are coordinated with other agencies, the DCI has the last word. Any dissent from the final estimate is included as a footnote. This is the last step in affording policymakers an independent analysis of national security issues.

—

When Ray Cline left for Germany, Russell Jack Smith, a longtime DI officer, replaced him as chief of the Directorate for Intelligence. At the time, the directorate was made up of four analytic and reporting units: the Office of Current Intelligence (OCI), the Office of Economic Research (OER), the Office of Strategic Research (OSR), and the Office of Biographic and Geographic Intelligence (OBGI). Of these, the OCI was the frontline operation, producing six days a week a daily intelligence summary in three levels of classification and a steady stream of memoranda on threatening trends and developments worldwide. At that time, OER concentrated on Soviet economic activity and production of military equipment, especially bombers and ICBMs. OSR maintained a watch on troop and aircraft deployments and various activities of Soviet and other military forces. OBGI produced reports of key foreign personalities, various background studies, and maps of strategic geographic locales.

In briefing outsiders on the intelligence directorate, Jack Smith described his shop as "the voice of CIA on *foreign* political, economic, and military affairs." He would then explain that in addition to producing annual, monthly, weekly, daily, and, on occasion, hourly intelligence disseminations, the DI ran two *overt* activities—Contacts, and the Foreign Broadcast Information Service (FBIS). The Contacts Branch was primarily concerned with the overt debriefing of businessmen and others who travel to areas of strategic interest. (This open activity is practiced by most of the world's intelligence services and foreign policy establishments.) The FBIS monitors a global range of foreign media—print, radio, TV—and publishes unclassified daily reports. The Central Reference office stores a wealth of intelligence data and maintains the Agency's extensive library.

I recall Allen Dulles's agreeing with Jack Smith's observation that an entire college faculty could be assembled from within the membership of the Directorate for Intelligence. This is surely true. The intellectual excellence and the professional qualifications of the area experts, researchers, scientists, and political analysts are unsurpassed within the government. But there is a certain irony in the remark: For all his professional expertise, Dulles tended to take the directorate for granted. He appreciated the value and quality of the product, but rarely addressed himself to the DI or any of its problems. This stands in sharp contrast to the major role Dulles played in shaping the operational elements of the Agency.

The analyst's daily task is to scan the material—virtually all of the information in his regional or functional discipline available to the U.S. government—for anything of immediate interest to the President, the White House staff, the secretaries of state and defense, or other senior officers. The longer-range data are filed for future use in "CIA Memoranda." These studies were of a deeper draft than the national newsweekly magazines, and laced with secret information not available in unclassified form. Moreover, owing to CIA's unique status—reporting directly to the President and lacking any responsibility for setting policy—these memoranda were characteristically objective and free from policy bias. In this respect it is understandable, for example, that Pentagon agencies, bearing the responsibility for national defense, were more inclined to emphasize the most threatening aspects in weapons development or military situations. In contrast, CIA analysts stressed what appeared to be the most likely outcome.

Like major news agencies and national newspapers, the DI and especially its OCI function on a twenty-four-hour basis, with deadlines ranging from weeks for interim studies to minutes in the case of the President's Daily Brief.

Here a confession. As much as I respected the intellectual heft, wisdom, and probity of the distinguished Board of National Estimates and especially the brilliant and colorful chairman, Sherman Kent, it never quite stilled the memory of my newspaper days in Berlin and inclined me to identify with the Office of Current Intelligence. For me the pressure of meeting urgent deadlines and responding immediately to developing crises always sparked a pleasant mnemonic echo. Indeed, Sherman Kent's salty tropes were strongly reminiscent of a newspaper office. His assessment of a tin-pot dictator's feckless effort to tidy up his government as akin "to gathering piss with a rake" is typical.

Casting aside the perceived—and I must admit the occasionally real—excitement of secret operations, the absolute essence of the intelligence profession rests in the production of current intelligence reports, memoranda, and National Estimates on which sound policy decisions can be made.

Chapter 23

—

A BONE
IN THE THROAT

There was another problem that became ensnared in the events that followed the President's murder. In outline, the case we first knew as FOXTROT was simple enough. Examined in detail, it was the most frustrating operation in my experience, and was to plague me from my post as deputy director for plans (DDP) through much of my service as director of Central Intelligence. The files consumed hundreds of pages of documentation and argument—two of the early studies ran to some twelve hundred pages. During my years at the Agency, no case was more baffling.

Operation FOXTROT opened in June 1962 when an urgent, Eyes Only cable was hand-carried to my office. Yuri Ivanovich Nosenko, a middle-level KGB operative temporarily serving as a security officer on a Soviet disarmament delegation visiting Geneva, had approached an American diplomat and asked to be introduced to a CIA representative. In the course of several clandestine meetings with an Agency officer, Nosenko volunteered to serve as an agent within the KGB.

From a security viewpoint, Nosenko's alleged background and Moscow assignment—he served in the American Department of the internal counterintelligence service of the KGB—made him an extremely attractive source. His targets were American diplomatic and consular personnel, journalists, and tourists in the USSR. As an agent, he appeared to offer an inside view of high-priority KGB operations against the United States. In Moscow, the KGB had created surveillance facilities which when focused would give an intimate, around-the-clock oversight of a target individual's everyday activity. Over time, this intense scrutiny enabled the KGB to identify any personal attitudes or habits which if manipulated and played upon by experts could lead to compromise and recruitment. No place on the globe were American personnel more exposed and vulnerable than in the Soviet Union.

For years the embassy personnel had been intensively briefed on how to protect themselves. Sophisticated audio devices were routinely dug out of embassy offices and private living quarters. Staff personnel were regularly warned away from KGB-sponsored social contacts. These briefings were helpful, but could no more solve the persistent security problems than the best medical advice has kept some people from smoking, boozing, or indulging in drugs. As in all secret intelligence, the key is "penetration"—the best possible security protection is a source in the opposition's counterintelligence component. Nosenko appeared to be just that. In our early meetings he named an American communications clerk who had been recruited, and pinpointed some fifty audio devices in the Moscow embassy.

Before he returned to Moscow, Nosenko specified that no attempt be made to contact him in the Soviet Union, and that future meetings be restricted to the times he accompanied Soviet delegations abroad. The Russian also said that he had no intention of defecting—he would not abandon his family in Moscow—but would contact us the next time he was abroad.

No matter what gifts they appear to bear, volunteers are always handled with extra caution. Initial reports are double-checked against reliable data, alleged motives are carefully sorted out, and the agent's background is thoroughly examined. Even before the first rush of excitement subsided, doubts about Nosenko had developed. Some of the "inside" information that looked so promising in the field had, upon examination at headquarters, proved to duplicate the data supplied by another KGB defector six months before Nosenko volunteered his services. This might be seen as confirmation that Nosenko was speaking the truth and knew what he was talking about. Viewed skeptically, it could also mean that the KGB was attempting to convince us that Nosenko was a bona fide walk-in by slipping us material they knew had been compromised by the earlier defector. Doubts about Nosenko's alleged career pattern and background also flared. If the Russian had been sent by the KGB, one purpose might be to deflect our interest from the reports of the earlier KGB defector and influence our other independent investigations.

It was nineteen months, and January 1964, before Nosenko returned to Geneva. To our complete surprise, and contrary to his earlier statement, Nosenko abruptly announced that he now wanted to defect immediately. He insisted that his security had been compromised, that he would be arrested if he returned to Moscow. Then, with barely a pause, he delivered another surprise. In the days following President Kennedy's assassination, Nosenko informed us, he had reviewed the entire KGB file on Lee Harvey Oswald's three-year residence in the USSR. Nosenko assured us that the KGB had found Oswald unstable, had declined to have anything to do with him, and he was not in any way involved in President Kennedy's assassination.

Coming some two months after the murder, when there was intense concern throughout Washington as to whether the Russians or Castro were in any way involved in the assassination, and when the Warren Commission was still scraping up every bit of information on Oswald, these allegations were a veritable bombshell. Nosenko's claim was the most important ever made by any previous defector, and with it the FOXTROT operation exploded into another dimension. Our suspicions notwithstanding, Nosenko's claim to have complete knowledge of Oswald's KGB file gave us no choice but to hustle him out of Geneva and into the Washington area for extensive debriefing.

Nosenko was brought into the United States under authority given CIA in Section 7 of the Central Intelligence Act of 1949. This provision states that in the interest of national security, and the furtherance of the national intelligence mission, as many as one hundred individuals a year can, with the authority of the director of Central Intelligence, and the concurrence of the attorney general and the commissioner of immigration, be admitted permanently to the United States without reference to other laws and regulations. This early Cold War legislation is clearly intended to facilitate the escape and prompt movement to safe haven of important agents or defectors. Once in the United States, these individuals are "paroled" in care of CIA and remain the responsibility of the Agency until they are granted citizenship or leave the country. CIA makes all defectors available for inter-

At the home of my McGarrah grandparents in Goshen, New York, 1915.
(Courtesy of Cynthia Helms)

Gstaad, Switzerland. At Le Rosey I did
double duty as goalie on both the hockey
and soccer teams.

Shirt, tie, and jacket
were customary at
Williams College, 1934.
*(The 1936 Williams
College* Gul*)*

RICHARD McG. HELMS
Permanent President
of the
Class of 1935

One of the few times my middle initials appeared
in print. *(The 1936 Williams College* Gul*)*

My press pass for the 1936 Nazi Party Congress at Nuremberg.

Dr. O. Dietrich has the honour, in the name of the Führer,
to invite you to a light luncheon on Sunday the Thirteenth
of September, Nineteen hundred and thirty-six.
You will be called for at seven a.m. at the Hotel
Württemberger Hof and driven to the S.A., S.S., and N.S.K.K.
Assembly in the Luitpold Arena and at the close of these
ceremonies to the Burg where luncheon will be served.

Nürnberg, Sept. 12th. 1936

Mr. Richard Helms

R.S.V.P.
to Mr. R. Hoffmann
Room 17. Württemberger Hof

Hitler had avoided the foreign press corps for some months before sending this surprise
invitation for lunch at Nuremberg.

Charles Lindbergh and the U.S. military attaché, Major Truman Smith, en route to a Berlin airfield. Smith had flattered Field Marshal Goering into showing Lindbergh how far the Luftwaffe had advanced over its British and French rivals. The Lindbergh-Smith report was an intelligence scoop. Incidentally, this is the first time my photograph appeared in the world press. *(UPI/Corbis)*

I spent some four years in a naval uniform and my only sea duty was an orientation cruise, after which I was assigned to an antisubmarine component of the Navy's Eastern Seaboard offices in Manhattan. *(Courtesy of Dennis Helms)*

While I was deskbound with OSS in London, Leading Seaman (!) Cynthia Ratcliffe, of the WRENS—specifically, the Women's Royal Naval Reserve Boats Crew—was in command of a launch and crew that ferried British naval brass from ship to ship in Plymouth Harbor. The casual pose conceals the regulation bell-bottom trousers. *(Courtesy of Cynthia Helms)*

Admiral William Raborn admired Allen Dulles, but I do not recall his having asked AWD's advice. *(AP/Wide World Photos)*

Mrs. Clover Dulles arranged Allen Dulles's funeral to reflect his interest in the continuity of the Agency. Among the honorary pallbearers were Colonel Lawrence White (right) and James Angleton (center, carrying ashes). I escorted Mrs. Dulles, who was followed by their children, their grandchildren, and AWD's sister, Eleanor Dulles.
(Courtesy of the Estate of James Angleton)

President Johnson summoned so many guests for my swearing-in by Judge Carl McGowan that at first I thought I had entered the wrong room at the White House.

No matter what the circumstances, LBJ always seemed to loom a bit.
(White House photo)

The seating at the Tuesday lunch was by strict protocol: Dean Rusk was at the President's right; I was at Rusk's right; the secretary of defense (here Clark Clifford) was at the President's left; General "Bus" Wheeler was to the left of his boss; and Walt Rostow, the national security advisor, was at the far end, between George Cushman and Tom Johnson.
(White House photo)

This was not one of the East Germans' most inspired propaganda efforts, and it had almost no resonance except among collectors of Cold War artifacts.

Although I played the game reasonably well for many years, this is the photo of me playing tennis that will be remembered. Had the East Germans been a bit more hip, this picture might have had more impact than the forged hundred-dollar note.
(Courtesy of Cynthia Helms)

William Casey, then
director of Central
Intelligence, presenting
me with the Donovan
Medal, on behalf of
the Veterans of OSS.
General Bill Quinn is
at the right. *(Courtesy
of the Veterans of OSS)*

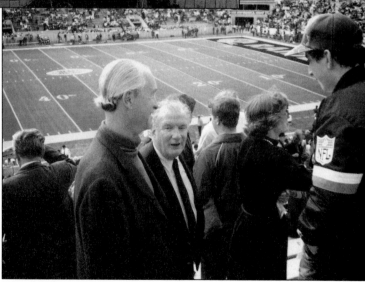

Absolutely the best way to watch the Washington Redskins was as a guest of
Edward Bennett Williams. *(Courtesy of Cynthia Helms)*

President Nixon's first visit to CIA. The body language says it all.
(Central Intelligence Agency)

Henry Kissinger had the
best grasp of intelligence and
security issues of anyone
on Nixon's staff.
(White House photo)

To The Honorable Richard Helms with best wishes Geo B.

At lunch in the Vice President's office. Aside from George Washington, the elder George Bush is the only President who had firsthand knowledge of the intelligence world. *(White House photo)*

Frank Wisner, in front of Hatfield, his home in England. Frank's role in the Cold War was unsurpassed. *(Courtesy of the Wisner family)*

Tom Karamessines, one of my most valued colleagues, with pipe in hand as always. *(Central Intelligence Agency)*

Des FitzGerald, an aggressive and high-spirited officer whose career was tragically cut short. *(Central Intelligence Agency)*

John Bross, an outstanding intelligence officer and treasured friend. *(Courtesy of Cynthia Helms)*

The presentation of ambassadorial credentials to the Shah was a rather formal undertaking.

There's more to riding a camel than can be mastered at a Fourth of July gathering at the embassy in Tehran.

Golda Meir at her home in Israel, 1971. She was one of the most impressive women I have ever met. *(Photo by Cynthia Helms)*

**Listening to Senator Frank
Church at a Senate hearing.**
(1978, The Washington Post.
*Photo by James K. W. Atherton.
Reprinted with permission.)*

**Edward Bennett Williams responding to the press after my 1977 trial in the
Washington District Court.** *(1977,* The Washington Post. *Photo by Gerald
Martineau. Reprinted with permission.)*

President Reagan
presenting me
with the National
Security Medal.
(White House photo)

RICHARD NIXON
October 24, 1983

26 FEDERAL PLAZA
NEW YORK CITY

Dear Dick,

    No one could have been more pleased than I
was to read that your outstanding service to the
nation has finally been properly recognized by the
White House.

    You suffered a great injustice simply because
you were carrying out the assignment which I felt
was vitally important to the nation's security.
The attempt to castrate the C.I.A. in the mid-
seventies was a national tragedy. Let us hope that
the recognition you have so justly received will
assist in reversing that negative trend.

    With warm regards,

                                    Sincerely,

                                    Dick

Mr. Richard Helms

This letter from former President Nixon marked the first time I had
heard from him since we shook hands at Camp David a few weeks
before I retired. *(Estate of Richard Nixon)*

At home, 1972. *(Courtesy of Karin Wartofsky)*

rogation by other U.S. agencies—the FBI questioned Nosenko soon after his arrival. It remains the Agency's responsibility to determine what we called the "bona fides" of these persons. This meant that we were to certify that the defector was the person he claimed to be, that his former position gave him access to the information he offered, that the reasons for his defection were plausible, and that there were no data suggesting the involvement of any foreign intelligence service in his defection.

It was not surprising that the KGB found Oswald too unstable to consider using for any operational purpose. Unstable, he surely was. But the KGB failure to take even the slightest security precautions before allowing Oswald to remain in the USSR did not square with Soviet security procedures as we knew them. Equally odd was the alleged failure of Soviet intelligence to question the ex-Marine on his military background. Had the Russians troubled to ask, they would have learned that Oswald had served in a radar unit on an air base that sometimes accommodated a U-2 aircraft, both topics of considerable interest to Soviet intelligence at the time. The assertion that the KGB did not trouble to investigate the possibility that Oswald was a CIA plant before allowing him to remain in the USSR also seemed highly unlikely. Nosenko's alleged knowledge of Lee Harvey Oswald seemed out of context with his professional responsibilities and assignment. Some of the details Nosenko offered on his own education and his military and intelligence careers were unconvincing.

If the conflicting elements of Nosenko's story had not been inflated by the allegation that he knew exactly how the young man who had murdered the President had been handled by Soviet intelligence in the USSR, the case would have been little more than a snarled counterintelligence problem, to be solved by close interrogation and further investigation. Nosenko's claim to knowledge of Oswald raised the case to national importance. If the Russian could be proved to be a legitimate defector, and his assurances concerning Oswald's handling could be proved entirely plausible, then the continuing suspicions of Soviet involvement in the assassination could be disregarded. But if Nosenko had been hurriedly briefed and dispatched to mislead us about any Soviet connection with the assassination, then the existing suspicions would be reinforced with consequences that, as I later testified, I thought would be "staggering." In March 1964 the Agency faced no greater problem than to resolve the allegations concerning the assassination of President Kennedy.

Unfortunately, no consensus could be developed within the Agency as to the truth of Nosenko's various stories. The counterintelligence specialists and some experienced operatives considered him to have been programmed to mislead us. Others tended to believe Nosenko, and to consider the transparently false discrepancies in his reporting to have been compounded by faulty memory, the determination to impress us with an exaggerated view of his knowledge and former position, language difficulties, fatigue, and emotional distress. All of these problems are common with defectors, and understandably so. The decision to abandon one's family, friends, homeland, career, language, and culture ranks highest on the roster of events most likely to cause the maximum emotional stress.

As deputy director for plans, responsible for all aspects of defector handling, it became clear to me that the Agency could not underwrite Nosenko's assertions by declaring him a bona fide defector. After consulting John McCone, I arranged an appointment with Chief Justice Earl Warren, head of the President's commission to examine the assassination of President Kennedy. We met in an empty office at the commission's headquarters in downtown Washington. I informed the Chief Justice that the Agency could not now, if ever, vouch for Nosenko's authenticity, and recommended that the Warren Commission not accept his assurances as to Moscow's innocence as of now. Warren was understanding, but obviously not pleased to learn that this important piece could not be fitted neatly into the assassination puzzle.

After some weeks, Nosenko's questioning was stepped up to what we called a "hostile interrogation." This harsh expression meant only that the interrogators would no longer appear to accept Nosenko's statements, but would challenge each and accuse him of falsifying some of his testimony. Nosenko remained unmoved, and the schism between those who believed him and those who did not continued to deepen.

In early April 1964, I met with Deputy Attorney General Nicholas deB. Katzenbach and other Department of Justice officials to clarify the Agency's responsibilities for the parolees as specified by the Central Intelligence Act of 1949. Katzenbach instructed William E. Foley, the Justice official most familiar with these matters, to double-check our responsibility, and to advise Larry Houston, the Agency's general counsel. Foley did this by telephone, and confirmed the basic parole agreement as executed in February 1955 by the attorney general and Allen

Dulles, then DCI. This agreement states that CIA is responsible for the care, supervision, and control of these special aliens in a manner "consistent with the internal security needs of the United States during continuance of their parole status."

As I was to testify before Congress in 1979,* establishing Nosenko's bona fides "became a matter of the utmost importance [to the United States] and, indeed to the world." The interrogation continued, with little or no progress, until it was decided to move him to a specially constructed building at one of our training areas. This meant that Nosenko could be held in strict solitary confinement while the interrogation continued. Conditions were spartan, verging on harsh, but no more so than solitary confinement in a maximum security federal prison. With the full weight of the President's murder hanging over our every action, Nosenko was subjected to various psychological pressures. Despite what has been reported in some of the literature, he was never drugged or subjected to any form of physical abuse, and was regularly examined by an Agency doctor.

Nosenko's testimony took various forms, and was sometimes contradictory, but remained essentially as he had first reported it—the KGB had never had any substantive contact with Oswald, and had nothing whatsoever to do with the assassination. There remained many obvious untruths in some of his other answers. At times, even his KGB rank came into contention—it varied from lieutenant colonel to the more plausible title of captain. In a rare exception to our usual practice, Nosenko was questioned by an earlier and trusted KGB defector, Lieutenant Colonel Peter Deriabin. He came to doubt many aspects of Nosenko's alleged KGB career, and in the end was not convinced that Nosenko had *ever* served as a KGB officer in the assignments he claimed.

After some seven months of intensive interrogation failed to elicit any substantive change in Nosenko's claims, I became convinced that further questioning would be fruitless and ordered a rapid windup of the case. This was not to be. The interrogation raged inconclusively through my tenure as deputy director under Admiral William Raborn, the new DCI,

*House Select Committee on Assassinations, *Report* (Washington, D.C.: U.S. Government Printing Office, 1979).

and on until after my appointment as director in June 1966. Late in 1967, when the case seemed no closer to resolution, I asked my deputy, Vice Admiral Rufus Taylor, to undertake an independent review of the case. After studying the immense files and talking with the concerned officers, Admiral Taylor informed me in October 1968 that he was not convinced how the KGB might have benefited by sending Nosenko to us. He recommended that Nosenko be accepted as a legitimate defector, and that his rehabilitation and resettlement should be accomplished in time for his full release in January 1969.

Because doubts remained as strong as ever in some quarters, I called a meeting of all the senior officers concerned with the case and asked each to comment on Admiral Taylor's report. Each of these officers recommended that Nosenko be released from CIA custody. Some differences—notably those of the Counterintelligence Staff representatives—remained as to whether Nosenko's authenticity had been conclusively proved, but the opinion of the majority of those present was that he still had some important services to offer CIA and should be retained under Agency contract. This was agreed upon.

In time, Nosenko received citizenship, assumed a different identity, married an American woman, and is now pursuing a new career in this country.

Some writers have alleged that Jim Angleton was responsible for Nosenko's confinement, extended interrogation, and the various attempts to prove that he was dispatched by the KGB. This is not true. From the beginning and until Admiral Taylor's investigation, Nosenko was the responsibility of the Soviet Division of the Directorate for Plans. The recommendation that he be held in solitary confinement was that of the division. Although Angleton was in the hospital at the time some of the critical decisions were made, he disagreed with the hostile interrogation and confinement of Nosenko. From the early months, Angleton's recommendation was that Nosenko be released, and his further activity monitored.

This case remains the most frustrating of any single espionage case in my intelligence experience. The sad fact is that if Nosenko had told the truth from the outset and throughout, he would not have endured the difficulties and neither would we.

Chapter 24

—

MOVING UP

It was early April 1965 when Marvin Watson, one of President Johnson's personal assistants, telephoned to ask if I was the Richard Helms who had been introduced to President Johnson at the National Security Council meeting a few days earlier. John McCone had taken me with him to the meeting for the express purpose of introducing me to the President. Apparently satisfied with my answer, Watson told me that I was to see President Johnson at the White House the following morning. This was a surprise. As deputy director for plans, I was two steep steps below John McCone, the DCI, and one rung below Lieutenant General Marshall "Pat" Carter, who had already logged three years as deputy director.

To the dismay of cabinet officers and agency chiefs, President Kennedy sometimes telephoned directly to one of their subordinates far down the pecking order. LBJ preferred to deal directly with his principal officers. I checked with McCone's secretary: Yes, the DCI knew the President had called.

From the outset of his tenure as DCI, I had got on well with John McCone. I admired the highly efficient way in which he ran his office, and respected his judgment and knowledge of the way things worked in Washington. We had an excellent working relationship, but I knew better than to ask if he or Pat Carter might also be going to the meeting. If the DCI thought I needed any more information on my summons to the

White House, he would have given it to me. The twenty-minute drive from McLean to 1600 Pennsylvania Avenue was not long enough for me to conjure up any plausible reason for this summons. There were the usual handful of routine operational bothers around the globe, but none of these could plausibly have come to the President's attention. I was acutely aware that for all of the effort we were making on Vietnam, we had yet to provide adequate access to the Hanoi leadership. If President Johnson wanted to underline his dissatisfaction, I reasoned, he would have started with John McCone before unloading on me.

It was a long ten minutes before a Secret Service aide led me upstairs and into the President's working office, which adjoined the more formal Cabinet Office. The President was hunched forward over his desk, a telephone in his left hand. He looked up, waved me to the chair close to his desk, and continued to speak into the phone. Like most Americans, at least at that time, I had grown up in awe of everyone who ever occupied the chair behind the desk in that office. I've never lost this attitude, and it was an effort to conceal it. At a distance of six feet, LBJ seemed almost an exaggeration of himself—huge hands, vast shoulders, massive head and ears.

President Johnson dropped the phone into its cradle and reached across the desk to shake hands. After a minimal but very courteous greeting, he came to the point. "John McCone has resigned, and I've decided to appoint Admiral William Raborn as the new DCI. Do you know him?"

"No sir."

"Well, you will. You'll be named deputy director at the same time." My complete surprise must have been obvious because the President waited for the news to sink in before saying, "You're not well known in Washington, or up on the Hill. The new job will give you a lot more exposure and a chance to get acquainted with some of the more important members of Congress. 'Red' Raborn has a first-class reputation with both Armed Services Committees because of the job—the fine job—he did bringing the Polaris submarine in under budget and ahead of schedule. I want you to go to every meeting with the admiral whether here or around town. You know the Agency. Red doesn't."*

---

*It was another of LBJ's secrets at the time but General Carter later told me that he had been named chief of the National Security Agency, a considerable promotion.

At this point I could not help noticing that the President's photographer, Y. R. Okamoto, had crept into the room and was crouched in a corner a few feet away from my chair. Okie always worked with available light, no flashbulbs and no noise.

"I'm going to make these appointments at the ranch when I sign the Elementary and Secondary Education Act into law," the President said. "You and the admiral are to be there, but I don't want any leaks. Marvin Watson will tell you how to arrange transportation."

I nodded, but before I could thank him, he said with heavy emphasis, *"No leaks."* With this second injunction, I dismissed the notion of mentioning my morning at the White House to any of my closest associates and even to my wife.

"Most of the press corps will be there for the signing, but this announcement will be a surprise, and no one's going to scoop me on it." LBJ's manner softened. "It will be in the schoolhouse—one room, near Stonewall, Texas, where I began my education." Then, almost stiffly, he declared, "As president, I believe deeply that no law I have signed or will ever sign means more to the future of America." No matter how formal this seemed, there was no doubt how deeply President Johnson felt about the bill.

At the ranch, Admiral Raborn and I succeeded in keeping a low profile as we dodged about in the crowd of aides while the President repeated his comment to me on the education act word for word. When he finished the signing, LBJ beckoned us to join him at the rope which had kept the press corps standing to one side. As the President announced McCone's resignation, a woman reporter gasped aloud, "Oh, no!" This heartfelt expression encapsuled both the journalists' frustration at being caught with an unexpected development miles away from a telephone and the President's delight at having caused it.

That afternoon, as the President dozed on the foredeck of a cabin cruiser on the lake near the ranch, I became acquainted with Senator Eugene McCarthy, the Minnesota Democrat who was well known for his sharply critical view of the Agency. But through the years since then, we lunched occasionally, and encountered one another at the usual Washington events, or as guests in owner Jack Kent Cooke's box at Redskin football games. McCarthy was always good company, intelligent and witty. His run for president petered out rather early on despite considerable support from the anti–Vietnam War faction. My guess would be that he never really wanted to be president, and that Gene was entirely too intelligent to think that it was a job made for him.

Oklahoma Congressman Carl Albert, then Democratic floor leader, was also along. Although he later became House majority leader, we rarely had any business to discuss. I remember him best for his great devotion to President Johnson and his efforts to support him in every way he could.

It was the first time I had met Lady Bird Johnson. She was hostess at dinner and later escorted us each to our bedrooms. At the time I did not realize how strong a lady she is, and how fortunate the country was in having her in the White House in the late sixties when the country was riven and President Johnson was under siege. She was best known as the champion of a program to beautify the country, but to those who came and went at the top of government, she was the lady of the house and the balance wheel on all occasions. She was especially concerned with the President's health and ever mindful of the massive heart attack he had suffered some years earlier. I recall President Johnson at one of the Tuesday White House luncheons declining dessert and muttering, "Lady Bird keeps reminding me that if I can't discipline myself, I can scarcely expect to lead the country."

On the way back to Washington on Air Force One, the President instructed me to "shake things up" at the Agency. It was less than clear to me exactly what he meant. Admiral Raborn and I were inheriting an organization that had been well tuned by John McCone, a man whose business experience had given him a matchless grasp of organizational efficiency and managerial responsibility. He had made all of the changes and adjustments that I thought necessary, and I believed it would be quite a while before I might be able to improve on any of them. My guess was that presidential directives to new appointees usually included the injunction to shake things up, on the theory that everything can be made better, maybe. Throughout our time together, the President never mentioned the matter again.

Vice Admiral William F. Raborn, Jr., a Naval Academy graduate, is the only DCI who stepped into office with no experience in intelligence. His highly successful naval career was almost entirely spent in weapons development. Lean and florid-faced, he came aboard with full military bearing. In the some fourteen months he served before retirement from the Agency in 1966, he tried hard to find his way in what was for him an uncharted area. He was expected to know about unknown places which had never previously come to his attention; he neither knew nor had even met any of the key CIA subordinates upon whose judgments and counsel he would have to depend; and he had no experience in dealing with the State Department or with Director Hoover at the FBI. Admiral Raborn was, of course, more familiar with the personnel and procedures of the Pentagon, but he had never met any of the Western intelligence chiefs with whom he would be in liaison. Admiral Raborn's effort and hard work notwithstanding, it was clear that President Johnson had thrust him into the wrong job. To his credit, I never heard Red complain.

Chapter 25

—

THE WAR WE WON

It was mid-June 1966 and one of the occasional Saturdays on which I resolved not to spend the morning in the office. There were errands to run in Chevy Chase, and I barely got home in time to pick up the telephone. John Macy, then head man at the Civil Service Commission, came right to the point. "The President is holding a small press conference this morning, only half a dozen reporters. He plans to announce three or four appointments, and among them, you're being named director of Central Intelligence." I managed to mumble a surprised acknowledgment before John went on to say, "Nobody knows anything about this, and you're not to mention it to anyone." There was no category of Top Secret Code Word, Cosmic, Eyes Only information any higher than the secrecy which President Johnson reserved for the name of anyone he planned to appoint to any office. The vaguest rumor was enough to make LBJ table the appointment.

Before I could assure John that the secret was safe with me, he added, "Sometimes the President decides at the last moment to postpone an announcement, so I mean what I'm saying—not a peep from you until you hear from the White House."

Within two hours my phone began to ring, not the White House but various friends calling to congratulate me.

For fear of being held up in traffic, and like a freshman on a date with a prom queen, I arrived at the White House early on June 30, the morning I was to be sworn in. As I walked up the stairs to the main floor, a segment of the Marine Band was tuning instruments in the foyer. Until three or four of a group of congressmen and senators stopped chatting and turned to congratulate me, I was convinced that I had stepped into the wrong ceremony. Not at all. LBJ had summoned the group and the musicians for my ceremony. After twenty years in Washington, this was a genuine and pleasant surprise.

—

As DCI, John McCone handled all significant relations with the White House, Bob Kennedy, Congress, State, and the Pentagon. It was only when McCone was out of town that General Carter assumed these duties. In contrast, Admiral Raborn insisted that I accompany him to most meetings with Congress, or at State or the Pentagon. I assumed that this was in keeping with President Johnson's intention that I become better known in Congress and at other departments and agencies. Whatever the reason, I appreciated the opportunity. There was one marked drawback. I could not make the trips to the East Asian and Pacific area that I needed to in order to acquaint myself with some of the countries I had never visited. Nor could I visit key officers in place throughout the area that I knew least.

There were problems aplenty in the USSR, Eastern Europe, and Near East, but from the early months of the Johnson administration, the political and security situations in the East Asian area—most importantly, Vietnam and Laos—were of increasing concern. CIA's role was expanding in bounds.

Aside from a relatively few—mainly OSS veterans—none of our operations officers had any significant paramilitary experience in the Pacific and Southeast Asian areas. We had an adequate depth of language competence in Europe, the Near East, and the Western Hemisphere. We were not tongue-tied in Southeast Asia, but competent linguists were in short supply. There was much training to be undertaken, and a sorting out of officers who could be expected to adapt to the political and cultural challenges of a completely new area.

Laos had first come forcefully to my attention in 1962 when I was appointed deputy director for plans. Until then, I had known the kingdom only as a small former French colony in a remote region—a hotchpotch of jungle and mountains squeezed between Thailand on the west, Vietnam on the north and east, China on the north, and Cambodia on the south, and plagued with conflicting ethnic and regional interests, feuding clans, and local warlords. Few areas in Southeast Asia are ridden with a more complex history or a more complicated tangle of political interests than this "accidental country," as one of my briefing papers described it. Lacking natural defenses, the ancient monarchy barely survived centuries of pressure from greedy neighbors, who saw Laos as a gateway to the richer lands they wished to appropriate. At one time or another, each of the neighbors had encroached upon the slender Laotian defenses. In our day, this happened most blatantly when North Vietnam (NVN) established the Ho Chi Minh Trail, the system of roads which began in the North, skirted the Demilitarized Zone separating the two Vietnams, and ran through the narrow Laos panhandle into South Vietnam and Cambodia. Without this pathway, the North Vietnamese might never have sustained their war effort in the South.

At the time, the second Geneva Conference was under way, with the contesting nations—the United States, USSR, China, and North Vietnam—still trying to negotiate a settlement among competing Lao factions and their various foreign allies. The neutralization formula for defusing the Laotian tinderbox seemed adequate on paper, and conceivably might have worked had the North Vietnamese honored it. But just as it had after the first Geneva Conference of 1954, North Vietnam failed to withdraw its troops from Laos. Some twelve thousand of them were left in the northern provinces, where they provided training and combat cadres for the Pathet Lao, the indigenous Lao communist force. This enabled the Pathet Lao to keep pressure on the weak, neutralist Royal Lao government, and freed the North Vietnamese troops to deepen their hold on Lao territory. Unobstructed, they continued to strengthen the Ho Chi Minh Trail. Cynical Americans referred to the trail as the "W. Averell Harriman Expressway." Harriman, then assistant secretary of state for East Asia and the Pacific, was the architect of the neutralization of Laos.

As specified at Geneva, the United States was obliged to halt all but very limited assistance to the regular forces of the Royal Lao government. Before the Geneva Agreement was signed, the White House authorized the CIA office in Vientiane to provide small arms to the Hmong (also referred to as the Meo) guerrilla fighters in northeastern Laos. This support was terminated, and all but two CIA officers were withdrawn. They were soon able to report that the Royal Lao armed forces were no match for the Pathet Lao and its North Vietnamese mentors. The Hmong highlanders who were willing to fight were primarily concerned with defending their homelands against the despised NVN force and the Pathet Lao. Like successful guerrillas everywhere, the Hmong knew their terrain intimately and were experts at ambush and hit-and-run forays.

By early 1963, the Hmong were experiencing serious difficulty as the strong NVN forces assumed more of the combat burden, and the Pathet Lao were relegated to the role of service troops. If the Hmong were to continue facing the superior firepower of their adversaries, they would need more weapons and training.

It was then that Prince Souvanna Phouma, the Laotian prime minister, quietly asked the United States for secret assistance. President Kennedy agreed, and at a Washington meeting in September 1963 assured the prime minister that the United States would never accept communist control of Laos and was determined to support Souvanna's government. President Kennedy then made CIA the executive agent for the paramilitary program in Laos. "Executive agent" was a new term that soon slipped into the lexicon.

Here a word on clandestine paramilitary activity. The notion that the CIA engages in any paramilitary or political activity on its own authority is so transparently false that only repeated press references to "CIA wars" make any comment necessary. To refer to U.S. clandestine support of the Laotian resistance to North Vietnam military invasion as "CIA's war" is as absurd as calling the war in South Vietnam the "Pentagon's war against North Vietnam."

The invasion of Cuba was conceived by President Eisenhower and authorized and directed by President Kennedy. The U.S. "secret" war in Laos, an indisputable violation of the Geneva accords, was authorized by President Kennedy and undertaken as a direct response to North Vietnam's initial violation of the agreements. Appropriate members of the Congress had full knowledge of Kennedy's action and were thoroughly briefed on CIA's responsibility for the paramilitary activity. In Washington, CIA's role was directed and monitored at every stage by the Special

Action Group formed by President Kennedy. In Laos, the paramilitary and associated activity was approved and directed by the U.S. ambassador in Vientiane.

A significant element in the success of these activities was the highly competent ambassadors who served in Laos. Ambassador Leonard Unger, who spoke both Thai and Lao, showed skill and courage in thwarting the series of attempted coups which threatened the moderate centrist government in Vientiane. On one occasion, when Souvanna Phouma had been seized and confined by rebellious generals attempting to force his resignation, Ambassador Unger left the embassy and sped to the house where the prince was held. Unger spotted Souvanna Phouma on a balcony and, shouting across a garden fence, assured him of U.S. support and urged him not to resign. The prince held firm, and the generals backed down. It was during Ambassador Unger's tenure that the Agency began its direct involvement in the war.

Ambassador William Sullivan succeeded Unger and oversaw a significant expansion of the scale and intensity of the U.S. operations. He had been Averell Harriman's deputy during the Geneva negotiations, and arrived in Vientiane with a good grasp of the situation. Sullivan oversaw the expansion in the scale and intensity of U.S. operations in Laos and focused U.S. airpower on the Ho Chi Minh Trail. This coincided with the continuing reinforcements of the U.S. ground forces in South Vietnam. It was at this time U.S. airpower began air support for the Hmong guerrillas. Sullivan was determined to preserve to the degree possible the fiction of Lao neutrality, and made no bones about keeping COMUSMACV (Commander, U.S. Military Assistance Command, Vietnam) and his staff at bay, and out of Laos. Bill's position was not particularly welcome in Saigon, but it was fully in keeping with U.S. policy as decreed by Washington.

Under the direction of these ambassadors, the CIA component served as a key element in the country team. With the substantial increases in the U.S. commitment to Laos, other agencies began to play important roles. The Agency for International Development (AID) was highly effective in propping up the weak Royal Lao government, particularly in providing food and medical support for the thousands of Hmong and other refugees displaced by the rolling tide of the guerrilla fighting.

The years 1967–68 were marked by a changing pattern in ground action. Instead of the traditional hit-and-run tactics, the guerrilla forces CIA supported were drawn into larger units and deployed against the most aggressive enemy forces. The firepower of the North Vietnamese regular units had been strikingly increased, and the lightly armed Lao forces were soon facing tanks and heavy artillery. The NVN incursions into Lao territory were deeper than ever before and covered a much broader area. During the dry season the NVN forces had mobility and pushed aggressively. Come the rainy season, they withdrew to the east and hunkered down to defend themselves against guerrilla attacks.

By 1969, when Bill Sullivan was replaced by Ambassador McMurtrie Godley, the level of combat in Laos exceeded anything envisioned in 1963, and it intensified steadily through the next four years.

I've often been asked why CIA, a civilian agency, should have been involved in a military operation this large and so obviously impossible to conceal. A fair question. The Agency did not reach out to assume a paramilitary activity of this scope. When it began, the operation was small and within CIA's ability to handle, and we did our best to keep it that way. In response to increasing demands, the operation grew in increments small enough not to have been widely recognized in Washington. The Agency's mandate to carry on was made clear to me by a succession of three presidents. Put simply, the Agency was instructed to do everything it could to sustain the independence of Laos and, consistent with this mission, to do all we could to support the U.S. effort in South Vietnam.

Every attack on the Ho Chi Minh Trail diminished the supplies available to the North Vietnamese forces in South Vietnam. Three of the best NVN combat divisions were tied down and under persistent guerrilla attacks in Laos. The NVN troops were supported by tank units, artillery battalions, and combat engineers. In 1973 the total NVN commitment in Laos was later estimated at 80,000 troops. Every NVN soldier in Laos was one less enemy in South Vietnam.

Basic to the presidential decisions to keep us at it was the fact that the Agency had already developed some unique resources in Laos. We also had great organizational and administrative flexibility. Almost from scratch we had developed a personnel cadre, limited in number, but with a sense of purpose and paramilitary skills particularly well suited to the mission. We had the full support of Air America, a highly efficient, ostensibly civilian airline controlled by the Agency.

The extent of Agency commitment and the outstanding performance of the Agency personnel in Laos came home to me in September 1970 when I visited Laos and saw it at first hand.

Laos, or at least the parts of the country where the war was being fought, has to be seen to be believed. The heavily forested mountains seem to go on forever, but it is the karsts that really catch one's eye. These great gray limestone shafts stand out above the terrain, often cloud-covered, sheer-sided, beautiful, and ominous. I saw them at close range on the flight north from Vientiane, and as we dropped into the mountain-rimmed valley called Long Tieng.

I've done my share of flying, but the pucker factor really kicked in when our tiny Volpar plane suddenly dropped over a 3000-foot stony ridge and made an abrupt ninety-degree turn. After a dismaying glimpse of a crashed C-47, we shot forward onto the landing strip at Long Tieng. This was the headquarters of General Vang Pao and the hub of the Agency's support structure for the fight against the North Vietnamese forces and the Pathet Lao. As we tumbled out of the plane, Lawrence Devlin, the Agency chief in Laos and my escort officer, pointed to the Skyline Ridge, which shrouded one side of the base. "That's the catbird seat, and the enemy wants it. As soon as they wiggle back near the top, they begin mortaring us. So far, we've been able to knock them off the ridge every time."

Larry's briefing was cut short as General Vang Pao stepped up to the plane. Stocky, cheerful looking, only five feet four, Vang Pao possessed a commanding military presence. After a salute, he welcomed us in a mélange of French and English. He led us across the runway to meet his staff officers and to review a company of Hmong troops. The famous Hmong guerrillas offered a near spit-and-polish, military appearance. I hadn't expected such a formal reception, but told him how much we admired the Hmong courage and their determination to resist the invaders. The general translated, and the troops cheered. We moved to the general's house for a *baci,* the traditional ceremony that marks most important occasions in Laos.

Sitting on the floor at nine in the morning, we were immediately surrounded by colorfully attired Hmong maidens and inundated by offers of candy and sweetmeats. This was followed by glasses of straight scotch, at room temperature. Politesse mandated that we down the whiskey in a single swallow. For a moment I thought we might be treated to the drink that had been inflicted upon a colleague who was being feted by a local chief in the South. It was a large glass of fermented rice wine, tarted up with a noggin of buffalo blood and a dash of warm water. Shades of James Bond insisting that his martini be shaken, not stirred.

After what would have served as a full meal anywhere on earth, a succession of Hmong men, senior people in the community, offered us round after round of fruit, hard-boiled eggs, chunks of chicken, and large slices of suckling pig. It was delicious, but not the best ballast for the extensive briefings that followed.

An intense session with Agency case officers stationed in the area was followed by a drive to Sam Thong, where AID had established a hospital for the wounded Hmong soldiers and civilians. A lasting memory is that of a boy no more than fourteen with an open abdomen wound. He was still clinging to the carbine he had carried into the firefight. His eyes wide open, he did not make a sound. Guerrilla warfare spares no one, aged or young.

En route back to Vientiane, our pilot was cleared to give us a glimpse of the Plaine des Jarres and the battlefield. It was late afternoon, and the October sunlight provided a spectacular glimpse of the area where the NVN anti-aircraft batteries were usually dug into the ridgelines. The rainy season had not ended, and the enemy had not yet returned from their rest areas farther east. Ironically, the plain gave me the impression of a vast golf course—soft, lush green fairways dotted with clusters of giant divots where bombs had fallen.

The light, slow-moving aircraft used for short-distance flights over the contested areas in Laos were near-perfect targets for anti-aircraft artillery, and even vulnerable to small-arms fire. The courage of the aircrews and our operations officers who made flight after flight in these fragile craft remains impressive. During those years, although our officers were expressly forbidden to engage in combat, the Agency personnel losses in Laos exceeded any that we had suffered elsewhere.

There are no bystanders in guerrilla warfare, and there are enough stars on the memorial wall in the Agency building to prove it.

In Vientiane I visited Ambassador Mac Godley. He was an action-oriented foreign service officer who had gained some of his considerable experience in the hostilities in Zaire. Mac was upbeat on our chances of preserving the Royal Lao government. He pointed out that the war in Laos had widened considerably, and that although the Royal Lao army did not amount to much, the ethnic elements—the Hmong, Kha, and Lao Theung—were giving a good account of themselves throughout Laos. Also important were the Thai volunteers, a force that eventually numbered some twenty thousand men, deployed throughout Laos. They fought under the direction of General Vang Pao in the north and General Soutchai in the Bolovens Plateau to the south.

At best, a brief trip into an area totally foreign to one's experience is little more than an orientation, an opportunity to glimpse working conditions and to touch base with the players. Only those who have spent time on ground as alien as Laos can have any substantive understanding of the work.

Vinton Lawrence was one of the first young officers CIA sent to Laos. He was not the most obvious candidate for the assignment he welcomed, and I doubt that his Princeton degree in art history fitted the desired profile of a paramilitary warrior. But for four years in the field—until I refused to let him risk another tour—his performance was outstanding.

When Vint arrived in early 1962, Laos was in a state of flux, verging on anarchy. The Agency's role was then restricted to providing the small arms requested by the Hmong. Vint's first task was to reconnoiter the deserted Long Tieng valley and determine if it was suited for an up-country headquarters and landing strip. The continuing peace talks in Geneva had made it desirable to move our existing offices away from the fishbowl that Vientiane was becoming. On his own, and two hundred miles from his supervisors, Lawrence decided that the valley would suffice.

It was only the arrogance of youth, Vint told me, that carried him through the planning, building, and then organizing of the outpost that within months became a settlement housing several battalion-size paramilitary units and their attendant families. Before our withdrawal from Laos, Long Tieng had become a working village of some thirty-six thousand inhabitants.

Long Tieng remained an advance post, with its headquarters still in Vientiane. Strategic planning and paramilitary support was centered on a base at Udorn in Thailand. This somewhat extended organization worked, but never quite achieved the status euphemistically referred to by the Pentagon as "the military chain of support."

William Lair, a quiet Texan and World War II veteran, was in charge of our Udorn office. He had already been in Thailand long enough to become fluent in Thai. It was Lair who opened our contact with the Hmong and first worked with General Vang Pao. Over the next five years, Bill was the key to our success in organizing the guerrilla force. He recognized Vint as the junior colleague he needed, and they soon learned that instead of relying on old models of paramilitary operation that might have worked elsewhere, they would have to improvise their own structure. This was a distinct advantage over the U.S. military who later arrived with knapsacks full of doctrine, little of which could be fitted to the reality of Laos and the Hmong guerrillas.

When the way was cleared for renewed military action, Thai paratroop teams took over the organization and training of the Hmong guerrillas. Some forty teams of young Hmong were formed, given as much leadership and military training as possible, and infiltrated into the operational zones surrounding the Plaine des Jarres and beyond. Once in place they watched, listened, and began to recruit local people as resident observers. Daily communication was by radio, and at night Lawrence would summarize the messages and add a daily situation report for Lair in Thailand.

It took months to develop the order of battle for both the Pathet Lao and NVN units in Laos. In theory, the next task was to organize the Hmong in military zones of operations, with a clear chain of command. Vang Pao pretended that the zone commanders were under his command. In fact, much of his time was spent flying from one area to another, trying to convince one recalcitrant village that it was essential to help a nearby village despite the feud that had existed for half a century. It was not in Hmong nature to conform to anything resembling a chain of command or to cooperate with any form of government beyond that of their immediate village.

As Vint put it, "Everything came down to families—why they would fight, why they would not fight, why some were straight, why some were crooked, why some became communists, why most supported Vang Pao."

The basis of Vang Pao's power was his ability to keep an anthropological and genealogical chart of these interconnections in his head. This allowed Vang Pao, Vint, and others to organize the zones from the bottom up. As the zones took shape, they turned out to be almost identical with those formed in the nineteenth century when the Hmong helped repel the Vietnamese incursion that threatened Luang Prabang and the Lao royal family.

Before my briefings were finished, I had a good idea of what a day in the life of an art historian and resident paramilitary advisor was like. The days that began before dawn were filled with meetings, bicycle trips, briefings, debriefings, flights to villages not marked on any map, and arrivals on windswept ridges where each landing was really a controlled crash. Vint admitted to being lucky to have walked away—more or less—from a half dozen "totals." The long return flights required weaving through the bad weather to reach the home strip before dusk. The courage of the young operatives and flight crews was of the highest order.

Another fact of life at Long Tieng was the long dinners with Vang Pao and local leaders who came from distant villages in part to see if what they had heard about the foreigners was true. The heavily spiced meals included "ferocious lashings of alcohol" and unique opportunities to practice the local dialects. When the social activity was over, all that remained was to check incoming radio messages and prepare the daily radio report to Udorn headquarters.

Aside from the operational aspects of life in Long Tieng was the responsibility for working up the infrastructure to support the 15,000 men—later more than 30,000—and their families. There were payrolls to monitor, rice drops for 250,000 people to organize, hospitals to establish, refugees to place and support. It was also necessary to establish a judicial system that could cope with the incidents that occurred when essentially nomadic loners were thrust into a melting pot with thousands of other nomadic loners.

The young men we had in Laos were an extraordinary bunch, sadly less heralded than they deserve.

—

In February 1973, at the time the cease-fire agreement was signed, I left the Agency. I did so with the conviction that we had done our job in Laos. The Royal Lao government still held approximately the same territory it had in 1962, when the Agency took to the field with the mission of keeping Laos intact and neutral, and a secondary task of providing support for our forces in South Vietnam. Laos was intact. The NVN troops and Pathet Lao occupied no more Laotian territory than they had in 1962. Some eighty thousand NVN troops, in three first-rate military divisions aided by separate artillery battalions, tank units, combat engineers, and support troops, were effectively tied down in Laos. When South Vietnamese resistance crumbled in 1975, the final assault on Saigon was spearheaded by two of these NVN divisions that had moved from Laos.

The Royal Lao government was fragile but still in power.

Our paramilitary operations in Laos were conducted by some two hundred Agency staff and contract employees. We had fulfilled our mission and we remain proud of it. We had won the war!

—

The debate in the American press about the "secret CIA war" in Laos comes down, as do many so-called secret things in Washington, to a question of whether or not the writer or his source knew the "secret." In Congress, Senator Stuart Symington, then a member of the Senate Foreign Relations Committee, probably knew the most about CIA activity in Laos. In October 1967 he chaired a meeting of the Senate Armed Services Committee in Room 212 of the Old Senate Office Building. At Senator Symington's invitation, Ted Shackley, then CIA station chief in Laos, briefed the committee at length. I sat to one side listening. Senator Symington praised the program as a sensible way to fight a war, and was the first to observe that CIA's annual budget in Laos was approximately what the U.S. military was spending per day in Vietnam. Ted and I were not surprised by Symington's remarks. The senator had been briefed several times and had visited Laos, where he stayed as Shackley's houseguest. Beginning in 1962 and continuing until 1970, some fifty senators had been briefed on CIA's activity in Laos.

In 1970 it came as a jolt when, with a group of senators, Senator Symington publicly expressed his "surprise, shock and anger" at what he and the others claimed was their "recent discovery" of "CIA's secret war" in Laos. At the time I could not understand the reason for this about-face. Nor have I since been able to fathom it.

The Paris peace agreement which ended American participation in the Vietnam War was signed in January 1973. When President Nguyen Van Thieu of South Vietnam balked at accepting the agreement, he was assured that the United States would retaliate if the North violated the cease-fire. In the end, Thieu had little choice but to sign.

This maneuvering was not lost on the Laotian authorities. They were also very reluctant to sign a similar cease-fire agreement, but in February 1973 they bowed to American pressure and accepted the assurances of U.S. retaliation against any possible North Vietnamese violation of the agreement. The Royal Lao government was then forced to accept a provisional coalition government fronted by the figurehead, King Savang Vatthana. This government included the communist Pathet Lao as a full participant. By 1975, the Pathet Lao had taken complete control. King Vatthana abdicated, and the Pathet Lao proclaimed the People's Democratic Republic of Laos. This was a sad end for a valiant effort.

The drastic curtailment of American military assistance which Congress almost immediately imposed signaled the end of resistance to the Pathet Lao and the North Vietnamese. Because the irregular forces CIA had supported—at the direction of three presidents—were not an official component of the Royal Lao armed forces, it was no longer possible to maintain them. There was no alternative but to disband the only effective fighting force the Lao government had. General Vang Pao was given limited aid in converting to civilian life, but he had no viable way to maintain his army of irregulars.

The support Vang Pao derived from the American presence in Laos ended in April 1975, when the North Vietnamese overpowered the South Vietnamese government and the United States abdicated its role in Southeast Asia. In Laos, the Pathet Lao, energized by the communist victories in Vietnam and Cambodia, asserted its dominance without opposition. For the Hmong this meant exile abroad or repression at a near-genocidal level at home.

Dr. Yang Dao said this to the French National Assembly on November 8, 1997: "Since 1975, more than 450,000 lowland Lao and highland Laotians have left their country for Europe, Australia, and America. More than three quarters of these have emigrated to the United States, some 200,000 of this group are Hmong."*

When I began this memoir, I realized that it would be impossible to mention any but a handful of Agency colleagues who served with distinction. There were simply too many. But in reviewing what I will always call the war we won, the extraordinary levels of commitment and

---

*Dr. Yang Dao received his Ph.D. in France. He is the first Hmong to have earned that degree.

outright bravery exhibited by so many colleagues were such that I cannot in conscience allow just a few of the many to pass without mention.

Bill Lair, quiet, soft-spoken, with a deep knowledge of Laos, opened our contact with Vang Pao and nurtured the relationship for years. Pat Landry was also a veteran in that effort. Young Vint Lawrence, with Lair, tried to keep General Vang Pao—who had started his military career as a sergeant in the French army—from overreaching. With others, Vint tried unsuccessfully to remind the Hmong fighters that the Americans would eventually go home.

Dick Holm pioneered the important Ho Chi Minh Trail–watching operations, and went on to Africa, where he was almost fatally burned in a plane crash. This happened sometime after his best friend—one of the anonymous stars on the memorial plaque—died in a helicopter crash in Laos. Will Greene was a superb paramilitary tactician. His death left an irreplaceable competence in our ranks. Howie Freeman came within inches of losing his life defending an Air Force installation from an NVN assault. After Laos, young Jim Lewis went on to Vietnam. After being wounded he was taken prisoner by the NVN and held in rough circumstances for more than a year. Jim and his wife were subsequently assigned to Lebanon, where they died in the terrorist bombing of our embassy. Jerry "D" worked for more than five years at Vang Pao's side and at great personal risk. When he left the Agency, Jerry went back to Thailand to help the Hmong refugees fleeing from the Pathet Lao. John "P" was killed when his helicopter was shot down after having infiltrated a team into NVN-held territory in Laos. John Kearns, a close friend of "P," rappelled from a helicopter in a vain attempt to recover the bodies of "P" and the aircrew. Kearns was killed in a North Vietnamese Army attack in South Laos.* The widows of both these men became CIA officers. Bill Buckley was our operations chief in Luang Prabang until he was transferred to Lebanon. There, he was kidnapped by terrorists and died under torture.

There are many more stories to be told and so many more comrades yet to be honored.

---

*CIA had no objection to disclosing the full names of the fallen. The abbreviated identifications are used at the request of the families involved.

Chapter 26

—

LOOKING DOWN

In mid-summer 1966, not long after I was sworn in as DCI, Carl Duckett, then the Agency deputy director for science and technology (DDS&T), undertook to brief me on the Agency's early effort to develop what he called "an imagery satellite with a real-time readout capability." The physics I learned at Williams College was of some help, but I realized I was getting only the gist of what Carl was telling me.

The next day, Carl was back in my office for round two. Before he could begin, I explained that although it might have been my fault, I had not understood many of the terms he used to describe his work. "From now on," I said, "you've got to use terms that I can understand well enough to visualize what you and your team are doing. Until then, the whole damn project is in the balance." Carl assumed—a bit rashly—that I was joking, and shifted gears. With the help of a glossary we created and Carl's infinite patience, my grasp of the project took shape.

Before becoming DCI, my knowledge of the science involved in the high-altitude reconnaissance projects came in fragments gleaned at meetings on other topics when Allen Dulles or Dick Bissell made glancing references to these ultra-secret, Eyes Only projects. I was, of course, fully cognizant of the stunning product of these operations.

During World War II, when he was the commanding general of

SHAEF (Supreme Headquarters, Allied Expeditionary Force), Eisenhower had become accustomed to the highest levels of intelligence on
every aspect of Hitler's armed forces and government. As president,
Eisenhower grasped the postwar espionage problems, and was keenly
aware that the vast wartime intelligence sources—broken ciphers,
agents in place in Berlin, scores of agents scattered throughout enemy-
occupied Europe, and daily aerial photoreconnaissance—were not available. He also understood that Soviet security measures were much more
sophisticated and even more pervasive than anything the Nazis had been
able to achieve. Eisenhower realized that, at best, it would take time to
effect any significant penetration of the USSR.

President Truman had authorized the Air Force and Navy to fly peripheral collection flights along the USSR borders. The results were useful but marginal. Worse, some two hundred airmen were killed or
captured in the course of these hazardous missions. President Eisenhower authorized the effort to continue, but knew that these flights could
not be expected to provide the data on Soviet military capability that he
considered essential. He was also concerned by the fact that the reconnaissance version of the B-47 looked dangerously like its twin, the
nuclear-armed B-47 bomber.

A committee chaired by James Killian, Jr., head of the Pentagon's
Scientific Advisory Panel and president of MIT, and a subgroup headed
by Edwin Land, president of the Polaroid Corporation, recommended
the development of an aircraft that could fly high enough to avoid anti-
aircraft fire and Soviet fighter airplanes. The new plane would require
sufficient fuel to fly a north-south route over the USSR and continue on
to safe haven. Cameras with extraordinary high-definition lenses and
new film would also have to be developed.

The urgent demand for hard intelligence on Soviet military capabilities and the need for the highest level of security to protect every aspect
of the new project governed Eisenhower's decisions. Because the President was acutely aware of how long it might take to push even an urgent
project through the prescribed Pentagon procedures, he ordered the program to be directed by CIA civilians, with strong Air Force support. Absolute security was essential—any leak would allow the USSR to
prepare new defense measures. To ensure this level of security, Eisenhower decided not to seek congressional approval. At his direction,

funds were allocated from the CIA budget. All knowledge of the project was restricted to an absolute "need to know."

On December 1, 1954, the Development Project Staff was established under the direction of Richard Bissell. The project was provided with its own communications system, and office space was established in Washington, several miles from the Agency headquarters. The staff included thirty security officers. In time, more than six hundred employees were stationed abroad.

The tight security prevailed until May 1, 1960, when a U-2 aircraft was knocked down over the USSR. At President Eisenhower's direction, no more U-2 flights over the Soviet Union were undertaken; a more capable aircraft was already in the works. The new vehicle was christened OXCART, rather a misnomer for a craft that flew 2000 miles an hour at 85,000 feet. At a secret air base in Nevada, I watched a midnight takeoff of this plane. The blast of flame that sent the black, insect-shaped projectile hurtling across the tarmac made me duck instinctively. It was as if the Devil himself were blasting his way straight from Hell. But OXCART was never used over the USSR; a "reconnaissance satellite" known as CORONA superseded it.

CORONA was vastly more complicated than the manned aircraft flights. The photo-satellite was propelled into orbit by a rocket. With its cameras programmed to turn on and off over various areas of the USSR, the satellite had to remain stable and on course until it completed the photo mission. The flight continued until reaching the precise map coordinates above the Pacific Ocean and a rendezvous with a high-flying aircraft. The satellite then ejected the cameras and film. If timing and navigation were perfect, the ejected bundle would be intercepted before plunging into the ocean.

I have never ceased to marvel at the amount of pure science, technical skill, imagination, initiative, and determination involved in achieving these results. CORONA ranks high in the history of American accomplishments. The fact that the project remained secret is in itself remarkable.

A final irony. After thirteen nerve-wrenching failures, the first successful CORONA flight occurred on the day that Gary Powers, pilot of the fallen U-2, was sentenced to prison by a Moscow court. On this flight CORONA returned with twenty pounds of film—and more, and better, photographs of the USSR than all of the U-2 flights combined.

As always in the intelligence world, one successful—against all odds—operation begets another often more daunting demand. We were soon informed that our magical triple play was entirely too time-consuming. Too many hours were involved in intercepting the stolen booty, flying it to Washington, and waiting for the lengthy processing. The time involved in this sequence seemed reasonable enough to me. Not so, said the impatient analysts. Something known as real-time readout was now deemed essential.

Fortunately for us all, Albert D. "Bud" Wheelon, one of the most outstanding of our score of genius-level scientists, was at home in Annandale, Virginia, watching the Washington Redskins blow a National Football League game in San Francisco. It occurred to him that if a Redskins fumble could be viewed across the country in real time, it should be possible to arrange such a transmission from an earth-orbiting capsule careening several hundred miles out in space. Indeed, why not?

Wheelon, who was the first chief of the newly formed Directorate for Science and Technology (DS&T), assigned the task to Leslie Dirks, a talented MIT physics graduate and former Rhodes scholar. Bud had recently recruited Dirks to run the Office of Science and Technology in the DS&T. This is not the place to recount the details, but by 1976 data from a satellite orbiting the USSR were transmitted to a relay satellite in a much higher orbit, from which it was then transmitted to a ground station in the United States. In effect, another spectacular triple play. The few seconds lost in this legerdemain fell within the definition of real time established by the persnickety consumers. The data flowed at the rate of over a hundred digital TV channels. Even more remarkably, the linkup was achieved on the first try.

A few months before the first successful satellite flight, the coordinated estimates of Soviet missile strength ranged from 140 to 200 intercontinental nuclear missiles. The first CORONA photographs reduced the count from 10 to perhaps as many as 25 ICBMs. CORONA flew 145 secret missions, with equally rewarding results. I was invited to CIA headquarters in February 1995 when Vice President Al Gore announced the declassification of CORONA. It was a treat to watch one of our Top Secret Code Word CORONA cameras being handed over to the Smithsonian Institution. More important, the declassification gave the project a second life.

From the first photographs in 1960, these reconnaissance satellites have continued to provide this government with the vital strategic intelligence needed for informed policy decisions. The military data protect our armies in the field. Policymakers can monitor compliance with international treaties, and evaluate natural and man-made disasters.

Today, the photographs are available to environmentalists, agronomists, geologists, cartographers, and dozens of other experts. The photographs show changes in the arctic ice cap, pollution in rivers, the effects of deforestation, the encroachment of deserts on once fertile land.

President Johnson once said, "We've spent between thirty-five and forty billion dollars on space . . . but if nothing else had come from that program except the knowledge that we get from our satellite photography, it would be worth ten times . . . what the whole program has cost. . . . We were building things we didn't need. . . . We were harboring fears that we didn't need to have."

Chapter 27

—

J. EDGAR'S FBI

J. Edgar Hoover had been in office forty-two years when I was appointed director of Central Intelligence. Given the pressure of other business, I decided that I might wait a few days before making the customary protocol call. I had met Hoover several times at social events, invariably when British, Canadian, or Australian intelligence and security visitors were in Washington on official business. On these occasions our chats were strictly social, no shoptalk, ever.

The day I first visited the FBI offices—as my grandmother would have said, "to make my manners," and to assure Hoover that CIA would continue to work closely with the FBI—Hoover greeted me cordially, and waved me to a chair directly in front of his desk. After a forty-five-minute uninterrupted history of the FBI in peace and war, J. Edgar stood up. We shook hands, and he wished me well in my new job. As I recall it, I did not say a word during his monologue. Nor did Director Hoover mention anything that in any way concerned our respective professional concerns. It was after this bizarre session that I decided not to seek any further one-on-one meetings with him.

A few months later, after a Tuesday lunch at the White House, I found Jim Angleton and Sam Papich, the FBI officer who handled liaison with the Agency, sitting in my outer office. Jim looked so glum and Sam so forlorn that I resisted the temptation to make a reference to "Death in the Afternoon," and summoned them inside.

The situation that Jim and Sam viewed as a serious crisis had surfaced a few days earlier in Colorado. In a routine discussion of the whereabouts of a missing college professor, one of the local FBI officers had inadvertently mentioned an inconsequential aspect of the case to the chief of the local CIA Contacts Division (overt) offices. When Hoover learned about this gaffe, he instructed Papich to demand that CIA identify the FBI officer who had made the mistake.

Angleton asked if we should comply with Hoover's demand. I refused. My strong feeling was that it was up to Hoover to ferret out his own agent. I did not want to put CIA in the position of finking on the slight slip of a career FBI officer.

When Hoover, who took great pride in keeping abreast of all FBI activity, no matter how marginal, learned that I had no intention of investigating the incident, he forthwith suspended all liaison between the FBI and the Agency. This was informal—that is, Hoover did not inform me officially or by letter; he simply instructed Sam Papich to stop coming to the Agency to exchange communications and discuss problems.

Jim and Sam both saw the situation as a much more serious crisis than I did. My reaction was conditioned by the fact that the last thing I wanted was an all-out contretemps with the FBI on such a trivial matter. Moreover, I decided that if J. Edgar wanted to punish me or the Agency, I did not, at the moment at least, see what might be done about it. I shrugged, and suggested that this episode might not be the end of the world as we knew it. After giving Jim and Sam the benefit of my reasoning, I suggested they go home, have a stiff drink or two, and wait to see what might happen. I assume that they accepted at least part of my advice.

It turned out that what J. Edgar had suspended was any personal contact between Bureau agents and their CIA counterparts. At the work level both sides got around the problem by exchanging memoranda in lieu of the usually more rewarding—and less time-consuming—personal meetings. This went on for several weeks until, without notice, things returned to normal, with FBI agents coming out to the Agency as usual. This episode struck me as an example of Hoover's determination to show that at all times he was fully in charge of every aspect of the FBI.

My first insight into J. Edgar's FBI came from Herman Horton, a Bureau officer who had left the FBI to join OSS and stayed on in CIA. Herman had actually worked in Hoover's office. From the early days, Hoover had insisted that all liaison between the FBI and other government offices, including Congress and the White House, be conducted by the responsible FBI agents visiting the offices of the other agencies. No outsider was to conduct business on Bureau premises. All liaison reports went directly to Hoover, and all outgoing correspondence was signed by him. I came to consider Hoover the most accomplished American bureaucrat of the twentieth century. I say this without irony. J. Edgar had a superb grasp of how things are done in Washington, and was informed in detail of every aspect of the FBI.

Hoover welcomed telephone calls from any senator, congressman, or high-ranking official, particularly one who might have been found misbehaving. According to Horton, it was Hoover's practice to "glad-hand" these callers. Not to worry, the miscreants would be assured, Hoover kept all such details in a secret file right there in his private office. I was never aware of Hoover leaking any significant intelligence or internal security data, but the bits of salacious gossip that often floated into the White House were another matter. And I know nothing of the alleged sensitive files that he personally kept. The fact that it was widely thought that J. Edgar kept such files was probably threatening enough to keep some potential sinners in check.

In the very early days, CIA conducted its own security background checks on prospective employees. When it became apparent that the FBI could handle this work more efficiently, the responsibility was turned over. In the United States, serious personnel security problems were handled jointly with the FBI and the CIA Office of Security.

When the CIA Counterintelligence Staff was established, Jim Angleton assumed responsibility for operational liaison with the FBI. Jane Roman, a veteran OSS X-2 officer, handled the daily meetings with Sam Papich. Hoover could not have made a better choice in selecting a liaison representative than Sam Papich.

Sam was one of the first FBI agents* to have worked undercover abroad. From 1941 to 1945 he had three undercover assignments in

---

*FBI officers are referred to as "agents" or special agents. FBI-controlled spies are "informants." In CIA, "agents" are spies. CIA operational personnel are "officers." To belabor the obvious, it has happened that an FBI agent was also a spy, and that a CIA officer was also an agent. In context, Robert Hanssen and Aldrich Ames come to mind.

Latin America. This gave him an informed understanding of the difference between police work at home and secret operations abroad.

Hoover was never comfortable dealing directly with foreigners. He restricted his few personal meetings with foreign officials to those from the United Kingdom, Canada, Australia, and New Zealand. He rarely if ever dealt personally with any of the other foreign services with which the FBI maintained relations. To my knowledge, Hoover had never stepped out of the United States.

In the early postwar days, liaison relationships between the Bureau and the CIA predecessor units were complicated by individuals smarting off. One side saw the other as cops, out of their depth in foreign operations. The others viewed the Agency staff as dilettantes, too delicate for the real world. Both were wrong. The respect and friendship that grew between Sam Papich and Angleton solved a great many problems, and served as the foundation for future relations at various levels.

One of Papich's earliest experiences with CIA came in a meeting with General Bedell Smith. Sam had gone to the DCI's office on a delicate counterintelligence matter. He presented J. Edgar's position, and General Smith exploded. "Does your boss really think he can send some bald-headed bastard in here to tell me how to run my business?" In deference to Beedle Smith's well-known ulcer problems, semi-bald Sam remained silent.

A few moments later, Smith got up from his desk and invited Sam into a small room adjoining his office. Coffee was served to Sam, milk to Smith. Cookies were shared. The air cleared, and Papich's relationship with Beedle was soon back on track and prospering. Months later, when General Smith was named under secretary of state, he asked that Papich replace the Bureau agent responsible for liaison with the department. Fortunately for the FBI and CIA, Sam managed to talk the general out of pushing his request.

By the late 1940s, we had achieved a reasonable and effective relationship between the two services. There were, of course, marked differences. The FBI was a national police service, and a good one. For decades the FBI's basic responsibility was solving crimes; domestic counterintelligence came second. CIA's operations activity was abroad. Differences in technique and methods became apparent when an FBI informant's activity took him abroad and the control of the operation was transferred to CIA. Similar problems occurred when a CIA-controlled agent's activity moved into the United States. Despite occasional misunderstandings, the relationship was always, at the least, more than adequate.

Another area of occasional disagreement came in the assessment of the bona fides of defectors and agents. In the Nosenko case, the differences of opinion between the Bureau and the Agency were mild when compared to the strife that existed within CIA, and to a degree within the Bureau. Less contentious were the respective evaluations of FBI-controlled agents in place in the Soviet intelligence services. As it was in Vietnam, it is not unusual for experts dealing with identical data to come up with divergent evaluations.

In the course of his service, J. Edgar made his share of enemies, and secretly disaffected superiors. President Nixon actually asked me how Hoover might be eased out of office. I understood his problem, but did not offer any advice. The bottom line was always attributed to President Johnson: "In the long run, I'd rather have Edgar on the inside pissing out, than on the outside hosing me down." Both Presidents decided to let nature take its course. It did, and Hoover died in 1972.

Since Hoover's death a few commentators and journalists have been bold enough to speculate on his possible homosexual bent. The image of the legendary G-man in wig and ball gown has even been conjured up by one writer. I know of no reliable evidence to support this allegation, and have no reason to believe that J. Edgar was anything but the self-contained fellow that he seemed to be. All I can contribute to the speculation is to point out that Hoover, a creature of habit, was almost never alone.

Hoover's daily routine rarely varied. An FBI car, driver, and bodyguard would pick Hoover up at his Thirtieth Street residence, drive to the apartment of his deputy, Clyde Tolson, on Massachusetts Avenue, and then to FBI headquarters. At noon, Hoover and Tolson would be driven to whichever restaurant was then their favorite. At the end of the day, the transportation routine would be reversed in time for early dinner and subsequent TV. This door-to-door transportation followed the same pattern when J. Edgar was on vacation—more often than not with Tolson.

In the Washington fishbowl, and even on holiday, I find it impossible to believe that anyone as well known and as easily identified as Hoover might have managed a clandestine sex life. J. Edgar Hoover's personal life could not have been more banal.

Eccentric? Yes. Very eccentric? Yes, indeed. An active homosexual? No way.

—

Chapter 28

BEYOND X–2

In his thirty-two years of active service, James Angleton remained relatively unknown beyond the confines of the secret intelligence world. It is all the more ironic that since Jim's dismissal from CIA, the only one of his Agency contemporaries to have inspired more public attention is Allen Dulles. Much of what has been published is unfair to Angleton, to the various DCI's for whom he worked, to the Agency, and to history.

At the time James Angleton relinquished his post in Rome, he was one of the few wartime OSS officers who remained in the field to become chiefs of station and who determined to make their careers in secret intelligence. Angleton's activity in Italy during the final months of the war had attracted General Donovan's attention and won praise from Allen Dulles in Bern. In the immediate postwar years, Angleton's work covered the spectrum of secret operations—liaison, intelligence collection on the new targets in Eastern Europe, Communist Party penetrations, counterintelligence, and communications. Some of the operations he established lasted years after his departure. By the time he returned from Italy in late 1947, Angleton was recognized as one of our outstanding field operatives. After a stretch of sick leave, he began work as a special assistant to Admiral Hillenkoetter, then DCI.

I met Jim in 1948 when he became a staff assistant to Colonel Donald

Galloway, then running the operational component, Office for Special Operations (OSO). Jim's area of responsibility was intelligence collection. It was in the process of attempting to push some of my correspondence through the occasional traffic jams in Colonel Galloway's office that I got to know Jim. We didn't always agree, but I profited from some of his insights, and I think he learned a bit about the operations climate north of downtown Milan. Nevertheless, we were both gratified when the Agency was reorganized in 1954. Frank Wisner became deputy director for plans (DDP), and at about that time I stepped up to replace Kirkpatrick as Frank's deputy and chief of operations. Bill Harvey moved from Staff C—then the counterintelligence component—to the communications intelligence assignment that would lead him to Berlin. Staff C became the Counterintelligence Staff and Jim was named chief, the job he most wanted and which he was to occupy until December 1974 when he was fired by William Colby. Contrary to some of what has been published, Angleton and Harvey were never competitors. Each followed a separate career path. They worked closely together and were friends—no matter that I have never encountered two men who differed more completely in experience, background, appearance, taste, and hobbies than this odd couple.

The best of Angleton's operational work is still classified and in my view should remain so. In his day, Jim was recognized as the dominant counterintelligence figure in the non-communist world. He succeeded in establishing an intimacy of counterintelligence and security liaison with the NATO powers and other non-communist countries that exceeded any that had previously existed in peacetime. In most instances these relations were at least as candid as those that existed under the blast furnace pressure of World War II. This was a considerable accomplishment and unprecedented.

In managing the Agency's liaison with the FBI, Jim's ability to maintain an even course and profitable relationship through the turf battles, bickering, misunderstandings, and collisions with the encrusted J. Edgar Hoover was outstanding. Jim's interest in Israel was of exceptional value. Various countries have honored their own officers and agents on postage stamps, and with official biographies and films. To my knowledge, only Israel has ever dedicated a monument to a foreign intelligence officer. In Jim's case, it is two monuments—one on a battlefield a few miles from Jerusalem, the other a plaque on a huge stone near the city center.

In the years since the collapse of the Soviet Union and the restructuring of the KGB into a domestic security organ and a separate foreign intelligence service, some of the KGB old boys have claimed, with knowing chuckles, that Angleton had turned out to be their biggest asset in the West. Not that Jim was a KGB agent, but that his alleged harebrained security measures had paralyzed the ability of the Western powers to operate against the USSR. And, incidentally, to protect the democracies from the depredations of the KGB and its sister services. This is less the opinion of ostensibly unemployed KGB hacks than blunt disinformation intended to warn the world's security services against ever again letting a deluded American talk them into wasting effort and money worrying about the KGB's offspring, the SVR. The Cold War is over, they remind us. The hatchets are buried, you democracies don't have a thing to worry about. Just relax, and let things get back to the way they were before that Gouzenko fellow walked out of the Soviet embassy in Canada with all those cables, and the lovesick Ms. Bentley began to blab a lot of nonsense. Indeed, why worry?

—

In the years we worked together, I got to know James Angleton well and to value him as a colleague and a friend. I remember him as one of the most complex men I have ever known. One did not always have to agree with him to know that he possessed a unique grasp of secret operations. As a friend remarked, Jim had the ability to raise an operational discussion not only to a higher level but to another dimension. It is easy to mock this, but there was no one within the Agency with whom I would rather have discussed a complex operational problem than Angleton. This notwithstanding, Jim's counterintelligence competence had to be balanced against an understanding of the many aspects of his personality.

I find it difficult to square the Angleton I knew with the images of Jim that appear to have been written by those who knew him slightly if at all. One element of the problem is that late in life Jim was not above spoofing uninformed supplicants who assumed they had outwitted him, and gulled their way into his confidence. This was less an intended disservice to history than a sardonic reaction to having been taken too lightly.

One of Jim's dominant traits was an obsessive approach to things that interested him. This was as apparent in his social life and hobbies as in his work—his commitment to counterintelligence was lifelong and relentless. Setting aside the responsibility for the routine security housekeeping encompassed by the all-purpose counterintelligence canon, Jim remained convinced that in peacetime it would be possible to achieve the level of counterintelligence practiced in World War II. Wartime security disciplines allowed both the Allied and Soviet services to stage brilliantly conceived and executed deception operations. The techniques involved in penetrating an enemy service and dousing it with enough disinformation and deception to turn its momentum and energy against itself cannot, however, be practiced on a broad basis or by inexperienced operatives. At some cost to his reputation, Jim continued to pursue possible instances of high-level peacetime deception. Given sufficiently high stakes, it is within the ability of sophisticated intelligence services to execute peacetime deception operations. Unless security can be maintained at an ultra-high level, such operations cannot be conducted on a broad basis or sustained indefinitely.

Jim went overboard from time to time. His conviction that the Sino-Soviet split was a mirage created by Soviet deception experts was interesting but simply not true. I let him push this view and arranged for him to express it to experts, including Henry Kissinger. When Jim failed to rally any support, I instructed him to knock it off, and to leave high-level political punditry to others.

Jim approached hobbies with the intensity he devoted to his work. His interest in fly-fishing led to collecting antique tackle and tying museum-quality specimens of trout flies. In an unguarded moment, I mentioned that my wife, Cynthia, and I would be vacationing with friends who planned to take us trout fishing. The next Saturday afternoon, Jim equipped us with some of his less delicate equipment and bundled us off to Battery-Kemble Park. For two hours, and to the amusement of a stream of passersby, we cast fly after fly in the general direction of a cluster of daffodils. Only when we were reaching the vicinity of our targets three out of five times were we allowed to call it a day.

Jim's interest in breeding orchids is as well known as his practice of controlling his inventory by bringing plants to friends. Cynthia telephoned to ask Jim why her favorite orchid seemed to languish. Too little of this, too much of that? she asked. Two days later, the postman delivered two single-spaced pages of possible remedies. The old-fashioned parlor game of charades, in which a member of one team had three minutes to mime a quotation or title proposed by the opposition, had a brief vogue in Washington. I recall Jim's confounding a party by guessing "Clot the bedded axle-tree" in thirty seconds and "Gamma Gurton's Needle" in less time.

Some critics have charged Angleton with having given away the store in his Washington liaison with Kim Philby. There is no doubt that Philby did immense damage to British and American interests, not the least of which came from his dealing with Agency and FBI officers who had little or no experience in coping with wily foreign liaison chaps. Jim was one of the most experienced CIA officers Philby encountered in Washington. I would guess that he was at least as accomplished as Philby in the tit-for-tat aspects of liaison. The hitch, of course, was that Philby—representing both the British and the KGB—had the vast advantage of playing on both sides of the net.

I have no doubt that the exposure of Kim Philby was lodged in the deepest recess of Jim's being. He had accepted Philby as a friend, and respected him as one of the most effective British operatives. This view was shared by Philby's English colleagues who had known Kim longer and more intimately than Jim ever did. The fact that Bill Harvey, who had no previous experience in dealing with the British, was the first Agency officer to be convinced of Philby's treason can only have intensified Jim's profound determination never again to be betrayed. Ironically, Harvey's dislike for Philby was fueled by a vulgar cartoon of Mrs. Harvey drawn by Philby's pal Guy Burgess.

The criticism leveled against Angleton since his dismissal by Colby seems to ignore Jim's accomplishments and the reasons General Donovan and six directors of Central Intelligence—General Vandenberg, Admiral Hillenkoetter, General Smith, Allen Dulles, John McCone, and I—valued his service. There were any number of channels, formal and otherwise, through which any of Angleton's *post facto* critics might have expressed their views of Jim's performance while he was still in office. I recall no one within the Agency having raised even a fraction of the criticism they began to express after his dismissal.

In the 1960s the White House appointed an interagency team to examine various CIA stations abroad. Discussions were concentrated on Agency operations against the USSR. A senior FBI officer accompanied the team. Not once was any complaint made against Angleton, nor was there any suggestion that he was in any way hampering operations.

In the 1970s the President's Foreign Intelligence Advisory Board (PFIAB) made a similar inspection. PFIAB members are appointed from private life by each president and given full security clearances. They are free to conduct any investigation they wish, and report only to the President. Again, a senior FBI man served as a liaison officer with the inspection group. The PFIAB members visited various field stations and poked thoroughly into the nooks and crannies of our Washington headquarters. No criticism of Angleton or the Counterintelligence Staff was raised in the field or in Washington.

I do not recall anyone in the Agency or elsewhere—board-certified in psychiatry or merely a self-recognized lay expert—ever diagnosing Jim as paranoid, or otherwise psychologically unfit for office. Extensive counterintelligence experience is likely to create a tendency in even the most sanguine officers to distrust some of what might be called received wisdom. In an imperfect world, we all need occasionally to be reminded that all that glitters is not necessarily eighteen-karat treasure.

One of the more difficult problems various writers have laid at Angleton's door bore the unhappy cryptonym MHCHAOS, most often shortened to CHAOS. During the Johnson administration and throughout my tenure under Nixon, CHAOS was my responsibility. Nothing in my thirty-year service brought me more criticism than my response to President Johnson's insistence that the Agency supply him proof that foreign agents and funds were at the root of the racial and political unrest that took fire in the summer of 1967. LBJ simply could not believe that American youth would on their own be moved to riot in protest against U.S. foreign policy. Nixon's reaction was, as always, more subjective, but he also remained convinced that the domestic dissidence was initiated and nurtured from abroad.

The broiling summer of 1967 had reached midpoint when President Johnson instructed me to obtain proof that the direction and funding of the antiwar movement and the domestic dissident political turmoil was coming from abroad. I explained that such an investigation might risk involving the Agency in a violation of the CIA charter limiting our activity to operations abroad and forbidding anything resembling domestic police or security activity.

LBJ listened for some fifteen seconds before saying, "I'm quite aware of that. What I want is for you to pursue this matter, and to do what is necessary to track down the foreign communists who are behind this intolerable interference in our domestic affairs."

I had no quarrel with LBJ's objective; his concern was legitimate. With tens of thousands of troops on the battlefield, the President's decision was obvious. It lay within the Agency's responsibility to determine if and how foreign powers might be provoking and funding antiwar and political dissidence within the United States.

The following day, I established the Special Operations Group (SOG) and named Richard Ober, a tall, levelheaded Harvard alumnus and third-generation oar on a winning crew, chief of the unit. I informed him that at the direction of the President, his group's sole purpose was to examine all the evidence from *all* possible foreign sources indicating any foreign support to domestic political dissidents, including student antiwar protesters. I then made SOG an appendage of the Counterintelligence Staff but not subordinate to Angleton. Political dissidence was scarcely a counterintelligence responsibility, but because the President had directed us to sail so closely to the wind, I wanted to keep this activity compartmented from other operational activity and firmly under my control. All of the Agency's CHAOS reporting went through me. Jim did not ask for this arrangement nor did I consult him before leaving this sensitive baby on the stoop beside his door.

In November, a month after a large demonstration on the steps of the Pentagon, the Agency forwarded its first report based on data the SOG had developed. However optimistically President Johnson may have opened his copy of the "International Connections of the U.S. Peace Movement," he can only have suffered a thundering disappointment. For all our effort abroad, we had not uncovered any significant foreign involvement or funding for any of the dissidence. I expected an explosive reaction from the White House, and in my darker moments thought there might even be a suggestion from the President that "we reason together for a few moments." LBJ's notion of reasoning together was the equivalent of discussing the ownership of a side of beef with a Bengal tiger.

There was no protest from the White House, only the demand that we intensify our search for foreign influence. At this juncture, we moved closer to infringing on our charter and produced a study, "Restless Youth." I forwarded two versions to the White House. One contained a domestic section and was restricted to the President and two of his closest advisors. In the cover letter to the President, I reminded him that he should "be aware of the peculiar sensitivity which attaches to the fact that CIA has prepared a report on the student activities both here and abroad." (When President Nixon asked for information on antiwar protests in early 1969, I sent a copy of this report to Henry Kissinger and the President with a similar caution in respect to the Agency charter. Nixon shared LBJ's conviction that foreign support was at the root of the political dissidence and antiwar activity.)

The pressure for results increased, and our efforts continued to expand. If there were any foreign support of the American dissident movement, it most probably would have come from the KGB, its sister services, and the North Vietnamese. Our existing foreign sources detected no such activity. If any artfully concealed support actually existed, we reasoned, it would likely be funneled through the European dissident student movements. If so, a well-cloaked American graduate student might wriggle his way deeply enough into the European movement to catch a glimpse of it. Two or three mature American volunteers acquired the necessary antiwar patina, and went abroad to continue their studies. They made contact with people who might be close to the most plausible foreign sponsors of the movement in the United States. Again, there was no trace of evidence to support the Johnson-Nixon convictions.

In this connection, a violation of our charter occurred when we accepted several reports from agents on the activity of the groups they had joined here in order to develop the camouflage that would give them access to the foreign dissident groups. This information was passed to the FBI. In strict compliance with the Agency charter, we should have destroyed these reports without allowing the FBI to see them.

Considering the pressure we were under, and the immense amount of material we were handling—some 7000 FBI files were studied and more than 300,000 of the names were incorporated into the CHAOS data bank—I think an assessment in the Rockefeller Commission* report is a

*See chapter 42.

fair judgment of our effort: "The Presidential demands upon CIA appear to have caused the Agency to forgo to some extent, the caution with which it might otherwise have approached the subject." Given the temper of the times, this was at the least a generous judgment. A more accurate assessment would have stated bluntly that without the President's insistence, CIA would never have investigated or reported on anything touching on domestic political violence.*

The Rockefeller report goes on to declare that the "proper functioning of the Agency must depend in large part on the character of the Director of Central Intelligence." The fact that significant areas of the Agency's activity must remain cloaked from public view magnifies the DCI's responsibility for keeping the President and appropriate congressional committees fully informed of all Agency operations, and has little to do with the DCI's character. The regulations, rules, and practices under which the DCI labors are as clearly established as those of other government agencies and departments. It scarcely needs to be stated that a DCI who, on his own, ignores or violates these boundaries should expect no more consideration than might be given the chief of any other federal agency or department. However obvious, this is a less than useful guide come crunch time, when a president orders his DCI to step out-of-bounds.

If, after reminding the President of the Agency's charter restrictions and suggesting any appropriate alternatives, the President remains insistent, what is the DCI to do? He is neither a policymaker nor a judicial officer. Has he the authority to refuse to accept a questionable order on a foreign policy question of obvious national importance? If the President's directive cannot be deflected, the DCI's responses range from acceptance to outright refusal and presumably resignation.

I faced two such instances. After having reminded President Johnson that he risked pushing me out-of-bounds, I agreed to attempt to find foreign influence in student and political dissidence in 1967. LBJ's determination to uncover the foreign sponsors of the dissidence was adequate reason for our initial investigation abroad. (As our effort continued, we erred in examining and analyzing domestic aspects of the problem.) In contrast, the police investigation of the Watergate break-in soon escalated into a vital domestic political issue. When President Nixon ordered

*The above-mentioned files were all destroyed by the Agency.

his White House staff—Messrs. Haldeman, Ehrlichman, and Dean—to direct me (via General Walters) to supply bail for the Watergate burglars, and to deflect the FBI's investigation of the crime, I instructed Walters to refuse their demands. Rather than force my resignation, and presumably face the likely intense public curiosity about the reasons for my leaving, President Nixon backed away.

One of the more publicized incidents attributed to Angleton by Agency critics is his alleged role in ruining the careers of various Agency officers with unfounded suspicions of their loyalty. I knew each of these officers and can vouch that they were well qualified for the positions they attained in the Agency, and could have expected further promotion. The security problems each encountered were quite different, and each officer was given every possible consideration. In the end, I had no choice but to accept a decision that in effect said each was innocent, but that the innocence could not be proved. This is the reverse of the verdict occasionally given in British law courts—"guilty but not proved."

In the very early days, my experience as a member of a board adjudicating a somewhat similar problem left me with a deep understanding of the complexity of each case. As DCI, there were no personnel problems that concerned me more than those of these four officers. Each officer was offered positions at his grade level elsewhere in the Agency and with the same promotion prospects offered in his original career discipline. The important difference was that the new positions would not require higher security clearances. The decision was a bitter disappointment to all, and each chose to retire with full benefits rather than accept a career change.

In arriving at this difficult decision, the Office of Security and the Counterintelligence Staff collaborated closely. The CI Staff was advisory. The basic recommendation rested with the Office of Security. The final decision was mine alone.

From the time in the SSU days when I was first involved in such drastic security decisions, I made every possible attempt to keep from having to dismiss an employee or radically to change his career path. But when all the evidence has been judged and innocence cannot be proved, there is no choice but transfer to less sensitive work, retirement, or dismissal without prejudice.

As evidence of the importance of staff security, it is worth recalling a few lines from the National Security Act of 1947. "In effect, *and notwithstanding the provisions of any other law,* the Director may, in the Director's discretion, terminate the employment of any officer or employee of the CIA when the Director shall deem it necessary or advisable in the interests of the United States" (emphasis added).

The tolerance with which the British service handled the case of the traitor George Blake, who was taken prisoner by the North Koreans and endured a severe hardship before offering his services to the KGB, is a sad example of the equities involved. Along with a mass of other data, Blake betrayed the Berlin and Vienna tunnel operations.

The most I can add to this difficult issue is that in the future I would have the Agency make it absolutely clear to every prospective employee that at any time in his career conditions might, through no fault of his, mandate either a career shift or dismissal. This might come from a security problem that cannot be resolved, a blown operation which results in widespread true-name publicity, or any other incident peculiar to high-security intelligence employment.

The widespread notion—spread in part by retired officers who should be better informed—that Angleton brought the Agency's Soviet operations programs to a halt in the last few years of his career is patently false. Defectors were welcomed, debriefed, and resettled. New operations were approved and went forward. The root of the allegations against Angleton appear to me to have been the decisions of the Soviet operations division to drop some long-standing activities of doubtful value in the interests of a new look and a change in operational emphasis. The Counterintelligence Staff had no part in these decisions.

Jim Angleton had his faults. He became too isolated late in his career, and failed to recognize some of the changes occurring within the Agency. He overvalued some sources, and became too focused on European problems. Jim should have left a better written record, and might have participated more directly in creating vitally important new counterintelligence training programs. Although Jim would have fought it with all his formidable strengths, I should have insisted that he step aside, and into a position where he could research his operational views and put them on paper. With it all, he served the country well and deserves a far better press than he has had.

Chapter 29

—

"FORGING" AHEAD

My first public appearance before Congress came in June 1961, a few weeks after the Bay of Pigs, when the Senate Internal Security Subcommittee opened a hearing on "Communist Forgeries." I was still officially Dick Bissell's deputy. Rather than attempting to explain all this, and because my name was *not* to appear in the published report, I was identified only as an "Assistant Deputy Director of the Central Intelligence Agency." It was a nonexistent title, and a notional step above my post.

The paper I presented was prepared by Angleton's Counterintelligence Staff. Aside from illustrating Moscow's well-honed ability to exploit the international media, I suspect that the staunchly anti-communist members of the subcommittee also hoped to generate some favorable press and to balance a bit of the criticism that followed the Bay of Pigs. For that reason, "Forgeries" was the first transcript of a Senate hearing ever to be translated into French, Italian, and Spanish.

From the early years of the Cold War, Moscow and its dependent communist services had plagued the United States with dozens of forged documents, usually prepared on official letterhead paper stolen or reproduced in Moscow. Each document was "authenticated" by the forged signature of one or more appropriately senior American officials. The forgeries invariably purported to show the sinister aspect of an alleged secret American activity or policy. The texts were relatively well prepared but quite easily shown to have been fabricated. Errors in format, spelling, syntax, and official titles were common. However obvious these mistakes or ludicrous the policy content, the allegations invariably reached a far greater audience than our subsequent crystal-clear—to us at least—proofs of forgery.

To avoid the appearance of coming directly from Moscow, the forgeries were most often slipped to left-leaning or communist-owned foreign newspapers. The sensational story would then be picked up and trumpeted by Soviet and Eastern European media. In due time the Western press would latch on.

Two interrelated incidents show how, with a minimum of discernible effort, Moscow was able to manipulate the world press. The first occurred in June 1961, and nearly resulted in the cancellation of a planned meeting between President Kennedy and Charles de Gaulle, the president of France. Before the dust settled in the second incident, a significant number of Americans had apparently been convinced that CIA and the Pentagon, supported by the "military-industrial complex," had successfully cooperated in murdering President Kennedy on November 22, 1963.

Moscow had long sought to tie the United States to France's strenuous efforts to suppress Algerian resistance to French colonialism. On April 22, 1961, a handful of French general officers, based in Algeria, attempted a coup d'état. A day later, the *Paese Sera,* an obscure Italian daily newspaper with ties to the Italian Communist Party, published a report claiming that the attempted coup had been supported by CIA. Twenty-four hours later, *Pravda, TASS,* and Soviet radio replayed the Italian story. The Western media soon followed. As always, with each repetition, the original allegation gained credibility. In France, the story peaked when *Le Monde,* one of the most influential newspapers in Europe, ran a lead editorial stating, "It now seems established that some American agents more or less encouraged" the French generals who had instigated the attempted coup.

Just how this judgment was "more or less" established was not disclosed. The fact that the U.S. embassy denied the allegation may even have underlined U.S. guilt in the eyes of the French left.

When President de Gaulle realized that the uproar threatened a scheduled meeting with President Kennedy in Paris, the French took action. Foreign Minister Couve de Murville stepped before the National Assembly in Paris and forcefully denied the allegations. President Kennedy's meeting with De Gaulle took place as planned.

It was in early 1967 that I received the first inkling of one of the more bizarre and troublesome incidents in my tenure as DCI. It came in a telephone call from the New Orleans district attorney, James Garrison— "Jim," as he referred to himself. I later learned that Garrison's given names were Earling Carothers. When visions of national political prominence first danced into his dreams, he arranged a legal change. Garrison asked me to come to New Orleans and testify in his investigation of the Kennedy assassination.

I had never heard of Garrison, and his investigation was news to me. After a noncommittal response, I arranged a meeting with Senator Richard Russell, then chairman of the Senate Armed Services Committee and the Senate Subcommittee on Security, both of which had oversight of CIA. His advice was succinct. "Do not go to New Orleans, pay no attention to anything Garrison says about anything. He is unstable." As I left his office, the senator said, "If he calls you again, tell me about it at once." I then went to Congressman Hale Boggs, Senator Russell's opposite number on the Armed Forces and Security Committees in the House of Representatives. He repeated Russell's advice with an emphasis on "unstable." With this, I assumed I had heard the last of Garrison. Wrong.

In February 1967 a New Orleans newspaper reported that Garrison had begun his investigation of the Kennedy assassination. Oswald had lived in New Orleans for a few months before the murder, but it seemed unlikely that the district attorney had uncovered any data that the FBI and Warren Commission had missed. Neither the FBI nor CIA was particularly concerned. Wrong again.

On March 1, 1967, Garrison announced that he had arrested Clay Shaw, a respected and well-known New Orleans businessman, and charged him with directing a plot that led to President Kennedy's murder. As Edward Jay Epstein points out, this initial newsbreak attracted little more press attention than a "flying saucer report."* Three days later,

---

*Counterplot (New York: Viking, 1968), p. 22.

Paese Sera—six years after its first big scoop but still an obscure Rome daily—again beat the world press with the news that Clay Shaw was more than a mere businessman. In fact, the paper alleged, Shaw was a CIA operative involved in a trade promotion organization, Centrale Mondale Commerciale (CMC). Moreover, the CMC was "a creature of CIA," and as such provided secret funds to support right-wing political activity in Italy. The Soviet press picked up the Italian story, and it was replayed in Paris by an organ of the French Communist Party (*l'Humanité*). Despite the foreign communist press coverage, American journalists were more restrained. In April the *Saturday Evening Post* published a long article demolishing Garrison's theories and sources. A few days later, a New Orleans daily headlined a story "Mounting Evidence Links CIA to 'Plot' Probe," sourcing the evidence to an influential Italian newspaper. The newspaper? None other than the *Paese Sera.*

The obvious question as to how this obscure daily uncovered such a story might have been raised in the Western press coverage. It was not. It was weeks before the allegation was challenged.

Thirty minutes after the first press reports, Clay Shaw's CIA file was on my desk. From 1948 until 1956 Shaw had (thirty-three times) volunteered information to the Domestic Contacts Service (DCS) of CIA. The DCS was an overt activity charged with interviewing Americans— usually businessmen—who in the course of their work and travel abroad frequently had access to information not readily available through other sources. The DCS relationship with these contacts was entirely voluntary and without compensation. Keeping in touch with the national business community is a widely practiced technique, often shared by the respective foreign offices and the national intelligence services in developed countries.

Clay Shaw was an intelligent and successful businessman with interests in South America and Europe. He spoke fluent French and Spanish, and was a keen observer. In 1948, Shaw founded the New Orleans International Trade Mart. In 1965 when he retired, the trade mart occupied a thirty-three-story building. He was an obvious contact for the New Orleans DCS office.

The file showed that one of Shaw's earliest reports concerned the commercial attaché in the New York offices of the new communist government in Czechoslovakia. The recently arrived Czech diplomat was attempting to expand Czech export trade through the New Orleans Trade Mart. Subsequent reports ranged from the efforts of Western European businesses to open trade with the Soviet bloc to the devaluation of the currency in Peru.

CIA contact with Shaw had ceased in 1956. As in occasional other cases, the file gave no reason for the lapse in contact. My guess is that Shaw lost interest, and that the New Orleans DCS office simply set his file aside. Had there been any misunderstanding or quarrel, it would certainly have been noted in the file.

The press firestorm that followed Garrison's initial "disclosures" gradually subsided as the more informed journalists began to poke holes in the many totally false statements and allegations stemming from the attorney general and his staff.

As some observers have suggested, Garrison's attempt to prove that Shaw was a CIA agent might have been resolved by Shaw's admission of his overt relationship and my testimony that he was by no stretch a CIA agent. I would also have testified that the Agency had no contact with or interest in the Centrale Mondale Commerciale. Had Shaw made such an admission, I would, of course, have confirmed it. On his own, Shaw decided not to mention his relationship with the DCS. As long as he remained silent, I would in no circumstance have disclosed it.

I think now, as I did then, that in the prevailing atmosphere, Shaw's decision was correct. An admission by him of any relationship with CIA would have added unquenchable fuel to the blaze Garrison had created.

In May 1967, Garrison issued a subpoena to me. I was to produce a photograph showing Lee Harvey Oswald—presumably arm in arm—with a "CIA agent" in Mexico City. There was no such photograph. I informed Senator Russell of the subpoena, and ignored Garrison's demand.

When Clay Shaw finally had his day in court, the jury pronounced him innocent of all charges after fifty-four minutes of deliberation. Two days later, Garrison struck back and again arrested Shaw. This time the crime was perjury. Before this charge was adjudicated, Shaw's attorneys sued to stop Garrison from continuing the prosecution of their client. The suit worked, and Garrison's case was thrown out of court. The verdict came too late. Garrison's malevolent campaign had ruined Shaw's life.

In retrospect, Garrison's shameless lies, fabrications, and distortions seem even more clearly self-serving than they did at the time. This is not the place to repeat the proofs of Garrison's unjustified allegations. Epstein's *Counterplot* demolishes Garrison's charges, and refutes his attack on CIA item by item.* More recently, *False Witness,* by Patricia Lambert, covers all of the data as well as detailed references to Oliver Stone's film *JFK.*[†]

Stone, who came back from combat service in Vietnam with a Bronze Star and a Purple Heart, established his reputation as a filmmaker with *Platoon,* a highly regarded film on combat in Vietnam. Apparently intrigued by Garrison's absurd conglomeration of theories and allegations in his book, *On the Trail of the Assassins: My Investigation and Prosecution of the Murder of President Kennedy,*[‡] Stone produced a "major moving picture." *JFK* is a hagiography of Garrison and his efforts to "solve" the Kennedy assassination. Stone appears to have accepted all of Garrison's allegations and composed an incident or two of his own.

As presented by Stone and Garrison, the assassination would have involved at least twenty persons. In real life, any of these presumably extraordinarily disciplined operatives might, with the passage of time, have been moved to sell his story for a several-million-dollar fee. But Oswald had no confederates, and there is no evidence to the contrary.

The movie was so skillfully produced that Senator Daniel Patrick Moynihan noted that a poll taken on the thirtieth anniversary of the assassination showed that three quarters of those questioned were convinced that CIA had murdered the President.[§]

Despite the unquestioned skill with which Stone presented his version of history, the film was harshly criticized by many reviewers. Typical of the more trenchant criticism is that of George Will in the *Los Angeles Times* of December 24, 1991. He describes Stone as "an intellectual sociopath, indifferent to truth" and a man who combined "moral

---

*Ibid.

[†](New York: M. Evans, 1998).

[‡](New York: Sheridan Square Press, 1988).

[§]Daniel Patrick Moynihan, *Secrecy: The American Experience* (New Haven: Yale University Press, 1998), pp. 219–20.

arrogance with historical ignorance." Will considers the film "execrable history and contemptible citizenship."*

Garrison's case was based on his imagination, rumors plucked from thin air and supported by the antic testimony of some witnesses who were at best no more stable than Garrison himself. Somewhere along his path, Garrison realized that no matter how implausible an allegation might be, the fact that it had been made meant that every time the lies were refuted, the charges were perforce repeated. The bigger the lie, the more often it is challenged by responsible persons. Rather than arguing, the demagogue ignores the points made by his opponents and attacks the motives of his critics. Joseph Goebbels knew this and so did Senator Joseph McCarthy.

After floating the initial charges of CIA's alleged activity and directing the communist media—and urging opportunistic journalists and sympathetic intellectuals—to keep things on the boil, the KGB could rest on its laurels. Garrison's scheming had taken on a life of its own. At this writing, the phony history is still alive and well, and will presumably live on indefinitely in the minds and books of careless "historians."

This Soviet operation, and I would be delighted to learn the KGB code name for it, is a textbook example of how, with a minimum of effort, the KGB covert action specialists were able to exploit a corrupt minor official and one of democracy's most precious components, a free press.†

---

*Quoted from *False Witness*, p. xvii.

†Max Holland's "The Lie That Linked CIA to the Kennedy Assassination," *Studies in Intelligence,* Fall/Winter 2001, unclassified edition (Washington, D.C.: Center for the Study of Intelligence, 2001), is a documented analysis of the *Paese Sera* and Garrison cases.

Chapter 30

SIX DAYS

Lyndon Johnson had no significant dealings with the Agency while serving as senator and later as vice president. Nor, to my knowledge, had he ever expressed any particular interest in CIA activity. This might have been expected to change overnight on November 22, 1963, when he succeeded President Kennedy. Far from it. Aside from giving me the impression that he did not share the Kennedys' obsession with Castro, LBJ's relations with the Agency were slowly to develop into a reasonable—despite a few sparks—and productive routine.

The first bump in the road came abruptly, and apparently out of the blue, when President Johnson accused me of being entirely too close to Joseph Alsop and leaking information to him. Joe was then a syndicated columnist at the *Washington Post,* and one of the most senior and best-known Washington press pundits. Washington deserves its reputation as a company town composed largely of the government, businesses feeding off the government, and journalists reporting on both. Chances are that anyone with a background in newspaper work who has been around the city as long as I have will have a speaking acquaintance with a dozen or so print and TV journalists on the national beat. I made it a practice to have lunch occasionally with various newsmen for no reason other than to show that I was in touch with the world beyond what some observers considered to be the totally closed bastion of the Central Intelligence Agency. I never encouraged it, but left it to the more surefooted station chiefs working abroad to do as much. There is a fine line between an innocent relationship and the public impression of attempting to influence the American press.

President Johnson lapsed deeply into the vernacular in characterizing Alsop and, before allowing me to say anything, ordered me to stay clear of him. I had known Joe for some time, though we could scarcely be described as being close. Johnson's assumption of my misprision caught me by surprise and I retorted vigorously. LBJ loosed another salvo, and I fired back. After a moment or two of silence, the President turned to another subject and business went on.

The lunches I recall having with Alsop consisted almost entirely of his discussing events in Vietnam. Joe, a hawk, was convinced that the United States would win that war. He was also so wrapped up in his own views that it was almost impossible to wedge a word into the flood of his discourse. Because I considered myself relatively well informed on Vietnam, I once tried to deflect Joe's lecture with a question about the book I had heard he was writing—a scholarly treatise on art.* This would have worked with most of the authors I've known, but after Joe's single sentence response—"I'm well into it"—we were back in Hanoi.

The fact that LBJ could scarcely have asked for any more well-informed or high-level journalistic support for his policy in Vietnam than that offered by Alsop may not have been enough to balance LBJ's knowing that Joe was one of the most prominent members of the "Georgetown set." In the eyes of those who did not consider themselves qualified for membership, the Georgetown set were, top to bottom, presumed to be liberal, snooty, well-to-do, and contemptuous of the mere mortals and their spouses who came and went with the change of administrations in Washington. LBJ was more rational on this subject than Richard Nixon, the prototype of an outsider's outsider.

Some days after this episode, we crossed swords again. LBJ jumped me on a different topic, again totally by surprise. After another sharp exchange of views and a standoff, we returned to business.

Later, I decided that although the President was indeed probing for in-

The Rare Art Traditions (New York: Harper & Row, 1982).

formation he thought would be sensitive to me, he might have been equally interested in testing my reaction to such sharp criticism. Whatever his reason, these were the only two such encounters in our long relationship.

Lyndon Johnson stepped into the White House determined to realize a legislative program as ambitious as Franklin Roosevelt's New Deal. From the beginning, the Great Society was the issue closest to Johnson's heart. He realized that the inherited Southeast Asia dilemma was a spear in his side, but in the early days of his administration LBJ showed little interest in any intelligence that did not point toward victory in Vietnam. Johnson's relationship with John McCone was correct, but as hard as McCone tried, he was never accepted into Johnson's intimate circle of advisors, and his views on policy were rarely if ever solicited. My guess is that the President never forgot that McCone was a conservative Republican. By April 1965, his patience exhausted, McCone resigned.

I got another glimpse of McCone's relationship with LBJ when Colonel Lawrence K. White, CIA executive director and comptroller, and one of the Agency's most respected senior officers, briefed me on Vice Admiral Raborn's account of his first session with Johnson. The President's final remark was an exasperated "And I'm sick and tired of John McCone's tugging at my shirttails. If I want to see you, Raborn, I'll telephone you!" This was insight enough into LBJ's initial lack of interest in the CIA product, and his reaction to McCone as a policy advisor.

In office, Admiral Raborn fared little better. The admiral did his absolute best, but he was neither born nor trained to be a director of Central Intelligence. It was as easy as it was unfair to make fun of him, but it was impossible for me to dampen it down within the Agency.

It was soon after my appointment that President Johnson first invited me to lunch. Early in his administration, LBJ instigated what became known as the "Tuesday lunch," a weekly gathering of his closest advisors—Secretary of State Dean Rusk; Secretary of Defense Bob McNamara (later Clark Clifford); General Earle "Bus" Wheeler, chairman of the Joint Chiefs of Staff; Walt Rostow, national security advisor; and George Christian, White House press secretary. Tom Johnson, deputy press secretary, took notes. Occasionally the Vice President or a senior general officer back from Vietnam would attend. Sometimes the Tuesday luncheons were on Wednesday; occasionally at breakfast on Thursday.

These luncheons were the hottest ticket in town. The Washington insiders who considered political scuttlebutt to be the coin of the realm recognized the Tuesday meetings as the ultimate in hard currency, and rightly so. As far as I know there was never a leak from any of these gatherings.

Because the sessions were unofficial, and the invitations for each meeting came directly from the White House, President Johnson was able to control attendance. At the National Security or cabinet conclaves, the President had almost no control of attendance. Any of the principal officers might bring along an assistant, or even a note-taker. The risk of self-serving leaks expanded exponentially with the number of persons present. On Tuesday, LBJ wanted a candid, uninhibited exchange of ideas, with no chance whatsoever of press leaks, and that's exactly what he got.

President Johnson never mentioned the reason for including me as a member of the group, but it seemed obvious that the intelligence and the estimates the Agency was providing had impressed him. It was the beginning of a relationship that would last long after LBJ's retirement.

—

Russell Jack Smith, former director for intelligence, has described my working relationship with President Johnson as "golden"—in the sense that it was close to the maximum that any DCI might hope to achieve.* However comforting, this assessment is too generous. It was not my relationship with LBJ that mattered, it was his perception of the value of the data and the assessments the Agency was providing him that carried the day. One thing is sure: once our relationship developed, I could not have asked for a more considerate chief and taskmaster than President Johnson.

For some time I had been cogitating about leaving my marriage to Julia. I knew that we had been growing apart and that it was probably my fault. The more I thought about divorce, the more complicated the problems seemed to be. Aside from the personal aspects, there loomed the question of the White House reaction to a presidential appointee being divorced while holding a job with far-ranging national security responsibilities. I realized that I would have to discuss the divorce with Presi-

*The Unknown CIA (Washington, D.C.: Pergamon-Brassey's, 1989, p 179.

dent Johnson. Obviously, this could only be done privately and without any of the omnipresent staffers taking notes. I knew from experience that personal secrets can be kept in the White House only if the President knows and wants it that way. The Style section of the *Washington Post* is a billboard for such insights.

After one of the Tuesday lunches in April 1967, I sidled close enough to LBJ to ask for a private meeting to discuss a sensitive personal matter. Without missing a beat, the President said, "See me as soon as I come into the office before my nap any afternoon." Fine, I thought, but how do I position myself close enough to any of LBJ's offices to know when the coast is clear? There is no spot in the United States where one is more certain to attract the attention of human watchdogs than loitering within sight of the President's offices.

It was luck that a few minutes after the next Tuesday gathering I managed to see the President entering the Oval Office unaccompanied. By the time I slipped through the door, LBJ was already in the Kennedy rocker, motioning me to a chair. "Mr. President," I said, "I am considering getting a divorce, and I want to ask you whether or not this would cause any political complication for you."

LBJ focused his attention full on my face and replied, "No, Dick, it will not be a problem for me." After expressing sympathy about the breakup, he added that although he appreciated my informing him, it had not been necessary. "You may be interested to know that not so long ago, Ambassador Ellsworth Bunker asked if his planned marriage to Ambassador Carol Laise would cause me any problem. I admitted that although it might be a first in the history of American diplomacy, it wouldn't cause me any problem."

—

As directors of Central Intelligence, Allen Dulles, John McCone, and Admiral Raborn were assigned individual security officers to live in their respective homes and remain on duty overnight. The prospect of a live-in security man in an apartment was obviously out of the question. I was fortunate to find temporary living quarters at the Bradley House, the men-only residential component of the Chevy Chase Club in Maryland. This was a blessing: not only was it financially within reach, but I could eat there, and come and go at all hours without attracting attention.

Each of my three predecessors also had an armed security man riding beside the driver of his Agency limousine. When it became my turn, I decided that the sight of a security guard obviously riding shotgun beside a chauffeur was more likely to suggest that a ranking official had come within range than to provide any additional safety. The Agency security office was well enough plugged in to the local police, the Secret Service, and the FBI to provide adequate safety without the additional guard. Today, security problems are vastly more complex. The differences between trained and motivated terrorists and a deranged individual are profound.

For the six and a half years I served as DCI, Ernest McCoy, my driver, and I traveled by ourselves, and without a "follow" vehicle. "McCoy," as he was universally known, possessed a level of discretion that would have become some of the more senior White House regulars. The only question I recall him ever posing concerned food. "Mr. Director, may I ask what you gentlemen get to eat at the White House?"

"If it is at lunchtime," I explained, "we eat in the family dining room, on the second floor. Lunch is prepared in the family kitchen, and we usually have a *table d'hôte* meal—a cup of soup and a light serving of fish or fowl. Dessert is optional, and all the food is tailored to LBJ's heart condition." McCoy nodded approvingly.

—

It is sometimes forgotten that the President of the United States is the DCI's only boss and principal constituent. No matter that the secretaries of state and defense, the national security advisor, the chiefs of the other members of the U.S. intelligence community, and a number of senators and representatives have claim on the DCI's services—it is the President who makes the appointment, approves the budget, and judges the DCI's performance. Every president is different, and during my tenure each shaped his administration's relationship with the Agency to his own needs and methods of work.

President Johnson was an omnivorous and demanding reader, but was impatient in the extreme if any oral briefing lasted more than a few minutes. If this limit was exceeded at a National Security Council meeting, LBJ would turn to chat with the secretary of state or defense, phone for coffee, or summon up a soft drink. I learned to say what I thought most important in the first minute or two of any briefing. Unless the President clearly showed interest, I would subside after delivering a few sentences fashioned like the lead in a newspaper report—who, what, when, where, why, and how.

In the past fifty-five years, no American president has suffered from a want of opinions, advice, facts, and factoids—solicited or otherwise—from sources ranging from the White House barber to the most sensitive intelligence reports. The wonder is that the White House has not collapsed under the weight of it all.

——

In early 1967 our reports showed that a crisis was building in the Near East, and that a military confrontation between Israel and Arab forces was a probability. Drexel Godfrey, then head of the Office of Current Intelligence (OCI), established a task force headed by Waldo Duberstein, a Near East expert, to monitor and report on the military developments in Arab countries on a daily basis. With this at hand, we were able to focus every appropriate resource on the developing crisis.

I had returned from a "Tuesday" breakfast at the White House in early May for my regular daily staff meeting. Jack Smith, then deputy director for intelligence (DDI), brought the meeting to attention with his opening remark that the Duberstein group had in the last twenty-four hours determined that war between the Arab and Israeli forces was imminent, and that Israel was likely to win it in from ten to fourteen days. For a moment, intelligence from the rest of the world slipped down on the roster of events demanding immediate attention.

At the breakfast, President Johnson had discussed the pressure he was under from Israel and the pro-Israel members of the U.S. government to radically reinforce our military and other aid to Israel. Arthur Goldberg, the ambassador to the United Nations in New York, was a strong and persistent advocate for additional military aid. To reinforce their plea for aid and more military support, Israeli representatives had circulated an intelligence estimate to various American officials and private persons casting considerable doubt on the ability of Israel's armed forces to defend themselves against the allegedly superior Arab forces. Because the Israeli data were so far at odds with our assessment, it seemed probable that the glum Israeli projection was meant to influence foreign opinion, and that more balanced evaluations of the situation were restricted to Israeli government officials.

CIA had earlier predicted that the Israelis could defeat any combination of Arab forces in relatively short order. The time likely to be required for such a victory remained contentious. The answer would depend upon who struck first and under what circumstances.

I asked Jack Smith and the Duberstein group to update their data and recheck the earlier estimate. In a few hours we had prepared a brief report outlining the present situation, refuting the Israeli claim to being outgunned and predicting Israeli victory within ten to fourteen days. Copies were rushed to the White House—President Johnson was in Canada for the opening of the U.S. exhibition at Expo '67—to Dean Rusk, and to Bob McNamara and General Wheeler at the Pentagon. From Canada, LBJ telephoned instructions for us to meet at the White House immediately upon his hasty return.

While we waited for the President, Dean Rusk, with a slightly sardonic expression, asked if I agreed with the report's conclusion of an Israeli victory in from ten to fourteen days. I said that I did. Dean then uttered his often-quoted remark: "All I can say is to remind you of the immortal words of New York Mayor Fiorello La Guardia—'If this is a mistake, it's a beaut!' "

At the conference table, LBJ read our estimate and asked if all present had read it. We had. After one more glance at the report, the President, peering over his reading glasses, went around the table again, asking each of us in turn if we agreed with the assessment. We did. LBJ then ordered General Wheeler and me to review the assessment and, in his words, "scrub it down."

There was only one change in our "scrubbed" assessment. After checking the original data and the latest reports, we shaved three days from the original estimate and concluded that the war might end within seven days. There remained another critical question: when would the war begin?

On the first of June, a senior Israeli official visited my office. I had known him for some time, and we met whenever he was in the United States. As I reported to President Johnson the following morning, my visitor had hinted that Israel could no longer avoid a decision. Israel's restraint, he felt, was the result of U.S. pressure and might have cost Israel the advantage of a surprise attack. Such an attack, he seemed to suggest, was likely to come quite soon. Unlike the pessimism stressed in the material Israeli representatives were circulating in the United States, my friend stated quite clearly that although Israel expected U.S. diplomatic support and the delivery of weapons already agreed upon, no other support was expected or likely to be requested.

In passing this information to the President, I added my own conviction that this visit was a clear portent that war might come at any time, with no advance warning. Three days later, Israel launched its preemptive attack. All told, we had presented the boss with a tidy package.

It was 3 a.m. on June 5 when I was roused by a call from the CIA Operations Center. Israel had launched its preemptive attack. Israel, Egypt, Syria, and Jordan were at war. The Foreign Broadcast Information Service (FBIS) had picked up open broadcasts that Israeli aircraft were attacking Egyptian warplanes on airfields in Egypt. I alerted Jim Critchfield, chief of our Near Eastern operations division, and Jim Angleton, who, in addition to his counterintelligence responsibility, handled some Israeli matters.

President Johnson had kept the congressional leaders informed of the situation as it developed, and was clearly impressed by the Agency's performance.

Throughout the six days of war, President Johnson held daily meetings in the Cabinet Room with a group of Near East experts, and Dean Acheson and Abe Fortas—neither of whom held any official position. In the midst of one meeting, LBJ suddenly fixed his attention on me in my usual seat at the end of the long table. "Dick," he snapped, "just how accurate is your intelligence on the progress of this war?"

Without having a moment to consider the evidence, I shot from the hip, "It's accurate just as long as the Israelis are winning." It may have sounded as if I were smarting off, but it was the exact truth, and it silenced the table. Only an amused twitch of Dean Acheson's mustache suggested his having noted my reasoning.

One of the most disturbing incidents in the six days came on the morning of June 8 when the Pentagon flashed a message that the U.S.S. *Liberty,* an unarmed U.S. Navy communications ship, was under attack in the Mediterranean, and that American fighters had been scrambled to defend the ship. The following urgent reports showed that Israeli jet fighters and torpedo boats had launched the attack. The seriously damaged *Liberty* remained afloat, with thirty-four dead and more than a hundred wounded members of the crew.

Israeli authorities subsequently apologized for the accident, but few in Washington could believe that the ship had not been identified as an American naval vessel. Later, an interim intelligence memorandum concluded that the attack was a mistake and "not made in malice against the U.S." When additional evidence was available, more doubt was raised. This prompted my deputy, Admiral Rufus Taylor, to write me his view of the incident. "To me, the picture thus far presents the distinct possibility that the Israelis knew that *Liberty* might be their target and attacked anyway, either through confusion in Command and Control or through deliberate disregard of instructions on the part of subordinates."

The day after the attack, President Johnson, bristling with irritation, said to me, "The *New York Times* put that attack on the *Liberty* on an inside page. It should have been on the front page!"

I had no role in the board of inquiry that followed, or the board's finding that there could be no doubt that the Israelis knew exactly what they were doing in attacking the *Liberty*. I have yet to understand why it was felt necessary to attack this ship or who ordered the attack.

The next crisis in the Six Day War came early Saturday morning, June 10, when President Johnson summoned me urgently to the White House Situation Room. Soviet Prime Minister Aleksei Kosygin had initiated contact on the "hot line" that supposedly linked the Kremlin directly to the White House. In those days, the White House Situation Room was in the basement, which meant that the President had to go outside, walk along the open colonnade from the Mansion to the West Wing, and continue down the stairs to the basement. The communications equipment—phones, Teletype machines, and cipher apparatus—was ranged along the hall outside the Situation Room.

At the time, and unlike the Hollywood versions of situation rooms, there were no flashing lights, no elaborate projections of maps and photographs on a silver screen, or even any armed guards rigidly at attention beside the doorway. The room itself was painted a bleak beige and furnished simply with an oval conference table and an assortment of comfortable chairs.

As I settled into my chair, Bob McNamara leaned over to give me

some background. Some minutes after he reached his Pentagon office—
as usual at 7 a.m.—there was a call from the Pentagon War Room.
"Chairman Kosygin is on the hot line waiting to communicate with the
President." "Why call me?" Bob asked. "Because the hot line terminal is
here in the Pentagon," the duty officer replied.

The "hot line" is not a telephone as it has been described in the press.
It is a dedicated Teletype device through which enciphered telegraph
messages can be exchanged between the incumbent head man in
Moscow (at that time the chairman of the Council of Ministers) and the
President in Washington. The system was established on the heels of the
Cuban missile crisis when it was realized that such a means of rapid
communication was a prudent precaution. The hot line had never been
used, and none of the officials most concerned remembered that it had
been installed in the Pentagon rather than in the White House Situation
Room. Bob had ordered Kosygin's message patched to the White House
and directed the immediate relocation of the cipher device.

Kosygin's message was indeed threatening. As President Johnson describes it in his memoir, the prime minister said a "very crucial moment"
had arrived, and spoke of the possibility of an "independent decision" by
Moscow. Kosygin foresaw the risk of a "grave catastrophe." Unless Israel unconditionally halted operations within the next few hours, the Soviet Union would take "necessary actions, including military." The
Russian also charged Israel with "ignoring all Security Council resolu-
tions for a ceasefire."*

For the next few minutes, each of us who had any knowledge of Russian checked the translation of Kosygin's message. Ambassador
Llewellyn "Tommy" Thompson, home briefly from his post in Moscow,
said, no doubt about it, the translation was accurate. There could be no
question that the prime minister had used the word "military" in the context of "necessary actions." The room went silent as abruptly as if a radio
had been switched off.

The President pushed aside his unfinished chipped-beef breakfast and
left. Dean Rusk and his deputy, Nicholas Katzenbach, departed for the
State Department. Tommy Thompson, Bob McNamara, and I remained
at the conference table. After taking another look at the translated mes-

*The Vantage Point (New York: Holt, Rinehart and Winston, 1971), p. 302.

sage, McNamara said, "Why not send the Sixth Fleet closer to the war areas—say a hundred miles offshore—instead of leaving it in orbit in the middle of the Mediterranean as it is now?" Ambassador Thompson nodded and pointed out that Moscow would surely view this move as a signal that the United States was not about to back down, and the unpublicized fleet movement would allow Kosygin to ease off without any chance of public embarrassment. I supported McNamara's recommendation by noting that the Russian "fishing trawlers," disposed as always within sight of the Sixth Fleet, would signal Moscow the moment it was apparent that the aircraft carriers and support ships were on the move.

The door opened and the President came back. McNamara outlined his proposal. After a few moments' contemplation, Lyndon Johnson nodded agreement, but did not say a word. McNamara picked up the phone with a direct line to the Pentagon. President Johnson later wrote, "There are times when the wisdom and rightness of a President's judgment are critically important. We were at such a moment. The Soviets had made a decision. I had to respond."*

It seemed impossible to believe that five years after the missile confrontation in Cuba, the two superpowers had again squared off, and that the Sixth Fleet, fully armed, would now move toward the battle and, not incidentally, closer to the Soviet warships already in the eastern Mediterranean.

There is something uniquely awesome about the moment a fateful decision is made. Tension in the room is taut as a violin string. One feels a visceral physical reaction. Our voices were so low we might have been speaking in whispers. Even the temperature in the room seemed to have chilled. Only the fact that each of us, the President included, had actions to take eased the stasis.

It was the world's good fortune that the hostilities on the Golan Heights ended before that day was out.

A few hours after the firing ceased, Jim Angleton and Jim Critchfield came to my office with an imaginative proposal they had roughed out. Critchfield had come up with the idea when an urgent cable from Jack O'Connell, our man in Jordan, sought our intervention with the Israelis

*Ibid.

after bombs had been dropped close to King Hussein's palace. This message was slipped to the Israelis and there were no further air attacks threatening King Hussein in Amman.

At the time, our reporting led us to believe that Moshe Dayan, who had been named Israeli defense minister days before the outbreak of war, was anxious to "undo the damage" caused by Jordan's intervention on the side of Egypt and Syria, and thought it much in Israel's interest to reestablish a stable relationship with Jordan. He also seemed to believe that an exchange with King Hussein in the existing circumstances might produce an accord of lasting value. With Egypt, Syria, and Jordan in political and economic disarray, there also seemed a possibility that the USSR might seize that moment to step into the Near East in a purposeful manner. As a counter to this possibility, Dayan might have recognized an opportunity to build an anti-Soviet alliance of Israel and the conservative Arab states of Jordan and Saudi Arabia.

Critchfield suggested that we pass this informal observation to the White House and State Department. I agreed, and Critchfield arranged to take it directly to McGeorge Bundy at the White House. Mac Bundy, President Johnson's national security advisor until resigning in late 1966, had been called back to the White House by the President as a temporary advisor during the six-day crisis. Bundy agreed to discuss the proposal with Nicholas Katzenbach at State.

The following morning, Katzenbach joined Mac Bundy for a meeting with Critchfield and Angleton in the Executive Office Building. Both Katzenbach and Bundy agreed that King Hussein was not prepared politically or legally for any such meeting. In the circumstance, they said, the Agency was to refrain from any follow-up discussions.

I thought at the time that this was a mistake, and I believe that events since have confirmed the possibility that in the prevailing atmosphere, secret negotiations involving the exchange of land for substantive peace treaties might have been productive. At no time, however, did I or any CIA officer argue against the State Department and White House decision.

The long-standing question of whether or not Israel has nuclear weapons and the gear to employ them did not play a significant role in the assessments made during this conflict. For my part, I had no reason to doubt that Israel has a nuclear capability. The notion that any nation less fearsomely armed can push Israel into the sea is, in my view, non-sense.

Threaded through my years at the Agency was the issue set forth in the book *Israel and the Bomb.** Avner Cohen, an Israeli citizen, undertook prodigious research in the United States and Israel to lay out what he believes to be the history of Israel's success in "going nuclear" under the guise of "nuclear opacity." He writes: "Nuclear opacity has been Israel's way of coping with the tensions and problems attending the possession of nuclear weapons. . . . Nuclear opacity is a situation in which a state's nuclear capability has not been acknowledged, but is recognized in a way that influences other nations' perceptions and actions."

In fact, the Agency's tracking of Israel's progress in this area was done in an appropriate fashion throughout the relevant time between 1950 and 1970. There is no need to underline the difficulty of establishing what was being done at the installation built at Dimona in the Negev. To use ambassador Chip Bohlen's often-quoted all-purpose trope, it was "like trying to catch a fart with a mitten." CIA was criticized for many alleged intelligence failures in my time, but this one never occurred. The top policymakers were kept adequately informed, and reacted positively to the Agency's efforts and coverage. It was no small chore to avoid leaks or mistakes in working on a matter so sensitive in view of the domestic and international politics involved. This is borne out when one notes that no responsible member of the U.S. government has ever felt it advisable to divulge facts on any explicit material regarding these matters. In sum, we did the job and were able to avoid the political pitfalls.

---

*Avner Cohen (New York: Columbia University Press, 1998).

Chapter 31

ARE THE LIGHTS ON?

Some months after my retirement, I had lunch with a colleague, a friend from OSS days and the former chief of a European station. He asked if I remembered an urgent cable sent in mid-1968 flagged with a code word marking it as a sensitive message on Vietnam, and addressed to him personally at his post in Europe. I reminded him that on any day in that turbulent year, a handful of such cables might have crossed my desk.

"It was an urgent, Top Secret query, a one-liner, no background at all," he said. I shook my head.

"I know damned well it was from you," he said. "Nobody else would send a cable like that to a station as far from Vietnam as I was." He paused. I waited.

"There was just one question: 'Are the lights on in Hanoi?' "

It came back to me and, in a way, the incident seemed to catch the feeling of that long decade.

John McCone (and Allen Dulles before him) considered his role as DCI to fall within the circle of policymaking, and took an active role in both the Kennedy and early Johnson eras. In contrast, I was convinced that my job as DCI was one of support, and I participated in policy discussions only when they involved action in the specific intelligence areas assigned to the Agency. At the Tuesday lunches and other lesser policy gatherings, my role was to keep the game honest. Policy advocates occasionally tend to overstate—or ignore—relevant data. I remained on the sidelines as policy discussions developed, and spoke up only when information crept into the dialogue which seemed to be at odds with the facts as I knew them.

The discussions in which I most often participated concerned the various pacification programs under way in South Vietnam. The Agency had been directed to provide liaison officers to beef up these far-ranging programs at the village, district, and province levels. These officers— many of whom volunteered for service in Vietnam—came from field posts all over the world, and although removed from Agency command, remained my responsibility. Few had knowledge of anything Vietnamese, and the most useful language any had to offer was fluent French—fortunately the second language in that former colony. As the war went on, English overtook French as the foreign language of choice.

At the usual Tuesday lunch, we gathered for a sherry in the family living room on the second floor of the White House. If the President, who normally kept to a tight schedule, was a few minutes late, he would literally bound into the room, pause long enough to acknowledge our presence, and herd us into the family dining room, overlooking Pennsylvania Avenue. Seating followed protocol, with the secretary of state at the President's right, and the secretary of defense at his left. General Bus Wheeler sat beside the secretary of defense. I sat beside Dean Rusk. Walt Rostow, George Christian, and Tom Johnson made up the rest of the table. It was probably a day after President Johnson had reluctantly agreed to a heavy bombing of the electric grid supplying power to the Hanoi area that I sent the cable to my friend.

LBJ never allowed the waiters to clear the table until the substantive talk had finished. On some days, the President would simply push his dishes aside to make room for the briefing charts and aerial photographs General Wheeler would fish from his briefcase. The discussions covered a wide range, but the emphasis was almost always on Vietnam. Opinions would vary on whether a proposed target was so close to populated areas that civilian casualties might result. Were the bombings around Hanoi and Haiphong damaging enough to North Vietnam's supply and distribution system to warrant the risks involved?

The selection of bombing targets while sitting safely in that comfortable dining room was a sobering experience. President Johnson was intensely aware of his responsibility for the pilots flying these missions. I learned that he would often go alone to his office in the West Wing of the White House in the middle of the night to find if there had been losses.

Throughout those long years, LBJ's handling of the war in Vietnam was castigated relentlessly and in the most violent terms. Only those of us who saw him regularly knew the agony he bore day after day without complaint. No one tried harder, worked with more intensity or more compassion than President Johnson. Despite this effort, he never forgot his dedication to the domestic programs, the Great Society.

I attended dozens of the luncheon sessions, and the one that occasioned my cable was no exception. The thrust of General Wheeler's briefing was, as always, a version of "mission accomplished." In this instance, the Air Force had "knocked out the grid and cut off electric power to Hanoi." As Bus gathered up his charts and photographs, and the luncheon broke up, the President signaled me to remain behind.

When the room emptied, LBJ asked what I thought of the briefing. I was well aware that Agency analysts often disagreed with the Pentagon on the relative success of bombing raids, code-named ROLLING THUNDER, and the most I might have said that day was that I was scarcely in a position to evaluate the photographs I had barely glimpsed. When LBJ felt strongly about making a point, he often moved within arm's length of his interlocutor. As we got up from the table and walked toward the door, he put his hand on my shoulder. "If as Bus just said, the bombers demolished the grid and destroyed the generators, am I right in assuming that the lights must be out in downtown Hanoi?" He took another few steps before saying, "Let me know about that tomorrow."

On the drive back to the Agency, and while phrasing an urgent cable to our station in Saigon, I jotted down the message to my friend, whose station was indeed as remote from Hanoi as any the Agency had. I admitted that I had forgotten about it, and asked how the former chief of station had dealt with the cable.

"As it happened," he said, "I'd been cozying up to one of the local gentry who I'd heard had a relative in Hanoi representing some business or other. I took him to lunch, and by the time we'd finished the wine, he mentioned that his brother was in Hanoi. Over coffee, I decided to ask him to telephone his brother and inquire if the lights were on. He had a pretty good idea what my job was, but not much notion of how we went about our business. I could see his espionage fantasies fading, but the most he said was that if he telephoned halfway around the world, his brother would think he was crazy. The best I could do was suggest that he congratulate his brother on an imaginary anniversary or some such. A couple of hours later, I sent you an urgent cable. 'As of twenty-three hours local, an untested source reported that the lights are on, repeat, the lights are on in Hanoi.' "

———

Vietnam was my nightmare for a good ten years. Like an incubus, it involved efforts which were never to seem successful, and demands which could never be met but which were repeated, doubled, intensified, and redoubled. It seemed I would never be free of it. Vietnam was invariably first and foremost with both Presidents Johnson and Nixon. On many occasions President Johnson would interrupt a discussion of an important problem in another area to press me for more intelligence on Vietnam. I recall Nixon saying, "Look, don't talk to me about this, that, and the other thing. There's one number one problem hereabouts and that's Vietnam—get on with it."

Vietnam was not new to us. An OSS parachute mission had effected contact with Ho Chi Minh and a coalition of resistance groups known as the Vietminh as early as March 1945. The OSS team was withdrawn after the Japanese surrender, and the contacts with the communist-led Vietminh lapsed. Some of the Americans who dealt closely with Ho in those early days saw him as a nationalist and idealist, a person whom the United States might profitably have supported. Ho's efforts to maintain his contact with American authorities were ignored and letters from Ho to President Truman were never answered. The fact that Ho was a proclaimed communist obscured the possibility that U.S. support for Vietnam's independence from France, and our economic help, might have provided the opportunity to influence the political orientation of his government. At the time, there were indications that Ho's passionate nationalism might have been nurtured to the point of overriding his communist convictions.

French Indochina was far from center stage in the months that followed the German and Japanese surrenders. The obvious problems with the Soviet Union and Eastern Europe had deflected interest from the lesser countries in the Far East, and General Douglas MacArthur's wartime refusal to allow OSS to operate in any of the areas under his command meant that there were few residual, in-place assets throughout the entire area.

The Japanese had moved into the French colony of Vietnam in 1940 with the concurrence of the Vichy French government. Throughout much of the war, the Vietminh was organized and led by Ho Chi Minh and Vietnamese communists. When the war ended, the French recognized Vietnam as a free state within the French Indochina federation but failed to implement substantive changes in the country's colonial status. This was not acceptable to the Vietnamese, and the Vietminh rallied the nationalists to resist French rule. Guerrilla warfare continued until 1949, when the French ordained an ostensibly independent Republic of Vietnam within the French Union. The Vietminh saw this as another half measure and intensified its guerrilla operations. It wanted genuine independence and would accept nothing less.

The struggle between the Vietminh and the French forces ended in May 1954 when, after two months of siege, the French garrison at Dien Bien Phu surrendered. In July, at a conference in Geneva, France and the Vietminh signed a cease-fire agreement, and established an International Control Commission to regulate the truce. The agreement specified the temporary division of Vietnam by means of a demilitarized zone running along the 17th parallel. The Communist Vietminh would govern the North, and the French-sponsored Emperor Bao Dai the South. National elections were to be held by July 1956. In the North, the Vietminh clamped down on the population, executed hundreds of anti-communists, and imprisoned even more dissidents. Thousands of non-communists streamed across the Demilitarized Zone to the South. There, a rigged election allowed a French-educated Vietnamese Catholic, Ngo Dinh Diem, to emerge as president of the Republic of Vietnam. Diem soon found reason not to push for the countrywide elections specified by the Geneva Conference and the North chose not to insist.

As the communists consolidated their rule in North Vietnam, they initiated a vigorous, underground political subversion campaign in the South. This was supported by the Viet Cong, a strongly motivated para-

military force largely infiltrated from North Vietnam. The political turmoil and the murderous Viet Cong activity paralleled the sharp increase
in the American commitment to the government of South Vietnam.

When I became DCI in 1966, I first had to cope personally with the
reality that the Agency bore two quite different responsibilities in Vietnam. The task of our analysts in the Directorate for Intelligence was to
judge the success or lack thereof of the U.S. military and civilian activities designed to win the war. The mission of the Directorate for Plans
was to spy upon and penetrate North Vietnam; to monitor and penetrate
the Viet Cong operations in South Vietnam; to train the South Vietnamese in counterinsurgency techniques; and, at the district level, to go
all-out to maintain the conviction that there was—in the worn phrase of
those days—light at the end of the tunnel.

As early as 1961, President Kennedy was determined to bolster the
failing government of Ngo Dinh Diem with strong U.S. military and
civilian support. It was some two years before it became apparent that irrespective of U.S. counsel and support, Diem was determined to go his
own way.

From the outset, the intelligence directorate and the Office of National Estimates held a pessimistic view of the military developments.
The operations personnel—going full blast in the effort to penetrate the
North and to persuade the South Vietnamese that their future depended
upon the government of South Vietnam—remained convinced that the
war could be won. Without this conviction, the operators could not have
continued their difficult face-to-face work with the South Vietnamese,
whose lives were often at risk. In Washington, I felt like a circus rider
standing astride two horses, each for the best of reasons going its own
way.

A few weeks after my appointment as DCI, we completed a 250-page
study, "The Vietnamese Communists' Will to Persist," which contained
50 pages of tables, charts, and graphs. It was classified Top Secret, with
maximum hold-down security code words added. The document went
directly to the President and secretaries of state and defense. The most
important finding was: "Nothing happening to the Vietnamese Communists as of mid-1966 is bad enough to make them stop fighting."

I knew that President Johnson was hungry for every scrap of solid
data that would suggest our policies were working, and realized that this

assessment could only add to the, perhaps literally, heart-rending pressures he was under. The fact that he never mentioned the document to me meant that this was one of his devices for keeping information close to his chest and using it as he saw fit. My conviction that he had factored the information and conclusions into his own appreciation of the Vietnam dilemma seemed confirmed when a few days later Walt Rostow, the national security advisor, telephoned to say that LBJ wanted me to brief Senators Mike Mansfield, Richard Russell, and J. William Fulbright on the study's findings.

We met in Senator Mansfield's office in the Senate. After presenting the core of the study orally, I handed each of the senators a summary of the key points so that they could read together precisely the language that was used in the study. It was soon clear that nothing in the document would change their positions. Senator Fulbright allowed that we should not become involved in what he believed was a civil war. Senator Russell stated that he would by himself "have come to essentially the same conclusions" as those of the study. Senator Mansfield's only comment was that he was particularly pleased that the Agency had "presented the President with such an objective and thorough report." No one had changed his views, but the President had played the game fairly, and given the senators an objective, if painful, independent analysis.

This episode was one of many that underlined my appreciation, or perhaps understanding, of the impossible problems President Johnson faced and the manner in which he coped with the running of an ugly war. It was at about this time that my deputy, Vice Admiral Rufus L. Taylor, testifying before Congress, mentioned civilian casualties as the result of our bombing military and industrial targets in North Vietnam. The following day, I saw the President on some other matter. As LBJ and I moved along the walkway from his office, he clasped my elbow and said, "The next time you or one of your fellas plans to mention civilian casualties in North Vietnam, I want you both to come down and have a drink with me before you go to testify on the Hill." There was no more sensitive subject for President Johnson than civilian casualties in that war.

In 1967, I caught another glimpse of LBJ in action when Senator George Aiken of Vermont, a venerable congressional landmark, and a longtime close friend of the President, suddenly found the White House door slammed shut. The senator, who was noted for his outspoken opinions, had made the mistake of publicly advising LBJ to "declare victory in Vietnam and get out." He was never again invited to the White House. Sometime later I asked Leonard Marks, LBJ's personal lawyer for twenty-five years and head of the United States Information Agency (USIA) under him, if this gossip could possibly be accurate.

"Oh, yes," said Leonard. "Let me tell you what happened to me. One morning while LBJ was still dressing and I was discussing a business matter he had called me about, LBJ abruptly said, 'Leonard, you look as if you have something on your mind, you're suddenly so silent.'

" 'Well,' I said, 'I was thinking about advising you to declare victory in Vietnam and get out.' Whereupon, the President stared at me for a few moments and then thundered, 'Get out, get out!' I gathered up my papers and departed. That was the last I heard from the White House—even notices of NSC and cabinet meetings stopped coming. Finally, I mentioned to my wife that I had about decided to resign since I was obviously completely out of favor. Dorothy's advice was to be patient, that LBJ was known on occasion to change his mind. A few days later, a phone call from Lady Bird invited us to a surprise birthday party for the President. As we went through the receiving line, I was startled to hear LBJ turn to another guest and extol the way I was running USIA.

"Sometime after that, I was bold enough to ask the President why he had been so rough on me. He shook his head, and said, 'You know, I secretly agreed with you and Aiken, but I knew I could not go that route without being torn apart by the Kennedys.' "

One day at lunch with Bob Strauss at the Metropolitan Club, I asked the Democratic oracle if he experienced anything like the way LBJ had treated Marks. "Of course," Bob said. "LBJ felt let down when someone he liked and trusted seemed to undermine his resolve not to let the U.S. be defeated."

Whatever reason LBJ had for pursuing the war as he did—and he seemed to have several reasons which he used selectively with different audiences—it is my hunch that he was driven by the heartfelt belief that he could not let the country fail. He simply could not tolerate the thought of being the President who presided over the first military defeat in American history.

Lingering in the background to some of the foreign affairs thinking during that turbulent time was President Eisenhower's belief in the "domino theory," which was valid in Europe during Hitler's early foreign policy successes, but to me seemed much less apposite in Southeast Asia. This, plus an overwrought concern for how China and the USSR might react in various circumstances, such as the U.S. launching a major ground attack on North Vietnam, led LBJ and his most senior advisors to take the greatest care in any initiatives. The prospect of possibly widening the area of hostilities was always present in LBJ's thinking. This resulted in the President feeling himself confined as well as confronted.

President Kennedy's supporters were much given to shaking their heads and opining that JFK would early on have withdrawn from Vietnam. That theory flies in the face of JFK's relentless determination to oust Castro and his government. In relative terms, once Cuba was free of nuclear weapons, there was little strategic comparison between the U.S. stake in Vietnam and the annoying Castro problem. What at the time appeared to me to be an excessive concern with Castro would surely have paled had JFK lived to face a conspicuous defeat in Vietnam.

In August 1968, I sent President Johnson an evaluation of the effects of the bombing of North Vietnam. The document stated that since March 1967 the Air Force had flown some ten thousand bombing runs over North Vietnam, a figure that nearly doubled those undertaken in 1966. After noting that these raids had increased hardship, and economic and logistics problems in the North, the report concluded that Hanoi still had managed to meet its essential needs, to continue the fighting in South Vietnam, and to move vital military and economic traffic.

The domino theory "believers" who cautioned that if South Vietnam fell to communism, Thailand, Cambodia, and Laos would topple in turn effectively drowned out those who disagreed. It was in this atmosphere that I asked one of our most sophisticated analysts, John Huizenga, chief of the Office of National Estimates staff, to prepare an assessment of the U.S. stake in the Vietnam conflict. He titled the paper "Implications of an Unfavorable Outcome in Vietnam," and without indicating his purpose, interviewed some thirty of the most informed persons in the Agency. In my cover letter to the President, dated some two weeks after the bombing assessment, I stated that although there was considerable diversity of view as to details and degrees of emphasis in this study, "there was much fuller agreement among those consulted than might have been expected on so difficult a subject." I explained that the paper was not an argument for or against ending the war, but an effort to assess the consequences of any unfavorable outcome for American policy and interests as a whole.

The thirty-three-page paper summarized the discussion with these assessments: an unfavorable outcome would be a major setback to the reputation of U.S. power and would to some degree influence and prejudice our other interests to a degree not easily foreseen; the net effects would probably not be permanently damaging to this country's ability to play its role as a world power; the worst potential damage would "be of the self-inflicted kind; internal dissension would limit our future ability to use our power and resources wisely and to full effect, and lead to a loss of confidence by others in our capacity for leadership"; the "destabilizing effects would be greatest in the immediate area of Southeast Asia," and "similar effects would be unlikely elsewhere or could be more easily contained."

The document closed with this observation. "If the analysis here advances the discussion at all, it is in the direction of suggesting that the risks [in an unfavorable outcome] are probably more limited and controllable than most previous argument has indicated."

I was fully aware that this document was as politically explosive as any we had ever prepared and took care that it got to President Johnson in a sealed envelope, with the blunt warning, "The attached paper is sensitive, particularly if its *existence* [emphasis added] were to leak." The intensity of the conflicting views on the conduct and purposes of the war were such that I wanted to be sure that LBJ would personally be responsible for any further dissemination, even to Dean Rusk, Bob McNamara, and General Wheeler. The mere rumor that such a document existed would in itself have been political dynamite.

President Johnson never mentioned the document to me, nor, to my knowledge, did he raise it with anyone else. As Bob McNamara rather politely pointed out, he first saw the document, which had been declassified, when he was researching his book.* Bob agrees with me in doubting that LBJ ever showed it to anyone.

I have always concurred with Harry Truman's conviction that the

---

In Retrospect: The Tragedy and Lessons of Vietnam (New York: Times Books, 1995), p. 293.

buck stops at the President's desk, but I must doubt that LBJ's persistent determination to keep not one but a number of "hole cards" to himself, concealed from his closest and most trusted advisors, was an effective, or even acceptable, way to discharge his office. As much as I liked and admired him, I must note that the political habits ingrained by his experience in local politics and in Congress served to diminish his acceptance of advice and counsel from which he and the country would have profited. The sad fact is that the President did not explore the likely consequences of an unfavorable end to the war in Vietnam even when they were presented to him as a reasonable gamble.

LBJ was in no sense a sphinx. Neither was he an oracle.

—

My involvement in Vietnam began when President Kennedy authorized a substantial increase in the commitment of U.S. advisors and military equipment to South Vietnam in expectation of increasing resistance to Ho Chi Minh's continuing military success and underground activity. Where there had been a unit in Saigon probing South Vietnamese government stability and intentions, there was now an effort to expand intelligence coverage in the countryside, in the Delta as well as north to the Demilitarized Zone. The operations officers were pushing hard to cope with the formidable Viet Cong operations and to support the Diem administration. The demand for additional officers in Vietnam was soon causing shortages in other critical areas.

One of the many aspects of secret intelligence that I brought to the attention of the White House several times is that operations officers at work overseas must have a backup system in Washington that will support their activity and provide a pool from which replacements may be drawn. The rapid expansion of our staff in Vietnam played havoc with our other personnel commitments. The administrative backup involved in relocating hundreds of officers and clerks working under a variety of cover arrangements stretched our support staffs to the limit.

It was in 1962 that we began a concentrated effort to penetrate the government of North Vietnam, and to break into and thwart its deeply grounded, subversive operations in South Vietnam. On form, civil wars create an optimum espionage venue. A common culture and language, family ties that stretch across the battle lines, massive social dislocation, and intense political convictions are among the most easily exploited elements in denied-area espionage operations. The common language and culture make it easy for an operative to assess and approach a potential recruit; cross-border family relationships offer a ready-made cover for operational communications; and the political, ethnic, and religious reasons for a civil war are strong motives for active participation.

In South Vietnam these factors proved to be a one-way street. The common culture and family ties greatly facilitated Viet Cong paramilitary and espionage operations in South Vietnam, but had only a slight impact on our efforts to recruit and run agents with access to the North Vietnamese governing and military hierarchy. In contrast to the strong political and nationalist ideals expressed by Ho Chi Minh and his administration, the series of weak governments of South Vietnam inspired little but pro forma anti-communist political support among persons who might otherwise have been motivated to assume the risks involved in espionage. In the months that followed our withdrawal from South Vietnam it became quite clear that many of the South Vietnamese who by day appeared loyal to their government were by nightfall active supporters of Ho Chi Minh's Hanoi regime. This might be taken as a counterintelligence or security problem. In fact, it ran much more deeply than that. For all its faults as perceived by Western observers, Ho Chi Minh's government offered the Vietnamese something that the politically weak governments in the South were never able to match. The faults and iniquities in the Soviet system that were so obvious to Western observers had little meaning and even less political resonance in a society as remote as that of Vietnam. Simple anti-communism was not much of a battle cry.

Another of the reasons the various "pacification programs" the United States initiated in South Vietnam failed was, as one of our officers has observed, that the Viet Cong had managed to become "custodians of Vietnamese anti-colonialism" and enjoyed a "near-monopoly of political energy among the South Vietnamese."*

In the ten years of our most intense efforts we tried every operational approach in the book, and committed our most experienced field operatives to the effort to get inside the government in Hanoi. What had

*Thomas Ahern, personal letter to me.

worked successfully against the USSR and its Eastern European cohort failed in North Vietnam. It is little comfort to describe how hard we tried, or to contrast it with our work in other areas.

One of the unique differences in operations against Hanoi and the USSR was the all but total absence of defectors who had had any reasonable access to Ho Chi Minh's policymaking structure. From the collapse of Nazi Germany until the end of the Cold War, the string of defectors from the military, diplomatic, and intelligence services of the USSR and the Eastern European communist administrations provided significant intelligence information. In addition, these sources gave us the background data we needed to facilitate the recruitment of penetration agents in place. The prisoners of war and the deserters from the Viet Cong and North Vietnamese military in South Vietnam were of some military value but offered little of strategic interest.

Within the Agency, our failure to penetrate the North Vietnamese government was the single most frustrating aspect of those years. We could not determine what was going on at the highest levels of Ho's government, nor could we learn how policy was made or who was making it. Along with the entire foreign policy element of the U.S. government, the Agency could not determine what might bring Ho or any of his principal officers to the table for face-to-face negotiations. As we eventually came to learn, the government of North Vietnam wanted a unified North and South Vietnam, independent of any foreign power, and would accept nothing less. In retrospect, I am convinced that there was nothing within our grasp which at that time might have brought about a reasonable negotiated peace.

Not the least of the operational and policy problems in Vietnam was our national ignorance of Vietnamese history, society, and language. As a tonal language, Vietnamese is at its best very difficult for native English speakers, and no crash course is likely to result in more than a basic competence. Beyond that, the ability to distinguish between polite agreement, delicate disagreement, sarcasm, and irony is not easily taught in a classroom. No series of background lectures can be counted on to replace serious study of the history and society of a distant country, and even this should be buttressed with a measure of in-country experience.

One morning at a meeting of President Kennedy's National Security

Council, I listened to a discussion of whether or not the immolations of Buddhist monks in South Vietnam was causing serious reflections on the existing Diem regime. Fritz Nolting, the former U.S. ambassador in Saigon, who had a more favorable opinion of Diem than prevailed at the White House, argued that the suicides would have little impact. Averell Harriman, assistant secretary of state for the Far East, disagreed strongly and carried the day. One Agency analyst summed up his years of dealing with some of Washington's Vietnam policymakers with a single lament: "They simply didn't know what they didn't know." Those who did know were too far down the line of command to have impact on the national-level policymakers.

Granted that the immolations were only one factor in the subsequent decision to favor the replacement of the Diem regime with a more effective leadership in Saigon, it was symptomatic of the lack of knowledge at the policymaking level of the underlying political and cultural forces arrayed against us. In retrospect, it seems clear that the fundamental mistake was the failure to comprehend that Ho Chi Minh represented fighters who for generations had struggled for their freedom and the independence of Vietnam from China, France, and Japan. The North Vietnamese leadership and population were prepared to fight, suffer, and die for as long as it might take to win. Because Ho Chi Minh felt he had been repeatedly cheated by the French, he had no intention of sitting down at a negotiating table with the United States merely to get the hostilities stopped. We bombed, we dispatched emissaries, we tried various maneuvers, but the North Vietnamese gave no positive responses. No amount of diplomatic or military pressure we might plausibly have devised would have moderated this position. To their credit, Agency analysts never agreed to the proposition that bombing North Vietnam would bring Ho's government to the negotiating table.

I was sometimes mesmerized by the mixture of domestic political considerations and foreign policy maneuvers. I particularly remember an exchange between Roger Hilsman and President Kennedy. Hilsman, who headed the intelligence component of the State Department, pointed out rather abruptly that a certain foreign policy decision would have an adverse effect on the political scene at home. Kennedy snapped back, "Let me worry about domestic politics. *You* help solve our problems in Vietnam."

At the Agency, William Colby, then assigned to the Far Eastern Division, caught John McCone's eye. Bill, the son of a professional Army officer, grew up on Army posts in Panama, China, and the United States, graduated from Princeton, and attended Columbia University Law School until commissioned in the Army in 1941. He volunteered for OSS after an injury interrupted his Army paratroop training, and in 1944 parachuted into occupied France with a Jedburgh paramilitary team. After weeks behind German lines, he returned to London and then led a sabotage team that parachuted into Norway. After the war, Bill was graduated from Columbia Law School. Following a brief hitch with a New York law firm, he joined the Office of Policy Coordination element of CIA when war broke out in Korea. Colby served in Scandinavia and in Rome, where he was deeply involved in political operations supporting center democratic parties in opposing Communist candidates. He was named chief of station in Saigon in 1960.

With a zeal that has been accurately described as "missionary," Colby promptly got on board what was known as the "Strategic Hamlet" program, which was designed to create a fighting peasantry, able to defend itself against the depredations of the Viet Cong. Diem's brother Ngo Dinh Nhu perceived the virtue of this effort which, at the beginning, enjoyed some success. Three years later, when optimists were pointing out that Viet Cong attacks on the villages had lessened, an American official based in a province noted that the attacks had subsided because there "were no longer any strategic hamlets worth attacking." Three quarters of the two hundred strategic villages had been destroyed.* At about this time, three paramilitary programs—Mountain Scouts, Combat Intelligence, and Border Surveillance Teams—utilizing members of the South Vietnamese military and closely supported by American military training officers, were established. Ambitious infiltration operations into North Vietnam were launched without discernible success. Parachute teams were captured or simply disappeared, and some of the radios that came on the air were obviously under hostile control. Serious security problems were encountered, and the entire program needed a counterintelligence overhaul and redirection, if not outright termination. With the

---

*Harold P. Ford, *CIA and the Vietnam Policymakers: Three Episodes, 1962–1968* (Washington, D.C.: Center for the Study of Intelligence, 1998).

arrival of increasing numbers of U.S. military forces, pressure mounted from the Pentagon for the Agency to turn these activities over to MACV, the Military Assistance Command, Vietnam, despite our strong advice. By December 1963, MACV assumed responsibility for these operations. We were in no position to refuse. The failed landing at the Bay of Pigs was taken in Washington as an indication that the Agency did not have the staff structure to handle major paramilitary operations.

Whatever value infiltration operations—by parachute, boat, or cross border—may have had before the advent of the modern police state with its high-speed electronic communications, it is doubtful that even well-executed infiltration operations have even a slight potential for collecting strategic intelligence. Paramilitary *resistance* operations are a different matter, and depend in large part upon the level of indigenous support and favorable terrain.

As the sixties melded into the seventies and the war dragged on with increasing ferocity, the division of opinion between those—primarily analysts—who were convinced that the war was being lost and the operations officers who could still see possible victory hardened. I did my best to preside over these disparate views. During those years we increased our staff personnel on the ground in Vietnam from some 200 to more than 600. Where there had been a small unit probing the intentions and stability of the South Vietnamese government, our objectives expanded to include intelligence coverage of the countryside from the Delta north into the Demilitarized Zone and across the border into North Vietnam. In addition to the staff personnel, we employed some 400 contract employees, many of them retired Army officers. CIA officers were assigned to the 44 South Vietnamese provinces and on duty in each of the 242 districts. These figures underline the fact that CIA was under pressure incompatible with secret intelligence operations. Our effort to use the Kennedy administration's favored counterinsurgency techniques to bolster what seemed to me to be developing into a military nightmare was a more than daunting task.

Outside the halls of government, sentiment against the war increased. Families were torn, emotions ran high. A medical problem kept my son Dennis out of uniform and in college for much of this time. Exposed as he was to the strong antiwar sentiments prevailing on every campus and in much of the media, Dennis had as strong feelings about the war as most of his generation, but he refrained from preaching or otherwise attempting to influence me. The most he ever said was, "Dad, you must know that most of my friends loathe this war, and hate the prospect of being drafted. In the long run, this will affect their attitude toward their government." This was not lost on me, but the most I could say was, "I know, Dennis, believe me, I know."

The notion held by many outside the Beltway that President Johnson and his closest advisors were somehow oblivious to the depth and intensity of the antiwar emotion was absurd, but no more farfetched than the conviction that any of us might have proposed a satisfactory solution to the dilemma. Aside from following the world and national press more closely than many readers, we also had the usual range of friends who offered opinions. At a college reunion in 1970, the wife of a classmate perched on the arm of my chair and launched a tirade so harsh and threatening that for a moment I thought she might use her sharp nails on my face.

As the war raged on, I was often reminded of a note extracted from a memorandum John McCone hand-carried to President Johnson in April 1965: "I think we are . . . starting on a track which involves ground force operations [that will mean] an ever-increasing commitment of U.S. personnel without materially improving the chances of victory. . . . In effect, we will find ourselves mired in combat in the jungle in a military effort that we cannot win, and from which we will have extreme difficulty in extracting ourselves."*

At the Agency there was a division of view, some of it generational, on the war and our role in it. On the core objective—to keep an unwelcome communist government from seizing by force of arms and subversion a relatively democratic part of Vietnam—there was slight difference. The obvious breakpoint was the extent of the effort the United States should commit to propping up an imperfect government that was unable to defend itself. Within the Agency, there was also an increasingly skeptical view of the domino theory as applied to Southeast Asia. It no longer seemed axiomatic that the forced reunification of Vietnam under Ho Chi Minh would oust the governments of Cambodia and Thailand, although the status of Laos was seen as more fragile. The National Security

*McCone, Memorandum for Secretary Rusk, Secretary McNamara, Saigon Ambassador Maxwell Taylor, and McGeorge Bundy.

Council was much more pessimistic, and at one point actually felt that the collapse of South Vietnam might even increase the threat to India, Australia, and New Zealand. This gloomy view was never shared by the Agency.

With the passage of three decades, I am relieved to be able to say that although the antiwar sentiment and convictions remained a matter of intense debate within the Agency, they did not bubble over into demonstrations or get in the way of daily work. The discipline that prevailed throughout those difficult years was a tribute to the caliber of Agency officers at the time. Concern for the combat troops was the strong motivating factor.

While I was still Admiral Raborn's deputy, I realized the extent to which Vietnam would occupy his everyday dealings with President Johnson. He needed more support than the Agency's organizational structure provided. The answer was to create a new job—special assistant for Vietnamese affairs (SAVA). It later proved to be as useful to me as it was to the admiral. The assignment went to Peer de Silva, a West Pointer who had left the military after World War II and who had served as chief of station in Saigon. At the time it was difficult to tell whether Raborn was more impressed by Peer's military posture or the aplomb with which he organized the torrential paper flow in the DCI's office.

When I replaced Raborn, SAVA was a going concern, and a blessing without which I could not have carried the responsibilities of my office while also spending the twenty-four hours a day on Vietnam as President Johnson expected. One day's schedule lingers in memory. A midnight telephone call summoned me to a meeting with President Johnson and his top advisors. It lasted from 2:40 a.m. to 5 a.m. This session was called by the President to meet with General Creighton Abrams, who had succeeded General Westmoreland as commanding officer in Vietnam, who had just been hustled to the White House from the airport. In LBJ's opinion, the general's analysis of the situation on the ground could not even be delayed until the break of dawn. There followed a ride to CIA headquarters in time to check the stack of overnight cable traffic and bolt a bit of breakfast before the Agency staff meeting at 9 a.m. I returned to the White House for lunch with the President at 1 p.m. and got back at my desk by 3 p.m. Four hours and fifteen minutes later I was on my way home. Aside from the time involved in the frequent drives back and forth from the Agency in Langley to the White House, my hours were not much different from those of the staff involved with Vietnam.

De Silva's replacement as SAVA was George Carver, a small man with horn-rimmed glasses, a puckish grin, and a boundless enthusiasm for work. He was bright, and the advantages of his education in both American and English universities were readily apparent. He thought fast, wrote voluminously and with great speed. George's nominal respect for those in high office did not temper the candid expression of his views, and he spoke as bluntly to the highest officials as he did to the members of his own staff. This did not endear him to everyone—within the Agency or without—but he did a superb job in one of the most difficult assignments CIA had to offer.

An example of George's straight-from-the-shoulder prose came in a 1967 cable he sent to me from a vitally important order-of-battle conference in Saigon. After describing his efforts to get the MACV, the U.S. military headquarters in South Vietnam, to agree to a higher estimate of Viet Cong strength in South Vietnam, Carver wrote: "So far, our mission frustratingly unproductive since MACV stone-walling obviously under orders . . . [my] inescapable conclusion [is] that [MACV] has been given instruction tantamount to direct order that VC total strength will not exceed 300,000 ceiling. Rationale seems to be that any higher figure would generate unacceptable level of criticism from the press. This order obviously makes it impossible for MACV to engage in serious or meaningful discussions of evidence." Carver's cable catches the intensity of the seminal debate over the strength—the order-of-battle (O/B) of the North Vietnamese forces in South Vietnam.

A significant element in the O/B problem in a guerrilla/paramilitary situation is the difficulty in deciding exactly who should be counted as members of the hostile force. The problem in South Vietnam was uniquely difficult. In conventional ground warfare O/B is clearly defined—squads, platoons, companies, battalions, and on upwards to army groups. In South Vietnam the enemy forces included relatively conventional regular army formations, guerrilla and paramilitary units of various shapes and sizes, headquarters echelons of assorted strengths, local militia units, self-defense outfits, supply and service troops, Communist Party cadres, individual terrorists, and agents in place. Aside from those fully occupied in the field, many of Ho Chi Minh's activists had day jobs ranging from clerks at MACV headquarters and the U.S. embassy to peasants in the fields, shopkeepers, locally hired employees of the foreign press and TV staffs, bar girls, and even domestic help. Any number could play, and there was no absolute litmus against which to sort one from another. Internal security in South Vietnam was an insuperable problem, and despite our efforts, an effective counterintelligence program remained beyond our grasp.

The discrepancy between the Agency's O/B estimates of the enemy military and guerrilla forces in South Vietnam and the more optimistic figures prepared by the MACV intelligence staff was one of the most persistent of the various intelligence bones of contention between the Agency and the Department of Defense. It had existed from the early days of our military involvement in Vietnam, and by 1966 had developed into a mean and nasty conflict. The Agency estimate of the North Vietnamese regular army strength in South Vietnam was always consistent with MACV's assessment. The rub came in estimating the number of Viet Cong and other irregular forces. MACV's early estimate of 100,000 to 120,000 Viet Cong irregulars in South Vietnam stood in contrast to the Agency's figure of 250,000 to 300,000 Viet Cong. The Pentagon and Agency estimates of the *combined* strength of the Viet Cong *and* North Vietnam's regular troops in South Vietnam were equally out of synch. MACV's estimate was a total of 250,000 ranging upwards to nearly 300,000; the Agency's calculation was of about 500,000—with some of our analysts holding out for an even more substantial figure. At the work level in the Pentagon and at MACV, various analysts supported the Agency's position. This notwithstanding, the MACV figures were accepted by the Pentagon, and the White House continued to use these estimates in public statements.

One of the reasons MACV stuck to the low order of battle figures was the traditional emphasis the military placed on counting the enemy forces that were clearly identified as military units, and to disregard the part-time irregulars who only occasionally might be called upon to stand and fight. There was also a significant political problem. The MACV staff had long claimed that the enemy was suffering such significant losses in South Vietnam that by mid-1967 the casualties might be expected to exceed the replacement capability. In view of the continuing increase in U.S. personnel and armaments in South Vietnam, any admission that the Viet Cong were actually gaining strength would obviously have stirred a severe public reaction on the home front.

The MACV estimates were heavily weighted by reports from South Vietnamese military sources. Because it was obviously in the interest of the South Vietnamese military to paint the best possible face on their efforts, the Agency put little trust in these reports. MACV also based its O/B estimates on information classified at a rather low level—observations made by U.S. troops in the field, aerial and ground reconnaissance, captured documents, and data from POW interrogations. Agency assessments balanced this material against data coming from more highly classified sources such as communications intercept. Although less than an art form, O/B estimates in a situation as complex as that in South Vietnam will always represent in part the opinions of specialists. And, in some instances, experts working from parallel data bases are likely to come up with different evaluations.

In January 1967, General Earle Wheeler, chairman of the Joint Chiefs of Staff, signaled his dissatisfaction with the conflicting estimates and convened a conference in which MACV, the Pentagon, the National Security Agency, and CIA were to rationalize their differences. Carver's outspoken cable cited earlier gives an eloquent impression of the atmosphere that marked the early hours of the conference. In time, an agreement—expressed in words rather than digits—was reached. The important conclusion was that the overall opposition to the United States in South Vietnam was "on the order of a half-million."* Although new criteria for estimating enemy strength were agreed upon, MACV found no reason to change its position, and continued to base its reports on its original optimistic estimates. In effect, the general commanding MACV had taken a "Command Decision" as to the facts bearing on the O/B problem, and his subordinates had no choice but to fall in line.

In 1967, Sam Adams, a keen young CIA analyst with a genealogical lineage going back to the founding fathers, was one of the first to leap into this imbroglio. He began by establishing his own criteria for determining precisely those who should be counted as members of the opposing force. Adams then made an intensive analysis of a mass of reports—

*Russell Jack Smith, *The Unknown CIA* (Washington, D.C.: Pergamon-Brassey's, 1989), p. 194. Smith was the CIA deputy director for intelligence throughout this period.

many of them from the notoriously unreliable POW interrogations—on the irregular forces in a single South Vietnamese district. From this, he developed a reasonably documented paper which to his satisfaction proved that the number of irregular combatants in that district was far larger than the figure that MACV had accepted. When this figure was pro-rated with other South Vietnamese districts it more than doubled the estimated enemy force. He then began a one-man campaign to have his work accepted as the official U.S. position on the enemy strength in South Vietnam. General Westmoreland and the military command in Saigon and the Pentagon were adamantly opposed to his position.

In the course of his campaign, Adams argued his position—without achieving consensus—through every pertinent echelon of the Agency. In the process, the issue became so involved that I asked the Agency's inspector general to conduct an investigation. His report was as thorough as it was complex. After studying it, I took the unusual step of appointing a special review board—wise men, all, each with different substantive experience—to review it. Vice Admiral Rufus Taylor, the deputy director of Central Intelligence; Lawrence Houston, the Agency general counsel; and John Bross, one of my closest advisors and a senior veteran of OSS and CIA, were as high level a committee as could be found within the Agency. Adams was also authorized to make his case with members of the White House staff.

When Adams, who was never less than totally convinced of his own judgment, failed to persuade Admiral Taylor and the others, he demanded that I arrange for him to confront President Johnson. I had no qualms in vetoing Adams's demand, and explained that since President Johnson was not an O/B expert, it would not be fair to subject him to any such briefing, no matter how artfully it had been developed.

Adams continued his crusade until it seemed to become more of an ego trip and obsession than a carefully reasoned opinion. In 1984, when General Westmoreland and CBS were locked in a libel suit over a TV documentary film concerning the alleged suppression of O/B data, the impression was given that the O/B conflict had somehow been hidden from Washington officialdom. At the time the O/B donnybrook was at fever pitch, I was convinced that every card-carrying member of the foreign affairs elements of the U.S. government in Washington and the concerned members of Congress were fully aware of the conflict. Aside from that, I had several times discussed the different estimates of the enemy strength in South Vietnam with President Johnson.

The responsibility for estimating the strength of the forces it faces in the field is traditionally, and properly, the responsibility of the military. Even in static positions with opposing forces in uniform, O/B estimates are a far cry from laboratory science. In paramilitary/guerrilla situations, O/B estimates are of necessity often based on extrapolations from shaky evidence, a process not to be confused with a test-tube DNA analysis. It was never my intention to insist that the Agency estimates—prepared by civilian staffs in Washington—override those of the military who were face-to-face with the enemy in the field. From the beginning, however, the President was fully aware of the marked difference in the Agency and Pentagon estimates of the enemy strength. Had LBJ wished, he might have recited these differences from memory, but he obviously did not wish to emphasize them even in his intimate circle.

I would, of course, have preferred to be able to give the President an exact agreed-upon figure on the strength of the enemy force. One slight consolation was my conviction that in the prevailing circumstances neither Ho Chi Minh nor General Giap, the North Vietnamese military commander, could have come up with a precise count.

Considering the immense pressure under which he labored, it is much to President Johnson's credit that never at any time did he request or suggest that I change or moderate any estimates or intelligence reports which did not support his administration's public evaluation of the situation in Vietnam. This could not have been said about the members of his staff who frequently challenged our work with infuriating suggestions that we "get on the team"—that is, trim our reporting to fit policy.

As director of Central Intelligence, it was my responsibility—as it had been my predecessors'—to report directly to the President. On a very few occasions, I handed reports of the greatest sensitivity directly to President Johnson, leaving him the option of informing the secretaries of state and defense, Congress, and any others as he saw fit. As a rule, I would direct reports of somewhat less sensitivity directly to the President and the secretaries of state and defense.

Throughout 1967 various military and civilian members of the Johnson administration appeared confident that American operations were reducing North Vietnamese forces to the point they would be able to wage only a limited war of attrition. Hal Ford, a senior member of the Agency's intelligence staff who drafted many of the Vietnam estimates, has noted some of these statements.*

In March 1967, Robert W. Komer, a special assistant to President Johnson on Vietnam, stated that aside from possible slipups, "major military operations might gradually fade as the enemy . . . put his emphasis on a protracted guerrilla level war." In November 1967, General William Westmoreland told the National Press Club: "Infiltration will slow; the Communist infrastructure will be cut up and near collapse; the Vietnamese Government will prove its stability, and the Vietnamese army will show that it can handle the Vietcong: United States units can begin to phase down." Walt Rostow, the national security advisor, urged Bill Colby in January 1968 to develop new analyses based on "totally different key facts, e.g. . . . that the gentlemen in Hanoi see the equation . . . as tending to indicate that one year from now, they will be in a considerably worse bargaining position than they are today: so that settlement now might be to their advantage."

A dispatch from the Saigon station in December 1967 noted that captured enemy documents called for "all out, coordinated attacks throughout South Vietnam utilizing both military and political means to achieve 'ultimate victory' in the near future" and suggested that this attack might fall during the upcoming Tet holiday. This accurate report did not stand out from other data—based on captured documents, prisoner interrogation, and troop movements—that had accumulated during the preceding weeks that indicated preparations for a major attack. Although the beleaguered Marine base at Khe Sanh, near the border with Laos, was considered to be a primary target, MACV issued a "maximum alert" for all its forces in South Vietnam some hours before the attack was unleashed.

On January 30, 1968, a bold North Vietnamese offensive broke out with simultaneous attacks on installations in Saigon, Hue, and most of the provincial capitals and major towns throughout South Vietnam. The strength of the attack—by some 80,000 troops and irregulars—surprised MACV, and to a considerable degree validated the Agency's view of the size and strength of the North Vietnamese forces in South Vietnam.

---

*Harold Ford, *CIA and the Vietnam Policymakers,* pp. 106, 107, 108.

Chapter 32

—

TURBULENT TIMES

The early January 1968 election of Alexander Dubcek as first secretary of the Czechoslovak Communist Party was good news, and strong evidence of the probable liberalization of Czechoslovakia. The first bad news of that tumultuous year came on January 23, when the North Koreans attacked the U.S.S. *Pueblo,* a naval communications intercept ship operating in international waters but close to the North Korean coast. After a brief firefight and four casualties—the ship was lightly armed and not equipped to defend itself—the *Pueblo* was boarded and taken into a North Korean port. The National Security Agency had cautioned the Joint Chiefs that the North Koreans had recently taken other belligerent actions in international waters, but the warning was ignored. Despite President Johnson's strenuous maneuvering to free them, it was some eleven months before the surviving crew and officers were released.

The next bad news came seven days later, at two-forty-five on the morning of January 30, the first day of the Tet lunar year holiday season, when Viet Cong commandos blasted their way onto the American embassy grounds in Saigon. This raid kicked off the North Vietnamese (NVN) campaign that became known as the Tet offensive. It was a bold series of well-orchestrated attacks by more than 80,000 fighters in five major cities, a hundred district and provincial capitals, and some fifty villages across South Vietnam. In the vicious battling that ensued, an estimated 58,000 NVN fighters died, and literally countless civilians perished. Hundreds were murdered as suspected sympathizers with either the northern forces or the government of South Vietnam as cities and hamlets were occupied and retaken by the contesting forces. The bulk of the NVN casualties were irregular forces, Viet Cong and others, with a lesser number of regular NVN troops. Eleven hundred Americans fell before the Tet offensive was beaten down.

Ho Chi Minh's best forces in South Vietnam suffered losses in numbers that would take more than two years to replenish. The quality and spirit of the replacements were never to match those of the cadres who died in the failed attacks. But what Hanoi lost on the battlefield it more than gained in a political victory. No matter how hard President Johnson had tried to convince the public that we were winning in Vietnam, it was now clear that he could no longer count on maintaining public confidence in an eventual victory.

The request of General William Westmoreland, commander of U.S. forces there, for more than 200,000 new troops to be added to the half million already serving in Vietnam provoked another CIA assessment of the enemy's "will to persist." No evidence could be found to suggest that North Vietnam would fail to match our forces in any likely escalation.

The news of General Westmoreland's request for the additional troops leaked to the press in early March, with the predictable public reaction. At a Tuesday luncheon, Clark Clifford, a Washington lawyer, former Truman aide, and longtime Democratic advisor, who had replaced Bob McNamara as secretary of defense, recommended that LBJ convene the "Wise Men" for an intensive post-Tet briefing. These men were an informal group of a dozen or so—among them, Dean Acheson, George Ball, McGeorge Bundy, Henry Cabot Lodge, General Maxwell Taylor—to whom LBJ occasionally turned for counsel. I arranged for George Carver to brief the group for the Agency. Major General William DePuy presented the Pentagon briefing, and Philip Habib spoke for the State Department.

Carver argued that although the Tet offensive had weakened the NVN forces in South Vietnam, the fighting clearly showed that the enemy was much stronger than had been estimated, and gave no indication of seeking peace. The following day, Dean Acheson, a hawk if ever there was one in that group, advised the President that, with two exceptions, the Wise Men's consensus was that Vietnam was a bottomless problem, and that it was time to begin to disengage. As he stepped out of the Cabinet Room, LBJ allegedly—and very plausibly—is said to have remarked, "Those establishment bastards have bailed out."*

President Johnson was so upset by the Wise Men's assessment and advice that on March 27 he summoned Carver and General DePuy to the White House to repeat their briefings for his benefit. Half an hour after this session, Carver returned to the Agency and slipped into my office to report. Slumped in a chair too big for him, George looked like the bedraggled sparrow that had taken a shortcut across a badminton court. The briefing, which may have been the longest LBJ ever sat through, had lasted more than an hour, punctuated by the President's frequent interruptions, "Have you finished yet?" In his typically unvarnished manner, George had presented a bleak but accurate view of the situation and again demonstrated that the NVN strength in South Vietnam was far stronger than had previously been reported by MACV, and that matériel and troop replacements were coming across the 17th parallel at somewhat greater levels than previously. He closed by saying in effect that not even the President could tell the American voters on one day that the United States planned to get out of Vietnam, and on the next day advise Ho Chi Minh that we will stick it out for twenty years. Why should anyone in North Vietnam believe it?

With this, LBJ rose like a rousted pheasant and bolted from the room. By the time Johnson came charging back, George's career expectations had faded away. The President, who was a foot and a half taller and a hundred pounds heavier than George, struck him a resounding clap on the back and caught his hand in an immense fist. Wrenching George's arm up and down with a pumping motion that might have drawn oil from a dry Texas well, Johnson congratulated him on the briefing, and on his services to the country and its voters. As he released George, he said, "Anytime you want to talk to me, just pick up the phone and come on over." It was a vintage LBJ performance.

Lyndon Johnson must have considered March 1968 the most diffi-

---

*James T. Patterson, *Grand Expectations: The United States, 1945–1974* (New York: Oxford University Press, 1996), p. 684.

cult month of his political career. The March 12 New Hampshire presidential primary set the stage. LBJ's name was not on the ballot, but the understanding of the Democratic Party was that LBJ would carry the day as a write-in candidate without having to campaign. Johnson received 49 percent of the vote, a slim 7 percent more than Senator Eugene McCarthy, an outspoken opponent of the war in Vietnam. Four days later, Senator Robert Kennedy, long regarded by Johnson as his most dangerous political enemy, announced his candidacy for president. Conventional Beltway wisdom had it that Johnson had lost both the hawks and the doves—the hawks blamed him for not crushing North Vietnam; and the doves detested the war and held the President responsible for every ugly aspect of it.

At a Tuesday lunch a few days after listening to Dean Acheson's advice, President Johnson shoved the Pentagon briefing material to one side. He glanced around the table, making eye contact with each of us in turn. He then began slowly to explain that he was in the process of making up his mind about running for a second term. He had not yet decided, but if he were not going to run he would make the announcement at the close of his TV talk, scheduled for March 31. I was not taken entirely by surprise, but the President's blunt announcement did shake me.

Without having any specific data to cite, I can say that in the course of my many hours in the White House, I had formed the impression that the mounting frustrations of his job had begun to tire the man I had thought to be indefatigable. I also sensed a growing concern about his heart condition. Lady Bird was as always the good soldier, but I have no doubt she spoke her mind in private.

In his March 31 TV talk, LBJ began with the announcement that he had ordered a partial suspension of bombing North Vietnam "in the hope that this action will lead to early talks." He continued, "We are . . . substantially reducing the present level of hostilities . . . unilaterally and at once." He then added that he did not believe he should "devote an hour or a day" of his time to "any partisan causes or to any duties other than the awesome duties of this office." The President closed by stating that he would "not seek, and I will not accept, the nomination of my party for another term as your President."

Three days later, the government of North Vietnam indicated its willingness to contact U.S. representatives in Paris to begin peace talks.

On April 4, Martin Luther King was murdered by an assassin with a high-powered rifle. Within hours violence had broken out in Washington—looting and arson raged in the black communities in the District of Columbia. Riots erupted in cities across the country, and as federal troops occupied the area around U Street a pall of black smoke obscured the sun in Washington and parts of Virginia and Maryland.

I was still living at the Chevy Chase Club, just across the state line in Maryland. To get home after a meeting with the President, I had to pass through military checkpoints in place along the route from the White House. It is difficult now to balance the emotions roiled by the realization that a half million troops were at risk in Vietnam, a country that many Americans might have difficulty locating on a map; that a semblance of martial law was in effect in Washington; and carnage and arson had erupted across the country.

In the days that followed, militant students took to the streets in this country, France, Germany, Italy, and Japan. In Czechoslovakia, the Prague Spring, a peaceful rejection of the communist government, blossomed briefly until cut down by Red Army tanks. In May, Hanoi accepted LBJ's offer and talks were undertaken in a CIA safe house in Paris. No significant progress was made, and when the NVN representatives refused to step away from their demand that we stop bombing—now clearly one of our most effective military means—the talks fizzled.

A wide range of political campaigning brought unusual candidates forward—among them, Eugene McCarthy, who did not seem much interested in campaigning. When George Wallace, the racist governor of Alabama, chose General Curtis LeMay—whose utilitarian weapon of choice was the atomic bomb—as his running mate, the *Washington Post* christened the pair the "Bombsy Twins." And after beating Gene McCarthy in the California primary, Robert Kennedy was murdered by a crazed Arab nationalist. Many thought that Bob, who appeared to have softened his attitude and broadened his political interests, might have won the Democratic nomination.

As orchestrated by Mayor Richard Daley, who authorized his police force to shoot to "maim" or "kill" the young political demonstrators, the Democratic National Convention in Chicago was all but upstaged by the violence outside the convention hall. Former vice president Nixon stepped back into national politics to win the Republican nomination on the first ballot. Nixon's choice of Maryland Governor Spiro Agnew as his prospective vice president struck many observers as a bizarre lapse of judgment for anyone as politically shrewd as Nixon.

And in Vietnam, the war raged on.

Sometime before the Tet offensive, I was surprised to find Robert Komer seated at LBJ's Tuesday luncheon table. Komer, a former CIA Near East analyst, had left CIA to join the National Security Council staff under President Kennedy. In March 1966, President Johnson had named him a special assistant on Vietnam matters. At the time, Komer was in charge of CORDS—in plain text, the Civil Operations and Revolutionary Development Support Staff—and stationed in Saigon. I had hardly picked up my napkin before the President turned to me and said, "I've approved the replacement of Bob Komer in Saigon by William Colby of your Agency." This was the first I had heard of this assignment and, to put it politely, I was irritated. Komer, who had a reputation for being impulsive, brash, and overly impressed with statistics of any sort, had not had the courtesy to let me know what he was planning to do, nor had Colby thought to mention it. In his book Colby notes that the appointment came as news to him.* This I must doubt. I've been around Washington too long to believe that a senior officer of one agency might be transferred across town to another agency, and offered the prospect of ambassadorial rank, without ever having been asked if he might so much as consider the proposition.

At the time, I had slated Colby to take over our Soviet operations division. Aside from the SAVA (special assistant for Vietnamese affairs) post, the responsibility for Soviet operations was one of the most important jobs the Agency had to offer. I managed to muffle my irritation by reminding myself that in the President's view, Vietnam came first in any calculation. Moreover, Colby had had considerable Vietnam experience.

It is probably just as well that Colby was assigned to Saigon. His lack of understanding of counterintelligence, and his unwillingness to absorb its precepts, would not have been compatible with the Soviet responsibility, and would surely have put him at loggerheads with Jim Angleton, his staff, and a number of senior operations officers. It was after Colby was appointed director of Central Intelligence that he asked Angleton to resign.

Honorable Men (New York: Simon & Schuster, 1978), p. 245.

Colby's transfer to CORDS meant that he had to request leave without pay from CIA and to be hired by the Agency for International Development (AID), an above-the-board government agency which was never part of CIA. Once in AID, Colby was assigned to CORDS. As much as this sounded like a CIA front, CORDS was nothing of the kind. It was a government-wide program established under AID, directed by AID personnel, staffed with a few State Department, U.S. Information Agency officers, and, in time, a seemingly ever-increasing number of CIA personnel.

It was under CORDS direction that the PHOENIX program was initiated shortly after the Tet offensive. It became an important part of the ill-named pacification program. (Rather than an attempt to "pacify," or even to quiet, the South Vietnamese countryside, PHOENIX was intended to *activate* and support armed resistance to the Viet Cong at every level from the most isolated hamlet to Saigon.) The program developed from earlier counterinsurgency efforts to arm and strengthen resistance to the Viet Cong terrorism.

From the beginning of the U.S. involvement in Vietnam, CIA attempted to combat and penetrate the North Vietnamese (NVN) secret organizations in South Vietnam. As a matter of convenience, we referred to all of the various clandestine NVN elements—guerrillas, terrorists, spies, Communist Party activists, and support personnel—as the Viet Cong Infrastructure (VCI). This involved our people working closely with the intelligence and counterinsurgency elements of MACV, the military command. Prisoners were interrogated, propaganda material monitored, and communications intercepted. We also maintained close liaison with the various South Vietnamese police, security, and intelligence organizations.

The basic Viet Cong objective was to destroy the South Vietnamese government at every level. Village leaders were murdered, and local defense force members were tortured and put to death. At the hamlet and provincial level, civilians suspected of any anti-VCI activity or sympathies were murdered. In the effort to wreck the economy, communications were interrupted, bridges blown, rail lines sabotaged, and crops destroyed. Young men were herded from villages and forcibly enlisted in the Viet Cong. On the threat of death, informers were recruited throughout the area and their relatives forced to supply and to hide Viet Cong units. Before the Tet offensive, our estimate of the VCI strength stood at well over 70,000 members excluding the regular NVN armed forces also active in South Vietnam. The VCI was a formidable force, and as savage as any in this century.

Like CORDS, PHOENIX was not a CIA program. It was a joint Vietnamese and AID program. As such, it played an important part in the efforts to eliminate Viet Cong guerrilla warfare in South Vietnam, and to harden the lines of communication and protect the population centers. PHOENIX had no forces of its own, and conducted no operations. It operated through the Vietnamese intelligence, security, police, and military organizations. Agency officers and lower-ranking Army personnel on detail to CIA served as liaison officers at various national, regional, provincial, and district offices manned and under the direction of the Vietnamese military, intelligence, and security personnel. Well-conceived efforts were made to recruit VCI personnel or encourage them to defect. Amnesty offers were well publicized and effective. Viet Cong agents were identified and their photographs circulated. Rewards were posted for the capture of VC personnel. Local defense teams were trained to the degree possible and well armed. As the Hanoi government was to admit sometime after the fall of Saigon, the early efforts of the PHOENIX program were successful, and of serious concern to the NVN leadership.

In testifying before a congressional committee in 1971, Bill Colby cited statistics supporting the overall success of the PHOENIX program: "From 1968 to 1971 some 17,000 [VCI] activists had chosen amnesty, some 28,000 had been captured, and some 20,000 had been killed." He then emphasized that "the vast percentage of these—over 85 percent—were killed in combat actions with Vietnamese and American military and paramilitary troops and only about 12 percent by police or other security forces."* Given these statistics—some 65,000 Viet Cong activists were eliminated from the VCI in South Vietnam—it is not surprising that Hanoi was seriously worried about the initial impact of the PHOENIX program.

The PHOENIX blueprint was a textbook plan for a counterinsurgency program, well tailored to the terrain. However, the program could not cope with the reality of the ineffective and lackadaisical Vietnamese

*Ibid., p. 272.

government. As with many plans created to strengthen the government of South Vietnam (SVN), after initial spurts of energy, and with the marked exception of some individual leaders at the local level, the SVN bureaucracy's attention would wander. As successful a program as PHOENIX was when guided by energetic local leaders, the effort could not develop into a national program without an equally dedicated and sustained level of support from Saigon. This was not often forthcoming, and in the longer run, the PHOENIX program failed.

Ho Chi Minh and his advisors had from the beginning successfully corralled the anti-colonial emotion of many Vietnamese. The pervasive presence in South Vietnam of numbers of brash, self-confident Americans who had but scant understanding of the local culture and customs, and who—given their brief assignments in Vietnam—could make little effort to learn the language, gave the VCI propagandists a ready-made manifestation of yet another imperialist foreign power bent on exploiting Vietnam for colonial purposes. The widespread American assumption that the South Vietnamese were both anti-communist and pro–Saigon government was wrong. There was a measure of anti-communist conviction in the South, but modest enthusiasm for the Saigon leadership.

Before it had run its course, PHOENIX had become one of the most controversial Vietnam programs. PHOENIX was directed and staffed by Vietnamese over whom the American advisors and liaison officers did not have command or direct supervision. The American staff did its best to eliminate the abuse of authority—the settling of personal scores, rewarding of friends, summary executions, prisoner mistreatment, false denunciations, illegal property seizure—that became the by-products of the PHOENIX counterinsurgency effort. In the blood-soaked atmosphere created by the Viet Cong terrorism, the notion that regulations and directives imposed by foreign liaison officers could be expected to curb revenge and profit-making was unrealistic. By 1971 and the introduction of President Nixon's policy of gradually turning the war over to the government of South Vietnam, PHOENIX had fallen by the wayside.

One of the problems in assessing the relative strength of the opposition forces in South Vietnam was what has become known as "quantification," a practice that became a quest for tangible proof that we were winning. Among other criteria this involved keeping count of the bridges blown along the Ho Chi Minh Trail, factories crippled in the North, weapons captured, enemy wounded, and bodies counted. In the most favorable circumstances this sort of bookkeeping might be expected to lead to optimistic figures. In the atmosphere prevailing in Vietnam—a weak central government, all too dependent upon U.S. support at every level—it was too much to expect some of the Vietnamese to provide candid assessments of their activity. On the American side, such reckonings were also prejudiced by the tendency—unconsciously influenced by the level of logistical support commanded by U.S. forces—to assume that the NVN irregulars in South Vietnam required more logistic provisions than was the case.

It was also difficult to comprehend the effectiveness of the Viet Cong supply channels, and to understand just how little it took for the VCI to make do. Bicycles laden with two-hundred-pound burdens could be wheeled along jungle trails that no level of air attack could interdict for more than a few hours. And in combat situations it is unrealistic to assume that battle-stressed troops will spend much time determining whether firefight casualties were members of the VCI or unfortunate bystanders.

In writing this, I came across a page of scribbled notes I had taken of a phone call from President Johnson to me late one afternoon in early March 1967 that seemed to catch his spirit and intense concentration on the war. I cannot say that the following is verbatim, but as a friend is fond of saying, it "near-as-damn-it" is.

The President: "Dick, I want two or three studies made for me. I want Bob [McNamara] to do some things, and Walt [Rostow], too. I don't ask for many studies from you, but with all these leaks about the bombing, I want you to get the best people you have, and assign a little task force to get me the following: the best estimate you have on how many people are pinned down by our bombing. They [presumably MACV] say 300,000 repairing railroads, bridges, and roads. . . . 100,000 coastal defense, maybe 125,000. . . . Second, I want to see how they have to travel at night because of the problem created by cleaning up in the day and all that kind of stuff. . . . I want twenty examples of what it costs them when we bomb. . . . I would like *anything* I can get on what the captured documents show, what the prisoners say about how many people they lost on their way down [from North Vietnam]. As I remember it, Walt said that a good many of the prisoners said they lost a third of their unit on their way down."

I forbore reminding LBJ that he averaged two requests a week for special studies, and said I would set up a task force and verify the estimated casualties along the Ho Chi Minh Trail.

President: "I want to see what evidence there is that our bombing is causing them [the NVN government] to stay in the war longer. . . . All the doves say that our bombing just stiffens their resistance, like in World War II and the Nazis. . . . I don't believe this, but if there's evidence to show it, I want to see it."

Although I knew what LBJ's answer would be, I asked when he wanted the material.

President: "As quick as you can. Tomorrow sometime. . . . Make it simple. . . . It ties down 500,000, 300,000, 100,000. . . . Number two . . . it costs them 5000 trucks, destroyed or damaged . . . and how many drivers are lost. . . . what I want to see is what it costs them . . . and if we do stiffen their resistance, *say so.*"

I said that I understood and would put it in the simplest terms.

President: "I'm going to be talking to a little group and I want that stuff right at hand."

"If I have it by five tomorrow afternoon is that time enough?"

President: "Yes."

And so it went, day after day.

—

I've been asked what a typical day was like during those turbulent months. In retrospect there were no typical days; only the atypical days come to mind. I recently unearthed a note scribbled on August 20, 1968. After checking my cable boards, the day started with a staff meeting in the conference room across the hall from my office. There followed a tour of the newly reorganized, and vitally important, Records Integration office. As I got back to my own premises, I found Dick Lehman, the chief of the Current Intelligence staff, waiting. He would not have arrived unannounced unless something had broken in the world press.

"The UPI ticker is carrying a bulletin that the top Soviet brass, civilian and military, are meeting in Moscow today. This time of year, they are usually on vacation in the Black Sea area. Something is up."

I signaled Elizabeth Dunlevy to rejigger my schedule.

"We have to wonder," Lehman said, "whether they are deciding to invade Czechoslovakia."

For several days, we had been monitoring the extensive maneuvers the Warsaw Pact forces had undertaken in East Germany.

"The distance from the maneuver area to the Czech border is just a skip and a jump," Lehman said. "I've alerted the Watch Committee."

I told Dick that I would mention this to the President at the Tuesday lunch that day. After checking to make sure that the newsbreak had reached everyone, I called George Carver to update me on the last twelve hours on Vietnam. Czechoslovakia notwithstanding, Vietnam was likely to be LBJ's first question to me.

Dean Rusk, Clark Clifford, Walt Rostow, Bus Wheeler, and LBJ's aide Tom Johnson were sipping sherry when the President charged into the room and made a beeline for Dean Rusk. They moved out of earshot to the big bay window and stood whispering. After a few minutes we moved into the family dining room. LBJ held forth on domestic unrest and the lack of military progress in Vietnam until I could find an opening to report on what CIA thought was going on in Moscow.

The President cut me short. "Dick, that Moscow meeting is to talk about us." Without another word, LBJ reverted to Vietnam. I hadn't the slightest idea what the President meant, but kept my peace.

The luncheon meeting ended as usual, with LBJ and Bus Wheeler huddled over maps and choosing bombing targets. Dean and I remained observers during this ritual. The moment the President left the room, I jumped from my chair and buttonholed Tom Johnson, who had taken notes. "What in hell is going on?" We stepped back from the table, as the others left the room.

Tom looked a bit uneasy, but said, "This is absolutely Top Secret Code Word, and you're not to say anything, or give a hint of knowing anything, but there's to be a joint announcement with the Soviets tomorrow on Strategic Arms Limitation Talks (SALT)."

This was not entirely news to me, but I nodded politely and asked if Tom had written my comment on the likely invasion of Czechoslovakia into the record. He had, and I went off to the Pentagon for a long meeting on the National Reconnaissance Office, an outfit then so secret that its name was only declassified twenty years later.

That evening I was dining at Normandy Farms, on the outskirts of Washington, with Cynthia McKelvie, whom I hoped shortly to marry, when my call gadget went off. The Warsaw Pact forces and Soviet tanks had rolled across the Czech border. The Prague Spring was over. LBJ had summoned a meeting at the White House at 10 p.m. We finished dessert, and I dropped Cynthia at her apartment before arriving at the White House and making my way to the Cabinet Room.

Clark Clifford, secretary of defense, greeted me with, "What did Dubcek do that caused the invasion?"

"It wasn't what he did, it was what he didn't do," I said. This was a rather glib response to the complicated political issues raised by the Prague Spring rebels who wanted to overturn communism and to whom Dubcek had offered some support rather than, as Moscow assumed, outright suppression.

As soon as we assembled, LBJ briefed us on his earlier meeting with Soviet Ambassador Anatoli Dobrynin, and the Soviet explanation of the invasion of Czechoslovakia. Dobrynin's excuses got short shrift. We began immediately to discuss canceling the announcement on the strategic arms talks scheduled for the next morning, and to determine how the incident might be kept from leaking to the press. This effort was successful. LBJ persuaded the Soviets to keep the decision to postpone the scheduled talks to ourselves at least until a more fortuitous time to make the announcement.

It was well past midnight before I began the drive back to Chevy Chase.

Chapter 33

—

OFF CAMPUS

I've never been particularly bothered by superstitions, but must admit that one of my darkest days as DCI came on February 13, 1967. With two Agency specialists, I had flown out to Las Vegas for a meeting with members of the Atomic Energy Commission and the opportunity to visit some of the atomic energy–related laboratories and plants. By the close of an exhausting day, we had moved along to Albuquerque, New Mexico. I was at the door to my hotel room when I glimpsed an agitated young communications officer rushing along the hallway. There was only one heavily sealed message in his briefcase. It was from the White House, and eerily succinct: "Return to Washington immediately."

It took fifteen minutes to determine that no commercial flights were available, and an hour for one of the Agency local contractors to slip me onto the company's private plane. The seemingly endless flight gave me ample opportunity to rack my memory for a trace of whatever pending crisis or flap might have prompted LBJ's urgent demand. A security officer met me at the airport, but once back at my desk it was another few hours before the White House returned my telephone call. All LBJ wanted was to be sure that I would be in my chair when an article in what *Time* magazine called the "little known, left-leaning, monthly journal, *Ramparts*" hit the newsstands. The magazine's full-page newspaper advertisements promised a candid exposé of CIA's role in supporting the National Student Association (NSA)—"a case study in the corruption of youthly idealism" and alleged proof of how the Agency "infiltrated and subverted the world of American student leaders."

The pending exposé did not come as a total surprise. In early January the Agency had obtained copies of a "gray" letter, and attached documents circulated by a heretofore unknown organization allegedly based in Vienna. In Agency jargon, a "gray" KGB letter made little effort to cloak the fact that it had been sent by any source other than a transparently notional organization. In contrast, a "black" letter was usually printed on the forged or stolen letterhead paper of a government organ or a bona fide civilian organization which in most circumstances had no idea it was being used in a propaganda campaign. In the Vienna mailing, the covering letter editorialized on the alleged fact that a CIA agent was active in the offices of COSEC (the Coordinating Secretariat of the International Student Conference) headquarters in Brussels. Copies of memoranda allegedly taken from the COSEC offices appeared to document the presence of the CIA agent and charged him with directing the activity of the student movement.

The use of forged or other documents in black and gray mailings was a familiar KGB technique. At the highest level, KGB operations of this nature were based on forged, highly classified documents allegedly written and circulated by senior White House, Department of State, Pentagon, or CIA officials. It was invariably possible to show errors in these otherwise carefully prepared forgeries, but as always the sensational charges lived longer than even the best proofs that the documents were false. The COSEC mailing alerted us to the presence of a Soviet sympathizer or, perhaps, agent within the secretariat, but did not attract any significant notice in the various newspapers to which it was addressed.

It was on the heels of this mailing that we learned that one of the NSA officers knowing of our financial support had, in a complete lapse of judgment, casually informed Michael Wood, an unwitting NSA member, of the Agency's funding arrangements. Subsequent efforts to contain the young man's reaction to the dreadful fact that his government was providing financial assistance to youth and students intent on curbing Soviet influence in the democratic world were to no avail. Wood was determined to hand his story to *Ramparts* magazine.

The stress of the war in Vietnam had already caused enough policy differences between the NSA leadership and the Agency for both sides to consider an amiable parting of the ways. There was no ill feeling on either side, and, given time, our parting would have been quiet and unremarked. But Wood's decision was not to be swayed. It would have been difficult to imagine a more cockeyed and distorted picture of the Agency's relationship with the NSA than that published by *Ramparts.*

As the incident blazed, I was reminded of a quotation attributed to Lenin at the time the New Economic Program was getting under way. In response to a question of why the Soviet Union should be trading with the democracies, Lenin remarked, "Don't worry, Comrade, when the time comes they'll supply the rope we hang them with."

I assumed that President Johnson would summon a meeting to cope with the coming *Ramparts* publication and what promised to be an international fracas. But LBJ left me the responsibility of pulling the Agency's scorched chestnuts away from the fire, and never expressed an opinion on how he might have preferred me to do it. I had no quarrel with his decision. It was an Agency problem from start to finish.

A day after the *New York Times* reported on the *Ramparts* story, the newspaper quoted LBJ's announcement that he had instructed CIA to cease all aid to youth and student groups, and that he had called for a review of all other Agency-funded anti-communist programs housed in nongovernment organizations. This prompted the *Times* reporter to speculate that CIA was also providing secret aid to "anti-Communist publications, radio and television stations and labor unions." This alerted the media to the probability that other CIA secrets were still in the closet. The most important Agency covert action programs had been in existence for some two decades, and were to varying degrees known to many members of Congress and numerous State Department and Pentagon officials, as well as several editors and other high-ranking executives in the publishing world. None of these activities had previously suffered any significant Western media exposure. No matter—the hunt was well and truly on.

Frank Wisner and I had several times discussed the necessity of phasing out CIA support to these projects in favor of replacing our secret underwriting with open funding from private organizations and perhaps some semi-official government sources. We both agreed, as Frank was fond of saying, "to find some words" which would convince the President that the time had passed when it was possible for the Agency to shield its relationship with these well-established organizations. Because other seemingly more urgent problems took precedence, we failed to follow through. So much for the adage against fixing things that aren't yet "broke."

Before the public uproar abated, the three operations that represented the most long-lived successes of the Agency's Cold War covert political action were at issue. Each of these operations had achieved goals that went well beyond the optimistic objectives that decorate many initial operational proposals. To differing degrees, each gained foreign policy objectives which at the time could not have been achieved if openly supported by the United States. The scope of these programs encompassed a wide—often left-of-center—spectrum of Western political opinion. The net effect showed dramatic evidence of the strength of democracy in contrast to the false face the USSR was presenting through its front organizations in the West.

The most ambitious of these operations, the Congress for Cultural Freedom, established rallying points for non-communist left intellectuals, provided for political conferences and seminars, and established more than a score of publications, the most important of which was the influential monthly magazine *Encounter.* Two other operations, Radio Free Europe and Radio Liberty, beamed timely, unvarnished news and sophisticated political analysis, respectively, to Eastern Europe and the USSR, while offering useful employment for émigré and defector political figures and intellectuals. Covert support to the National Student Association enabled young American activists to counter Soviet domination of the worldwide youth and student political activity, and provided scholarships at U.S. universities for hundreds of Third World students. These activities ran effectively until the *Ramparts* disclosures rocked the Agency, Congress, and media.

During the inception of these programs, I was fully occupied as the division chief responsible for operations in Central Europe. It was when I stepped up to be Frank Wisner's chief of operations and deputy that I shared with him the supervision and daily control of these and other CA operations. My initial concern was to tighten the security practices protecting our support of these operations. This was a relatively simple matter in contrast to the considerable problem of covering the sources through which funds were being funneled into the organizations. In the earliest days, and in the rush to respond to the administration's insistence that the Agency get quickly onto the field which the Soviets had dominated for years, mistakes were made.

The most critical error was in inadvertently allowing a linkage in the sources of the funds that were provided to the various organizations the Agency was authorized to support. On examination, it was apparent that the compromise of one such channel would almost certainly contaminate another, and in sequence another, and another. But by the time I focused on this, there seemed more risk in attempting to dismantle the existing channels than in slowly phasing them out in favor of open funding from private organizations with some overt government support. I banned any expansion in the use of the existing funding mechanisms, but it was a mistake not to have insisted on the Agency beginning at once to make the necessary changes.

Even now that the battle is over, the notion that supplying no-strings-attached funds that would allow American student volunteers to take on Cominform apparatchiks at the height of the Cold War does not meet a rational definition of corrupting or subverting anyone's "youthly" idealism. At the time, the *Ramparts* exposé struck me, as it does today, as an irresponsible and self-serving bit of "gotcha" journalism. When the Agency initiated these programs, covert action was the *only* alternative to abandoning the fight against Soviet political subversion in Europe and throughout the Third World. By 1947, the USSR had achieved effective control of East Germany, Poland, Hungary, Bulgaria, Romania, and the Baltic states. In February 1948 a political coup replaced the Czechoslovak democratic government with a Communist dictatorship. In Italy, the Communist Party and the associated leftist elements appeared strong enough to vote themselves into power in the national elections scheduled for April 1948. The French Communist Party was expected to exceed the 28 percent of the vote it had mustered in the 1949 elections. By 1950 the USSR had also established and was secretly supporting a panoply of well-conceived international front organs.

This dismal political picture was further darkened by the success the Soviet Union was achieving in penetrating, influencing, and, in some cases, controlling foreign institutions ranging from organized labor to university students, and even to a semblance of Boy Scouts. Beyond this, almost any Western political or social cluster with a grievance, a "peace" banner, or merely an empty purse could hope to partake of the Kremlin's funding in return for accepting the political direction provided by the Cominform and KGB.

In the USSR and Eastern Europe, where membership was less than optional, the well-funded youth and student organizations were directed by overage leaders striving to make a place for themselves in the Communist hierarchy. (Before he was named KGB chief, Aleksandr Shelepin served as Komsomol chairman—in effect, the Soviet youth leader.) The French and Italian youth movements were thoroughly penetrated and subjected to the direction provided by party members. In the Third World, many student organizations were loudly pro-Soviet. Funds were readily available for travel, and handpicked, well-coached delegates were positioned to help dominate international conferences and rallies.

The National Student Association was founded in 1947 by a group of American students who had been shouted down by communist activists running the 1946 World Student Congress in Prague. The NSA remained loosely associated with the communist-dominated International Union of Students until the communist coup in Czechoslovakia and the brutal squelching of student protest caused a complete rupture. NSA was represented on some three hundred college campuses, and squeaked along on dues payments and minimal contributions from private foundations—the climate for tax-deductible contributions to any possibly left-of-center youth organization having been poisoned by the rant of extreme right-wingers.

After his graduation in 1949, one of the NSA activists joined the Agency. Before he had finished training, he approached the covert action staff and underlined the scope and effectiveness of the Soviet youth and student activity. A project was prepared, White House approval was granted, and the appropriate senators were briefed on our plan to underwrite—in large part—specific NSA expenses with Agency funds funneled through private foundations. The NSA blossomed.

In addition to travel expenses for NSA delegates to world conferences, and annual meetings of foreign youth and student organizations, scholarships were provided for foreign student leaders to study at American universities. After graduation, some of these young foreign nationalists went on to play leading roles in the political movements in various Third World countries and the United Nations.

The impact of the NSA was most clearly to be seen at the Soviet propaganda festivals in Vienna in 1959 and Helsinki three years later. For the first time American students, in collaboration with other democratic representatives, were in a position to take on the apparatchiks in public and at their own level. As a result of this counterattack, the Soviet representatives and their student front personnel scuttled off the field in Vienna and later in Helsinki. After a trouncing in Finland in 1962, Moscow was unable to sponsor any future youth festivals outside Eastern Europe.

The notion broached by *Ramparts* that CIA had, on its own authority, somehow funded such an ambitious covert effort while incidentally corrupting the idealism of American youth fired an intense editorial reaction in the press. A Harvard dean called it "a poisonous business." Senator Eugene McCarthy compared it to an unspecified activity of Hitler. The more responsible levels of criticism were dampened to a degree when Senators Richard Russell and Robert Kennedy stated plainly that the student program was well known, had been approved by Presidents Eisenhower, Kennedy, and Johnson, and had been fully cleared with Congress. As useful as this was with the more thoughtful press, the trite truth is that sensational charges linger longer than any after-the-fact proof that the allegations are false.

As the storm of media attacks on the Agency neared its peak, I was startled to find a flattering sketch of myself on the cover of *Time* magazine. The Agency and I both would have preferred a bit less coverage than the five-page lead article, "The Silent Service,"* contained, but on the whole it was a fair treatment and, I think, helpful. *Time* also slipped, and offered the scandal's sole, faintly amusing moment when it explained that the handful of NSA officers who over time had been briefed on the Agency funding were known in CIA jargon as being "witty." Some of the students were undoubtedly witty, but the Agency term for an outsider who had been briefed on a secret project was that he had been made "witting."

From the beginning Wisner and I agreed that the best way to handle the project was to leave both the tactical and strategic planning to the

Time, Feb. 24, 1967.

student leaders. They understood the problem at the ground level, and had the brains and gumption to deal with it. Through our relationship with the two or three senior NSA officers who were security cleared and briefed on the Agency's financial support, we were able to monitor the expenses and to offer routine guidance. Aside from this, the NSA was in the hands of the students. Any substantive political intervention by the Agency would have lessened, if not destroyed, the impact of the project. The notion put about by some of the "shocked" critics of the program that CIA was somehow using the students for espionage was absurd. None of the students had or might plausibly be expected to gain access to the intelligence the Agency was seeking. Moreover, no operations officer in his right mind would have attempted to slip an espionage harness onto these bright and politically rambunctious activists.

The *Ramparts* publication and ensuing press hysteria effectively put an end to Agency support to the NSA, and in time to the Congress for Cultural Freedom, Radio Free Europe, and Radio Liberty. The boldest of these operations was the Congress for Cultural Freedom. The events that led to the congress began at a conference at the Waldorf-Astoria Hotel in Manhattan in March 1949. As one of a string of Soviet-initiated and -supported "cultural" meetings, some eight hundred intellectuals and artists gathered to protest American "warmongering" and to be cautioned by the composer Dmitri Shostakovich and other Soviet delegates against the "hatemongering," and the thrust for world power of the new American "fascists." Clifford Odets denounced "fraudulent reports of Soviet aggression," while ignoring the Soviet military occupation of Eastern Europe and the Baltic states.

The Waldorf meeting was one of the first postwar Cominform-sponsored propaganda efforts staged in the West. Despite the presence of Aaron Copland, Lillian Hellman, Norman Mailer, Arthur Miller, and Odets, New York City was not the place for the meeting. For all of the hair-splitting and nuanced political differences between the intellectual, academic, ethnic, and recent refugee groups, New York also housed a solid and well-informed non-communist consensus. The Cominform promoters and their front men were taken by surprise when Sidney Hook, Mary McCarthy, Dwight MacDonald, and a dozen anti-Stalinist intellectuals punctured the Soviet propaganda balloons with a series of pointed questions that provoked strenuous debates as to what was really going on in the USSR and the areas of Eastern Europe occupied by the Red Army.

In Washington, Frank Wisner, who had barely got the Office of Policy Coordination up and running, realized the potential importance of rallying a group of well-established non-communist left scholars, intellectuals, and émigré political figures. The potential value of such a counterforce was obvious—it was the likelihood of melding such ardently independent individuals into any organization that seemed remote. (Sidney Hook once remarked that he could not recite the multiplication tables without infuriating somebody.)* After consultation with the White House, Wisner offered covert Agency support for an upcoming State Department–sponsored conference in Paris—the "International Day of Resistance to Dictatorship and War." The French Communist Party professed outrage at the meeting but might have saved its breath. The neutralist flavor of many participants and the anti-American enthusiasm of the French delegates effectively diluted this response to the Cominform's defense of Stalin's dictatorship. Paris was the wrong venue for the April 1950 meeting.

A subsequent venture, partially funded by the State Department and quietly by CIA, in Berlin proved more effective. The some two hundred sponsors and delegates represented many of the best-known non-communist writers and political activists. Among them were François Bondy, Sidney Hook, Arthur Koestler, Melvin Lasky, Malcolm Muggeridge, Carlo Schmidt, Ignazio Silone, Stephen Spender, and Manes Sperber. The conference opened in June 1950, the day after North Korea launched its invasion of South Korea. Some four thousand Berliners— few of whom had any illusions about Soviet reality—joined the delegates and sponsors at the opening meeting.

In considering the success of this conference, the State Department and the Agency decided that if the Congress for Cultural Freedom was to have a future, it could not be known as an official mouthpiece for U.S. foreign policy. The potential value of the congress would depend upon its political independence and ability to rally the best available non-communist left intellectuals—the persons most likely to make a success of the congress. President Truman, already under attack for being soft on

*Peter Coleman, *The Liberal Conspiracy* (New York: Free Press, 1989), p. 34.

communism, could not be expected to ask the U.S. Congress for funds to support any organization which his conservative Republican opponents would perceive as a grab bag of left-wing intellectuals, many of whom were outspoken critics of some aspects of U.S. foreign policy.

Despite the objections of the State Department and Pentagon officials who had organized and promoted the Berlin meeting and the organization of the congress, overt U.S. support was withdrawn. Henceforth, funds for the congress would come from private subsidies, with substantial covert support funneled through the Agency.

In the years that followed, the congress, under the leadership of Michael Josselson, took on and bested the Soviet efforts to subvert the political and intellectual life of the non-communist world. Josselson was born in Estonia in 1908. His family, members of what has been called the "Baltic Diaspora," emigrated to Germany at the time of the Bolshevik Revolution. After graduation from the university in Berlin, Mike moved to Paris to work as the European representative of such American firms as Saks and Gimbel's. In 1936 he emigrated to the United States and obtained citizenship in 1942. After military service in a Psychological Warfare unit, he remained in Berlin as a Cultural Affairs officer. It was there that he became a charter member of the Congress for Cultural Freedom and attracted the attention of CIA. In 1950, Mike was named executive director of the congress. He held this post until his retirement in 1967.

As one of the founding members, Mike Josselson deserves a large measure of the credit for keeping the congress intact and focused on its original missions. His ability to manage relations between such a wildly assorted, unruly, genius-level intellectual and political prima donnas, while simultaneously overseeing some twenty politically hefty journals and refereeing innumerable conferences and seminars, was quite simply phenomenal. That he spoke fluent English, Russian, German, and French, and could make his way in a handful of other languages helped, but was only one element in the rare combination of his extraordinary intelligence, political wisdom, and full measure of administrative competence. Mike's devotion to duty came at the expense of his health. After a series of heart attacks, he retired to Geneva, where he died in 1978.

There is no doubt that the problem of attempting to hide his relationship with CIA from his close associates and friends was a considerable additional burden for Mike. With the passage of time, the slim cover for Mike's CIA relationship tattered. The attacks ignited by the *Ramparts* disclosures tore Mike's double life to pieces. He deserves much more recognition for his role in the Cold War—and it was a war—than he will ever receive.

Chapter 34

TALK RADIO

In late 1948, even before the Congress for Cultural Freedom took shape, James V. Forrestal, the secretary of defense, George Kennan, the director for policy planning at State, Robert Joyce, who had returned to State as a policy advisor after OSS service, Frank Wisner at CIA, and a group of private citizens in New York incorporated the National Committee for Free Europe. At the suggestion of Dean Acheson, the secretary of state, former ambassador George C. Grew was elected chairman of the New York group, which among others included General Eisenhower, Allen Dulles, then still in law practice in New York, and Adolf Berle, an assistant secretary of state under President Franklin Roosevelt.

The committee's first objective was to provide useful employment and a rally point for some of the prominent Eastern European political figures and intellectuals who were scattered among the thousands of refugees streaming into Austria and West Germany. Many exiles were well known in their homelands, but only a few had the language or work backgrounds that offered a reasonable prospect of useful employment at their professional level. Like the working-class refugees, the white-collar group were anxious, even desperate, to find work. Many were uniquely qualified to select and prepare the news and editorial comment that the Eastern European governments were most determined to censor.

Another, but not insignificant, value of these exiles was the operational and research data offered by their intimate knowledge of their homelands. The Committee for a Free Europe—later to be better known as Radio Free Europe (RFE)—received continuing contributions from private and business sources, but the projected scope of the committee operations meant that substantial secret government funding would be required.

As soon as the Agency project was drafted and the National Security Council had briefed appropriate members of Congress, the pressure on CIA intensified. The communist bloc population were to be immediately convinced that they had not been forgotten. The first step would be to provide Eastern Europe with uncensored straight news. Pending the time needed to establish broadcast facilities, the use of leaflet-carrying balloons was authorized.

For some time I had been convinced that the invention of radio had put two traditional secret intelligence utensils permanently on the shelf. Mother Nature may have had spies in mind when she perfected carrier pigeons, but by the end of World War I, pigeons had no more status than dead ducks, and further research in the military use of propaganda-bearing balloons was shelved. Short-range, across-the-lines balloon propaganda operations were used to some slight effect in World War II and, to a lesser degree, in Korea. In 1951 the possibility of floating propaganda-laden balloons over the Iron Curtain was fostered as a standby until radio broadcasts could be gotten under way. The notion was bold enough to attract Frank Wisner's support. Aside from the obvious possibility that rogue winds might shower downtown Budapest with balloon loads of hard-hitting news in Czech, I confess to not having been convinced that even the most news-starved citizen would risk a stiff jail sentence by rushing to pluck pamphlets from a nearby bush.

Wisner disagreed with my prejudice. The prospect of blanketing Eastern Europe with timely propaganda material fascinated Frank, and it was balloons away! A forgotten trove of weather balloons was uncovered. Meteorologists were rallied to research upper-level air currents, and to map altitudes at which prevailing winds might offer access to targets in Poland and Czechoslovakia. Pilot balloons were rigged so that they could be monitored from the launch sites to test the altitudes offering the most likely target access. Ballooning techniques and facilities improved to the point that by 1953, 60,000 balloons could be launched in a single campaign. The use of balloons capable of carrying 400-pound loads was abandoned because of the hazard to aircraft.

One of the more ingenious methods of releasing the propaganda over the desired target involved dry ice and some fancy calculation. On platforms dangling beneath the balloons, open boxes containing tens of thousands of loose pamphlets were supported on one side by blocks of dry ice. By the time the balloons reached the target area, the ice was calculated to have evaporated to the point that the boxes would tip over, spilling the pamphlets into the wind. Meanwhile, RFE radio stations were coming on air.

Even the best operations are sometimes blessed with a light side. The Agency's elongated transparent plastic, high-tech balloons bore an eerie resemblance to the fanciful science fiction sketches of visitors from Mars. As secret intelligence luck had it, two of these balloons wafted far off course and landed upright, side by side in a village square in rural Austria. It took the local priest to convince a clutch of village grandmothers that the odd couple were neither Heaven sent nor invading Martians.

Our balloon barrages created a longer-lasting and more furious reaction from Eastern European authorities than the much more effective RFE broadcasts. Along with protests on the diplomatic level and at the United Nations, attempts were made to shoot down the balloons with anti-aircraft fire. When this failed, propeller-driven aircraft were used— jet fighters proved too fast to target the slow-moving targets.

By the mid-1950s, the pugnacious balloon operations, which had been controversial from the beginning, had become an anachronism in the eyes of all but the true believers. Radio was the accepted cross-border communication means of choice.

While preparing its own transmission facilities, RFE attempted to buy radio time from two powerful commercial stations: Radio Luxembourg and Radio Monte Carlo. When neither station was willing to risk losing its audience by interrupting entertainment programming with an occasional hour of news transmitted in any of the Eastern European languages, the committee turned to RIAS (Radio in the American Sector) in Berlin for advice. RIAS, an official U.S. government station, had won a wide audience in East Germany. The down-to-earth advice from Berlin confirmed that of the broadcast experts being assembled in New York. To hold an audience and compete with the communist-controlled broadcasts, Radio Free Europe would have to create Eastern European versions of the NBC and CBS commercial stations.

In addition to the straight news and political comment prepared by native writers, and read by native speakers, the RFE broadcasts would have to be spiced with bits of sports, popular music, and cultural programs. All of the material was to be independently prepared by Polish, Czech, Hungarian, Romanian, and Bulgarian staffs supervised by substantively competent (and, when possible, linguistically qualified) Americans. Albania, one of Frank Wisner's more obscure enthusiasms, was initially on the broadcast list. Reason prevailed, and Frank was talked out of attempting to influence the million and a half Albanians, many of whom lived without radios.

Unlike the broadcasts offered by the Voice of America—many of which were written by staff employees, translated, and aired by native speakers—the RFE programs were to simulate as closely as possible material that might have been broadcast from within the target areas had there been no censorship. This was a tall order.

Those of us who were still establishing the postwar espionage service wondered if Frank Wisner and his relatively inexperienced staff appreciated the task they were undertaking. Monitoring editorial material in five different languages, presiding over émigré personnel who did not share a common language, and ironing out century-old Eastern European attitudes and prejudices were a formidable undertaking. Finding politically savvy and linguistically qualified supervisors, while also recruiting the exile editors and writers able to produce the substance of programs, was no less daunting a prospect.

Wisner persevered. On July 4, 1950—a scant thirteen months after the Radio Free Europe Committee was established in New York—RFE transmitted its first program: thirty minutes of news expressed in idiomatic, accent-free Czech. Some five weeks later, broadcasts had been initiated to Romania, Hungary, Poland, and Bulgaria.

In practice the policy guidance supplied by State and the Agency was thrashed out at daily staff meetings. As soon as news and editorial content were decided, the exile editors and writers prepared scripts for immediate broadcast. Because the editors and writers often brought full measures of national, ethnic, and religious attitudes to their work, news and editorial comments were strictly separated. In contrast to the straight news programs, editorial articles favoring one or another faction were always signed. After-the-fact editorial control was maintained by random sampling and close scrutiny of the various programs.

Care was taken lest any of the writers and editors confuse the Eisenhower administration's political campaign oratory and slogans—"rollback" and "liberation"—with actual foreign policy for Eastern Europe and the USSR. The strictly enforced standing injunction was that the radios were never in any way to provoke internal revolt by suggesting or implying that assistance would be given the rebels. The White House, State Department, and Agency were of one mind on this issue.

One of the early decisions was to concentrate the news broadcasts on internal developments within the target countries, and to leave the big-picture, world news coverage to the Voice of America and the BBC. Security-cleared American staff personnel had access to classified intelligence reports. This material was reinforced by the questioning of refugees, still fleeing across the borders, access to defectors, and close contact with key figures in the emigration. The straight news and perceptive comments on local developments within the Communist bloc were the basis of the reputation RFE was able to maintain with its audiences.

Staffing and broadcast content were but part of the undertaking. Sites which would offer optimum radio reception throughout Eastern Europe had to be researched. At times it seemed that the dickering for permission to build powerful radio stations anywhere but in West Germany would exceed the life span of the most dedicated negotiators. Radio transmitters were not all that had to be arranged. Office space and housing had to be found or constructed; once selected, personnel—some one thousand in Munich—were to be security vetted, and employment contracts had to be written. Aside from the negotiations at the diplomatic level, CIA was responsible for the entire activity, and for masking the covert funding.

Within the Agency, Frank Wisner's relentless dedication to his duty was a primary factor in pulling it all together. Tom Braden, a newspaperman and OSS veteran, joined the Agency as Frank's chief for this activity. Others, without compensation, spent hundreds of hours pushing the program into being and nurturing it through the difficult early months. John Richardson, who gave up an important investment banking career to become RFE president, was highly effective. He went on in government to serve as an assistant secretary of state. Peter Miro, a skilled radio engineer, was equally effective. Among others were Frank Altschul, Howard Chapin, Frederic Dolbeare, John Hughes, Robert E. Lang, Allen Phenix, DeWitte C. Poole, Charles Spofford, and H. Gregory Thomas. None has been given the recognition he deserves.

At the time these projects were undertaken, CIA operations were still divided between the Office of Special Operations (OSO), responsible for intelligence operations, and the newly formed Office of Policy Coordination (OPC), charged with covert action. In 1951, I stepped up from my job as chief of Foreign Division M (FDM) with responsibility for Central Europe to the Office of Special Operations. At the time, Allen Dulles, who had left his New York law practice to join CIA, was chief of OSO. Lyman Kirkpatrick, another OSS veteran, was Dulles's chief of operations, and I was Kirk's deputy.

As RFE got under way, Frank Wisner tried more than once to lure me across the line into OPC. I was still digging into the operations in areas beyond my earlier beat and getting to know the people, many of whom were new to me. I had no wish to leave that job unfinished in order to assume a completely new and extremely ambitious effort. Frank and I finally agreed that I should stay put.

I've always thought that the people who were to be charged with specific responsibilities were more important than the often elegant bureaucratic wiring diagrams that are assumed will fit any individual into an organization. Nevertheless, as Willy Loman's widow observed, "attention must be paid." In August 1952, General Bedell Smith, the director of Central Intelligence, merged the Office of Policy Coordination and the Office of Special Operations into a single unit, the Directorate for Plans. Allen Dulles moved up to become General Smith's deputy. Frank Wisner became deputy director for plans (DDP), and Lyman Kirkpatrick was named Frank's chief of operations. I was promoted to be Kirkpatrick's deputy.

I first met Cord Meyer when he succeeded Tom Braden as the Agency man responsible for our International Organizations branch. He was one of the most memorable of my colleagues. Cord's parents had married in

France during World War I—his father a fighter pilot, his mother a Red Cross nurse. Cord was graduated from Yale in three years. A month later, he volunteered for the Marines, and by February 1944 he had fought his way ashore on Eniwetok Atoll, and later Guam. In July 1944 a War Department telegram informed his parents that Marine Lieutenant Cord Meyer had been killed in action. In fact, Cord had suffered a near-fatal head wound. While still on the battlefield, a Marine doctor assumed his patient had but a few seconds to live, and had made what Cord later called "a premature diagnosis." After bouts of plastic surgery and the loss of an eye, Cord faced a serious decision. Fragments of metal were still embedded in his remaining eye. In time, these might corrode and destroy his vision. The alternative, another operation, might also cost him his sight if it failed. Cord refused the additional operation and was discharged in New York City.

As a junior member of the U.S. delegation, Cord attended the San Francisco convention which established the structure of the new United Nations organization. He served two years as chairman of the United World Federalists before enrolling at Harvard with plans to complete a Ph.D. and to finish a book-length manuscript. Cord's experience with the Soviets in San Francisco had sparked his interest in Soviet propaganda and communist front activity. By the outbreak of the Korean War in 1950, Cord had tired of academe and thought of a diplomatic career. Friends at State were discouraging—Cord was so publicly identified with the World Federalist movement that he would be too controversial for the department. Cord turned to Allen Dulles, whom he had known socially in New York. He accepted Allen's job offer at the moment Frank Wisner was establishing the Office of Policy Coordination.

Cord was one of our more easily recognized members—tall, prematurely gray, and, like a French cabdriver, rarely to be seen without a cigarette dangling from his lips. I did not understand how Cord tolerated the smoke drifting from the smoldering cigarette until I realized that it was always on the side of his reconstructed eye. It was not until 1953 when Cord was denounced to the FBI as a security risk that I got to know him well. I served as a middleman, helping Cord work his three months' passage through the security bureaucracies. Even in the climate poisoned by Senator McCarthy, the charges against Cord were preposterous, unevaluated allegations made by untested sources. A year later, after another, this time mercifully minor organizational change, Cord was named staff chief for all covert action operations.

In 1967, when the *Ramparts* charges were still front-page news, the *New York Times* published a biographical profile that attempted—rather unsuccessfully—to explain what made Cord change from an idealistic world federalist to a senior CIA official. The following day, a colleague received a call from Daniel Dodson, then a professor in the English department at Columbia University. Since 1947, the professor said, he had waited for a book by the young author of the *Atlantic Monthly* short story "Waves of Darkness." It was, he said, one of the finest pieces of American writing to have come out of World War II. Until he recognized Cord's name in the *Times* story, he had assumed that equally fine novels would be forthcoming. At the time I had not read the story—it is indeed an extraordinary literary achievement.*

———

Within weeks of its inception, Radio Free Europe became a primary target for each of the communist intelligence services. Operations ranged from penetration of the editorial staffs to sabotage of the facilities and attempted murder. Exiles were subject to blackmail threats against relatives still within reach of the communist security services. Eastern European agents posing as dissidents were inserted into the refugee flow with instructions to find work in RFE. Munich became a lively counterintelligence battlefield, replete with double agents, defectors, saboteurs, and assassins. It was in the sorting out of the security problems and defensive counterintelligence operations that I moved closer to the staff engaged in this vital covert action activity.

When the West German government agreed to the broadcasts, the first RFE transmitters were established in Bavaria. The day-to-day RFE programming was centered in Munich, with policymaking split between the offices in New York and Washington, and the political advisors in Munich. The distances between these offices, and the strong-minded personnel in each, made for intense, sometimes ear-splitting policy debates. Despite the wear and tear, the results seemed to me to be optimal.

---

*Cord included "Waves of Darkness" in his book, *Facing Reality: From World Federalism to the CIA* (New York: Harper & Row, 1980).

We soon learned that broadcasts from Germany were easily and quite effectively jammed from within the target countries, so the radio engineers went back to the drawing table. The best locations for transmission to Eastern Europe were found to be near Barcelona and a bit north of Lisbon. Strenuous negotiations bore fruit and the stations, employing some four hundred staff, were established.

At about the time RFE was getting under way in 1951, the State and Defense Departments and the National Security Council agreed that Frank Wisner should rally another group of private citizens in New York. Their task would be to form an organization similar to but separate from RFE. The new corporation, the American Committee for Freedom for the Peoples of the USSR, was to enlist émigrés from the Soviet Union to "aid the worldwide Russian and nationalistic emigration in its effort to sustain the spirit of liberty among the peoples of the USSR." The corporation would also "aid the emigration in seeking to extend understanding of the West within the USSR." This was another towering order, which at best could be fulfilled by beaming news and sophisticated analysis programs into the Soviet Union. Broadcasts were to be offered in Russian and many of the national minority languages. As with RFE, financial support was ostensibly to come in part from interested private sources. In fact, CIA would provide cover for the substantial official U.S. funding.

Howland Sargeant, a former assistant secretary of state in the Truman administration, was highly effective as chairman of Radio Liberty. Aside from the regular policy and operational meetings I attended with Agency and New York staff, there were semi-annual dinners. These New York occasions were a curious combination of serious policy discussions and, in a broad sense, a pep rally. It was perhaps a bit of luck that I always managed to sit beside Mrs. Sargeant, more widely known as the movie star Myrna Loy. There was no more lively dinner companion or effective antidote to long evenings of high policy talk than that polished actress.

Keeping the various Eastern European political and ethnic groups from one another's throat at RFE was a cinch in comparison to the complex relations separating the political particles spawned by the Soviet Union. Between the numerous non-Russian ethnic entities—ranging from the Armenians, Azerbaijanis, Belorussians, Georgians, North Caucasians, to the Turkmenistani—there sometimes seemed to be more bad blood than water coursing down the Volga. Aside from the ethnic groups were numerous political parties—the Nazi-tainted Vlassovites, the rightist NTS, and a dozen or more lesser phratries. The most common term used in discussing the exiles was "splinter faction." As the splinters split into sub-splinters—the dozen or so Ukrainian elements never coalesced—a friend suggested that one more split might reduce the entire emigration to sawdust.

In speaking lightly of the difficulties faced by the Agency staff struggling to fashion a semblance of unity in the emigration, it is easy to forget that the glue which eventually held some of these elements together was largely composed of the sweat of the activists who fashioned what became known as Radio Liberty.

Allen Dulles kept himself closely informed on developments in Eastern Europe and the USSR. He did his best to stand as a buffer between the well-informed and heavy-hitting members of the New York committees and those of us responsible for the daily broadcast content and support activity. There were times when caught between a sizeable rock in New York and the hard place represented by the Washington-based policymakers that I understood Lucky Pierre's problem. The senior members of the New York group were not accustomed to having to debate their decisions with anyone, least of all a handful of mere government employees some three hundred miles to the south, and a few score subordinates on the far side of the Atlantic.

One of the least-remembered RFE achievements came in late summer 1956 when William Griffith, the Munich-based policy advisor, and his deputy, Paul Henze, spotted a changing mood in Eastern Europe, and gave warning of a likely confrontation between the indigenous populations and the Soviet forces in East Germany, Poland, and Hungary. Cord Meyer briefed Allen Dulles on this speculation and attempted to get this impression across to the State Department and Agency analysts. Neither Dulles nor the reigning specialists were convinced by the RFE analysis, and were content to assume that as in the past, the communist authorities would maintain effective control of their Eastern European "allies." When the outbreak of violence in Poland and open revolt in Hungary proved the RFE analysts were correct, Allen Dulles rebuked Cord for not having pressed the RFE position hard enough.

When RFE and Radio Liberty got fully under way, they collected vast amounts of information on the communist countries. Monitoring stations maintained twenty-four-hour coverage of all broadcasts originating behind the Curtain. Local newspapers, journals, and other publications throughout the Soviet bloc were meticulously studied by highly qualified analysts. In addition, the radios maintained news bureaus throughout Western Europe, and were able to debrief travelers and question defectors and refugees from the target areas. Despite repeated charges that the radios were running agents and spies, no such activity was ever undertaken. It would have been foolhardy to risk the integrity of the radios by attempting to mix espionage with the overt activity. As the data and analysis gained strength, Western journalists became regular visitors to the research facilities in Munich.

One incident that mandated my eating crow in respect to propaganda-bearing balloons came in 1954 when Colonel Josef Swiatlo, a senior officer in the Polish security service, defected to the CIA post in Berlin. Swiatlo was intimately well informed on the inner workings of the Polish government and its relationship with Moscow. In addition to radio programming, hundreds of thousands of pamphlets detailing Swiatlo's inside data were strewn across Poland by balloons. By December 1954, Swiatlo's information had blown General Stanislaw Radkiewicz, the Polish minister of security and one of the most powerful members of the Polish government, and three of his top aides out of their Warsaw offices. The security forces were reorganized but with diminished authority.

The most serious test of the radios' ability to hew to the agreed-upon policy of not encouraging futile resistance to the Soviet occupation forces came first in 1956 when CIA obtained copies of Khrushchev's secret speech to the Twentieth Party Congress in Moscow. The *New York Times* published his bold attack on Stalin in February. The full text and analysis were aired by both radios, and, to the degree possible, printed texts were circulated (yes, sometimes by balloon) throughout Eastern Europe. In May, Jakob Berman, a Stalinist, acting premier in Poland, was forced to quit. In June, a spontaneous worker uprising was put down by the heavy-handed Polish security police. This open revolt surprised the West as much as it did the Polish authorities.

In the following weeks, the Polish government promised reform and improved living conditions for the workers. This fed the Polish appetite for more freedom and by October 19, Wladyslaw Gomulka, a relatively moderate communist, fresh from prison, was readmitted to the Polish Central Committee. The PCC promptly relieved Soviet Marshal Konstantin Rokossovsky of his post as "Polish" defense minister and Polish army commanding officer, and expedited his return to Moscow. This was more than Khrushchev had bargained for, and with Vyacheslav Molotov, Anastas Mikoyan, and Lazar Kaganovich, enplaned for Warsaw and a confrontation with Gomulka. Unless Rokossovsky was reinstated, Khrushchev declared, the Red Army would put things straight. Gomulka refused, and pointed out that the Polish workers were already armed and prepared for a scrap. Khrushchev backed down.

Throughout these tense hours, when open warfare was a strong possibility, RFE consistently cautioned the Polish people not to press the demands—free elections and the immediate withdrawal of the Red Army occupation force—that would force the USSR's hand. Gomulka was elected first secretary and proposed a compromise which the Soviets accepted. In the midst of these negotiations, Gomulka suspended the internal jamming of RFE broadcasts—a strong indication that he welcomed the calming RFE programs.

Jan Nowak, one of the surviving leaders of the 1944 Polish revolt against the German occupation, was chief of the RFE Polish desk in Munich. His firm hand ensured that RFE continued to counsel the Poles against what Cord Meyer referred to as "the suicidal romanticism that had marked earlier Polish revolts." With the able help of Bill Griffith, the Munich political advisor, the Polish desk performance was brilliant.

Things went less well in Budapest.

In October, sparks like those which ignited the bloodless revolt in Poland set Hungary ablaze. Rallies organized by university students attracted enough popular support to force the replacement of the widely despised Mátyás Rákosi as first secretary of the Hungarian Communist Party and the granting of a few slight political concessions. This palliative worked no better in Hungary than in Poland, and by October 22, 300,000 protesters were in the Budapest streets, and Hungarian workers were arming themselves. Hungarian military units were soon to turn against their Soviet "comrades in arms," and when security police posts were attacked, some of the survivors joined the protesters. The Communist government fled from Budapest, and Imre Nagy, a moderate reformer, took office as premier. On October 24, Soviet tanks, supported by elite combat troops, battled their way into Budapest. By late November, the Russians had captured Nagy and spirited him out of the country for trial and execution.

The Hungarian people had won their revolution but lost their war against the Red Army.

The free world and many Communist Party members were appalled by the post-Stalin violence. Moscow soon realized that the USSR had lost more sympathy and support than at any time in its history. A full-strength counter-propaganda attack was quickly mounted. The first blast came from—one might say, of all places—Bucharest. This was followed by remarks of the Soviet delegate during a Security Council debate in New York. In short, the USSR alleged that it was the subversive RFE broadcasts, directed from the United States, that played the key role in preparing and provoking the armed conflict. Today, it is difficult to believe that anyone with access to a free press might be led to believe that a series of broadcasts could possibly cause a nation, presumably delighted to live under the thumb of the USSR, to make an all but barehanded attempt to expel an occupation force backed by the then strongest military establishment in the world.

Yet the Bucharest allegation and its many offspring in the Western press got wide and repeated circulation. Three separate investigations—by the State Department, the West German Foreign Office, and the Agency—showed the RFE Polish desk to have remained completely within the tightly written policy guidelines. The hours spent going over the mass of data on the RFE Hungarian desk response to the revolution revealed one violation, an apparently innocent rebroadcast of an editorial opinion expressed in a British newspaper. Considering the emotional impact of the doomed Hungarian effort to shake free of the Soviet Union, this is a commendable record.

Chapter 35

—

GOING PUBLIC

For some time before the *Ramparts* disclosures hit the fan in February 1967, Frank Wisner, Cord Meyer, and I had been aware that the slim security shield protecting the fact that federal funds were financing Radio Free Europe and Radio Liberty had seriously eroded. No amount of security tinkering can be counted on to contain the circle of compromise in any long-lasting secret activity involving numbers of people and extensive funding. Employees come and go, gossip is exchanged, slight security infractions pile up, and if the initial funding arrangements were rushed, basic security will become increasingly fragile. The number of knowledgeable members of Congress and congressional staffs increases with each change of administration.

After some two decades of expensive activity, any interested observer could only have deduced that no plausible measure of private funding would have met more than a fraction of the RFE and Radio Liberty overhead.

Ironically, it was the success of RFE and Radio Liberty that made it difficult to reinforce security. The risk of tampering with complex and highly successful operations going at full blast is akin to that of fixing something that is not yet broken. As we saw it, the only possible solution would be to arrange a means of acknowledging overt U.S. government support without destroying the impact on the audience. Aside from Senator Fulbright and a handful of others who were prepared to knuckle under, no one in the Johnson administration, and certainly none of the New York founding fathers, was interested in muzzling the radios. And no one was prepared to take on the problems and risks that would certainly be involved in trying to sell some semi-federal version of RFE and Radio Liberty to a less than enthusiastic Congress. Reluctantly, Cord and I agreed that rather than risk an upheaval, it would be best to let the security dog doze. Or so we thought.

Twenty-four hours after the initial *Ramparts* disclosure, a second *New York Times* front-page story noted that when President Johnson announced that he had stopped all secret aid to student groups, he also ordered the Agency to review all CIA financial aid to private anti-communist organizations. James Reston, head of the *Times* Washington office, observed that LBJ's action placed other Agency operations—aid to anti-communist publications, radio, and labor unions—"in jeopardy." With this, even more cats were tumbled out of the bag.

President Johnson had been well briefed on the Congress for Cultural Freedom, the Free Europe Committee, RFE, and Radio Liberty. Given the problems already on his desk, LBJ showed no particular interest in the details of successful projects, two of which had rocked along for some twenty years. He agreed with our estimate (shared by State) of the considerable impact these operations were having in Eastern Europe and Russia, but his enthusiasm was never more than tepid. When the *Ramparts* data surfaced, I had the impression the President was more concerned with the fundamental legality of passing official funds through various private channels than the effect the *Ramparts* fallout would have on the future of the Agency projects.

As the torrents of op-ed abuse continued to flow, Mike Wallace, a CBS-TV news correspondent, joined the attack and charged CIA with having used every citizen who contributed to the funds solicited by the RFE as "cover." This had a curious side effect. As corporate president of CBS, Frank Stanton, a stouthearted patriot, was Wallace's employer. Stanton was also chairman of the executive committee of the Free Europe Fund.

In a successful effort to head off an all-out Senate investigation of CIA clandestine funding, President Johnson appointed a special three-

man committee to review relationships "between CIA and American educational and private organizations operating abroad." The committee
was also to recommend ways which government assistance could be
provided to allow these organizations "to continue their proper and vital
role abroad." Under Secretary of State Nicholas deB. Katzenbach, my
old friend Secretary of Health, Education and Welfare John Gardner, and
I were the only members. Katzenbach later remarked that when appointing us, LBJ assumed that I would want *all* the CIA projects to continue,
that John Gardner would insist that everything stop forthwith, and that
Nick would serve as referee.

We met in Katzenbach's office at the time he was also acting secretary of state. John sat at one end of a sofa and I at the other. Katzenbach,
a large and impressive figure, loomed over us from behind a desk the
size and heft of a pool table. He was slow moving, but his darting eyes
and occasional smile—sometimes genial smirk—were ample proof that
he never missed a detail. John Gardner, uncommonly bright, with both
feet squarely on the ground, and by then an icon in the educational
world, was formidable in debate. The atmosphere was occasionally
frosty but never ill-spirited. On the positive side, we came up with a succinct and effective recommendation: "It should be the policy of the
United States that no federal agency shall provide any covert financial
assistance or support, direct or indirect, to any of the nation's educational or private voluntary organizations." Unfortunately, the committee's statement that the covert assistance to private American groups was
a necessary and appropriate reaction to the communist front organizations was ignored in most of the press coverage.

For me, the least welcome of the committee conclusions was that, in
view of the publicity and editorial ranting, it would be necessary to terminate *all* such secret grants. This, it was assumed, might "avoid any im-
plication that because governmental assistance was given covertly it was
used to affect the policies of private voluntary organizations." The drastic cutback was intended to make it plain that the "activities of private
American groups abroad are, in fact, private." My observations about
babies and bathwater both going down the drain were to no avail.

On the positive side, we battled our way to the sound recommendation "that the Government should promptly develop and establish a
public-private mechanism to provide public funds openly for overseas

activities of organizations which are adjudged deserving, in the national interest, of public support." We wisely did not attempt to frame any such public-private institution, and shrewdly proposed that the President form another committee to deal with the problem. We wound up our recommendations with the warning that the new outfit "would have to be . . . and be recognized as . . . an independent body, not controlled by the government."

President Johnson accepted our recommendation that another committee be appointed to fashion a more nearly acceptable public-private mechanism for funding worthwhile projects. He named Secretary of State Dean Rusk as chairman of an eighteen-man committee with membership drawn from Congress, the executive branch, and private life. I was not the least surprised when this committee wrestled itself to extinction in its failed attempts to find a means of filling the void left when the Agency was ruled off the field. The complex of tangled events that led to the hyper-moral editorial judgments and sanctimonious posturing of some public officials had resulted, as Cord Meyer put it, in "unilateral political disarmament in the face of a continuing Soviet pressure."*

It was 1973 before the Board for International Broadcasting was finally established. This was in marked contrast to Wisner and his New York supporters, who created both RFE and Radio Liberty from scratch in a matter of weeks.

The details of the efforts to establish the broadcasting board are well and fairly given by Sig Mickelson in his book *America's Other Voice.*† Before becoming president of RFE, Mickelson was president of the CBS News Division and its chief executive for news and public affairs. Senator Fulbright continued his attack on RFE and Radio Liberty until the end. As chairman of the Senate Foreign Relations Committee, he described the radios as "an instrument to keep alive animosities of World War II." History suggests that the only sure way of *ending* such animosities is for one nation to abandon its principles, jettison its arms, and surrender. Fulbright notwithstanding, President Johnson had no intention of surrendering anything to the Soviet Union. In March 1967, LBJ accepted our recommendations as policy.

Facing Reality (New York: Harper & Row, 1980), p. 106.

†*America's Other Voice: The Story of Radio Free Europe and Radio Liberty* (New York: Praeger, 1988).

The decision that there was to be no further covert funding of any U.S. educational or private voluntary organizations was to a degree modified by "surge funding"—before the President's directive became effective, RFE, Radio Liberty, and the Congress for Cultural Freedom were provided with a sufficient budget to carry on until arrangements for future funding could be determined. President Johnson and appropriate members of Congress agreed with this carryover solution.

The extended fallout from the *Ramparts* scandal, and the exposure of the Agency role and mechanisms involved in funding these organizations, threatened to compromise other covert action operations around the world. If security leaks were to be stanched, an immediate evaluation of all covert action projects was an essential first step. President Johnson directed that this be accomplished "in short order."

In 1965, when I was promoted to deputy director under Admiral Raborn, Desmond FitzGerald, then chief of the Western Hemisphere division, moved up to replace me as deputy director for plans (DDP), with responsibility for worldwide operations. Des was an aggressive officer who had previously served in the Far East and as headquarters chief of the FE division. He had a distinct flair for covert action and was not easily persuaded by conventional thinking or tripped up by outdated procedures. After a brief but pointed discussion, I directed Des to review each covert action operation and to dismantle every such activity that might be terminated without any significant loss. He was also to evaluate the security of each operation and to close any that lacked sufficient security footing. I asked to have the report in my hands within a week.

Minutes after Des left, another senior officer, fresh from an overseas inspection trip, came through the door. He briefed me at some length before confiding that he had discovered that the Agency office in one of the lesser-developed countries had used the funds left over from a marginal covert action project for a most graphic poster campaign. Unfortunately, he admitted, the campaign had not been cleared with me or anyone else in Washington. The explicit graphics, he explained, were necessary because the intended audience was illiterate. It had been a long day and I braced myself for more bad news.

For decades, I learned, peasants living on the outskirts of the capital had once a week sold their produce on the city streets. At the close of business, it was the peasant custom to buy a bottle of the local firewater, and to drink as much as possible before curling up on the sidewalk. In time, the peasant would wake, lower his trousers, defecate, and totter along home. This sequence of events was portrayed on the posters, with an explicit picture of the possible consequences. Only when the head-quarters man stepped from the capital's best restaurant and narrowly missed putting a foot in the redolent proof that the campaign had failed did he agree that the $260 salvaged from the abandoned project had at the least been spent with the best of intentions. I managed a faint smile, suppressed the thought of briefing Congress on this transgression, and realized it was past time for me also to get along home.

In the week that followed, Des reviewed hundreds of covert action projects with the responsible division chiefs and headquarters desk officers. Canceled out of hand were the marginal activities hastily undertaken in the go-go days when "the Russians are coming" was the Washington watchword. Aging projects with most energy spent were put to rest. Operations which, despite the efforts of the case officers, showed only a chance of achieving success were less easily throttled. Each dismantling presented unique problems. Well-motivated indigenous activists had to be assured that the closing of their activity did not signal a change in U.S. policy. Mercenary agents, accustomed to a monthly tax-free income, had to be left with a smile and a delicately shaded caution against any threat of tattle-telling. Within the Agency the impact of the cutback was traumatic. Months of hard work were swept aside in reviews lasting but a few minutes. But the decks were cleared for new projects and security fences were effectively reinforced.

In November 1967, when the editorial attacks had subsided from flood stage, President Johnson asked me to remain behind after one of the Tuesday lunches. Without the slightest preface he said, "I won't fund those radios of yours any longer."

Taken totally by surprise, I blurted, "You can't do that!"

My spontaneous response had gone so far beyond the customary White House protocol that we both lapsed into silence. Until that moment I had assumed that although LBJ had never expressed interest in either of the radio projects, he was not opposed to them. By the time I realized that my spontaneous reaction had come as much of a surprise to the President as his announcement had to me, I began to recover my wits. LBJ listened for the usual two or three minutes before interrupting.

"All right, Helms," he said. "If on your own, and without any support from me, you can get the Senate to play ball, I'll agree." He loosened his tie in preparation for his after-lunch nap. "Just don't forget that you're not going to have any help from me."

In the course of our work together I had learned that one of President Johnson's quirks was his tendency to react immediately, and without any staff consultation, to the views that some trusted chum had expressed orally. It would have helped in framing our response to know who had soured LBJ. I was unable to uncover a clue.

It took a bit more than three weeks to select and brief the members of Congress having to do with appropriations who would support the radios, and whose views were most likely to impress the President. Senator Russell was an obvious choice, with Senator Milton Young of North Dakota as second witness. Congressmen George Mahon of Texas, Frank Bow of Ohio, and Glenard Lipscomb of California completed the cast. Each volunteered to support the Agency's request to continue federal funding until other arrangements could be made. As usual, Senator Russell was outspoken in his support and admitted to wondering "what all the ruckus" was about. The consensus of this group was that this was not the time to reduce our efforts to influence our Eastern European and Soviet audiences.

In the opening paragraph of my letter forwarding the news to the President, I was more mindful of my manners than when he first dropped the bomb on me. "You will recall," I wrote delicately, "that at lunch . . . we discussed the future of Radio Free Europe and Radio Liberty . . . you expressed a willingness for me to consult those leaders of Congress having to do with appropriations" and that in doing so I was to make sure that my approach "would not constitute a request by you for this money or a charge against your congressional program."

The funds were appropriated and LBJ never again mentioned either of the radios to me.

Now, some thirty years after the firestorm of criticism of Radio Free Europe and Radio Liberty, it is easier to judge the impact of these operations than it was at the time the naysayers were holding the high ground. In a letter to Radio Liberty on its fortieth anniversary, Russian President Boris Yeltsin wrote: "It would be difficult to overestimate the importance of your contribution to the destruction of the totalitarian [Soviet] regime." Mikhail Gorbachev wrote: "Radio Liberty always broadcast much which was essential to people in Russia and in Europe." In a letter to President Bill Clinton, Václav Havel, president of the Czech Republic, said: "On several occasions I have, on behalf of Czech citizens, expressed gratitude for RFE's help in our people's resistance to the communist regime." These *post facto* comments support the more difficult impact assessments we were able to make before Eastern Europe and Russia shook off the shackles.

Before Cord Meyer left for an overseas assignment, I had the pleasure of awarding him the Distinguished Intelligence Medal. Cord accepted the decoration on the part of the others who had contributed so much to these programs.

———

A few weeks before his death, I visited Allen Dulles in his Georgetown house. Through the years of his retirement there were often bits and pieces of unfinished business. As DCI, I always welcomed the opportunity to handle some of them myself and to use the occasion for a chat. Allen's gout had flared and, as always, he resorted to the well-worn carpet slippers. We had finished our shoptalk and were sitting in the solarium which he used as his retirement office. It was dark by the time we set aside the tea that his wife, Clover, had brought. I was about to leave when Allen, pipe in hand, motioned me to stay.

"You know, Dick," he said, "for some time now, there's been something I've wanted to say." Dulles reached for a match to relight his pipe; I wondered how many hundred—perhaps a thousand—times I had watched him lend emphasis to a conversational point by using his pipe as an actor might to ensure he had focused the audience's attention.

"Before it's too late," he said, "I want you to know that I think my not giving you the DDP job was my greatest mistake."

It was the last chance we had to speak. No matter how succinct the message, I was deeply touched.

Dulles died in January 1969.

Chapter 36

PRESIDENT NIXON

Four days after his election, Richard Nixon proposed a meeting with President Johnson to sound out any pressing problems and to give some of Nixon's staff a notion of how things were arranged within the White House. It was mid-afternoon when Secretary of State Dean Rusk, Secretary of Defense Clark Clifford, General Earle "Bus" Wheeler, chairman of the Joint Chiefs of Staff, and I gathered in the Cabinet Room to wait for LBJ and the President-elect.

Dean Rusk took charge. "Mr. Nixon is coming by himself—no aides. We'd best deploy ourselves so that he doesn't find himself alone on one side of the table." With this, he signaled Bus and me to sit on either side of the chair which he reserved for Nixon. I took the seat on Nixon's left. LBJ and the President-elect arrived promptly.

Dean opened the meeting by asking, rather boldly I thought, if the President-elect had yet chosen a secretary of state. Nixon shook his head. "No, but I'm obviously thinking about it," he replied. "I can assure you that there's no lack of aspirants. It may also interest you all to know that even Scotty Reston is among them." At the time, James Reston, chief of the *New York Times* Washington Bureau, was one of the best-known newsmen and political pundits in the country. The notion that he had signaled interest in being secretary of state seemed completely out of character. Whatever Nixon's purpose in dropping this bit of information, the result was five sets of simultaneously raised eyebrows and a moment of surprised silence. Dean brought us back to reality by opening a discussion of problem number one, Vietnam. Nothing surprising was raised and the meeting was soon adjourned.

As I was gathering my papers, LBJ stuck his head back into the room and said, "Wait here, I want to talk to you." I sat down, opened my briefcase, and tried to concentrate on some of the documents. No use, my attention was elsewhere. I had logged my share of time in Washington, had known President Kennedy, and had spent a great many hours face-to-face and on the telephone with President Johnson. Despite this experience, I have never shaken what I suppose may be an adolescent feeling of awe in the presence of a president. My reaction is compounded of respect and admiration: respect for a man who for at least four years, twenty-four hours a day, bears such responsibility; and admiration for the political skill that won him the office and must shape so many daily decisions. In history, no more than a handful of men have had a fraction of such power. For me, sitting for thirty minutes alone in the Cabinet Room, waiting to be called into the Oval Office, was not conducive to concentrating on a sheaf of papers, Top Secret or otherwise.

My reverie was broken when an aide beckoned from the secretary's office which connects the Cabinet Room to the Oval Office. LBJ was standing. "Sorry to keep you waiting but I wanted you to know that Nixon has for the second time asked me about you. I told him, 'Helms was a merit appointment, I've no idea how he voted in any election and I have never asked what his political views are. He's always been correct with me and has done a good job as director. I commend him to you.' " LBJ walked to his desk before saying, "That's it, Dick." As I thanked him, LBJ picked up the telephone and eased himself into the handsome leather chair. I slipped out the side door to the Oval Office, again wondering how many hours a day LBJ spent on the telephone.

Four days later, I was summoned to a meeting with Nixon. Unlike the previous three transition teams that had taken offices in Washington, the Nixon group had chosen quarters on the thirty-ninth floor of the Hotel Pierre in New York City. This was inconvenient for the rest of us, but from the President-elect's point of view, it was presumably far enough away from LBJ's staff to avoid any unsupervised fraternization. To make sure that Nixon and his staff were kept completely in the daily intelligence loop, R. Jack Smith, the DDI (deputy director for intelligence), was to remain temporarily in New York. He would handle the daily briefings and assume responsibility for the highly classified documents involved.

H. R. Haldeman, Nixon's chief of staff, was surprised when Jack told him that security regulations required the Top Secret data to be kept in a vaulted area under twenty-four-hour guard. Haldeman, whose manners were as bush as his brush haircut, directed Jack to an unfinished room in the cellar of the nearby American Bible Society building. An Agency security team did the necessary refitting.

I arrived at the Pierre on schedule, and in a few minutes a Secret Service man ushered me into the suite Nixon was using as his office. He greeted me with a smile and handshake, and introduced me to John Mitchell, who was standing nearby. We sat down, Nixon and Mitchell side by side, across a coffee table from me. After a passing reference to the White House meeting, Nixon said he had heard well of my performance as DCI and that he wanted me to stay on. He added that he would also ask J. Edgar Hoover to remain and commented that the previous administrations' practice of keeping these two appointments out of the political arena was sound. I remarked that I thoroughly agreed with that policy.

Nixon then asked me to keep silent until the official announcement was made. Mitchell, who was already flagged as the likely attorney general, remained silent throughout our brief meeting. We shook hands all around and I departed, using a freight elevator to avoid the photographers and reporters staked out in the hotel lobby. Our meeting was on November 14. It was not until December 18 that the announcement was made.

I was pleased to be reappointed, but it did little to shake my long-standing impression of Nixon's antipathy to the Agency. Within a few days, another straw in the wind drifted across my desk. In the course of a phone call, Jack Smith told me that Nixon did not appear to be reading the President's Daily Brief—the single most important daily intelligence publication. Worse, if he were reading it, he apparently didn't like it.

In Washington, the weeks following the election of a new president and the appointment of his cabinet and other advisors can best be described as "fraught," particularly in the minds of those who overnight might find themselves out of a job. My dictionary offers various definitions of "fraught" ranging from the archaic "freighted with or loaded" to the more pertinent "bearing promise or menace." In respect to the incoming Nixon administration, the Washington atmosphere seemed more fraught than usual.

I had first met Nixon, then Vice President, in November 1956 at the time of the Hungarian revolution. Allen Dulles and I briefed him before he left Washington for Vienna. Nixon was preparing to represent President Eisenhower at a meeting concerning aid for the Hungarian refugees then flooding into Austria. Our second meeting came when as President-elect, Nixon visited Washington to meet President Johnson. In the course of one of their sessions, LBJ summoned me and said, "I want you to be sure that Mr. Nixon gets all of the intelligence you are giving me, starting right now."

One of the first adjustments the Agency makes at the advent of a new administration is the shaping of a daily Top Secret intelligence summary to the specific needs and wishes of the incoming president. President Truman had initiated what he called his daily newspaper—a summary of the most important cable and dispatch traffic and intelligence reporting of the preceding twenty-four hours. This Top Secret document was also circulated throughout the government to the high-ranking officials involved in foreign and defense policy. In various formats, with but slight substantive changes, this document continued through the Eisenhower administration.

By the time President Kennedy settled in, he realized that the White House was so burdened with information from State, the Pentagon, and the Agency that there was a risk that some vital intelligence might never reach the top of the appropriate in-tray. JFK asked for a single, concise summary of the most important "*all source*" reports from the intelligence community. The result was a daily document that included summaries of *all* the most highly classified and sensitive intelligence of the preceding twenty-four hours.

At the time, the highest security classification was known as Top Secret/Code Word. In practice, the slug—as we called it—"Top Secret/Code Word" was followed by a noun, so scrupulously chosen that even the most intuitive intruder could not associate a glimpse of the code word with the subject matter it protected. In my day there were a dozen or more of these tightly compartmented classifications of information. Aside from the President and a few others—usually the secretary of state, secretary of defense, and national security advisor—no other government official was automatically cleared for "all source" reports. The lesser recipients of specific code word data had to have a clearly established "need to know" the substance of the compartmented report. Compartmentation, as we called it, is one of the most effective means of protecting sensitive data. Even today, I hesitate to pick a typical code word to illustrate the system. As surely as Heaven gave us little green apples, it would be my luck to pick a five-letter noun that is in current use.

At the outset, the JFK briefing was known as the "President's Intelligence Check List," otherwise, PICL—pronounced "Pickle" by those involved in preparing the document. In time this evolved into the "President's Daily Brief," otherwise the "PDB." As I recall it, President Eisenhower had wanted his daily summary at reveille. JFK liked to read the Pickle on arrival at his desk. President Johnson wanted the PDB in late afternoon and often read it in bed. Neither Jack Smith nor I was ever sure how often Nixon even glanced at his PDB.

The Top Secret/Code Word daily briefings that JFK shared with the secretaries of state and defense were hand-carried to each recipient by a Directorate for Intelligence officer who was prepared to answer any questions the reader might have. With the exception of the President, the officer courier was required to wait—slow or preoccupied readers notwithstanding—until the recipient had read the document before carrying it back to the Agency vault. Clumsy indeed, but efficiency and security are absolutely incompatible concepts.

One Sunday morning, the precious few recipients of the PDB were startled when the *New York Times Magazine* section featured a photograph of LBJ, propped up in bed, reading the PDB with the Top Secret/Code Word slugs plainly to be seen. Presumably to the dismay of the *New York Times*'s KGB readership, the Agency security office managed to change all the Top Secret/Code Word slugs by Sunday lunchtime.

When in 1965 I stepped up to be deputy director of Central Intelligence, Admiral Raborn, who was not familiar with any of the Agency personnel, left the choice for my replacement as deputy director for plans to me. I was in no rush to fill the job, and wanted to be sure that the new DDP could function on his own while I was concentrating on the elements of the Agency that were relatively new to me. In time the choice narrowed to Thomas Karamessines, who was my deputy as DDP, and Desmond FitzGerald, then a division chief. Within the plans directorate there were so many differences between the score or so of most senior offices that an outsider might well wonder whatever activity brought such an odd bunch together. That said, there was no difference more vast than that separating Tom Karamessines and Des FitzGerald.

Des was gifted in every sense of the word. He was very bright and operationally aggressive—not to say dashing. Hail Citizen Nixon: Des was also a full-fashioned charter member of the East Coast establishment. There were times when I was convinced that Des was on first-name terms with everyone ever mentioned in *both* the Social Register and *Who's Who*. He was also an exception to the OSS legacy of officers, most of whom, because of their World War II experience, might be described as "Eurocentric." Des's military and early Agency experience was in Southeast Asia, China, and Japan. His most recent command responsibility was in Latin America with an emphasis on Cuba, the area of keen interest to the Kennedy administration. This put Des in contact with his friend President Kennedy.

Thomas H. Karamessines, or Tom K, as he was universally known within the Agency, was cut from different cloth.* Tom was born on Staten Island, the son of Greek immigrants. He worked his way through Columbia University and Columbia Law School in the days before the war when tuition fees were hard to come by. In 1941 he signed on as a deputy assistant attorney under Thomas E. Dewey, who was then heading what was known as a "racket busting" office in New York City. One of Tom's fellow lawyers was William Rogers, later secretary of state.

When Tom enlisted as a private soldier in 1942, his background and fluent Greek brought him to OSS. He was assigned to counterespionage in X-2 and commissioned. He remained in the military as a major on assignment to SSU until CIA was formed. Tom was short, not quite stocky, had jet black hair, and was rarely seen without his pipe. Soft-spoken, un-

---

*When Jim Angleton's full name became known within the Agency, a friend noted that a powerful name was obviously one of the criteria for senior operations officers— James Jesus Angleton, William King Harvey, and Thomas Hercules Karamessines.

obtrusive, and extremely perceptive, he was an excellent judge of people and had a keen operational sense. We worked closely together, and he had my confidence.

At the time, my guess was that the corridor gossips were betting on Tom as my choice to be deputy director for plans. It was perhaps typical of Des and Tom that while Tom never raised the possibility of promotion with me, Des came into my office to make a straight-from-the-shoulder bid for the job. This notwithstanding, Des was my choice, and Tom remained in place as deputy to the DDP.

I could not suppress the memory of my reaction when I was Frank Wisner's deputy and Allen Dulles chose Dick Bissell rather than me as Frank's replacement. It was typical of Tom K that he never gave the slightest indication of his disappointment.

Des FitzGerald had scarcely served a year as DDP when in July 1967 he collapsed on a tennis court. His sudden death, quite possibly hastened by his strenuous wartime service in the Pacific, was a severe loss.

The shock that followed was still being felt when I appointed Tom K to replace Des.

It was not until late January 1969 that Tom Karamessines, Cord Meyer, then Tom's deputy, and I were called to the White House for our first formal briefing of President Nixon. We met in the Cabinet Room. Henry Kissinger, fully established as national security advisor, sat at Nixon's side. I had first met Henry when he came to Washington to study an aspect of the Berlin problem. We were not together long enough to become acquainted, but Henry came across as the thoughtful, well-informed Harvard professor that he was. We did not meet again until Nixon appointed him national security advisor. It occurred to me then that Nelson Rockefeller might have suggested the appointment to Nixon.

We gave the President an overview of our most productive operations, and closed with a discussion of the more risky activity. In passing, I noted that the most important operations are not necessarily the most chancy. Nixon appeared affable, and was quick to ask pertinent questions. As we gathered our papers and were making our way from the office, the President—in what I later realized was a rare jovial moment—called out, "But don't get *caught!*"

The full irony of that advice came home to us some thirty months later when a band of President Nixon's private operatives were themselves caught in the Watergate premises of the Democratic National Committee.

My first substantive meeting with Henry as national security advisor came on the heels of the session with the President. Henry spoke first, advising me of Nixon's edict that effective immediately all intelligence briefings, oral and otherwise, were to come through Kissinger. *All* intelligence reports? I asked. Yes. National Intelligence Estimates? Henry nodded, and went on to explain that Nixon also wanted me to leave the National Security Council meetings immediately after my weekly intelligence roundup. I was not to be present during the policy discussions that followed.

By the time Nixon stepped into the White House, I thought I had more fully fathomed the reasons for his negative attitude toward the Agency. Nixon was, and remained, convinced that an element in his losing his first presidential election was the data he thought Allen Dulles slipped to Senator Kennedy alleging that there was a sizeable gap between the U.S. and USSR missile capability. The allegation was false, but Nixon was not to be dissuaded. A more rational reason for some of Nixon's antipathy was his negative reaction to Allen Dulles's enthusiasm for advocating policy positions in meetings with President Eisenhower and his staff. This is one opinion that Nixon and I shared: the DCI must refrain from taking sides in policy debates. CIA's most important responsibility is to present the President with the best possible data on which decisions can be made. The unvarnished intelligence and the National Estimates of its importance must be presented accurately, no matter whether the material supports the incumbent administration's policy or not.

Another aspect of Nixon's attitude appears to have come from deep within his personality. He seemed to dislike and distrust persons who he suspected might not put personal loyalty to him above all other responsibilities. This obsession sometimes seemed combined with deep suspicion of people Nixon thought might consider themselves his social superior. Nixon never appeared to have shaken his early impression that the Agency was exclusively staffed by uppity Ivy Leaguers, most of whom lived in Georgetown and spent every evening gossiping about him at cocktail parties. The explanations for these attitudes, which in some cases seemed to blind his judgment, is best left to board-certified medical specialists.

Whatever Nixon's view of the Agency, it was my opinion that he was the best prepared to be President of any of those under whom I served—Eisenhower, Kennedy, and Johnson. Each had great strengths, but as I saw it, Nixon had the best grasp of foreign affairs and domestic politics. His years as vice president had served him well.

As Henry continued to talk, I realized that, in effect, Nixon had reverted to an expanded semblance of the National Security Council that President Eisenhower had established. Neither President Kennedy nor President Johnson was much interested in the NSC, and made little use of it. Under Nixon, and with Henry Kissinger's leadership, the NSC assumed a much more significant role in policymaking. The personnel strength quadrupled in size and grew in substance, with the addition of a number of excellent analysts detailed to the White House from the Agency and State. Various NSC subcommittees were formed with experts also borrowed from the Agency, State, and Defense. The most important of these bodies was the Senior Review Group, which studied policy recommendations before they were presented to the full NSC. Jack Smith was an obvious choice to represent the Agency as a member of this senior group.

In the course of attempting to shape our product to the requirements of the new administration, Jack's initial conviction seemed confirmed. Nixon was not reading the PDB—still the most important daily intelligence document in Washington. I agreed with Jack's suggestion that he raise the topic with Kissinger, with whom we were developing a working relationship. Jack arranged a meeting, and by luck found Attorney General John Mitchell in Henry's office. When Jack raised the question of the PDB, Mitchell got up to leave. Henry requested him to stay, and asked if he knew what Nixon thought of the PDB. Mitchell said he thought that Nixon considered the document too far-ranging, and that it covered areas which were of slight interest to the White House. He added that Nixon had once said he had trouble sorting fact from opinion in the PDB.

Jack then asked if Nixon wanted just the facts and no interpretation. Mitchell, who was less than expansive at the best of times, was downright laconic with relative strangers. He grudgingly allowed that Nixon was a lawyer, and lawyers always liked to have the facts first, with the opinions to follow. It was not much to go on, but Jack began refashioning our efforts accordingly.

Nixon's decision that I was to decamp before the National Security Council began discussing policy matters struck me as shortsighted, and not merely because of any anguish the group might suffer from my absence. Minus the director of Central Intelligence, there would be no one left standing who on occasion might be able to "keep the game honest" by pointing out that some of the bona fide NSC members were making too freely with dubious data.

At the next NSC session, I was preparing to slip gracefully away when Nixon invited the group, one and all, for lunch with him. In the NSC meetings that followed, I thought that Nixon had either forgotten his initial ukase or had clearly changed his mind. I was thereafter allowed to remain at table as the NSC went on about its policymaking business. Sometime later I was told that Melvin Laird, secretary of defense, had interceded with Nixon, and insisted that the DCI be present at policy discussions.

Very early in my career I realized that secret intelligence is not for the fainthearted. From the mortal peril of organizing resistance and stealing secrets in police states to dealing with one's own government, secret intelligence can be a lethal version of a rugged contact sport. In the Johnson administration, the near nightmare of balancing the conflicting Pentagon and Agency views on the strength of the North Vietnamese forces in South Vietnam had been resolved. But blood was on the floor and walls before a compromise that did not violate the integrity of the estimate had been agreed upon, and President Johnson was provided with the most accurate possible estimate of the North Vietnamese forces. In September, an equally explosive issue came to the flash point in the Nixon administration.

A New England–born colleague characterized the battle between the Agency and the Nixon Pentagon over the capabilities of the newest Soviet intercontinental ballistic missile (ICBM) as a "real pea-whistler." He explained that in Maine there were two varieties of pennywhistles available at every corner candy store: one cost a nickel, the other a dime. The price difference was mandated by the presence of a dried pea in the luxury whistle. For some reason the pea raised the volume of the classy whistle to an excruciating level. Hence, any top-of-the-line product was referred to as a "pea-whistler."

The Agency had designated the USSR's new ICBM as the SS-9. It was the first Soviet MIRV (multiple independent re-entry vehicle). A MIRV is a rocket that carries more than one warhead, each of which separates from the mother rocket before striking individual targets. Our data on the SS-9 were too scant to permit a firm estimate of its capability. The first issue was the throw weight. How much of a load could the MIRV carry? The Air Force, impressed by the SS-9's bulk, granted it an enormous capability. Our experts thought it less powerful. The Pentagon military analysts considered the weapon to be highly accurate. The Agency team disagreed. Although all the disputants agreed that the SS-9 was built to transport three independent atomic warheads, there was more to come.

In mid-1969 the Nixon administration was pushing for congressional approval of a multi-billion-dollar program to develop an anti-ballistic missile (ABM). On form, and if such a defense weapon could be perfected, the ABM program would provide rockets which could detect and destroy incoming ballistic missiles. Critics of the ABM program described it as a bullet intended to shoot down another bullet. The Pentagon, with its eye on convincing Congress that an American anti-ballistic missile was an essential defense need, decided that each of the three SS-9 atomic warheads had its own independent guidance system that would steer it to pre-selected targets. If anything was likely to unleash the dollars needed to create an ABM, the specter of a score of SS-9s delivering sixty precisely guided missiles in one volley should have carried the day.

Agency analysts disagreed, and remained convinced that any such independent guidance capability was beyond the grasp of Soviet science, and the research and testing so expensive it might unhinge the USSR's economy. As the estimates' battle raged—and this is not too strong a word—the Pentagon retreated a bit. Perhaps the three warheads would not have independent guidance systems. Even so, twenty SS-9s, each loaded with three powerful atomic warheads—to be flung like fistfuls of golf balls in a predictable pattern that would cover most of the chosen targets—could be presumed to destroy all the Pentagon silos enclosing the Minute Man rockets. CIA still disagreed: the Russians did not have and were not likely soon to achieve even that level of guidance capability.

As Jack Smith has pointed out,* this led to another even more vital conflict. Was the USSR striving to achieve a first-strike capability? In military terms, "first strike" means much more than landing the first blow. A successful first-strike ICBM salvo will demolish the enemy's ability to return fire. By definition, a first strike is a knockout blow.

The Agency position was firm. The USSR was not seeking a first-strike capability, and the SS-9 was some four years away from its first testing.

Secretary of Defense Melvin Laird was not persuaded by the Agency view of the SS-9 capability. Having been argued to a standstill by CIA, the Pentagon turned to TV. Displaying a variety of charts, Pentagon spokesmen illustrated the SS-9 "footprint," a homely military term for the predictable pattern in which the individual warheads would presumably return to earth. This, it was explained, would be accurate enough to demolish the U.S. missile silos. These briefings and press leaks, some of which charged the Agency with a bias against the Pentagon position, raised the debate temperature to a boil. At one point, I was moved to instruct Agency officers that under no circumstances were they to make any public statements—pro or con—on the issue.

In early September the Agency submitted the annual updating of the earlier Top Secret National Estimate of Soviet ICBM capability ("Soviet Strategic Attack Forces"). A brief paragraph in the updating reaffirmed the earlier estimate—the USSR was not seeking a first-strike capability. It also stated that the Soviets had not yet produced an SS-9 for testing, and expressed doubt that this could happen before 1974. As always, this document was presented to all of the relevant U.S. intelligence and policy offices for coordination. It was produced with many dissenting opinions cited in footnotes. The Nixon administration reacted at once. Mel Laird was about to give a speech outlining the administration's policy on first strikes and MIRVs. Where, he demanded, did CIA get off contradicting Nixon's policy?

---

*Russell Jack Smith, *The Unknown CIA* (Washington, D.C.: Pergamon-Brassey's, 1989), p. 207. This is an excellent text on the Directorate for Intelligence, and a fundamental document in CIA history.

When Laird's complaint hit my desk, I summoned the Agency experts. Not one of our analysts or weapons specialists agreed with the Defense Department position. The resulting standoff was as difficult a policy problem as I had faced. I realized that there was no convincing evidence in the Agency or at the Pentagon which would prove either position. Both positions were estimates—speculation—based on identical fragments of data. My decision to remove the contested paragraph was based on the fact that the Agency's estimate—that the USSR was not attempting to create a first-strike capability—as originally stated in the earlier detailed National Estimate would remain the Agency position. The issue came down to whether or not the initial estimate needed to be stressed in this updating of the original document. In the interest of allowing the Defense Department analysts and weapons experts to state their position, I agreed to drop the disputed paragraph.*

An important factor in my decision to compromise with the Defense Department position was my long-standing conviction that it is a serious mistake for any intelligence service ever to assume that it has achieved absolute wisdom. I disagreed with the Pentagon position, and could not suppress the feeling it was tainted by the Nixon administration's determination to develop an anti-ballistic missile. Although the Agency's initial estimate would stand, I concluded that the Defense Department analysts and weapons experts should have ample opportunity to state their position.

At the height of the debate the atmosphere was further poisoned by a remark attributed to senior members of the administration: "Whose team is CIA on?" In other words, "Let's all get together and trim the evidence to suit the wishes of the politicians."

Aside from Jack Smith, whose view of the situation coincided with mine, the decision did not sit well with the Agency analysts and experts. In their view, I had compromised one of the Agency's fundamental responsibilities—the mandate to evaluate all available data and express conclusions irrespective of U.S. policies. Pertinent to this discussion is the fact that the President is under no obligation to accept any intelligence estimate at face value, nor is he required in any way to

---

*Ironically, Thomas Hughes, head of the State Department intelligence office, reinstated the dread paragraph as a footnote, regretting its omission in the original text.

follow it. The President's responsibility is to act in the best interest of the country. I was not prepared to stake the Agency's entire position on this one issue—in an average year CIA was making some sixty estimates, very few of which ever reached the President's level of concern. I was convinced we would have lost the argument with the Nixon administration, and that in the process the Agency would have been permanently damaged.

The final step in the MIRV conflict was taken by Henry Kissinger when he informed me that the National Security staff would examine all the data and come to its own conclusion. Jack Smith and Abbott Smith, head of the Office of National Estimates, conferred with Kissinger. Henry was clearly in no mood to accept the Agency position as stated in the study. Jack's offer to rephrase the data that Henry had considered biased was refused. The NSC staff would make its own evaluation. Several days passed before we learned that this staff had made no changes in the CIA estimate of the SS-9's performance.

The Agency's estimate that the USSR would not have a MIRV/SS-9 first-strike capability for some four years was borne out in 1974 when the Soviets tested their first MIRV. The timing of this test tallied nicely with the Agency's original estimate.

As the dust settled, the Agency encountered another collision with the Nixon administration.

Chapter 37

—

SIHANOUKVILLE

The strenuous tussle over MIRV capabilities and the SS-9 coincided with, but did not interrupt, the Agency's battle to produce the necessary intelligence on North Vietnam. We were trying every operational skill in our arsenal to penetrate the policy levels of the government of North Vietnam. I kept a high standard of staff personnel in Vietnam, and the best of the Agency operatives around the globe were focused on Hanoi. Nothing worked. And there was no satisfaction in the knowledge that we had done our best. In the years since President Nixon closed the door on Vietnam, I have yet to uncover any means that we did not exhaust in the effort to reach Hanoi.

Strategically, one textbook approach to countries as alien to our culture as Vietnam might require a ten-year commitment. It would take that much time to develop a sophisticated cadre of language and area experts prepared to make their career in such remote areas. In a decade, the right operatives might achieve command of the necessary languages, and the desired in-country familiarity with the cultures and terrain. With commitment and effort, there might develop personal relationships—and identity of interests—strong enough to survive political fallings-out that might follow. The possibility of funding such an effort in half a dozen likely areas and finding personnel willing to make the necessary commitment to the job would be a major undertaking. In the absence of any such unrealistic strategic commitment, the tactical solution is obvious. Do not intervene on the ground unless prepared to make an all-out effort. And do not count on a secret intelligence agency being able to pull political folly away from the blaze.

Given a choice, I would have picked a less dramatic proof of my conviction that intelligence services have never come close to possessing divine insight. But no such luck, Sihanoukville it was to be. For years the Agency and the various military intelligence services had been monitoring the North Vietnamese incursions into Cambodia and attempting to determine the amount of Chinese military matériel coming through the Cambodian port at Sihanoukville en route to the North Vietnamese forces.

There was no doubt that North Vietnamese troops and Viet Cong guerrillas slipping down the Ho Chi Minh Trail would dodge across the border into Cambodia to regroup, refit, and catch their breath before continuing. The open questions: how many troops are in transit, and how much matériel are they toting? The Agency estimate was that some four or five times more matériel was coming down the trail than before ROLLING THUNDER, the Air Force's widely publicized attempt to interdict the traffic. This antagonized the military staff in Vietnam (MACV) and the Pentagon, and can only have dismayed President Johnson.

In contrast to the CIA's glum estimate of the traffic on the Ho Chi Minh highway, our estimate of the Chinese-supplied matériel transiting Sihanoukville was almost exactly half the tonnage that MACV and the Pentagon analysts had determined. Both the Pentagon and Agency teams worked from the same data—scraps of hearsay, lowest-level agent reports, and unreliable prisoner-of-war interrogations. Neither MACV nor the Pentagon analysts saw reason to give ground to the equally entrenched Agency experts. In almost every respect this was a sour replay of the "First Strike/SS-9/MIRV" controversy: competent experts in honest disagreement.

As with everything in Vietnam, there was intense pressure from all sides. At a morning staff meeting, I asked, in the absence of any new information on Sihanoukville, how we might at least resolve the controversy over the existing data. Jack Smith's suggestion that he go to

Saigon and talk with the MACV experts was immediately agreed upon. He would determine how the MACV staff arrived at its estimate, and learn if, by any good fortune, the military had come upon an informed source that CIA did not know about.

Jack was impressed by the quality of the MACV analysts and their straightforward presentation of their position. The data were almost identical with the Agency's. And as Jack reported, "Alas, it was the same shoddy, low-grade information we were using." The MACV deduction remained firm: twice as much matériel was flowing through Sihanoukville as CIA estimated. In May 1970, Secretary Laird and General Wheeler testified before Congress using the figures that contradicted the Agency estimate.

Dawn broke in late June, when CIA operatives recruited an agent with direct access to the bills of lading that provided documentary evidence on the shipping passing through Sihanoukville. It was a classic bit of espionage, involving spies, secret writing, radio communication, special cameras, and film. The result was a steady flow of documentary intelligence on the Chinese arms shipments moving through Sihanoukville to staging areas in Kompong Speu and eventually to the "Parrot's Beak" and Vietnam. Photographs of the bills of lading were supplemented with local agent sightings of the after-dark off-loading of the equipment. At one point, CIA bought a truck which was accepted into the convoys that were moving the arms shipments.

The carefully recorded data showed conclusively that the Sihanoukville matériel was much more than the CIA estimate, and, if anything, a bit more than the MACV-Pentagon figures. In one outstanding espionage operation, we managed to prove that the CIA estimate was more than 50 percent off base.

Jack Smith gave me the good news at my morning staff meeting. He claims that I accepted it without flinching—and might well have added that I did not trouble to wipe the egg from our collective faces. The report went immediately to the White House and Pentagon. And Jack's staff undertook a postmortem.

In a more perfect world, after criticizing our initially poor performance, a more perfect leader might have managed a word of encouragement for having, against formidable odds, achieved an impressive bit of long-range intelligence collection. It would have been too much to expect anyone to remark on CIA's immediate admission of our initial error. As it was, the Sihanoukville incident appeared to be taken as further evidence of the Agency's bias, and even sympathy, for what some of the White House staff referred to as the "McNamara position on Vietnam."

The worst result of the corrected estimate was the bludgeon it gave Agency critics to belabor any future intelligence estimates that did not reinforce the administration's policy. "But what about your estimate on Sihanoukville?" was to become an all-purpose argument clincher.

Chapter 38

—

NIXON VS. ALLENDE

In contrast to my work with Presidents Kennedy and Johnson, I rarely saw Nixon. When we did encounter one another, he was often affable and always businesslike. The atmosphere at National Security Council meetings was quite different. At these gatherings, Nixon often found fault with the Agency and spared me little criticism. This was certainly within his prerogative, but his views might occasionally have been tempered with some acknowledgment of the Agency's competence.

As a rule, Nixon's instructions were conveyed to me by Henry Kissinger, or his deputy, Colonel (later General) Al Haig. As far as I ever knew, they were effective messengers. As national security advisor, Kissinger ran his own, exceptionally well-staffed shop. Staunch as he was in his own strong opinions, Henry quickly became secure in his relationship with the President he could scarcely have known when chosen for the job. Al Haig always struck me as the very definition of a highly competent chief of staff. There was never a detail that he failed to grasp or an error he did not put straight. Aside from an occasional lapse into obscure but colorful Army slang, he was always precise and to the point. "Let's snake-check this one," Al was fond of saying. I learned that every morning, on certain Army posts, prudent soldiers carefully examined their boots lest a chilly reptile had found a snug sleeping place.

One of Kissinger's important services was his ability to articulate President Nixon's foreign policy views. At NSC meetings, Nixon would often speak at some length on his foreign policy plans or concerns. Curiously, for a lawyer and experienced public speaker, Nixon often rambled from point to point, out of context, and at length. No matter how closely the NSC members paid attention, these off-the-cuff remarks were sometimes bewildering and hard to follow. It always came as a surprise to me when in a press briefing a few hours later, Henry Kissinger would express Nixon's earlier discourse in a well-organized and lucid form. It was only later I learned that when Nixon prepared for a public address, he would draft his remarks on legal-size yellow pads and, in the process of editing, in essence memorize the speech. It was when he was speaking in-house that Nixon was prone to wander.

In National Security Council meetings and other such gatherings, Nixon appeared actually to enjoy disparaging various elements of the executive branch. It often seemed as though he were setting himself and the White House staff in an adversary position against the rest of the government. It was an odd attitude: as the ultimate boss, he presided over it all. Nixon trusted few. It was as though he felt beleaguered by his own subordinates. And maybe he was at times and in some instances. But he had the power and the responsibility to correct it.

At one time, Nixon admitted to me that he wanted to get rid of J. Edgar Hoover, and asked if I had any suggestions. I had none. Like President Johnson, Nixon was not prepared to take the political heat involved in any such move. With his election to a second term, Nixon saw his chance to establish the kind of control of the executive branch that he wanted. He nominated a few officers as counselors on the White House staff. Their task was to keep an eye on selected cabinet departments. He also wanted to plant White House staffers in various departments in positions from which they could report regularly to the White House. This effort to seize a more firm day-to-day control of the government collapsed and disappeared in the storm that followed the Watergate break-in.

At best, Nixon seemed perpetually cranky in his relations with CIA. He appreciated the fact that the Agency could adequately monitor an arms control treaty, but with the passage of time became sour as gall about our inability to shunt Salvador Allende aside from the presidency of Chile.

Throughout my tenure under Nixon, candid glimpses of his attitude came to my attention and to that of other senior CIA officers. In the course of Henry Kissinger's first post-election meeting with the President, Nixon took care to denounce CIA as a group of "Ivy League liberals" who "had always opposed him politically."* Other all too candid glimpses of Nixon's attitude came frequently to the attention of the Agency's upper- and mid-level officers. At the lowest level, these remarks included ludicrous allegations—CIA personnel housed themselves in Georgetown and spent off-duty hours at cocktail parties making sport of Nixon. If our several thousand employees and their families actually lived in Georgetown, there would have been but standing room for one and all. On a more significant level, Nixon's allegedly expressed wonderment as to what "those idiots out there in McLean are up to" could only poison the atmosphere. Face-to-face, Nixon usually affected a somewhat more benign attitude.

In contrast to the repeated criticism, I was surprised to read Nixon's comment on me as recorded on a bit of the famous White House tapes.[†] It came on May 11, 1973, at the height of the Watergate crisis. Nixon is conferring with White House Chief of Staff General Al Haig. "Helms's ass is out there," Nixon says. "His whole career is out there." After a few words on General Walters, Nixon continues, "Helms would never agree . . . to falsify cops and robbers things. He's never going to say that he participated in a cover-up." There may be some less favorable judgments on the tapes, but I've not come across them.

It was soon after Nixon's first inauguration that it began to seem that what he wanted from CIA was intelligence reports and estimates most likely to support his foreign policy and domestic positions. In effect, he wanted a claque underwriting and applauding his policies. Dislike for the bearers of bad news is, of course, universal. No president can have been more disheartened by bad news from the battlefield than President Johnson. But like President Lincoln, LBJ accepted bad news and moved along accordingly. Nixon showed little interest in an independent intelli-

---

*Quoted from Christopher Andrew, *For the President's Eyes Only* (New York: HarperCollins, 1995), p. 350.

[†]Stanley I. Kutler, *Abuse of Power: The New Nixon Tapes* (New York: Free Press, 1997), p. 477.

gence service. The ink that puts this opinion to paper does not flow easily, the more so because of my conviction that on foreign policy issues, Nixon was an extremely well informed president. Whatever my faults and the possible shortcomings of the Agency's senior officers, the explanation for Nixon's persistent deriding of many who were in the best position to serve him and his administration must rest deep within the personality of Nixon himself.

—

To most Americans, and to me before 1962, the word "Chile" conjured up the image of a small democratic country stretched alongside Argentina at the southern tip of the Western Hemisphere. Today, however, I still associate Chile with some of the most unpleasant aspects of my professional life.

Almost from its inception in 1947, CIA activity and objectives in the Western Hemisphere were overshadowed by the more demanding concerns in the USSR, Eastern Europe, the Far East, and the several hot spots in the Near East and Africa. By 1959, the advent of Castro brought Cuba abruptly to the attention of the Eisenhower administration. In 1961 the Bay of Pigs reinforced President Kennedy's conviction that there should be no communist governments in the Western Hemisphere.

For some 150 years, and with only a handful of brief interruptions, Chile was known as one of the more democratic and stable countries in Latin America. The constitution provided for a multi-party political system based on open elections. Presidents served a six-year term and were not allowed to succeed themselves in office. Unlike many others in the hemisphere, the Chilean military maintained a hands-off relationship with the government; there was a developing middle class, and women had begun to play a more active role in public life. At my first briefing on Chile, I recall the young desk chief reminding me that I should not confuse the political terms used by the European labor movements with those in Chile. The European parties were essentially democratic/labor-oriented reformers working within the existing democratic parliamentary systems. From its birth in 1933, the Chilean Socialist Party was dominated by far-left Marxist-Leninist ideologues, with the sometimes openly expressed objective of destroying the existing "bourgeois society."

In 1962, President Kennedy directed CIA to provide covert support to the Christian Democratic Party. More than $200,000 was authorized. It is not much of a sum these days, but it was quite hefty at the time. The Kennedy concentration on Castro, and the need for containing Cuban efforts to export their revolution to South America, meant that Chile loomed large. From 1962 until 1970, under Presidents Kennedy, Johnson, and Nixon, the policy governing CIA operations in Chile was simply to preserve the democratic constitutional system. When subsidies were given, the funds were used to strengthen the democratic elements committed to economic and social reform. Covert propaganda alerted the Chilean voters to the danger of the Soviet-supported popular front strategy and countered the heavily subsidized Soviet and Cuban propaganda machines. In Chile, as in many other areas, the political parties most likely to share and support the U.S. objectives were democratic and left of center.

As the 1964 election approached, I met daily with my deputy, Tom Karamessines, and the desk officers concerned with Chile. It would take time and a delicate hand to establish the mechanisms—press and radio outlets, financial support—necessary to help underwrite Chile's democratic government. Our efforts were carefully coordinated with the Kennedy White House and embassy in Santiago.

Eduardo Frei, the competent and popular leader of the Christian Democratic Party, was elected president in 1964 with a comfortable margin. His plan to initiate various reforms attracted the favorable attention of both the Kennedy and Johnson administrations. The Alliance for Progress granted Chile a net of some billion dollars in aid—more per capita than any other country in the Western Hemisphere. Early in the 1964 election campaign, the Johnson administration directed CIA to pass $3 million to Frei's Christian Democratic Party. The following year, President Johnson authorized CIA to commit another $500,000 to help block the election of a dozen far-left candidates for Congress.

In office, Frei found it easier to promise reform than to put the programs into practice. The left-wing Christian Democrats were dissatisfied because Frei had not pushed through the more ambitious programs. The right-wing members of that party were alarmed by the scope of some of the reform measures. The resulting discord splintered the Christian Democratic Party and triggered an unwelcome polarization in Chilean politics.

When President Nixon took office, he inherited the policy of the two previous administrations that had both openly and covertly opposed the possible election of Salvador Allende. The prospect of an Allende government in Chile was a clear threat to our national interest. In a three-way election, it appeared most likely that the two non-Communist parties would split the anti-Allende vote and allow a Socialist-Communist government to step into office.

As the 1970 presidential election loomed, three candidates were chosen. On the right, the National Party chose Jorge Alessandri, a respected establishment figure. Alessandri had been president from 1958 to 1964, and was thus able to run again. The Christian Democrats picked Radomiro Tomic, a slightly left-of-center candidate.

Salvador Allende, a founding member of the Chilean Socialist Party and an avowed Marxist, was the choice of the Popular Unity coalition. Following Moscow's lead, the Chilean Communist Party and the Socialists had combined with leftist fragments to form a version of a European popular front called FRAP. Allende was outspoken in pushing hard-line, Moscow-inspired programs. If elected, he would expropriate land and basic industry, and end "American monopolies." The independent judiciary was to be subordinated to a "Popular Assembly," and a "national system to promote a popular culture" would be established. Nor did Allende blush at larding his speeches with large chunks of policy lifted verbatim from the Chilean Communist Party programs. He also took care to make sure that the electorate understood one of his most deeply felt convictions: "Cuba in the Caribbean and a Socialist Chile in the southern cone will make the revolution in Latin America."

Moscow responded by showering Allende and his party with funds. By our count, even Castro handed Allende some $350,000 taken from the lean Cuban treasury.

In mid-April 1969, some eighteen months before the presidential election, there were several significant storm warnings. President Frei recognized that the popular base of his Christian Democratic Party was eroding, and began moving to the left. Allende's support within the Congress was increasing, and the prospect of a three-corner presidential race between two conservative candidates and the Allende front had become even more discouraging. Chances were strong that Tomic and Alessandri would split the democratic vote, leaving Allende with at least a plurality in the national election.

Several times, we warned the Nixon administration that if the United States were to undertake a serious covert action in the 1970 presidential election, we would have to get under way. There would be much more involved in this campaign than funneling funds to the non-communist parties.

I no longer have a record of the exact date, but it was at about this time that Senator William Fulbright, chairman of the Foreign Relations Committee, summoned me to his office at the Senate. I knew he was aware that in the 1964 presidential campaign the Agency had given political and financial assistance to Frei and the Christian Democratic Party. Now, Senator Fulbright wanted to know if CIA was about to undertake a campaign against Salvador Allende and the Popular Unity coalition. At the time, it appeared that Fulbright knew that the Nixon administration had approved a lightly funded campaign which involved nothing but a covert propaganda effort. It was obvious that he was opposed even to this level of activity, but did not think it would be worth a fight with the Nixon administration to make an issue of it. As I was about to leave, Fulbright said, "Dick, if I catch you trying to upset the Chilean election, I will get up on the Senate floor and blow the operation."

The Agency's most formal alert came on April 15, 1969, when I raised the problem at a meeting of the 40 Committee.* I bluntly stated that if CIA was to be directed to attempt to influence the election, it was time to begin. There was no response from the White House. Later that year, I repeated my argument. If a serious effort was to be made, it must begin at once. Again, the White House failed to take notice.

Here, Henry Kissinger's and my memory differ. Henry writes that the Agency should have insisted more firmly that the situation was desperate, and that if action was to be taken, CIA would need a *maximum* of advance time.† I think CIA spoke often and loudly enough. In Henry's

---

*The 40 Committee was the National Security Council component that passed on covert action operations for the NSC. The committee was first known as the Special Group and later as the 303 Committee, each with the same responsibilities.

†*White House Years* (Boston: Little, Brown, 1979), chap. 17.

and my mutual defense, there were more than enough problems and crises elsewhere to keep us both occupied—Vietnam, Cambodia, Laos, airplane hijacking, Middle East cease-fire violations, Soviet intentions to build a submarine base at Cienfuegos in Cuba, plus the usual garden variety of lesser bothers.

In the interests of compromise, and if Henry will agree that he and his staff should have listened more attentively, I will grudgingly admit that the Agency might have *shouted* even more loudly. In the event, the National Security Council, the State Department, and the White House dropped the ball.

I first thought to include CIA among those who fumbled, but in retrospect the intelligence estimates were correct and timely. Furthermore, the ambassador to Chile, Edward Korry, could scarcely have been more prescient in his comments. Had the Agency protested more vigorously against the Nixon administration position, it would have risked stepping into the policymaking field.

It was not until March 1970—some six months before the election—that the 40 Committee authorized CIA to spend $135,000 on what it referred to as "spoiling operations." This less than felicitous expression meant only that the Agency was to cause enough squabbling within the Allende fold to fragment the movement. In late June, the 40 Committee increased the budget to $300,000. Posters were printed, news stories planted, editorial comment encouraged, rumors whispered, leaflets strewn, and pamphlets distributed. The thrust of this effort was to show that an Allende victory risked the destruction of Chilean democracy. It was a strenuous effort, but the discernible effect seemed minimal. The cost and extent of this activity was but a fraction of the Soviet and Cuban effort in Chile.

As the Nixon administration began to focus on Chile, the State Department's Latin American Bureau took the position that any financial aid to the parties that might block an Allende/Socialist/Communist election victory must be found *within* Chile and that no support should be given to any one candidate. Aside from the fact that there was not the slightest hope that significant funds could be scraped up in Chile, the effect of canceling any U.S. government support to the democratic elements would surely signal a lack of concern for the problems likely to result from a Castro-Allende axis. This abrupt U.S. laissez-faire attitude was also certain to cheer the many radical elements in Chile's neighbors—Argentina, Bolivia, and Peru. The notion that neither of the democratic parties should be supported meant that their split vote would hand the election to Allende.

In contrast to the State Department's position, Ambassador Korry was steadfast. In a message to the department he said, in effect, an Allende electoral victory would be the first incidence of a heretofore democratic country voting to place itself under communist rule. He predicted accurately that although an Allende government would initially act legally, it would use the excuse of defending itself against the United States (or as Allende expressed it, "public enemy number one") to institute "profound changes" within Chile, and a foreign policy shackled to Cuba and the USSR.

Here an observation on the presidency in the twenty-first century. Except for George Bush the elder, who served for some twelve months as director of Central Intelligence, no American president in a hundred years has had but a slight idea of how clandestine operations are conceived and run.* What presidents do know about secret intelligence seems most often to come from high-spirited movies, novels, press coverage, and, occasionally, bits of Washington "insider" gossip. Nothing wrong with that, except that none of it—and rarely any nonfiction— gives the slightest idea of the dreary routines and the vast amount of time involved in establishing a sound covert action or espionage operation.

The importance of a minimum of such understanding is to be seen in what Nixon finally wanted—and expected—in Chile in the weeks before Allende was inaugurated. Nixon had no notion of the maneuvering and caution involved in *secretly* organizing and building cover for the operations he demanded, nor was he disposed to consider any of the pitfalls involved in attempting to establish this activity overnight. This reluctance to accept advice on secret operations appeared to have been poisoned by Nixon's now-familiar preconceived attitudes. CIA was never really "on the team." The Agency had failed at the Bay of Pigs. It had neither pene-

---

*As an accomplished general officer, President Eisenhower dealt extensively with the highest levels of intelligence product, but had had no reason to concern himself with the details and mechanisms of secret intelligence operations.

trated the government in Hanoi nor erased North Vietnamese activity in the South. If CIA could not succeed in any of these efforts, what use could it be? The too frequent response to estimates or data that did not fit policy assumptions was another reference to Sihanoukville.

In keeping the Agency at arm's length, and even though filtered through as competent a national security advisor as Henry Kissinger, Nixon denied himself the firsthand knowledge that I think is essential to any president. At the time Nixon took office, CIA had an extraordinary technical collection competence, an abundance of skilled intelligence analysts and research experts, a secret operational capability that was only occasionally matched by any opposing service, and an expanding mass of background and research data probably unique in history. Given the extent and depth of our overt and secret activity, I remain convinced that CIA's failures—however painful—should be judged in comparison with the Agency's overall performance. Alas, and no matter what level of competence any intelligence service might build, it is not likely to encompass walking on water.

Some six weeks before the September election, the CIA Office of Current Intelligence (OCI) produced a blunt estimate—the race between Allende and Alessandri, the two strongest candidates, was a dead heat. Neither candidate could count on gaining a majority. This OCI document was followed by a National Intelligence Estimate, "The Outlook for Chile." In sum: if elected, Allende would eventually create "a Chilean version of a Soviet style East European Communist state." I agreed with the estimate, but doubted that it would take Allende as long as the projected two or three years to bring about a communist state.

The election was indeed close. Allende won 36.3 percent of the ballots—actually a slight decline from his tally in the 1964 election. The runner-up, Alessandri, got 34.9 percent, and Tomic 27.8 percent. As predicted, the two democratic parties had knocked one another out of the ring, leaving a probable victory to Allende.

As Ambassador Korry reported, "Chile voted calmly to have a Marxist-Leninist state, the first nation in the world to make this choice freely and knowingly."* All this by a margin of some one percent of the vote.

---

*Kissinger, *White House Years,* p. 653.

In Chile, if no candidate wins a *majority,* it becomes the responsibility of Congress to choose between the two candidates with the most popular votes. In the past, the Congress had always opted for the candidate with the largest electoral vote. The runoff decision was scheduled for October 24. This left the Agency with a few hours less than fifty days to achieve what might have been accomplished had we begun twelve months earlier.

However long foreseen, the now probability of an Allende administration appalled Nixon. Henry Kissinger wasted no words in describing the President's reaction to Allende's victory—"Nixon was beside himself."* And no matter what the evidence, in Nixon's opinion CIA had again failed Nixon.

Four days after the election, a grouchy 40 Committee met to consider likely strategies. I reported that the Chilean Congress would probably confirm Allende's election, and suggested that once he was in office, his domestic political opponents would soon fold. Then, while attempting to make it clear that this was not a policy recommendation, I said that unless action was soon undertaken, there was little or no chance that even a military coup could succeed. Henry Kissinger and Attorney General John Mitchell both agreed with my position.

On September 12, Ambassador Korry cabled the State Department that there was little chance that the Chilean military would move to keep Allende out of office. That day, I again advised the NSC that there was only a slight possibility that senior elements of the Chilean military would move against Allende. Moreover, I noted that the Agency lacked the means of motivating the military to intervene.

Two days later, the 40 Committee met again. They directed the embassy and the Agency to intensify political and economic measures with propaganda making plain the painful consequences that would follow an Allende takeover. This was too little and too late. The $250,000 contingency fund also authorized by the 40 Committee was merely too late.

The following afternoon, I was summoned to the Oval Office for a meeting with Nixon, Henry Kissinger, and John Mitchell. Armed with the pad and pencil I carried at every meeting, I sat in the chair to the right

*Ibid., p. 671.

of the President's desk. It was at this meeting that Nixon raised the stakes.

As I testified to the Church Committee some years later, "the President came down very hard . . . he wanted something done, and he didn't much care how and . . . was prepared to make money available." The notes—now well publicized—that I hastily scribbled show Nixon's directive was straight to the point.

> One 10 chance perhaps, but save Chile
> worth spending
> not concerned risks involved
> no involvement of Embassy
> $10,000,000 available, more if necessary
> full-time job—best men we have
> game plan
> make the economy scream
> 48 hours for plan of action

President Nixon also instructed us three to keep all knowledge of this directive from the secretary of state, the secretary of defense, Ambassador Korry, and the CIA chief in Chile. In my post–World War II career, this was the most restrictive security hold-down that I can remember.

Without reminding Nixon that there would be no more than thirty-eight days from the time I got back to my own office to the moment Chile's Congress would vote, I tried to give him some idea of the problems and risks involved. Standing mid-track and shouting at an oncoming locomotive might have been more effective than attempting to inject caution into this fifteen-minute White House session.

Truman had lost China. Kennedy had lost Cuba. Nixon was not about to lose Chile.

Henry Kissinger has pointed out, Nixon "was given to grandiloquent statements on which he did not insist once their implications became clear to him. The fear that unwary visitors would take the President literally was, indeed, one of the reasons why Haldeman controlled access to him so solicitously."* This is well said and, of course, quite true. But

*Ibid., p. 674.

I do not consider myself to have been an unwary or even casual recipient of instructions given by the President from behind his desk in the Oval Office. President Nixon had ordered me to instigate a military coup in Chile, a heretofore democratic country. Moreover, the knowledge of this presidential directive was to be kept from the U.S. officials most directly concerned. Within CIA this directive was to be restricted to those with an absolute need to know. And I was to report to the President through Henry Kissinger.

By what superior judgment was I to leave the White House and then decide that the President did not mean what he had just said? Nixon had eased himself along the corridors of power for more than two decades, time enough, one might think, for him to have some notion of the impact his direct orders would have upon his senior subordinates. I was quite capable of scrubbing the garnish of hyperbole from the core of the President's instructions. I did not presume to have the authority to tamper with the President's obvious intent.

To my knowledge, Nixon did not inform anyone in Congress of his orders to me. My opinion is reinforced by the fact that the always reliable and ultra-discreet Senator Russell was seriously ill and, in effect, out of office at the time.

Five years later, in the course of the publicity generated by Senator Frank Church's hearings, the terms "Track I" and "Track II" emerged as shorthand references for the secret maneuvering to block Allende's taking office. Track I encompassed all of the activity conducted under the responsibility of the 40 Committee. Track II covered only Nixon's most secret decision to instigate a military coup, and to restrict the knowledge to Kissinger, Mitchell, and me. In Chile, although President Frei has denied it, the Track I covert political, economic, and propaganda activity was, to a degree, undertaken with his implicit knowledge. To my knowledge, Track II remained closely guarded until Senator Church began his hearings.

A word about my crib notes taken at the Oval Office meeting. When I was retired from CIA, I left a few items which I considered classified, but personal and yet important enough to preserve in the custody of the Agency. The small packet was to be held in secure premises and under my name. Or so I thought. After his appointment as DCI, William Colby apparently did not feel the need to consult me on its disposition.

While I was still in Tehran as ambassador, Colby handed the packet to the Church Committee for scrutiny and, incidentally, whatever political use Senator Church might make of the documents. I mention this as a caution to those who believe that the security of secret government operations can be kept indefinitely, or even for a reasonable time. Congress is composed of members who keep their mouths shut and those who do not. More specifically, there will always be those in Congress who think they have a constitutional—not to say God-granted—right, without consultation with anyone, to expose any operation or activity of which they do not approve. In context, Senator Fulbright's threat comes to mind.

To implement the instructions given me in the Oval Office, I summoned an early-morning meeting with Tom Karamessines and two of his senior staff. It was a bleak session; no one present thought there was any reasonable chance to keep Allende from the presidency. In the time remaining, we agreed that the only faint possibility of blocking Allende's election was a military coup.

In the days that followed, we renewed and intensified our contacts with those in Chile who might be in a position to inform us of any coup plotting. In late September, our Santiago office reported that there was no indication that either President Frei or the Chilean chief of staff, General Rene Schneider, appeared to be considering any action. In early October, however, General Roberto Viaux, who had been retired after an ill-conceived coup attempt in 1949, informed us that he was again constructing a "*golpe*"—coup in Spanish. Viaux was less than impressive—one of our operatives thought him a bit "far out"—but he seemed determined to take action.

On the basis of the "do anything" directive, we continued to listen to Viaux, but refused his request for a sizeable airdrop of arms and ammunition. The notion that a group of senior army officers would need an airdrop of foreign arms to stage a coup was not an encouraging indication of Viaux's potential. But to keep the pot on the fire, we advanced some funds, and a life insurance policy to protect Viaux's family in the very likely event that things were to go wrong. After subsequent discussion, it became clear that Viaux's plans were not likely to carry the day. Henry Kissinger agreed with our conviction.

Coincidentally, another Chilean general was moved to action. He asked for tear gas and submachine guns. Although there seemed little possibility of this coup succeeding, three weapons were handed over. But before this group could act, a fragment of General Viaux's original band of *golpistas* attempted to kidnap General Schneider. In defending himself, General Schneider was mortally wounded. At this point, the group that had been upstaged by the Viaux splinter group gave up planning its own coup and returned the three unused weapons.

In sketching these developments, I realize that it must seem that Chile was the Agency's only priority. As important as Chile was to U.S. responsibilities and interests in the Western Hemisphere, the problem was largely contained within that area. On a daily basis, Chile occupied less of my time—and perhaps less of Henry Kissinger's concern—than, for example, the vast problems in Vietnam, Cambodia, and Laos. In my position, the ongoing supervision of technical and human intelligence collection operations targeted on the USSR, Eastern Europe, Asia, and the Near East was relentlessly demanding.

President-elect Allende was sworn into office on November 3, 1970, and soon began to implement his promises. U.S. policy returned to an appropriate level of "cool but correct" diplomatic, political, and economic relations with a country whose government was in almost every respect at odds with ours. In my remaining months in office, Allende continued his determined march to the left, but there was no further U.S. effort to instigate a coup in Chile.

President Allende continued in office until September 11, 1973—some seven months after I had been replaced as DCI—when General Augusto Pinochet overthrew him and moved the Chilean government from the far left to the extreme right. In the course of the coup, Allende died—by accident or suicide—of a bullet wound. Chile was the loser at both ends of the political spectrum.

There were, of course, lessons to be learned from this experience. It sometimes seems that the best way to identify the most important lessons to be learned is to count the number of times a lesson must be relearned. There are three lessons to be relearned in respect to Chile and Tracks I and II. If a major covert action is to be undertaken, ample time must be allotted for preparation; if *any secret* U.S. contact is made with an individual or group thought to be planning a coup or revolution, it will be all but impossible to convince the plotters that this contact does not indicate U.S. support; and, finally, unless the fate of the nation is at stake, an intelligence service should try to avoid being saddled with the command, "do something, for Heaven's sake, do *anything.*" When such hasty operations begin to come unstuck, the highest authority is most likely to have forgotten its early command.

Chapter 39

—

HANDSHAKE
AT CAMP DAVID

My assumption that on Election Day 1972 the President and Henry Kissinger would be fully occupied offered an opportunity to invite General Al Haig for lunch. As Henry Kissinger's deputy, Al handled many of the nuts and bolts involved in the Agency's daily contact with the Nixon White House. He was a near-perfect intermediary, with immediate answers to most questions, and never fudging when he didn't have an immediate response. There was no idle chitchat, and no time for gossip in Al's office.

I had often been Al's guest at the White House mess, but had not been able to lure him out to the DCI's dining room on the seventh floor at the Agency. As we relaxed over coffee, and agreed on the apparent certainty that Nixon would be reelected, I asked what the future might hold for me.

"I haven't any insight into what the President will do about appointments," Al said. "But why don't you just wait and see what develops as things settle down. If you want to stay on, you might do so, and later, leave at your own convenience."

I indicated that I would almost certainly stay on if asked. I did not, however, add that Cynthia and I had pretty much decided that I would leave government sometime after the election. It had long been apparent to me that I was not one of the Haldeman/Ehrlichman favorites, and I had come to suspect that Nixon's two courtiers had strongly opposed the President's allowing me to remain in office for his first term. My impression of the President's attitude was amply borne out in some of the Nixon White House documents released in March 1998. An item from an Associated Press account quotes some of H. R. Haldeman's (September 1972) handwritten notes on Nixon's goals for a second term: "Helms has got to go. Get rid of the clowns—cut personnel 40 percent. Its info worthless." Clearly, Nixon held CIA to a higher account than he did his personal band of "plumbers" who were taken in flagrante in the course of a nighttime incursion, at the unprotected national headquarters of the Democratic Party, at the Watergate in Washington, D.C.

Nixon wasted no time in shaping his new administration. At a cabinet meeting in which those at the table might have expected a few moments of cheer to celebrate the election result, Nixon asked one and all immediately to prepare their letters of resignation. This coincided with a similar order that *all* presidential appointees promptly draft their letters of resignation.

Over the years, the appointment and dismissal of the Agency leadership had been handled by presidents in a personal and private manner. Unlike other presidential appointees, it had become customary for the DCI and the director of the FBI to remain in place during a change of administration. In keeping with this practice I did not submit my resignation to Nixon. When General Vernon Walters, my deputy, asked, I advised him not to offer his resignation.

On November 20, a routine message from the White House summoned me to a meeting with Nixon at Camp David. The bureaucratic confusion following the numerous resignations had died down. Several budgetary matters were under discussion, and I briefed myself and collected the necessary papers before going to the Pentagon heliport for the flight up the Potomac River. None of the handful of fellow travelers were known to me, or appeared interested in attempting conversation in the noisy helicopter.

I was met by a security officer who escorted me to Aspen Lodge. On the short walk, I noticed George Shultz headed for another building with a bundle of papers under his arm. Only on the return flight did it occur to me that George and other White House staffers might be discussing job changes.

Haldeman met me at the door—I was about to say, greeted me, but "met" is the right word—and guided me into the Aspen sitting room. The President rose from a small sofa, we shook hands, and I took a chair. As usual, Haldeman assumed his place at the President's left.

Small talk was never one of Nixon's social strengths, but he launched our chat with several rambling, disjointed observations before beginning to assure me how much he appreciated the fine job I had done during my tenure as DCI. After noting that I had been appointed by President Johnson, a Democrat, Nixon got down to business. He was eager for new ideas, and wanted "new blood" in his second term. I had been at the Agency for a long time. It was time to make some personnel changes. He wanted my reaction to his plan to appoint a new DCI. Even before Nixon reached this point, I had tumbled to the fact that there was to be no discussion of the budget. However surprised, I said I fully understood that I served at the President's convenience, and that changes were to be expected. I added that the Agency policy required personnel to retire at sixty. I would reach retirement age in March 1973. Nixon seemed surprised both at the Agency policy and at what I had assumed to be the indisputable fact of my age. He was also unaware that from OSS to CIA I had served some thirty consecutive years in intelligence. Nixon apparently thought that President Johnson had brought me into the Agency.

At this point I suggested that it might be best if I remained at the Agency until March 30, my sixtieth birthday, and the time when Agency policy specified retirement. This would remove the DCI appointment from other, predominantly political appointments. After some discussion of details, Nixon agreed to postpone my retirement until spring.

In passing, I asked if Nixon was considering an Agency insider as my replacement, but he obviously had no intention of either asking my advice or revealing any of his own plans. As my earlier remarks began to sink in, Nixon paused as if he were shifting gears. Would I, he asked, be interested in becoming an ambassador?

This came as a total surprise to me—and probably to Haldeman. I admitted that since the thought had never crossed my mind, I would like a little time to consider it.

"If you were to accept such an appointment, where would you want to go?" Before I could respond, Nixon said, "What about Moscow?"

I moved from being surprised at having been dismissed from office to being floored by the prospect of wintering in the Moscow embassy. "I'm not sure how the Russians might interpret my being sent across the lines as an ambassador."

"That's a good point," Nixon said. "But what about some other country?"

To this day I'm not sure why Iran came to mind, but it did, and I said, "Tehran might be a more plausible choice, but I'm not sure but what it's time to leave government and to try something new."

Nixon brightened. "Iran sounds good, I've got something else in mind for Joe Farland." At the time, Ambassador Joseph Farland was in Tehran.

"In any event, I will have to talk to Cynthia before deciding on anything."

I agreed to keep my dismissal to myself, with the promise to let the President know my decision in a few days.

We shook hands.

I headed back to the chopper.

The next morning at a National Security Council meeting, Henry Kissinger asked what had happened at Camp David. I was silent for a moment because I thought he surely knew, and I did not want to violate Nixon's request that I keep my dismissal to myself. Henry bristled a bit and snapped, "If you won't tell me, I'll call Haldeman." With this, I gave Henry the facts. His surprise was genuine.

Without a warning from the White House staff to me, the President swore in several members of the new administration on February 2, 1973. Among them, James Schlesinger was named director of Central Intelligence. The timing caught me by surprise. I had barely time to get my things out of the office and to assemble as many colleagues of all ranks as possible for a farewell session in the Agency's new building.

A few days later, I encountered Haldeman. "What happened to our understanding that my exit would be postponed for a few weeks?" I asked. "Oh, I guess we forgot," he said with the faint trace of a smile.

And so it was over.

Chapter 40

—

TRICK QUESTIONS?

A few days after leaving CIA, I was summoned to testify before the Senate Foreign Relations Committee. It was an open session to consider my appointment as ambassador to Iran—ambassadors are appointed by the President, but require "the advice and consent of the Senate." Early in the questioning, Senator William Fulbright, the committee chairman, asked if this was the first time I had ever appeared before the Foreign Relations Committee in *open* hearing. I replied that this was indeed my first appearance at an *open* hearing. "In all these years?" Fulbright posed his question with heavy emphasis on "all these years." I replied in monotone, "All these years."

The senator then asked if I thought it wise for the Senate to have held my earlier appearances in executive session. I said yes. "Are you," he then asked, "under the same oath that all CIA men are under that when you leave the Agency you cannot talk about your experiences there?" I said, "Yes, sir, I feel bound by that." Fulbright asked again if I felt bound by this oath. I replied: "I think it would be a very bad example for the Director to be an exception."*

Senator Fulbright and other senators had for years attempted to wrest

*Quotations from Thomas Powers, *The Man Who Kept the Secrets* (New York: Knopf, 1979), pp. 272–73.

some responsibility for CIA oversight from Senator Russell and his Senate Armed Services subcommittee on CIA. Russell had persistently and forcefully kept them at bay. In late 1971 when Senator Russell died, Senator John Stennis replaced him as chairman. Stennis made a game effort to continue Russell's policies, but he was no match for Fulbright, who now had a free hand.

On February 7, 1973, two days after the relatively tame open session, the Senate Foreign Relations Committee met in executive session (a meeting closed to the press and public) again to consider my appointment. After a few desultory questions on training police officials and superficial queries on the Watergate scandal, Senator Fulbright announced that "it would be appropriate" that I be sworn as a witness. I raised my hand and swore "to tell the whole truth and nothing but the truth." I was then subjected to a closer questioning on the Agency than I had ever previously experienced.

Senator Stuart Symington, a member of both the Senate Armed Services subcommittee on CIA and the Senate Foreign Relations Committee, asked three direct questions.

"Did you try in the Central Intelligence Agency to overthrow the government of Chile?"

"No, sir," I said.

"Did you have any money passed to opponents of Allende?"

"No, sir."

"So the stories you were in that war [*sic*] are wrong?"

"Yes, sir."*

It had been my custom after any testimony before Congress to review the session with Larry Houston, the CIA general counsel. He found no problem with the bulk of my testimony but thought I might have a problem with my categorical response to Symington's questions on Chile. I disagreed. In the first place, I reminded Larry that Senator Symington had been thoroughly briefed on the operations that Presidents Kennedy, Johnson, and Nixon had directed the Agency to undertake in Chile. The only ex-

---

Hearings before the Committee on Foreign Relations, United States Senate, on the Nomination of Richard Helms to Be Ambassador to Iran and CIA International and Domestic Activities (Washington, D.C.: U.S. Government Printing Office, 1974), quoted from Powers, p. 232.

ception to this, I added, was Nixon's last-minute (Track II) order that I direct the Agency to intensify operations to prevent President-elect Allende from assuming office in Chile. At that meeting Nixon ordered me to keep his instruction from the secretary of state, the secretary of defense, the ambassador in Chile, and anyone in CIA who was not directly involved in this activity. I also reminded Larry that six of the senators present at the hearing were not officially authorized to question me on any CIA activity.

Larry remained doubtful.

Because Senator Symington knew the answers to the questions, I could not understand why he posed them. And in the decades that followed, I've yet to determine why he wanted my answers on the record. Symington had, of course, done much the same thing when, at a Senate hearing in 1970, with a group of other senators, he professed "surprise, shock and anger" at what he and the others claimed was their "recent discovery" of "CIA's secret war in Laos." Not only had the appropriate members of Congress been fully briefed on the Agency role in Laos, but Symington had twice visited Laos, stayed with our chief of station, and been extensively briefed by CIA officers, the ambassador, military attaché, and various Laotian officials.*

Sometime after John McCone resigned as director of Central Intelligence, he told me that he had chided Senator Symington, an old friend, for having asked the questions on operations in Chile when he knew what my answers must be. Moreover, as Symington well knew, the past activity was still very sensitive because of ongoing operations. Why had he put me on the spot? McCone asked. The senator did not answer. Later, McCone told me that this was the last time Senator Symington ever spoke to him.

A few days after this hearing, I also testified before Senator Frank Church's Subcommittee on Multinational Corporations. In response to a direct question, I denied that CIA had any contact with the Chilean military establishment during my tenure as DCI. It was an open session, and my response was mandated by my earlier testimony on Chile, and the fact that the committee had no authority over any CIA activity.

The Senate approved my appointment, and Cynthia and I began preparations to leave Washington.

*See page 261.

Chapter 41

—

ONCE PERSIA

Twelve hours before Cynthia and I were scheduled to leave for my assignment as ambassador to Iran, the director general of the foreign service telephoned with the news that President Nixon had ruled that diplomatic appointees, if kidnapped, would not be ransomed by the American government. This bon voyage message was in laconic contrast to the pleasant ceremony at which my family and a few friends watched Secretary of State William Rogers swear me in as an ambassador.

Because Cynthia was still recuperating from a serious operation, we decided to break the long flight to Tehran, and to spend a day with my brother Pearsall and his wife, Marianne, at their home in Geneva. At 3 a.m. Pearsall knocked on our bedroom door: the American embassy in Bern had an urgent telephone message for me. At that hour I scarcely expected good news and I was right. The State Department wanted me to know that Black September, an Arab terrorist group, was planning an operation against me. This was not the first time in the past few months that I had received such threats, and I went back to sleep. Cynthia had no such luck. She was still awake when Marianne called us for breakfast.

When we arrived in Tehran, the Shah was on holiday over Now Ruz, the Iranian New Year, and I was free to make the obligatory protocol calls on all the foreign embassies in Tehran. The experience ranged from straight vodka with the Soviet ambassador and his wife in mid-morning to an exhausting array of hors d'oeuvres prepared from an American cookbook by the chef at the United Arab Emirates. Warm soft drinks were the beverage of choice at most embassies.

I had first met the Shah in 1957 when I visited Tehran to negotiate permission to place some sophisticated intercept equipment in northern Iran. The location, on high hills overlooking the Soviet missile ranges in the Kazakhstan area, made it possible to intercept the telemetry used to control the rocket flights. On that visit, the Shah acted as his own chief of intelligence—I was later to learn that His Majesty always acted as his own DCI. Our meetings went well, and the Shah authorized the installation. Later, when I was *en poste* in Tehran, my channel to His Majesty was via Assadollah Alam, the Shah's longtime confidant, advisor, and minister of court. Alam arranged things, but in the nearly four years that followed, he never sat in on any of my sessions with the Shah. We always met tête-à-tête, with no note-takers or advisors.

One session with the Shah remains firmly in mind. We had several times discussed the secret help the United States, Israel, and Iran were giving the Kurd separatists in their struggle against Iraq. Using equipment supplied by the United States and Israel, the Iranian military were lobbing long-range shells over the mountains and into the area where the Iraqi forces were fighting the Kurds. The shelling was causing significant casualties among the Iraqi troops. Although the Kurdish chieftain, Mullah Mustafa Barzani, continued to plead for more support for his people, the Shah was becoming increasingly restive about the drain on Iranian resources. In March 1975 the Shah decided to head the Iranian delegation to a meeting of the Organization of Petroleum Exporting Countries in Algiers. This was a surprise because it was unusual for the Shah to attend such a meeting, even when other chiefs of state were likely to be present.

On his return to Tehran at 2 a.m. on March 7, the Shah was, as always, greeted by a group of his ministers. While still on the tarmac, he briefed the ministers on the outcome of his negotiations with Saddam Hussein, then the number two man in Iraq. These *negotiations* came as a total surprise, and the moment the news reached the embassy I asked for a meeting with the Shah.

The Shah began by pointing out that his father, Reza Shah, had agreed to a treaty with Great Britain that placed the demarcation between Iran and Iraq on the border of Iran rather than in the *Thalweg,** the deepest part of the Shatt al-Arab, the confluence of the Tigris and Euphrates Rivers. The original border, the Shah said, had been demeaning to the sovereignty of Iran, and he was pleased to have obtained Hussein's agreement to change the line to the *Thalweg*. The Shah also convinced Hussein to allow Shiite pilgrims to visit the Moslem holy places in Iraq, Najaf and Karbala. In return, the Shah agreed to halt the shelling of Iraqi troops, to cease supplying ammunition and equipment to the Kurds, and to open the Iran-Iraq border, which had been sealed with Iranian troops.

I was, of course, aware of the impact this news would have in Washington, but as ambassador I was scarcely in a position to rain on His Majesty's parade. It was a done deal, and the most I might do was to inform Washington. When the Shah finished explaining his rather dubious success, I asked how the talks with Hussein were conducted.

"Oh," he said, "we met for two days with Algerian President Boumedienne as go-between."

"But Hussein speaks only Arabic—how did you talk to him?"

"I spoke French to Boumedienne, and he spoke Arabic to Saddam."

So much, I thought, for formal negotiations, with maps, diplomats, note-takers, and expert interpreters at hand. The Shah was clearly proud to have righted a wrong and to have enabled the Shiite pilgrims—as many as ten thousand a year—to visit holy sites. He could not have known that the Shiites would use their pilgrimage to smuggle audiocassettes bearing incendiary anti-Shah sermons of the Ayatollah Ruhollah Khomeini and other exiled mullahs into Iran. The cassettes were quickly duplicated and distributed to mosques throughout Iran. The sermons contributed to the undermining of the Shah's standing, and ultimately to his leaving Iran.

In Tehran security was about as good as one could wish. The embassy is in a twenty-five-acre compound surrounded by high walls and protected by local police. The Agency had assigned a security officer, Jim Cunningham, to accompany me whenever I left the compound for the city or to visit the provinces. My driver, Haikaz, an Armenian, had saved the life of one American ambassador by a clever and courageous bit of

---

Thalweg is the diplomatic term for the world's maritime borders.

driving. As an added precaution, our vehicle, a shabby beige Chevrolet, was weighted with considerable armor plating. Cynthia was assigned another inconspicuous car and her own security officer.

As ambassador, my relationship with the Shah was as much as might be asked for. Our conversations were lively, though many times we had no choice but to agree to disagree. The polite give-and-take was always tempered by the Shah's knowledge that, in the end, he was, indeed, His Majesty. Our meetings ranged from wherever the Shah happened to be to sessions in his private offices, formal diplomatic dinners, and receptions. At one of the major holidays, the Shah provided a buffet dinner for more than a thousand guests. I was standing with a plate in one hand and a glass in the other when an aide beckoned me to the Shah's side. With plates, forks, and glasses in our hands, and in full view of the entire diplomatic corps and the Tehran social set, we talked shop for some ten minutes. My relationship prospered in part because the Shah had always been well impressed by the quality of the CIA people he had met through the years.

A few days after the Yom Kippur War broke out in October 1973, six Gulf states raised the price of oil some 70 percent. Soon afterwards, Saudi Arabia declared an embargo on oil sales to the United States. The reaction in Washington was prompt and vociferous. Those of us as far away as Tehran were hard pressed to make diplomatic ends meet. As ambassador I was asked to have Iranian oil provided to the U.S. naval force in the vicinity of Bandar Abbas and permission for Navy aircraft to use a nearby air base for its P-2 aircraft. It took some doing but the Shah came through. He also sent his energy minister to Saudi Arabia to ask the Saudis to call off the embargo, to no avail.

In the mid-seventies the Shah funded a deluge of orders for billions of dollars worth of high-performance U.S. aircraft. Both State and the Department of Defense were concerned about the impact this would have on relations throughout the area. The more informed Iranians and even the clergy were outspoken in protesting the Shah's insistence on pushing through what seemed to be a senseless expenditure. But in 1980, when Saddam Hussein's army finally did march into Iran, it was this expensive equipment that kept Iran and the mullahs from losing that long, bitter war.

In spring 1976, Cynthia and I decided it was time to begin to think about leaving Iran and government service. It would be a wrench leaving many friends and a fascinating country, but we had had enough of diplomatic life. Also, I wanted to leave before the November election to be sure that my departure would not be taken as refusal to serve under the next president, whoever he might be. Henry Kissinger, then secretary of state, had scheduled a visit to Iran, and I thought that might be the time to inform him of my plans.

"Strenuous for everyone but Henry," is the only way to describe an official visit by Secretary of State Kissinger. His energy was inexhaustible. At 11 p.m., after a day of end-to-end meetings with foreign statesmen, local dignitaries, American ambassadors summoned from their nearby posts, and a diplomatic dinner party, Henry would summon a secretary or two, and begin to dictate a blizzard of official communications. By breakfast, he would again be up and at it. Only Henry's relentless humor and good nature forestalled a complete collapse of the embassy staff, the upper brackets of Tehran's officialdom, and the diplomatic corps. In the hectic hubbub of events, Henry agreed to my plan to resign in the fall, although the actual announcement was to be made only on the eve of the presidential election.

In the time since I left Iran, I've often reflected on how so many things went wrong in the later years of the Shah's rule. However important a figure he was in the Middle East, the Shah was burdened with one considerable drawback. Iran is predominantly a Shiite entity in an Arab world dominated by Sunnis. This had the effect of isolating Iran and the Shah from the rest of the contemporary Moslem world. The Shah was determined to modernize Iran. In doing so, he neglected to develop a political system that would accommodate the changes and development while also providing for the improved well-being of the largely illiterate and impoverished general population.

The gap between the educated, wealthy minority and the other thirty million Iranians widened. There was no structure between the upper brackets of the Iranian government, business, and social worlds. Students returning from a university education abroad could not find work. Corruption was rife, foreign businesses flourished, and entrepreneurs fattened on profits which never trickled down to the working class. In suppressing dissidence and active resistance to the Shah's rule, Savak, the Iranian security and intelligence service, inflicted its power ruthlessly. I was never sure whether the Shah knew the extent of Savak's brutality. In time, it was obvious that the Shah was becoming increasingly autocratic and isolated from the population.

Foreign businessmen flooded Tehran. Few had any knowledge of the country; fewer could speak a word of Persian. James Bill, then a professor of Iranian history at the University of Texas, pointed out to Cynthia that the *New York Times* index from 1965 to 1975 contained 195 references to Iran—that is, 32 fewer than to Ethiopia, a country of significantly less world importance. By the time I left Tehran it was becoming clear that Iran was headed for serious trouble. It began with widespread demonstrations and rioting in 1978 and exploded in January 1979 when thousands gathered in Tehran to denounce the Shah and to force him into exile. The man who had effected such major changes in his thirty-seven-year rule found himself without a constituency.

Cynthia and I left Tehran in December 1976. Ironically, the only time we got to ride in the ambassador's traditional big black Cadillac, with the flag flying from the front fender, was on the way to the airport at the end of my tour in Iran.

In November 1979 the U.S. embassy in Tehran was attacked and occupied by revolutionary groups. The negotiations for the release of our embassy personnel failed, and President Jimmy Carter launched what seemed to me a desperate scheme for a military team to break into the embassy compound, free the prisoners, and fly them all to safety. When I was first in Tehran as ambassador, I had reviewed and, to various degrees, changed the security of our buildings there. In the ensuing three years, I became familiar with every aspect of the physical security of the embassy compound—from the locks on doors, to the vaulted areas, to the exits, emergency and otherwise. In the planning for the desperate (in my opinion, impossible) operation, which with a sad loss of life foundered in the desert without reaching Tehran, none of the White House tacticians thought to ask me a single question.

In 1979, Cynthia and I went openly but discreetly to visit the Shah late in his confinement at a New York hospital. He was already ill with cancer and had been allowed entrance into the United States only after considerable ugly negotiation. His bitterness was apparent. He could not understand why the United States had abandoned him, and had permitted everything that he had done to be undone by the mullahs. I could find no easy response when, propped up in bed, the ashen Shah asked, "Why did you do this to us?"

As we continued to talk, Cynthia asked, "But why did you leave Iran?" Without hesitation, the Shah said, "To avoid bloodshed—that is the difference between a king and a dictator."

The Shah died in July 1980 in Egypt, where he had kindly and courageously been granted political asylum by President Anwar Sadat.

Chapter 42

UNZIPPING
THE AGENCY

It appeared to me that James Schlesinger, my successor as DCI, came to office with firm instructions from Nixon: Jim was to shake up the Agency, trim it down, and rid it of what Nixon perceived to be the existing regime of anti-Nixon Georgetown dilettantes and free-range liberals. Aside from presumably making CIA a more effective service, this was also to make the Agency a more responsive element of the Nixon administration. Nixon appeared to be convinced that the Agency had shaped itself into a gentlemen's club dominated by the senior members of the plans directorate—in effect, as one writer reported it, my "Praetorian Guard." More recently, in browsing through some of the post-Nixon memoirs and the White House tapes, I found reason to believe that in his more eccentric moments, Nixon also imagined using the Agency for *domestic* covert action operations.

The number of senior CIA staff whom Nixon might have classified as upper-bracket society gentry was no greater than any other element of the foreign policy establishment in the United States. A few of our ancestors may have waded ashore in the seventeenth century—someone should have reminded Nixon that dukes and their duchesses rarely emigrate—but most of us were the offspring of the immigrants who disembarked in the centuries that followed. Others were born abroad. Nixon's suspicions notwithstanding, Ivy Leaguers did not dominate the Agency establishment; there was a proportionate number of state university, private, and community college graduates.

There is no doubt that some of the Agency personnel were at the least reserved about Nixon and his administration. The Agency was not, however, universally "anti-Nixon," and the average was probably not much different from that of any other segment of the Washington foreign policy establishment. More to the point, and personal domestic political preferences notwithstanding, there is only one president at a time, and we all had worked for each in turn—Truman, Eisenhower, Kennedy, and Johnson. Despite President Nixon's suspicions, until the Watergate break-in and the failed cover-up, neither Nixon nor his associates were treated any differently from their predecessors.

As the debris from the Watergate cover-up continued to fell his appointees, Nixon was forced to shuffle and restaff his administration. Among the changes mandated by the various resignations and firings, Nixon named James Schlesinger to replace Elliot Richardson as secretary of defense on May 17, 1973, and on the same day turned CIA over to the deputy director, William Colby. For the record, James Schlesinger served as DCI for four months—from February 2 to June 2, 1973.

Colby's promotion to DCI was announced at the time of Schlesinger's transfer to the Defense Department, but he was not sworn in until early September. This meant that General Vernon Walters, the deputy director, was acting DCI from May until Colby's formal swearing-in sixteen weeks later. Legal niceties notwithstanding, Dick Walters eased himself to one side, and Colby functioned as DCI from the time his appointment was announced. In the twilight of the Nixon era, Colby's swearing-in was simply forgotten until on a visit to California, Dick Walters reminded the President of the oversight.

Jim Schlesinger, a tough and aggressive executive, was not a stranger to intelligence organizations in Washington. In 1971, when Schlesinger was still serving as deputy director of the Office of Management and Budget, Nixon had ordered him to make an extensive examination of the national intelligence community. Schlesinger also worked at the Rand Corporation as director of strategic studies, and had been chairman of the Atomic Energy Commission for the three years before he joined CIA. During his brief tenure as DCI, Schlesinger moved to make changes in the organization and operations of the Agency. It was in this period that some one thousand employees, a significant number of them from the operations element—now called the Directorate for Operations (DO)—were fired, retired, or caused to resign. The abrupt and unnecessarily callous dismissal of so many of the staff had the obvious effect on the spirit of all concerned. The bond between the CIA management and personnel—an essential element in the security of any intelligence agency—was seriously damaged.

Some of the discharged employees were eligible for retirement and pension. Others were not. Some of those who left took with them a store of language, operational skills, and area knowledge which, even with their possibly diminished energy, might usefully have been retained—if necessary by some contrived "on the shelf" arrangement. Intensive foreign language study has always been neglected in the United States. The situation has improved, but even today, when Spanish is heard in many areas of this country, fluent Spanish-speaking college graduates are in short supply. In operations, intelligence production, research, and estimates activity, prospective recruits with a command of the languages spoken throughout Eastern Europe, Asia, the Arab world, the Far East, and the sub-Saharan Africa areas are much more difficult to find.

Schlesinger's seventeen weeks as DCI coincided with a series of embarrassing public disclosures ranging from the negligible charge of training Tibetan guerrillas in Colorado in an alleged violation of the CIA charter forbidding operations within the United States,* to having supplied operational equipment that was used by White House operatives Howard Hunt and G. Gordon Liddy, a former FBI employee, to burglarize the offices of Daniel Ellsberg's psychiatrist. Ellsberg was the Department of Defense official who leaked the highly classified Pentagon Papers to the press. My deputy, Marine Corps General Robert Cushman, who authorized handing over the equipment, had failed to ask what use the Nixon operatives planned to make of it. (He also neglected to inform me.) When Judge Matthew Byrne, conducting Ellsberg's trial, was in-

---

*Training foreign agents within the United States is scarcely to be equated with running secret intelligence operations in the Colorado mountains. Aside from the unwelcome publicity, the more serious result of this disclosure was that it tipped the Chinese to the fact that CIA was preparing agents for work in Tibet.

formed that the defendant's phone had been tapped and his psychiatrist's offices burglarized, he declared a mistrial. Ellsberg walked free.

Under intense presidential pressure, the Agency had also overstepped its charter in preparing psychological/medical profiles of Ellsberg. These at-a-distance studies of various foreign, political, and intelligence figures had proved a useful extension of the routine diplomatic and military reporting. Although I think the Agency was the only element of the government to have developed this particular technique, and despite the fact that Ellsberg had disclosed a mass of Top Secret material, some of it touching on CIA, I should have insisted that the White House find someone in the medical or academic community who might have attempted such an assessment.

Neither Schlesinger nor Colby had any knowledge of Ehrlichman's demand that the operations support material be provided to Howard Hunt. (It was only when Hunt's demands for exotic operational devices escalated that General Cushman informed me, and further cooperation was refused.) Colby's previous assignments would not have given him access to anything as remote from his previous responsibilities as knowledge of the Ehrlichman-Hunt problem, nor the White House demand for the Ellsberg profile. Had Jim Schlesinger asked during either of our two thirty-minute meetings, I would gladly have disclosed this and any other aspect of CIA–White House relations of interest to him. (It is now my understanding that Jim had asked the White House to respect the originally scheduled date for my retirement—my sixtieth birthday, March 30. Had this been done, Schlesinger and I would have had ample time for whatever discussions he might have wanted.)

As it was, Schlesinger and Colby were blindsided, and Jim reacted vigorously to the newsbreak which came two days before his appointment as secretary of defense. As DCI, he issued an order, recommended and written by Colby, for all senior Agency officers immediately to report any current or past activity that "might be construed to be outside the legislative charter" of the Agency. In addition to the senior officers, the DCI's order directed "every person presently employed by the CIA" to report on any such activity as might be known. Former employees were also solicited to report their recollection of any such past activity.

The making-a-clean-breast intent of this directive, surely the first in intelligence history, is abundantly clear: to make certain that nothing like it ever happens again. Less clear was the standard to be used in judging the activities which might fall legally beyond the Agency's legislative charter. The National Security Act of 1947 was deliberately cast in terms vague enough not to offend the elements of Congress and the public who might be shocked at the thought of the United States admitting that it was arming itself with a national intelligence service. Colby's directive left it to CIA employees, present and past, to decide which activity might conceivably be illegal, unjustified, improper, or perhaps distasteful. It is difficult to believe that the members of any of the world's foreign intelligence services might be able to decide precisely the activity that fell legally within their national charter—even if such a charter might exist.

The directive was so broadly phrased that it risked inciting disgruntled employees, as well as those who might have grudges to settle, to step forward. As Cord Meyer expresses it, "Very few human institutions in this world, from the American Civil Liberties Union to the Boy Scouts, could survive in good working order" after suffering such an instruction.*

The result was a 693-page collection of allegations by employees from entry-level clerks to the most senior staff officers over a period of twenty-five years. Someone dubbed the resulting documents the "Family Jewels." The term was a corruption of OSS usage. While in Switzerland during World War II, Allen Dulles kept the data on his most sensitive sources and German contacts in a book-size looseleaf binder. The only member of the station who had access to it was Allen's personal secretary. Senior officers were briefed that in any emergency, the notebook was to be the first document destroyed. The individuals cited in the book were known within the station as the "Crown Jewels," and the notebook was referred to as the "Family Jewels." Allen's rage, had he been alive to learn that the term had been turned upside down by one of his successors, might well have blown the roof off the Agency's new building.

Colby did not inform President Nixon or, later, President Ford of this explosive collection. This neglect is in sharp contrast to his briefing of the Senate and House committees on the data a year before the document first leaked.

Facing Reality (New York: Harper & Row, 1980), p. 161.

Another astonishing fact is that in the sour atmosphere prevailing in post-Nixon Washington, it took fifteen months—and a headline article in the December 22, 1974, *New York Times*—for this bundle to explode. Within five weeks, three separate federal government investigative groups were established. First off the mark was a bipartisan commission formed by President Gerald Ford on January 4, 1975. The group was chaired by Vice President Nelson Rockefeller, supported by seven distinguished private citizens, including Ronald Reagan, John T. Connor, C. Douglas Dillon, Lane Kirkland of the AFL-CIO, and Erwin Griswold, former dean of Harvard Law School.

This blue-ribbon group was "to determine whether the CIA has exceeded its statutory authority . . . [and] determine whether existing safeguards are adequate to preclude Agency activities that might go beyond its authority and to make appropriate recommendations." President Ford notes in his memoirs that he also wanted to avoid "unnecessary disclosures [that] could cripple the agency's effectiveness, lower its morale and make foreign governments extremely wary about sharing vital information with us."* This perceptive and well-stated objective failed largely through DCI Colby's single-handed thrusting of highly sensitive, classified data upon the Rockefeller Commission and subsequent congressional investigating committees.

The Senate formed the Select Committee to Study Government Operations with Respect to Intelligence Activities on January 27, with Senator Frank Church at the helm. Not to be left on the outside with its nose pressed against the CIA windows, the House of Representatives formed its own Select Committee on Intelligence Operations, chaired by Congressman Otis Pike, on February 19.

After Colby replaced Schlesinger as DCI, he established a policy that Senator Church and his staff were to be given access to all the documents, irrespective of classification, that the committee might think useful. Rather than wait until the committees asked for data, Colby was prepared to supply whatever such documents—internal memoranda, directives, dispatches, cables, and files—he thought the Church Select Committee (and subsequently the Pike Committee) might find useful. As director of Central Intelligence, it was Colby's sworn responsibility

---

A Time to Heal (New York: Harper & Row, 1979), p. 230.

to protect "CIA sources and methods." Moreover, Colby made this decision without consulting or informing either the President or the national security advisor.

It was after Colby's early appearances before the Vice President's commission that Rockefeller took him aside and asked, "Bill, do you really have to present all this material to us? We realize that there are secrets you fellows need to keep and so nobody here is going to take it amiss if you feel that there are some questions you can't answer quite as fully as you seem to feel you have to."* This warning and the DCI's legal responsibilities did not affect Colby's determination to continue dumping CIA files on the Rockefeller Commission, and subsequently the Senate and House committees. The fact that the Soviet and other foreign intelligence services were surely studying the disclosures with microscopic attention was also apparently ignored by Colby.

The DCI's unilateral actions effectively smashed the existing system of checks and balances protecting the national intelligence service. As Henry Kissinger points out, "In ordinary circumstances, the Director of Central Intelligence would have sounded the alarm against excessive disclosures inimical to national security. The President, in consultation with the Director and the Secretaries of State and Defense, would have sought to develop some criteria by which to define transgressions and confine investigations to these subjects."† As in the past, this would have protected security secrets and opened the way to establishing procedures to prevent any further such abuses.

The Rockefeller report noted that in the course of its twenty-eight-year history CIA had engaged in some activities that should be criticized, that some were unlawful invasions of the rights of Americans and should not be allowed to happen again. Press coverage of the Rockefeller report failed to stress that a number of these questionable activities were initiated or ordered by the various incumbent presidents. Seventy-five percent of the "domestic spying" incidents were security investigations of persons affiliated with the Agency. Only fifteen such investigations concerned persons not directly connected with CIA. This is a less than impeccable performance, but not all that bad considering the security atmosphere pre-

*William Colby, *Honorable Men* (New York: Simon & Schuster, 1978), p. 400.
†*Years of Renewal* (New York: Simon & Schuster, 1999), p. 320.

vailing throughout the darkest days of the Cold War and the many years involved.

I recall only two instances in intelligence history in which the files of intelligence services were as thoroughly ransacked as those of the Agency during these three investigations. Shortly after the Bolsheviks took power in Russia, the files of the Okhrahna—the imperial Russian intelligence and security agency—were thrown open to the public. The purpose of this hasty action was presumably to convince the Russian people that the czar's government had used all manner of illegal secret operations to spy upon and destroy all political opposition to its rule. It was only when the Soviet security services realized that the newly formed Polish intelligence service had helped itself to all of this data that the barn doors were closed. Veteran Polish intelligence officers admitted that this information helped in their early successful penetration of the USSR. The second such instance came after the surrender of the Third Reich, when the victorious Allied and Soviet intelligence services assigned scores of researchers to the tons of Nazi files that had escaped destruction.

The Church Committee began its investigation with what seemed to be reasonable precautions in the handling of classified data. CIA and other agencies involved in the investigation were allowed to delete sensitive portions of documents before handing them to the investigating staffers. Unfortunately, this precaution was often nullified by the tight deadlines imposed by the senator for delivery of the documents. In the time available it proved impossible for the reviewing staff to consult with other officers who might have a more informed opinion of the sensitivity of the specific material. Throughout this exercise senators like Charles "Mac" Mathias and John Tower struggled to keep the committee on focus and to avoid the most serious, and often gratuitous, security compromises. Their good counsel and cautions were persistently overridden by the enthusiasm that some of the others had for making headlines with the data supplied by CIA and Senator Church's persistent grandstanding.

One of the more revealing illustrations of Church's approach to "Study Government Operations with Respect to Intelligence Activities" surfaced in one of his early questions at the first *public* hearing with DCI Colby. With an appropriately grim visage, Church asked, "Have you brought some of those devices which would have enabled CIA to use this [a previously discussed poison] for killing people?" Given this presumably out-of-the-blue question, one of Colby's side men promptly produced a clumsy pistol equipped with an unwieldy telescopic sight. DCI Colby described the device as a "Nondiscernible Microbioinoculator." It was presumably supposed to convince worldwide audiences to stay tuned—the senator and DCI were hand in hand about to make a clean breast of CIA's past. And as surely as the sun sets in the west, the world press leaped to attention.

Lost in the blaze that followed was the fact that this preposterous "dart gun" was not a CIA concoction but the product of a Defense Department employee. As Henry Kissinger explains, it was in an effort to recoup some of the cost of developing this gimmick that the military had attempted to convince other, less lethally armed agencies to purchase a few.* At CIA, the free-sample Microbioinoculator was relegated to a locked closet. Until glimpsing the device on the front page of a newspaper, I had never seen it. Sometime later, a colleague and small-arms expert remarked that the pistol would be more effective if thrown rather than fired at a prospective victim.

By October 1975, Church had completed his work. (Before the senator finished with me, I had testified for some hundred hours.) President Ford, who had a much more informed knowledge of the intelligence and security equities than he has been given credit for, tried to keep Senator Church from publishing his report. The President was convinced that the ensuing discussions of the mountains of classified data Church had amassed would play neatly into the hands of the anti-American elements throughout the world. He also knew that in the heat of the worldwide reaction to the material Church was preparing to disclose, little attention would be paid to the committee's final findings: With the exception of Nixon's Track II operation, CIA had functioned under appropriate congressional oversight and White House control and direction. The report placed heavy emphasis on the five assassination "attempts": Castro in Cuba, Rafael Trujillo in the Dominican Republic, Ngo Dinh Diem in South Vietnam, Patrice Lumumba in Congo/Zaire, and General Schneider in Chile. Also mentioned was the fact that in eight months of dra-

*Ibid., p. 328.

matic investigation, Senator Church had managed to determine that CIA had never assassinated anyone.

Senator Church refused President Ford's request not to publish his committee's report on the flimsy grounds that the committee had voted to release the report after a closed Senate session. The report was printed, and by late November 1975, copies of the report were given to each senator.

In the prevailing climate, the sad fact was that most of the accusations of wrongdoing were immediately accepted and trumpeted as facts. Moreover, the accusations were far more widely propagated, and lived much longer, than the eventual denials. And many of these accusations still echo in the press and public mind.

Congressman Pike headed a staff of fifty. From the beginning, it seemed to me that he affected a strong anti-intelligence attitude. This was a shrewd position in at least one aspect—there were more headlines to be gained by parading alleged misdeeds than by digging deeply enough to question the validity of the alleged transgressions. And to stay abreast of, or even occasionally to outshine, the more senior and somewhat more security-conscious Senate committee, the Pike allegations had to be freshly minted scandals.

At the time, it was my impression that none of the staff employees of either congressional committee had any significant experience handling classified data, background in intelligence, or knowledge of security procedures in general. The ultimate irony of this sorry episode came when DCI Colby, who had provided the committees with hundreds of classified CIA documents, lost his pucker. In his book he refers to the Pike Committee staff as a "bunch of children who were out to seize the most sensational high ground . . . and could not be interested in a serious review of what intelligence is really all about." As for the congressman himself, Colby said: "He accepted without change the ragtag, immature, and publicity-seeking committee staff that had been gathered for the investigation."* To be fair, I must note that Colby also credits Pike with having started with three questions: How much does intelligence cost, how good is it, and what risks are involved? Alas, Pike did not come within sight of any answers to these questions. His young staff reminded

*Honorable Men, pp. 431–32.

me of a group of brats who, having broken into their school, celebrated the adventure by trashing their classroom.

Congressman Pike finally stubbed his toe when he refused to agree not to make public five different intelligence estimates on a situation in the Near East. The consensus of the U.S. intelligence community was that the publication of these estimates would compromise its ability to monitor and evaluate certain situations. When the Pike group published the information on September 1, President Ford reacted sharply. In an open hearing the following morning, the assistant attorney general reminded the Pike Committee that the President was responsible for national security and foreign relations. He then directed the committee immediately to return all classified materials previously furnished to the committee and that in future "all departments and agencies of the executive branch . . . [are] to decline to provide . . . [the Pike Committee] with classified materials."

In Pike's opinion, this raised a constitutional issue as to whether a congressional committee could on its own release classified data prepared by the executive branch. He refused to return any of the documents Colby had provided. Six days after the assistant attorney general's order, Pike released more classified documents. Some were designated "Eyes Only," and others contained the names of CIA personnel serving abroad. Pike subsequently subpoenaed the DCI to provide additional data on highly sensitive communications intelligence and the National Security Council to provide a mass of highly classified 40 Committee data on covert action operations. As the all-out battle lines became clearly established, Secretary of State Henry Kissinger stepped upon the parapet. Loud and clearly he proclaimed that President Ford was entirely correct in withholding classified information from a congressional committee that refused to obey the legally instituted classification system established by a long-standing presidential order. It was at about this time, mid-October, that the tide turned.

A *New York Times* editorial declared the Pike Committee to have been acting "contrary to public interest." In a letter to the *Washington Post,* George Kennan strode into the fray with strong support for President Ford and Kissinger. The battle raged on, and the seriously irresponsible disclosure of classified documents continued—various promises and compromises notwithstanding. The tragic murder of Richard Welch, the

CIA station chief in Athens, on December 23, 1975, contributed to the changing press and public reaction to the Pike position. Dick Welch's name (as well as his address and assignment) was one of those disclosed in the compromised CIA material. In late January 1976 the House of Representatives voted to block the release of the Pike Committee report until President Ford could certify that it contained no harmful classified data. No matter, the report was leaked.

In February the *Village Voice,* a weekly New York journal not previously noted for its coverage of congressional or foreign affairs, published a version of the Pike report. Daniel Schorr, a CBS journalist, subsequently admitted that he had slipped his copy of the document to the *Village Voice*—possibly because he could not find a more suitable outlet. As a journalist, Schorr was under no legal obligation to reveal the source of the stolen document.

President Gerald Ford attended the burial ceremony of Dick Welch at Arlington National Cemetery with honors due to a man murdered by political activists while assigned to the U.S. embassy in Athens.

Chapter 43

—

STORM WARNINGS

I was quietly getting on with my ambassadorial duties in November 1975 when Henry Fowler telephoned to say that he and George Ball were in Tehran on business and would like to drop by and say hello. Henry Fowler, known to his friends as Joe, had been secretary of the Treasury under President Johnson. George Ball was number two at the State Department under Dean Rusk and had attracted considerable attention for publicly opposing the war in Vietnam. Joe and George had both practiced law and were popular and distinguished figures on the Washington scene. We were friends of long standing, and lunch at the residence offered a good chance to pick up on the most recent Washington gossip.

Before we had settled down for a drink in the library, Joe, like many of our Iranian visitors, made a close inspection of the American Indian paintings Cynthia had borrowed from the National Museum of American Art in Washington. He was not long in getting down to business. "If you are going to do any more testifying in Washington," he said, "you'd better get yourself a good lawyer." There may be more effective ways of souring the last sip of one's sherry, but none comes to mind.

During the process of obtaining Senate approval of my appointment as ambassador, I testified before the Senate Foreign Relations Committee, Watergate Committee, and Multinational Corporations subcommittee. At the time, I saw no need for an attorney, and thought that the presence of such a guardian might give a misleading slant to my testimony. To my surprise, it was these hearings which seemed to concern my two visitors more than my subsequent appearances before Senator Frank Church and his Select Committee to Study Government Operations with Respect to Intelligence Activities, the group that was to become better known as the Church Committee.

My tenure in Iran was plagued by sixteen strenuous round trips to Washington. I accompanied the Shah on an official visit, and made another trip to testify on Watergate. Most of the remaining visits were devoted to Senator Church. I recall at least one session with the House Select Committee on Intelligence Operations, also known as the Pike Committee. These sometimes all but back-to-back trips and the hundred or so hours of testimony on incidents that I could scarcely recall were at the least exhausting.

In those days, if the weather and flight connections were perfect, the trip from Tehran to Washington, with a change of aircraft in London, averaged from seventeen to eighteen cramped, chairbound hours in the air. Combined with the time spent scuffling from one aircraft to another at Heathrow, this made for an exhausting experience. Along with reading, picking at microwaved delicacies, and glancing at the films shown on previous trips, I had ample time for what might at best be called contemplating the verities. Any hitch in the weather or flight schedules might add as much as five hours to the total. "Boredom," "stress," and "wear and tear" are words that come to mind.

In Washington, friends insisted that I stay with them rather than at a hotel. This helped to keep my internal clock on one setting and minimize some of the exhausting jet lag. It also made it easier to face as many as four hours attempting to cope with remarks such as "But Mr. Ambassador, *you* signed this CIA cable!" After glancing at the cable, I often had to reply, "Yes, Senator, that is my signature. On some days, I may have signed as many as twenty cables. Now, years after the fact, I doubt that I can recall any one of them." This is not an exact quote but it is close enough to give the flavor of the questioning. After two or three such days, I was free to "hop" another interminable trip back to the embassy.

Before Senator Church had had his fill, I testified before his committee for, as best as I can now remember, some thirty times. In the moments of relative rest during the senator and his ample staff's fulminations, I found it increasingly difficult to suppress my ever stronger inclination to shout, "Do you really think that CIA would undertake an operation of that importance on its own authority, and not at the direction of the President, and without the knowledge of the National Security Council? And without informing appropriate members of Congress?" But I did no shouting.

Time surely heals many wounds and often softens judgments. That said, it remains my opinion that Senator Church operated his committee at a level of self-serving hypocrisy unusual even for other run-of-the-mill presidential hopefuls. For his own purposes, Church affected to assume that CIA ran most of its sensitive operations on its own initiative and authority, and without the President's knowledge. Church would also have had his TV audience and the print media believe that the Agency operated behind the back of the national security advisor and his staff. At one of his dramatic heights, Church described CIA as a "rogue elephant"—presumably rampaging both Washington and foreign capitals.*

———

At our luncheon in Tehran, I had no sooner finished subjecting George Ball and Joe Fowler to my opinion of the Church Committee than they returned resolutely to their original thought.

"We've been hearing things about you around town," Joe said. George nodded agreement and added, "A good lawyer—just to be on the safe side." By the time we moved along to the dining room, I learned that the rumors concerned the Justice Department investigation of me, which might lead to my indictment for perjury. This was startling news and I readily agreed to find someone to represent me in Washington. At table, I could barely focus on the conversation centered on the waves still roiling in the wake of Nixon's resignation, and Gerry Ford's slight prospects in the upcoming presidential election.

*In the committee's final report to the Senate, Church—in a rare statement not fashioned as a sensational sound bite—quietly admitted that his committee had found that CIA was *not* a "rogue elephant."

Within a few hours I reached Edward Bennett Williams on the telephone. He had the reputation of being one of the best trial lawyers in Washington. Over the years we had become friends, although my work could scarcely have been more distant from Ed's high-powered law practice and his prominence in the hierarchy of the Democratic Party. One element in our relationship was our mutual interest in the Washington Redskins football team—Williams a part-owner, and I but an enthusiastic fan. Redskin tickets are more difficult to come by than an invitation for an informal supper with the folks at Buckingham Palace, but Ed always made space available for us.

Telephone connections between Tehran and Washington were at best squawky, but I managed to present my problem to Ed. Would he consider taking me on as a client? "Of course, Dick. And, I'll handle it myself from here on." This lifted my spirits, but I knew the road ahead would be bumpy. It did not occur to me that it would involve my indictment and conviction.

Chapter 44

—

WELCOME HOME

Cynthia and I left Tehran in December 1976. After a pleasant New Year's stop in Morocco, we went on to Washington. The few days involved in "signing out" were a suitable anticlimax to thirty years of government service. The first hurdle in the path to what I had assumed might be an easy transition to private life came in two weeks when the Justice Department issued its report on the "Investigation and Prosecutorial Decisions in Respect to Central Intelligence Mail Opening Activities in the United States." This concerned a CIA-sponsored project started in 1953 and closed in 1973 involving the opening of selected mail to and from the United States and, primarily, to the USSR. From the outset the project was cleared by the postmaster general. All of the results of this program were immediately shared with the FBI.

The reasoning behind the project was our knowledge that Soviet intelligence had satisfied itself that no such mail opening existed within the United States and thus might have been lured into inexpensive and speedy communications offered by the open mail. It was not that we expected to find clear text intelligence and operations messages. Rather, we hoped to uncover highly sophisticated secret writing and enciphered communications. Western security services had found that Soviet agents operating under unofficial cover, and without diplomatic immunity, were usually equipped with excellent secret writing devices, and many sent some messages by open mail. Although the net result of the operation was less than we hoped, two agents and various counterintelligence leads were uncovered.

After discovering that the program had been cleared by the postmaster general, the Department of Justice decided not to undertake any effort to prosecute the individuals involved. The department's final report says in part: "It would be mistaken to suppose that it was always clearly perceived that the particular mail opening programs of the CIA were obviously illegal. The [Justice] Department believes that this opinion is a serious misperception of our nation's recent history, of the way the law had evolved, and the factors to which it responded—a substitution of what we now believe is and must be the case for what was." Another relevant sentence reads: "Although the Department is of the firm view that activities similar in scope and authorization to those conducted by the CIA between 1953 and 1973 would be unlawful if undertaken today, the Department has concluded that a prosecution of the potential defendant would be unlikely to succeed because of the state of the law that prevailed during the course of the mail opening problem."

In short, the Department of Justice took into account the security problem which the White House and others knew the country faced during the height of the Cold War.

Almost coincidentally, the press accounts of the Rockefeller Commission investigation and the Church Committee Senate hearings stirred a hornet's nest of legal suits against me personally in my former role as director of Central Intelligence. The variety of suits which U.S. citizens and their lawyers can devise when inspired by a glimpse of secret files is staggering. Fortunately for me, many of these suits fell within the responsibility of the Department of Justice. This meant that my defense in those cases would be handled by lawyers approved of and paid by Justice. Other suits were handled by Edward Bennett Williams and some of his highly competent assistants. At one point, I asked Ed what the criteria were for deciding whether the Department of Justice or his office was to handle a specific case. He thought for a moment before saying, "I *can* answer your question, but life being short, the brief answer is that Department of Justice decides which office is to handle whichever case any which way the Department of Justice chooses." All of these suits were eventually dismissed, but the nervous energy expended, hours squandered, and the legal costs to the government and my own lawyers were considerable.

Despite the early warning given me by George Ball and Joe Fowler about the intention of the Justice Department to take me to court, my problems continued to multiply. The Justice Department had, reluctantly I learned, determined to prosecute me on the basis of two separate instances of my testimony in congressional hearings in connection with my appointment as ambassador. The two hearings occurred in February 1973, when the Senate Foreign Relations Committee questioned me on covert action operations in Chile. The second charge against me was based on an open session of Senator Frank Church's Subcommittee on Multinational Corporations, also in February 1973, when I denied CIA had any contact with the Chilean military establishment during my tenure as DCI. (The details are in Chapter 40, "Trick Questions?," pp. 413–15.)

During the early months of 1977, Ed Williams declined to tell me how the legal case against me was proceeding. Gregory Craig, whom Ed referred to as his sidecar rider (and who was later to serve as President Clinton's legal advisor during the impeachment fracas), also kept the secret. It was wise of them. Had they done otherwise, it would have been a very bleak several months.

In September, I learned that DCI Colby had provided the Department of Justice with some sixty documents concerning CIA operations in Chile. These documents had been assembled at Colby's direction by three mid-ranking CIA officers—as far as I know, none had a law degree. Without exception the documents were classified Secret or Top Secret. In the letter transmitting this material, Colby suggested that I might have committed perjury in testifying before Congress. Also included with this material were the full details of Track II, Nixon's last-minute instruction for me to instigate a military coup in Chile. I soon learned that Colby had done this without any reference to President Gerald Ford or the national security advisor at the White House—the two officials under whom the director of Central Intelligence serves and to whom he is obligated to report. I might add that Colby also neglected to inform me. On the basis of these documents—which included my scribbled notes on the Track II meeting with Nixon—the Justice Department had little choice but to consider prosecuting me on two separate instances of my testimony.

When news of my indictment became public, a number of friends and colleagues asked why I had not simply asked that the hearing go into executive session so that I could respond openly. Even when answering my former colleagues who were bound to respect the security issues involved, my answer was complex. First, I had been ordered by President Nixon not to discuss the Track II aspect of the Chile operations with anyone but Nixon, Henry Kissinger and his staff, and the Agency personnel who were directly involved in the operation. I was sure that if I asked for the hearing to be moved into a closed session, the press would have been alerted to the likelihood that there were still pertinent data to be uncovered on the Agency's role in Chile.

Aside from violating the presidential instruction, I had very quickly to factor in the further possibility that my candid account of what went on in Chile might leak—even from such a sequestered meeting. President Allende was still in office. Any disclosure by me of the details of the Agency's past activity in Chile would certainly endanger the lives of those who had cooperated with us at the time, as well as those who might still be active in the anti-Allende efforts. I also remembered Senator Fulbright's earlier promise: "If I catch you trying to upset the Chilean election, I will get up on the Senate floor and blow the operation." Later, Fulbright underlined his position by stating, "I pay no attention to the assertion that CIA can only testify on operational matters before the Senate Armed Services Committee."

Last, I had sworn to protect CIA sources and methods from unauthorized disclosure. To my knowledge only Senator Symington, among those present at the hearing, was officially authorized to have access to this information.

Like the captains of square-rigged sailing ships, I was caught between wind and tide in a narrow channel with no room to maneuver.

———

There is a certain irony in my relations with Senator Fulbright. A few weeks into my tenure as DCI, the Agency press relations officer suggested that I sign a letter to the *St. Louis Globe-Democrat* complimenting the newspaper on a recent editorial supporting a Senate vote to continue to restrict the handling of CIA matters to Senator Russell's Armed Services Committee and its subcommittee on CIA, and not to share them with the Senate Foreign Relations Committee. After a quick glance, I signed the letter and went back to dealing with my more appropriate responsibilities. A few hours later, I learned that the editorial I had so casually praised was entitled "Brickbats for Fulbright," and in the body of the text was a reference to the senator as being "crafty." So much for getting off on the right foot in a new job.

An hour before signing this letter, had anyone asked, I would have said no DCI has any business writing letters commending editorial comments in any newspaper. An hour after signing the letter, I would have said the same thing. To this moment, I have no idea what manner of preoccupation might have caused such a complete lapse in judgment.

I rushed to apologize to Senator Fulbright. He was understanding and more than courteous in accepting my apology. In the course of making my amends with other concerned senators, I was again impressed by the fact that irrespective of their sometimes intense political differences, senators are all members of the same club. To attack—inadvertently or otherwise—one senator is to attack them all. It is also true that despite the strongest political differences, personal relations within the Senate are almost without exception, polite, tolerant, and, at the least, ostensibly friendly. This attitude also governed my long relationship with Senator Fulbright. Despite our strong difference of opinion on how the Congress should maintain appropriate oversight of CIA, we remained friends.

—

It was not until September 10, 1977, that, on instructions from Assistant Attorney General Benjamin Civiletti, in charge of the Justice Department's Criminal Division, that Allen Carver, the leading Justice Department lawyer, presented the case against me to Ed Williams, my lawyer. The briefing took two hours. Williams subsequently discussed the case with the attorney general, Judge Griffin Bell.

Two days later, I met with Williams and Craig at their offices in Farragut Square. After informing me in detail of their discussions with the Justice Department, Ed said that we had a choice of pleading nolo contendere and accepting the attorney general's offer or going to trial. The offer, which at the time nearly floored me, was that in pleading "nolo" as Ed put it, I would retain my pension and not be subjected to imprisonment. Until that moment I had not considered the possibility of being sent to prison. After further intense discussion, we decided to consult Clark Clifford, the venerable lawyer, public servant, and advisor to several presidents. I had known Clark for years—he had served as chairman of the President's Foreign Intelligence Advisory Board, and as a counselor on personal matters.

We met in Clark's office. Hollywood could not have constructed a movie set more impressive than these offices. Not by accident, the picture window behind Clark's desk offered a glimpse of the White House.

It was when Ed Williams brought Clifford up to date that I learned that Colby had declassified and delivered to the Justice Department every piece of paper—no matter how highly classified—on covert action and intelligence collection operations in Chile. I was literally stunned, and scarcely ready for Ed's statement that we were now at the point of decision. Clark Clifford took a deep breath and asked what I wanted to do. It was a few moments before I said, "Cynthia and I discussed this last night. We agreed that I should go on trial."

This surprised Clark. After a pause, he launched into a depressing description of the costs and time that such a move would involve. He closed his remarks with what for me was the clinching argument. "Going before a District of Columbia jury on a matter as complicated and unusual as this case runs the very real risk of getting you convicted."

The discussion that followed was enough to convince me that the lawyers were right. I was not prepared to risk both a prison term and the loss of my pension. After thirty years of government service, during which time I had lived on my adequate but less than handsome civil service wages, the pension was vital. All told, it had been a grim afternoon.

At two-forty-five, Monday, October 31, 1977, I appeared before the Honorable Barrington D. Parker. With me were Edward Bennett Williams and Gregory Craig, "lawyers on behalf of the defendant." The government was represented by Benjamin R. Civiletti. The purpose of this "action" was thought by both Civiletti and Ed Williams to be my sentencing. Not at all, we learned. After considerable judicial maneuvering and discussion, it was clear that Judge Parker did not agree to my being sentenced on that occasion, what with the courtroom being nearly empty of spectators and the press.

It was not until November 4, when the venue was crowded with both press and spectators, that Judge Parker was prepared to give me a verbal whipping. He opened his remarks with his observation that I stood "before this court in disgrace and shame."

Without any reference to the unusual circumstances surrounding my case, he continued: "You considered yourself bound to protect the Agency whose affairs you had administered and to dishonor your solemn oath to tell the truth before the Committee." He then noted that to lie when "obligated to testify forthrightly, free of false, inadequate, incomplete, and evasive testimony," was "to disobey and ignore the laws of our land." He went on to remind me that "public officials at every level, whatever their position, like any other person, must respect and honor the Constitution and the laws of the United States. There is no exception to or qualification of this principle."

My sentence: a $2000 fine and two years in jail, with sentence suspended.

Feeling, if perhaps not looking, ashen, I followed Ed Williams out of the courtroom and into the gauntlet of press. Ed provided the reporters with a quick comment. "Helms will wear this conviction like a badge of honor." A reporter picked this up and asked if I agreed. "I do indeed, and I don't feel disgraced at all. Had I done anything else, I would then have been disgraced."

Judge Parker's legal case against me has had a long life in print. At the Kennedy School of Government at Harvard, it is used as text for discussion: "The Two Oaths of Richard Helms." In the years that followed I was often bemused when lawyers at legal depositions asked me if it were true that I had been convicted of "perjury." Conviction for perjury is a felony. My failure to testify in public "fully and completely" before a congressional committee was a misdemeanor.

Later, on the morning of my sentencing, I went to the Kenwood Country Club for one of the regularly scheduled luncheons of CIRA (the Central Intelligence Retiree Association). The news of my conviction had been on the radio, and to my complete surprise, every one of the several hundred guests rose and applauded thunderously. It had been a really rotten day, and I hoped that I managed to mask at least some of my emotion.

Before the luncheon, someone had fetched two large wicker baskets. Despite my remonstration, the baskets were rapidly circulated and soon filled with checks and cash that exceeded my $2000 fine. I managed later to return some of the checks, and forwarded the overflow of cash to an Agency welfare fund. These were moving, never to be forgotten moments.

A few days later, I went to Ed Williams's offices. He brushed my thanks to one side, and frowned as I asked how much I owed him. "You don't owe me anything, Dick," he said. "And I really mean it." Aside from being one of the best lawyers in Washington, he was also known for being among the best compensated.

A decade later, at a *National Geographic* reception, Cynthia and I were moving along a receiving line a few steps behind Judge Griffin Bell, President Carter's attorney general, who had decided how the government would handle my case. He turned, greeted us warmly, and noted that he and former senator Sam Nunn had just come in from Atlanta where they had attended a ceremony honoring the late senator Richard Russell. At one point, Judge Bell said, "If Senator Russell had been alive, you would not have had that legal trouble over testimony before congressional committees." I allowed, a bit ruefully, that he was correct.

Sam Nunn, who had heard Bell's remark, told me later that Judge Bell was "probably right, but a written record in an oversight committee is much more valuable in such cases."

This was Sam's polite way of saying that the knowledge which Senator Russell kept in his head should have been on record in his committee. I could only agree.

—

Chapter 45

BROWSING

While reading a recent magazine comment on President Lyndon Johnson, I was reminded of the last time I had visited him on business. LBJ had called President Nixon and asked that someone come out to the ranch and bring him up to date on foreign affairs. I welcomed the invitation and the opportunity to visit LBJ and Lady Bird on their home ground. Taking the Agency's propeller-driven aircraft meant getting under way early in the morning, but the plane was easily accommodated on the landing strip at the Johnson family's Texas spread.

LBJ settled into a chair in the sunroom, tilted back, and thrust his feet up on a stool. Ten minutes into my briefing on Vietnam and the rest of the world—a briefing several minutes longer than LBJ would have tolerated while in the Oval Office—it became obvious that he was losing interest. As I was closing down, he interrupted.

"Dick," he said, "what do your luncheon notes show about who was responsible for cutting back on the big increase in troops the Pentagon wanted in Vietnam?"

"If you mean at one of the Tuesday lunches," I said, "it was you. After listening to a discussion of the Pentagon recommendations, you said flatly that you were not going to commit any more troops."

"That's exactly what I remember," Johnson said. "I knew damned well that I made that decision." He grunted and pulled himself erect in the chair. "It's just that now they're telling me that Clark Clifford's claiming he took the lead that day."

"That's definitely not the way I recall it," I said.

"When you get back to Washington, take a look at your notes and give me a ring."

"But Mr. President, I don't have any notes. You had forbidden it." For a moment, I half suspected that this might have been a sly probe to find out whether I had a stack of Tuesday luncheon memoranda. "You were constantly reminding us that everything said at the luncheons was completely off the record."

LBJ shook his head and uttered a deep sigh. "I know, but I always assumed that you guys kept notes anyway." President or ex-President, he was always vintage LBJ.

It was clear that Lyndon deeply resented the allegation that anyone else, particularly Clark Clifford, who at that time had been secretary of defense, might have made the difficult decision.

I had to refuse LBJ's tempting invitation to have a swim before leaving for the long trip back to Washington.

The last time I saw LBJ and Lady Bird was also at their ranch. Before departing for Iran, Cynthia and I were en route to Mexico for a vacation, and we stopped for a visit. Lyndon looked much the same but appeared to be slowing down slightly. Sadly, I noticed that he had again begun to smoke. We exchanged the usual Washington gossip and did a little reminiscing. I particularly remember LBJ wishing me well in my new assignment and promising that he and Lady Bird would visit us in Iran as soon as we were comfortably in place. As ever, Lady Bird was an attentive hostess and always unobtrusively supportive of her husband. More than anyone I recall, LBJ still personified the cliché "larger than life."

Ironically, it was sometime after I left government that I first got to know an incumbent President socially. In 1983, I was still running Safeer, my consulting firm, when President Reagan awarded me the National Security Medal in the Roosevelt Room at the White House. I was more than pleased by the award, the highest decoration in the security field. Vice President George Bush, one of my successors at the Agency, was also present. The award also brought a letter of congratulations from ex-President Nixon. It was the first I had heard from him since we shook hands at Camp David.

For some time after the White House ceremony, I worked with Nancy Reagan as head of her anti-drug program, Just Say No. It was two years later that our social relationship slipped into high gear. Cynthia and I had become acquainted with Rex Harrison when he came to Tehran to participate in an international film gathering. In 1985, when he and Claudette Colbert were in Washington starring in a play headed for New York, we invited Rex and his wife, Mercia, for dinner. With the help of Michael Deaver, the White House chief of staff, we also invited the only other actors we knew—the President and Nancy Reagan. At the time, I had logged some forty years in Washington, long enough, I thought, to have a sound notion of how things were done thereabouts. Not so.

The proceedings began with a top-to-bottom inspection of our house by a handful of Secret Service experts. The attached garage was deemed a bit narrow for Secret Service purposes, but it was decided that, with some practice, one of the White House drivers could back the President's limousine into it without necessarily damaging the vehicle or our otherwise serviceable garage. Within the house, the kitchen and the living and dining areas were carefully examined, and chairs suitably safe for the President were chosen. This was not a question of weight-bearing strength, but rather to deny a line of sight for any assassin possibly lurking in the neighborhood. Scrupulous electronic probing presumably eliminated any hidden surveillance possibilities. I say "presumably" because it had been my experience that the most up-to-snuff secret audio and other clandestine monitoring techniques always seemed to be a step ahead of the counter-surveillance teams.

The Secret Service then alerted all of the neighbors along the street to a "happening" that required them not to park in front of their dwellings from 6 p.m. to midnight, by which time our mystery guests would presumably have left for home. Everyone cooperated in good spirit. This allowed ample space for the (by Cynthia's rough count) twenty-three vehicles involved in the President's entourage—a communication van, radio units, a decoy limousine, an ambulance, motorcycles, and miscellaneous prowl cars—to navigate and park.

The final step was oversight of the food and drink. At the risk of possibly compromising any still useful security precautions, I will admit that before any drink was poured, food put on the table, or coffee brewed, ample precautions were taken. I wondered how civil service regulations might describe the job that in time past was known simply as "food taster."

The motorcade arrived punctually; the President and Nancy made their way into the fortress without incident. I dutifully indicated the chair that had been selected for the President. Without the slightest hesitation, Ronald Reagan slipped into another, more comfortable chair.

—

My first invitation to the annual dinner of the Gridiron Club came in 1967. The fifty journalist members of the club use the white-tie event to singe, but not burn, a few of the hundreds of invited guests. I had hoped to rest quietly, far to the side of the scaffold on which more prominent guests were expected to suffer. Not at all. I learned that my job at the Agency was only cover. My actual job was writing schoolbooks, and my name was really McGuffey. This was a clever but rather stretched pun, which I thought might have slipped past most of the guests. My middle name, which I have seldom used, and which it is unlikely most of my acquaintances would have known, is McGarrah. There followed a joyous rendering of a song set to the tune of "The Sweetheart of Sigma Chi," but with twisted lyrics. Entitled "The Sweetheart of CIA," it described "the girl of my dreams" as "a snake-eyed girl," and then noted that "the cloak on her back is a subsidized black" and "her bank account continues to mount." In context, I got off easily.

In 1969, Dean Acheson and I drove together to another Gridiron dinner. It was almost midnight before the guests were toasted and I could find Dean in the dense crowd. We agreed that it was time to leave, but then Dean hesitated. "First, I want to pay my respects to the new President," he said. As I followed him to the suite where President Nixon was holding court, I remembered the relentless antagonism with which these two men had confronted each other during the McCarthy era. As secretary of state, the highly competent Dean Acheson was pilloried—Nixon referred to him as the "Red Dean." Various Nixon enthusiasts, including senators and congressmen, demanded Dean's resignation on the grounds that he was a communist sympathizer. Years later, in his memoirs, Acheson referred to this as "the attack of the primitives."

I stood back a bit when Dean, the next in line, leaned forward, extended his hand, and in a deep voice said, "Mr. President, I am Dean Acheson." "Thunderstruck" best describes Nixon's appearance as he struggled to understand why this distinguished statesman should feel he needed identification. "Yes—I know," he finally blurted.

It was a nifty lesson in Washington establishment manners.

—

It is tempting, in closing, again to praise the staff who were so influential in guiding the Agency through the turbulent early days and shaping this country's first national intelligence service: Larry Houston, from OSS and CIG to CIA, a peerless general counsel, dealing every day with unprecedented legal problems; Colonel Lawrence "Red" White, a superb executive director and comptroller; Tom Karamessines, the most steadfast operations officer; Albert "Bud" Wheelon, scientist extraordinaire; and Sherman Kent, the flamboyant Dean of Intelligence, with red suspenders and a vocabulary to match.

Among the legion of operatives, analysts, scientists, and scholars whom I have had to refrain from giving at least a bit of the credit they have so richly earned are two who deserve special mention:

John Bross, one of our most distinguished officers, graduated from Harvard Law School in 1933, and for six years practiced law in New York City. In 1942, he was one of the earliest OSS volunteers; he was the first American to graduate from the British commando training school in Scotland. The officer students—who wore no insignia of rank—were relentlessly subjected to rough treatment by the rugged, noncommissioned commando instructors. Hardy Amies, the English fashion designer, was one of John's fellow trainees. After an exhausting day, the pair limped back to their quarters. John and Amies were commiserating over the treatment that "Bob," the roughest instructor, had inflicted. Amies flung himself on his cot, spluttering, "I'd like to see that bastard Bob design a hat!" Although he was a solid ten years older than his English classmates and had been injured in a parachute jump, Bross graduated first in his class.

In London, John was chief of the OSS mission to the United Kingdom, Norway, and Denmark. After the war, he rejoined his law firm in New York. He returned to government in 1949 as deputy to the general counsel to the U.S. High Commissioner for Germany, and he joined CIA in 1951. He headed the Eastern European Operations Division until 1957, when he became chief of our offices in Germany. On his return to Washington, he served as chief of the DDP Senior Planning Office, as CIA comptroller, and then as deputy to the DCI for national programs evaluation. He retired in 1971, but remained as a consultant until 1988. Throughout his career, John handled some of the most difficult and intricate jobs in the Agency. His performance was never less than outstanding.

Bronson Tweedy will be more than miffed to find that I have violated his determination to slip into retirement unnoticed and without responding to any of the pressures to share his inside view of the history to which he contributed. Brons began his intelligence career in the U.S. Navy, interrogating captured Nazi U-boat survivors. After the war, he returned briefly to his Madison Avenue career; by 1947, he knew it was no longer for him, and he joined the Agency. I was lucky to have known him from the earliest days of his career—first as a case officer in Europe, then as chief of station. Brons returned to Washington for a staff assignment, and then went to Austria as chief of one of our busiest Cold War offices. After a senior headquarters assignment came another CIA station. Before he retired, Brons had also served as chief of two area divisions. His last assignment, for which he was singularly well qualified, was deputy to the DCI for the intelligence community.

It was my good fortune that throughout Bronson's various Washington assignments, our houses were closely enough situated to make carpooling possible. The hours we spent threading our way through traffic allowed me the full benefit of his friendship, wide experience, and levelheaded and highly perceptive comments and counsel.

———

In keeping with CIA regulations, some of which I instituted, this manuscript was submitted to the Agency for security clearance. As with all former employees, the Agency has requested that I remind readers that the opinions I have expressed are not necessarily those of the Central Intelligence Agency.

INDEX

After his retirement, RICHARD HELMS lived in Washington, D.C. He died in October 2002.

WILLIAM HOOD was born in Maine and entered the military in 1942. After serving in the Armored Force and military intelligence, he volunteered for the Office of Strategic Services; he was at the London headquarters of OSS until 1945, when he joined Allen Dulles in Switzerland. He remained in OSS carryover units until CIA was formed. He served abroad and as chief of station, with responsibilities involving Eastern Europe, the USSR, and Latin America, and was executive officer of the Counterintelligence Staff when he retired from CIA. He has published three novels and a nonfiction book, *Mole.* He divides his time among New York City, Maine, and East Hampton, New York.